So You Want To Be An Interpreter?

An Introduction to Sign Language Interpreting

Fourth Edition

So You Want To Be An Interpreter?

An Introduction to Sign Language Interpreting

Fourth Edition

Janice Humphrey
Bob Alcorn

H & H Publishing Company
Seattle, WA

So You Want To Be An Interpreter?
An Introduction to Sign Language Interpreting
Fourth Edition
Textbook with CD Study Guide

Copyright ©1994, 1995, 2001, 2007 by
H & H Publishing Co.

Printed in the United States of America
Cover: Design Point
Printing and binding: Paragon Group

ISBN 0-9767132-6-8

H & H Publishing Co, Inc.
330 SW 43rd St., Suite K #172
Renton, WA 98057
206-338-2596 (v)
425-438-1010 (fax)

handhpublishing@comcast.net

Table of Contents

CHAPTER ONE: The Importance Of Communication 1
The Communication Process 1
Contextual Environment..3
Communication In Action 4
Grammar And Meaning 6
Message Construction...6
    Speaker/signer Goal 6
    The Context Of Message Conveyance...................8
    Degree Of Directness...9
    The Clarity Of Message Construction....................9
Powerful/powerless Speech 12
Responsible Language 15
Linguistic Register...16
Chapter Review 29

CHAPTER TWO:The Influence Of Culture On Communication.
35
Definitions Of Culture 35
The Role Of Culture..37
The Relationship Of Culture And Language 39
Two World Views...39
Cultural Identity 44
The Influence Of Cultural Affiliation On Communication.
45
Significance For Interpreters...................................51
Chapter Review 52

CHAPTER THREE: Working In Multicultural Communities ... 57
Interpreting With People Who Identify Primarily With
Deaf Culture 59
Interpreting With African American Deaf People 66
Interpreting With Deaf Hispanic People 68
Interpreting With Native Deaf People[21] 71
Summary 76
Chapter Review 76

CHAPTER FOUR: Identity And Communication
In The Deaf Community 83
Identity And Labeling 83
The Multilingual Nature Of The Deaf Community 88
Contact Varieties In Sign Communication 96
Others That Aren't On The Chart 97
Summary..102
Chapter Review 103

CHAPTER FIVE: Cultural Frames: Schemas,
Beneficence And Audism.. 109
Stereotyping, Oppression And The Deaf Community .111
Characteristics Of "Benefactors" (Oppressors)........ 114
How Does Audism Affect Deaf People? 119
Viewing Deaf People As Different............................123
Chapter Review 124

CHAPTER SIX: Oppression, Power And Interpreters.........131
Liberation Movement..131
Power And Oppression 132
Humor 133
The Impact Of Oppression On Interpreters 136
Advocate Or Ally..140
Chapter Review 142

CHAPTER SEVEN: The Work Of Interpreters 147
    Basic Terms 147
    Looking At The Work Of Interpreters.......................154
    Chapter Review 163

CHAPTER EIGHT: How We Approach Our Work................171
    Helper Philosophy 171
    Machine (Conduit) Philosophy 173
    Communication Facilitation...................................176
    Bilingual-bicultural 178
    Summary...184
    Chapter Review 185

CHAPTER NINE:The Challenge Of Mediating ASL & English ....
189
    Specific Linguistic Considerations For
    ASL/English Interpreters 189
    Conveying Meaning 194
    Word Order/Grammatical Structure 207
    Implications Of Word-order 209
    Grammatical Structure For Interpreters 209
    Negation/affirmation 212
    Voice 214
    Noun/verb Modifiers 216
    Affect Markers 220
    Numbering Systems 222
    Chapter Review 224

CHAPTER TEN: The Process Of Interpreting 233
Process Models...233
The Process Of Interpreting: A Closer Look 235
    Take in Source Language 236
    Analyze Deep Structure Meaning 238
    Apply Contextual/Schema Screen 243

Formulate/Rehearse Equivalent Message 246
Produce Target Language Interpretation 247
Process Multi-tasking And Monitoring 249
Chapter Review 253

CHAPTER ELEVEN:The History And Professionalization
Of Interpreting... 261
How It All Began..261
The Establishment Of RID 262
The Establishment of AVLIC 266
RID Certification 270
AVLIC Certification 279
EIPA 283
A Look At The Field Of Spoken Language Interpretation
283
The Emergence Of Sign Language Interpreter Education
Programs..284
A Revolution In Interpreter Education 286
Legislative Initiatives 287
Chapter Review 289

CHAPTER TWELVE: Principles Of Professional Practice.....299
What Distinguishes Professionals? 299
What Are Ethics? 301
Guidelines For Professional Conduct......................302
Interpretation Of The Code.................................305
Learning To Make Ethical Decisions......................310
Practicing The Principles.....................................312
The Foundation Of Ethics: Knowing Yourself...........318
Support Groups And Mentors 319
Chapter Review 321

CHAPTER THIRTEEN: Where Interpreters Work 325
Interpreting In Educational Settings 325
Interpreting In Employment-related Settings 337
Interpreting In Religious Settings 341
Working With Deaf Interpreters 346
Interpreting In Medical Settings 348
Interpreting In Legal Settings 353
Interpreting In Mental Health & Psychiatric Settings 359
Interpreting For Conferences 361
Interpreting In Theatrical Or Performing Arts Settings.. 364
Interpreting In Social Service Settings 371
Interpreting In Personal Settings........................... 372
Interpreting In A Team 376
Chapter Review 379

CHAPTER FOURTEEN: Basic Business Practices 389
The Job Market.. 389
Pay Rates 391
The Cost Of Doing Business................................. 393
Preparing To Do Business.................................... 394
Threats To Staying In The Field............................. 398
Chapter Review 400

APPENDIX A: The Claggett Statement 403
APPENDIX B: NAD-RID Code Of Professional Conduct 409
APPENDIX C: AVLIC Code Of Ethics & Guidelines
for Professional Conduct 419
APPENDIX D: Kohlberg's Stages of Moral Development............ 428

GLOSSARY... 430
REFERENCES AND RESOURCES 447
INDEX 478

PREFACE

Bob Alcorn and I began the first edition of this book in 1984 with a single goal in mind of conveying sign language interpretation as the captivating, challenging, exciting and critically important discipline that it is. Years of teaching and working as interpreters had convinced us that it was possible to communicate the fascinating complexities and the immediate impact of this subject without being too simplistic or, alternatively, so theoretical and academic as to become dull and inaccessible. We wanted to inspire critical thinking, deepened insight and to entice readers with the intrigue of working as an interpreter. The enthusiastic response of instructors, students and professional practitioners has been very gratifying, encouraging this fourth edition in an effort to update and enhance the information provided.

The first and second editions were a true partnership between Bob and myself -- Deaf and hearing, consumer of interpreter services and interpreter practitioner, male and female perspectives. When Bob passed away in 1996, I was left to prepare the third and fourth editions alone. I have tried throughout to honor Bob's philosophy and the values that supported our original work, including a deep respect for members of the Deaf community, as well as the profession of sign language interpretation. Enjoy!

Jan Humphrey

THANKS!

This book has benefited from the work of the entire community of scholars involved in the study of interpretation, linguistics of ASL, sociolinguistics, muticulturalism, diversity and communications. I have learned much from conferences, journals, books and conversations with fellow interpreters, interpreter educators, interpreter practitioners and Deaf community members. Of course, I am particularly indebted to the many individuals who have read various drafts of this book, provided suggestions, criticism, references and encouragement. Each of them has made the book a better one and I thank them all. I cannot name each of you, but of particular note are:

- Individuals who have attended workshops I have taught since 2000 -- you were my greatest guinea pigs!

- Teachers and students from various interpreting programs who have asked questions and made suggestions;

- Charlotte Baker-Shenk, Janice Jickels, Cheryl Palmer, Karen Malcolm and Debra Russell

- Ophelia Humphrey and Kristina Stratton -- editors extraordinare!

Chapter One

The Importance of Communication

 Interpreters are professional communicators. For that reason, it is imperative that interpreters understand the communication process as a whole, and the way messages are constructed. Once we have an understanding of message construction and communication in general, we must apply that knowledge to our work as interpreters.

Communication is complex and imprecise, yet it is essential for life, health, and the development of one's sense of self. We also rely on communication to meet the critical social needs of inclusion, control, and affection.[1] Experiments have demonstrated that human beings require physical contact and communicative interaction to survive.[2]

Communication is the primary way relationships are formed and maintained. It affords us opportunities to affect the behavior of others and provides an avenue for feedback from others regarding our actions and ideas. Some assert[3] that the only way we learn who we are and develop a sense of self is by interacting with others through communication. Obviously, if you want to be an interpreter, effective communication is a foundational tool.

The Communication Process

Communication cannot be viewed as a linear process in which information and ideas flow one at a time in only one direction. This is rarely the case. Rather, communication is usually an interactive and dynamic process in which communicators simultaneously send and receive multiple and overlapping messages.

Consider, for example, the following scenario:

As soon as she hears the words spoken by Josh, Ruth begins to send nonverbal messages indicating her level of comprehension, interest, agreement, etc. Josh receives those non-verbal messages while still speaking and simultaneously begins to send his own nonverbal messages along with his spoken message. He might for instance check his watch or shift forward in his chair as he speaks. Ruth's reactions communicate to Josh, letting him know if his goals are being achieved or not. They may also prompt Josh to interrupt himself to modify, clarify, speed up or otherwise change the message being sent.

Throughout the interaction, Ruth is trying to understand the intent of the message she is hearing by deciphering the meaning of the words, as well as the accompanying nonverbal elements used by Josh.

This whole process is complicated by the fact that the words or signs we use to communicate our ideas are never an exact representation of the mental concept itself.[4]

Furthermore, many of the nonverbal aspects of a message — facial expressions, gestures, body posture,

vocal tones and so on — are communicated unconsciously. It is these nonverbal elements that carry the bulk of the meaning of a message. In English, only 6% of the meaning is found in the words, 39% of the meaning is in the vocal intonation, and 55% of the message is conveyed in the accompanying gestures, body language and facial expressions used.[5]

It should also be noted that each act of communication takes place in a **contextual environment** which includes both:

✦ The physical location where the interaction is taking place.
✦ The personal history each participant brings to the event.

In most cases both participants share a physical location, but the amount of shared personal history varies according to the topic of communication and the roles of the individuals involved. Sometimes there is little or no overlap, especially among people of different cultural or linguistic backgrounds. In other situations, the individuals involved have similar backgrounds, experiences and knowledge. Thus, they share some environmental elements. As an interaction takes place, participants may acquire new information that allows them to interact with increasingly greater overlap, depending on their background, level of interest and other factors.

Contextual Environment

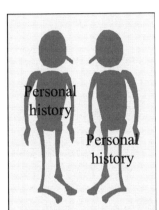

Communication takes place in a contextual environment made up of the physical location and the status of each participant. Each participant brings his or her own personal history. Some components of personal history overlap due to common background & knowledge. The degree of overlap varies depending on the topic of communication. In addition to the physical location and personal history, there is also a level of "noise" in every communication environment.

In this context, noise is not simply an unpleasant sound, but anything that distracts the participants in an interaction from their communication. Noise can be external, physical, physiological or psychological. Examples of **external noise** include the flickering of an overhead florescent light, the squeal of a poorly connected microphone, or the incessant coughing of someone in the room. **Physiological noise** refers to biological factors that interfere with communication, such as illness, exhaustion, or hunger. **Psychological noise** exists, to some extent, in the heads of all participants in the communication environment. Examples include internal stress, personal judgments about the other participants, and random thoughts that pop into one's mind. Noise from any of these sources can distract the communicators, making concentration, participation and understanding difficult.

COMMUNICATION IN ACTION

It should be noted that communication is imprecise at best because of the human element involved. There is no guarantee that the receiver will decode a message in a way that matches the sender's intention. Good communicators learn to think analytically, listen effectively and express themselves clearly in the signed, spoken and written forms of the languages they use. These are prerequisite skills for anyone seeking to become an interpreter.[6]

Effective communicators strive to achieve their goals in ways that maintain or enhance the relationship between the participants. To do this, they use a variety of styles that reflect their personality and personal values. It is also important to remember that communication competence is situational and depends considerably on the cultures, personal history and relationships of the individuals present. What might be effective in one setting, could be disastrous in another. In part, this is due to the fact that each culture has its own definition of communication competence. Being aware of these differences and modifying your communication to reflect the various cultures represented in an interaction is a challenging but worthwhile goal.

It is important to remember that communication is **relational** — it is done *with* other people. Effective communicators must develop a variety of interpersonal skills and sensitivities that enable them to interact with other people in satisfying ways. Your "people skills" are perhaps more critical than anything else in moving you toward the goal of becoming a professional interpreter.

Language is a marvelous communication tool. Due to its symbolic nature, however, it is not a precise vehicle. **Pragmatic rules** help us make sense of the language we encounter in our interactions with others and determine the meaning of the utterance within the given context. For example, the phrase "see you later" can have a variety of meanings including:

> ➤ "I hope I never see you again"
> ➤ "I'll see you at our prearranged clandestine place" or simply
> ➤ "Good-bye," although there is no plan to actually see the addressee again

The intended meaning is determined not by the words or signs themselves, but by a variety of contextual factors including:

- ✦ Who made the statement
- ✦ The location in which it was said
- ✦ The tone of voice and the accompanying nonverbal behaviors
- ✦ The relationship between the sender and the receiver

In order to determine meaning with consistent accuracy, interpreters must have a wide range of experience and knowledge.[7] Pragmatic rules are numerous and quite complex. A 1992 study[8] detailed 24 different pragmatic functions of humor alone, including:

> ➤ Showing the speaker's sense of humor
> ➤ Entertaining others
> ➤ Decreasing another person's aggressive behavior
> ➤ Easing the disclosure of difficult information
> ➤ Expressing feelings
> ➤ Expressing aggression

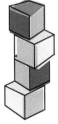

Grammar and Meaning

Communicators must construct messages in a grammatically correct way in order to make sense. However, after the meaning being conveyed has been extracted from a sentence and understood by the listener, the specific grammatical structure no longer serves any purpose. This is because grammar is not needed to retain the information carried in an utterance. Thus, it is critical for interpreters to understand how messages are constructed in order to extract meaning from the utterances they are expected to interpret.

MESSAGE CONSTRUCTION

When someone is ready to communicate an idea to another person, they automatically take several things into consideration.

In this chapter, we look at several of those factors, each of which influences how we construct a message. These factors are the speaker's goal, the context of the message conveyance, the degree of directness desired, use of powerful/powerless speech, responsible language and the linguistic register.

SPEAKER/SIGNER GOAL:
The "Why" of Message Construction

We communicate for a number of social purposes and it is important to realize that not all communication is intended

to convey information. For example, when two people greet each other in passing with "How are you?" their goal is to acknowledge each other, not actually seek information about each other's well-being. Other goals for communication might include:

> ➤ To have fun and enjoy ourselves;
> ➤ To help others and let them know we care;
> ➤ To feel included and less alone;
> ➤ To put off doing something else;
> ➤ To unwind or relax;
> ➤ To get someone else to do something;
> ➤ To influence or persuade others.

FIG. 1-1 SPEAKER GOALS		
Advising	Challenging	Fighting
Flirting	Bullying	Placating
Humoring	Clarifying	Nurturing
Scrutinizing	Delaying	Evading
Encouraging	Needling	Rationalizing
Convicting	Accepting	Threatening
Giving	Surveying	Baiting
Helping	Asking	Resolving
Informing	Grieving	Introducing
Supporting	Joking	Maintaining
Urging	Nagging	Buying
Guiding	Preparing	Seducing
Reinforcing	Justifying	Explaining
Entertaining	Goading	Inspiring
Demonstrating	Teasing	Prompting
Questioning	Hinting	Verifying

A prerequisite of effective communication is having a goal — a reason behind the statement being made or the question being asked. In the absence of such a goal, words, sentences and even whole diatribes can be expressed, but there will be no underlying blueprint. People listening to such a message will quickly become confused or frustrated because they are unable to determine the intent of what is being said.

The way language is used to achieve these goals varies from culture to culture. Within each culture, accomplished communicators are those who are able to use language to achieve the full range of speaker goals in culturally appropriate ways.

THE CONTEXT OF MESSAGE CONVEYANCE:
The "Who" and "Where" of Message Construction

Another factor that we consider when preparing to communicate is the context of the interaction — who are we communicating with and where is the communication taking place.

The question of *who* we are communicating with is of great significance because everybody carries some level of status with them into an interaction. The status may be obvious — the accented English of a sales clerk, the robes of a judge, the tattered and stained clothing of a street person. Or, it may be invisible — a patient at an AIDS/HIV clinic who is the CEO of a large company; the fourteen-year-old at the local arcade who is a student at Harvard; a chief of surgery wearing street clothes rather than a medical jacket.

Social and cultural norms dictate how we interact with people of equal status as well as those of higher or lower status. Because each communicator hopes to accomplish a specific goal, awareness of the status of participants is important in formulating a message.

For example, let's say I am a person of lesser status than the person to whom I am speaking — perhaps a tourist crossing the border into another country speaking to the border patrol. If my goal is to placate, rather than offend, I will select a certain way of phrasing what I wish to convey, out of deference to the status differentiation. My goal will also require making choices regarding eye gaze, volume of speech and physical posture to

support my goal of placating. I could violate status-defining behavior — refuse to answer the guard's questions, touch or stand
too close to her/him in violation of the established norms for
physical distance/space, etc. — and my goal would probably be
undermined. Likewise, I could use language in such a way that
I might undermine my goal to placate. Examples include shout-
ing or using a loud volume of speech, incorporating inappropriate expletives, or demonstrating disrespectful facial expressions
and body language.

It is important to note that the appropriate response to status
also varies from one culture to the next. In some cultures, for
instance, looking someone in the eye demonstrates respect. In
other cultures, the same behavior is interpreted as disrespectful, especially when done by a younger person to an elder. An effective communicator must be aware of various cultural norms
and expectations when attempting to achieve a specific communication goal.

The location — or the "where" — of the interaction also influences message construction. The dynamics, for example, may be
different if the interaction is taking place in private or in front of
others. This is because people sometimes feel they must "save
face" in front of others, lest their status be undermined. If the
interaction is taking place in a private setting, status rules are
sometimes more flexible. An employee might be able to have a
heated debate with a supervisor behind closed doors that would
lead to dismissal if held in front of other employees

DEGREE OF DIRECTNESS:
The Clarity Of Message Construction
When constructing a message, we may choose to communicate clearly and explicitly or we may choose to obfuscate our
meaning for some reason. People often profess a preference for
clear communication, but there are a number of reasons to use
less direct or implicit communication. Some of the factors that
determine how clearly a message will be expressed include the

goals of the speaker, the context of the interaction and the cultural norms of politeness.

If, for example, the norms in which one is reared dictate that it is impolite to ask for a gift directly, the speaker will most likely *hint* about a request rather than state the message overtly. Thus, your teenage daughter (whose birthday is next week) may say to her boyfriend, "I *love* that artist — I sure would like to get a copy of his new CD." In the context of their relationship (boyfriend/girlfriend) and the shared factors in their communication environment, the boyfriend will probably *deduce* that your daughter wants that CD for her birthday.

In another situation, someone may have done something they knew was against the rules. When challenged by a teacher, parent or other person of authority, they may give an indirect response rather than confessing overtly what they have done. For example, a teacher asks "Did you take that from my desk?" The student may hedge with, "Uh, no ... I was just looking at it."

Below are four types of language usage that can produce imprecision, sometimes causing miscommunication but at other times supporting the speaker goal of being vague.

Equivocal language is the deliberate use of words, signs or phrases that can be interpreted in more than one way in order to mislead someone. An example of this is saying to a friend who is sporting a new hair-do, "It's really different!" rather than saying, "It looks weird" or "I don't like it." Equivocations can be relatively innocent in some cases, but can lead to serious misunderstandings at other times.

Euphemistic language is the use of socially acceptable terms and phrases in place of blunt, descriptive ones. When we refer to "the powder room" rather than "the room where women urinate and defecate," we are using socially prescribed euphemistic language. Another example is saying that someone "has gone to a better place," instead of directly stating that he or she has died.

Abstract language refers to degrees of imprecision in communication. The less specific something is, the more *abstract* it is. High level abstractions are sometimes used to form a type of "verbal shorthand." This permits people to communicate information without going through a detailed list. For example, a speaker can say "I have to clean the house today," and listeners will understand what that entails without the speaker having to itemize each chore on his or her list. English is a language that supports abstractions. It is replete with compact lexical items or abstractions, including such terms as:

➤ Camping
➤ Drugs
➤ Multicultural
➤ Weapon

Abstractions are also used to be deliberately vague, permitting the speaker to hint at their true response without being too confrontational. However, the use of abstractions often leads to unclear and confusing interchanges.

For example, when you ask what to wear to a special event and the reply is "Well, the dress is *formal* but not *too formal*," do you have any idea what kind of clothing to wear?

Passive voice refers to a statement in which the person or thing performing the action is not overtly stated. "The car was wrecked," for example, is a statement in passive voice form. We don't know who crashed the car, we simply know the result of some action was the wrecking of the car. Other examples include:

✦ The president was shot.
✦ My friend has been lied to.

✦ A phone call was made.

In all of these examples, we know what action was taken and who the recipient of the action was, but we do not know who the actor was — who did the shooting, lying or phoning. English uses passive voice fairly often, especially informal speech. This sentence construction allows a speaker to do such things as concealing the identity of the responsible party, discussing something that happened for unknown cause; and emphasizing the *result* of an event over the cause.

If you want to be an interpreter, it is important to recognize when someone is deliberately attempting to be vague and when they are trying to communicate clearly. Further, you must develop a range of language skills in order to make appropriate interpreting choices — using clear, non-abstract terms when a speaker is being clear and precise in their communication, and appropriate euphemisms, equivocation, etc. when that is the most equivalent choice. Awareness of your own use of English and ASL, as well as the way others use these languages, will help you when you engage in the work of interpretation.

POWERFUL/POWERLESS SPEECH:
The Credibility of a Message

Language is powerful. It shapes and mirrors the perceptions of its users. It reflects the level of affiliation, attraction and interest a speaker feels toward a subject. It influences the listeners' perceptions of the speaker's power. There are several communication patterns that make a person seem less powerful and less confident about what they are saying. These include hedges, hesitations, intensifiers, polite forms, tag questions and disclaimers, all of which are described in Fig. 1-2.

FIG. 1-2 Powerless Forms of Language[9]		
PATTERN	DEFINITION	EXAMPLE
Hedges	Qualifiers that weaken the statement being made.	✦ I'm sort of hungry. ✦ She's kinda mean. ✦ I guess I could do it.
Hesitations	Fillers preceding and during an utterance.	✦ Like, you know ... I was wondering ... uh ... if you could like uh ... help me.
Intensifiers	Unnecessary modifiers added to an utterance which obscure the message	✦ I'm really so very happy to see you. ✦ It's truly an absolute honor to meet you!
Polite Forms	Words and phrases used for more than simple politeness	✦ Excuse me, I was wondering ... if you don't mind ... I mean, I don't want to impose but ... could you help me?
Tag questions and "up talk"	Question tacked onto the end of a statement. Also includes using "up talk" at the end of a sentence which makes a statement sound like a question.	✦ She did a good job, didn't she? ✦ We ought to move on, shouldn't we? ✦ I think I'll go to college (?-up-talk) ✦ Yeah, I've finally made up my mind (?-up-talk)
Disclaimers	Qualifying phrases which weaken the validity of the statement being made	✦ It's only my opinion but I think this is OK. ✦ I'm not sure but I think we could move on.

Speakers who consistently incorporate these features come across as uncertain and lacking in confidence. As a result, people view them as less credible and believable. Look at the statements in Fig. 1-3 and note the difference in power reflected in each.

FIG 1-3 Comparing Powerful/Powerless Forms	
POWERFUL	POWERLESS
I need an appointment with Mr. Choy, preferably sometime today or tomorrow.	I kinda need to see Mr. Choy ... umm ... I don't want to impose but ... umm ... if it isn't too much trouble, maybe I could see him ... errr ... soon?
I asked for this appointment today because I need to discuss the terms of our contract.	Thank you so very much for meeting with me today. I really appreciate it. I uh ... sorta need to discuss ... uh ... the terms o our contract ... if that's okay with you?

Which speaker in this interaction do you think will get the secretary's attention and respect and, ultimately, the appointment? And which speaker will be more successful in negotiating the terms of the contract? Research indicates that using powerful language will result in people viewing you as a more dynamic, capable, authoritative and socially attractive person.

However, the rules defining powerful and powerless forms of language vary from culture to culture. In Japan, for example, speakers are expected to fill their utterances with ambiguities, hedges and qualifiers to show respect to others, a cultural mandate no less valid than the Western value of appearing confident and self-assured. Mexican culture places great emphasis on cooperation, resulting in regular use of hedging in order to make everyone feel comfortable.[10]

Even in cultures that value assertiveness and self-confidence, powerful and assertive language must be balanced with being culturally appropriate and courteous. If you are too authoritarian, you are likely to be viewed as aggressive, intimidating, bossy or rude. Further, there are times when you may deliberately use more polite (and consequently less powerful) forms of language because it is more effective in accomplishing your goal.

RESPONSIBLE LANGUAGE:
Accountability in Message Construction

Language can be used to indicate the speaker's willingness to take responsibility for his or her statements.[11] Within English-speaking North American mainstream culture, this is done in at least two ways: the use of "I" statements and the avoidance of "but" statements.

"I," "You" and "It" Statements

An individual reflects personal responsibility for a message being delivered when using "I" statements, such as "when our discussions become overly emotional, I feel uncomfortable." "It" statements are often used in an attempt to avoid responsibility, as in "it isn't right to get so upset." "You" statements can place negative judgment on the person being addressed, such as "you make me feel uncomfortable when you get too emotional." Notice how a single idea can be expressed in each of the three ways to produce a very different impact on the listener, as illustrated in Fig. 1-4 below.

Fig. 1-4 Examples of "I", "You", "It" Statements	
It bothers me when you pay for me.	"It" statement
You shouldn't pay for everything!	"You" statement
I feel uncomfortable when you pay for everything.	"I" statement
It isn't right for kids to watch so much TV.	"It" statement
Your kids shouldn't watch so much TV.	"You" statement
I believe television adversely affects the moral development of children.	"I" statement

"But" Statements

When the word "but" is used to join two statements, the second statement cancels or limits the statement that preceded it. Examples include:

15

> ➤ "It's a really good class, but I always get bored about half way through.
> ➤ "You've been a good employee, but I'm going to have to let you go.
> ➤ "She's been a good neighbor, but I'm glad to see her moving.

"But" statements are frequently used as a strategy when a person is trying to soften the actual message being delivered and/or avoid personal responsibility for the content of the message.

LINGUISTIC REGISTER: Degree of Formality in Message Construction

All languages have registers that allow speakers to modify the language in order to convey levels of formality or degree of familiarity between participants.

Register determines:

- ✦ Turn-taking and interaction between the sender and receiver of the message;
- ✦ Complexity and completeness of sentence structure;
- ✦ Choice of vocabulary;
- ✦ Use of contractions;
- ✦ Volume of speech or size of signs;
- ✦ Rate (i.e., speed) of speech or signs;
- ✦ Clarity (i.e., diction, enunciation, etc.) of signs or speech;
- ✦ Speaker goals;
- ✦ Use of fillers and hesitations; and
- ✦ Allowable topics of discussion.

For example, the English features listed below, are associated with lower English registers.[12]

Feature	English Example
Contractions	I'd She's
Phonetic assimilations	Whadif Shouldda Gotta
Hesitations/fillers	Er Umm Uhh
Corrections	I mean I should have said

An early linguist[13] divided linguistic registers into five levels of formality, each with specific characteristics and unwritten rules. These include frozen, formal, consultative, informal, and intimate. These divisions are useful in understanding the concept of register; however, they can be misleading because there is no discrete demarcation between one register and the next. Shaw,[14] an interpreter who has done some study in the area, notes that registers have certain ranges with definable properties but lack discrete boundaries.

For that reason, we typically describe relative degrees of formality, saying a text is "high consultative" or "low formal," rather than saying "this is clearly formal." Keeping this in mind, let's look AT some linguistic registers.

Frozen
A frozen text is one that is the same each time it is rendered. Examples include a Robert Frost poem, the Lord's Prayer, the national anthem, and the oath administered to the incoming officers of an organization.

Settings Where This Register Is Used
Frozen texts are typically used in weddings, funerals, swearing-in ceremonies, sports events and religious ceremonies. Frozen register is most commonly used in formal settings like a wed-

ding or where large groups of people are gathered to engage in an activity together, such as a graduation ceremony. Frozen form can also be found in the entertainment setting in the form of songs, poetry or established comedy routines like the famous "Who's on First?" sketch.

Vocabulary and Sentence Structure

Because it is "frozen" and may have been handed down through the years, the vocabulary and sentence structure of formal texts are sometimes archaic. "Our Father which art in heaven, Hallowed be thy name," for example, uses old English terms and poetic sentence structure. One modern sample of a frozen text is the Miranda Warning used by the police to inform suspects of their legal and constitutional rights prior to questioning them. Here, the sentence structure appears to be fairly simple: "You have the right to remain silent. Anything you say can and will be used against you in a court of law." However, closer scrutiny reveals that there are compound and complex meanings hidden within that sentence structure which makes access to the intended meaning challenging at best.

Frozen register is unique because the meaning is often found more in the ritual surrounding the words or signs used than in the words or signs themselves. The meaning in the Miranda Warning, for example, is found more in the fact that it is be-

ing read by a police officer as you are being handcuffed and led to a police car than in the comprehension of the actual words.

Also, no one at the ballpark really sings the national anthem with an impassioned focus on the meaning of each word. If someone *did* sing with utter conviction and patriotic zeal "Oh say, can you *see* by the dawn's *early light...*" Or "O! *Canada!* Our home and *na-*

tive land! True patriot love in all thy sons command...," the people around him or her would think it very odd. *The message or meaning in a frozen text is in the ritual — the accompanying actions.* In the example of the ballpark, the meaning is in the fact that 10,000 people from all walks of life are standing together, with their hands over their hearts, looking at the flag.

Turn-Taking Rules
There is no actual turn-taking when traditional frozen texts are used. However, audience members may sing or recite in unison or there may be a prescribed response — a collective "Amen" at the end of the Lord's Prayer or a cheer at the end of the national anthem, for example.

Rate And Volume
The rate of a spoken or signed presentation is slowed slightly and signs and speech are more clearly enunciated. This is due primarily to the presence or participation of an audience, not because of an increased focus on the meaning of individual words or signs being uttered.

Signs are often produced in a larger signing space and microphones will typically be used to project a speaker's voice in order to ensure that all audience members have access to the message. Increasingly, you may also see large TV screens projecting the image of the speaker or signer to the audience.

Common Speaker Goals
Goals that prompt the use of frozen text usually include one or more of the following:

+ To unite a large group at the beginning or end of an event (e.g., singing the national anthem or reciting a pledge of allegiance);

+ To evoke reverence or stimulate individual memories related to a particular text (e.g., singing a familiar wedding song or a hymn at a funeral); and less often,

✦ To deliver a formal proclamation (e.g., the Miranda Warning).

Formal

The formal register refers to the type of language used when one speaker addresses a fairly large group of listeners, with virtually no turn-taking or linguistic interaction between the speaker and the audience. This may include such events as a minister delivering a sermon, the president of the university delivering a welcome address to an auditorium full of new students, or the keynote speaker's comments at a large conference.

Settings Where This Register Is Used

The settings in which a formal register is used can be quite varied, including sports arenas, auditoriums, theaters, hotel ballrooms and churches. These settings are commonly marked by a physical separation between the speaker and the audience, which often includes a raised platform with five feet or more between the front of the platform and the first row of seats. Other settings have even greater physical separation. For example, the graduation ceremony of a large university may be held in a sports stadium where some audience members are several hundred feet away from the speaker.

Turn-Taking Rules

Because of the physical distance and other cultural phenomena, there is virtually no informal or spontaneous turn-taking when formal register is being used. For example, when a minister is delivering a sermon, parishioners are expected to sit and listen, not to ask impromptu questions. In some settings, though, there may be a structured question and answer session at the end. In these cases, those asking questions are often required to leave their seats, go to a microphone, and stand while presenting their question or comment. The speaker or a moderator controls the turn-taking and generally adheres to pre-established guidelines. For example, there may be a requirement to alternate or rotate the order of questions taken from one microphone to another to reflect a balance of "pro" and "con" questions or statements. The speaker or moderator will decide on a time limit for the question period and can arbitrarily end this interactive portion of the meeting.

The absence of interaction between presenter and audience members or limiting this interaction to a formal question and answer session, along with other factors, typically creates a psychological distance between the speaker and the listeners. Lighting in these settings sometimes puts the audience in darkness and prevents the speaker from seeing the faces of those being addressed. This contributes to the sense of psychological distance in these settings.

Vocabulary/Sentence Structure
The sentence structure in formal register tends to be compound and complex. The insertion of some frozen texts is common and there is a tendency to use "ten dollar" words and two-handed signing forms. In English, there is a greater tendency to use passive voice and rhetorical questions.

However, presenters at formal interactions may deliberately attempt to close the physical and psychological distance between themselves and the audience by incorporating some consultative and informal register behaviors. They may, for example, move from behind the podium for a portion of the address. They may incorporate humor, personal anecdotes, or less formal sentence structure and vocabulary selections to give the illusion of a less formal interaction.

Rate And Volume Of Speech/Speed Of Signs
Public speaking and signing demands clear diction and well-enunciated articulation, requiring a deliberate and slower-than-normal rate of production.

Signing space is enlarged and the volume of speech is increased in order to permit the message to be carried to all members of the audience.

Typical Speaker/Signer Goals

The goals prompting the use of formal register often include one or more of the following:

> ➤ To inspire or encourage;
> ➤ To teach or instruct;
> ➤ To recognize or honor;
> ➤ To sell or convince; or
> ➤ To move to action.

Consultative

When consultative register is used, one of the individuals involved in the interchange has "expert" status or an enhanced command of the topic at hand, yet there is a desire to interact with the listener or audience to confirm that communication has taken place.

Settings Where This Register Is Typically Used

Consultative register is generally used in one-on-one or small group interactions, commonly between service providers ("experts") and their consumers. This may include individuals such as health care providers and patients, lawyers and clients, teachers and students, or mental health practitioners and their patients. A unique feature about consultative register is that the register seems to follow the individual of expert status in interactions with consumers no matter what the physical setting is. For example, a doctor will typically maintain consultative register, turn-taking rules, sentence structure, etc. when dealing with a patient regardless of where the interaction takes place.

Vocabulary /Sentence Structure

Complete, compound sentence structure is the norm in consultative register. Utterances are often marked with professional or technical "jargon," terms that have specialized meaning within the particular technical or professional field of the "expert."

Slang and informal forms of address are not generally acceptable.

Turn-taking Rules
There is a variety of unwritten turn-taking rules in consultative register that vary depending on the personal style of the person of status. In some educational classes, for example, a student is expected to raise her/his hand before asking a question or inserting a statement or observation. In other classes, students wait for eye contact, a head nod or some other kind of recognition from the teacher before speaking. In the doctor or lawyer's office, the patient/client typically waits until the "expert" asks if there is a question or until there is a lull in the explanation being made to take the floor. Consumer interruptions when the expert is speaking are generally considered rude and unacceptable unless there is some type of emergency.

There are times when you may encounter the linguistic behaviors and turn-taking rules typical of formal register. This is true when give-and-take interaction is discouraged or disallowed between the person of status and their students, patients or clients. Even though there may not be much physical distance between the consumer and the "expert," a psychological separation is created leading to reduced or strictly regulated turn-taking. In this event, we would consider the linguistic register to be formal rather than consultative, even though the setting (classroom, doctor's office) is consultative in nature.

Rate And Volume of Speech/Size Of Signs
These features will be dictated by the physical environment, characteristics of the participants and the personal style of the speaker. Enunciation is expected to be clear and articulate but not as precise as that required in formal and frozen registers. However, if participants are unfamiliar with the language or specific terminology being used, the rate of production may be slowed. Because this register is typically used in one-on-

one and small group interactions, the physical distance is not usually significant to the volume of speech/size of signs will be reduced compared to that of formal register. There may be settings, however, where physical noise or visual distractions require increased volume/size.

Rules of Interaction

There are typically prescribed physical distances between the parties in a consultative exchange. This influences acceptable greeting and leave-taking behaviors, as well as distance during the interaction. Shaking hands is acceptable in most cases but is not always mandatory or appropriate. Although the doctor may conduct a physical examination or banker may learn intimate details about one's financial well being, it is not appropriate for them to hug their patients or the customers at the beginning or end of a professional interaction.

The status of each participant may vary depending on the setting where the consultative exchange is taking place. If a plumber goes to see her/his lawyer, the attorney is the expert and the plumber will follow turn-taking, sentence construction, etc. expected in the attorney's office. If, however, the attorney has a clogged drain and calls the plumber, the plumber now holds expert knowledge and the attorney follows appropriate turn-taking, sentence construction, etc., when interacting with the plumber who comes to her/his home.

Typical Speaker/Signer Goals

The goals prompting the use of consultative register usually include teaching, informing, instructing diagnosing, descriing demonstrating and/or explaining.

Informal or Casual

When informal or casual register is used the participants involved have equal status. This typically involves neighbors with neighbors, church members with church members, etc.

Settings Where This Register Is Used

Informal register is commonly used when neighbors, co-workers, students, or colleagues are chatting as peers or equals. Thus, the settings where this register is used are limitless because it is the relationship between the individuals, rather than the physical space, that dictates the register.

Vocabulary/Sentence Structure

Sentences are slightly truncated resulting in some fragments, as well as run-on sentences within informal exchanges. Likewise, slang and improper grammatical forms are frequently used.

Turn-taking Rules

Turn-taking is much more fluid and a certain amount of interrupting to take the floor is acceptable in most cases. Participants often "finish each other's sentences" or presume what the other person was going to say. This behavior is possible because — unlike the turn-taking rules in some registers — corrections and clarifications can be made immediately if miscommunication or an incorrect assumption has been made.

Rules For Interaction

In many cultures, physical touch is more likely to be a part of an informal interaction — a special handshake, slapping each other on the back, or even exchanging hugs in greeting or leave-taking. The physical distance used with informal register is often fairly close.

Rate and Volume of Speech/Size of Signs

The casual nature of the interaction often results in a more rapid rate of speaking/signing, as well as less precision in enunciation and production. These exchanges usually happen when the parties are close in physical proximity, seated at a table in the restaurant, chatting over the backyard fence, or standing at the water cooler in the office. Therefore, the volume of speech and size of signs is significantly reduced.

Typical Speaker/Signer Goals

The use of informal register can be motivated by a multitude of speaker/signer objectives including:

> ➤ To tease or cajole;
> ➤ To inquire or inform;
> ➤ To share or borrow; and
> ➤ To give or take.

Intimate

This does not mean the individuals involved are sleeping together! Intimate register refers to communication exchanges that take place between individuals who have a shared history or experiential base that influences the communication dynamics. You may have been with several friends or coworkers when one of them said, "Right! *For a fee ...*" and the others in the group break down with laughter. When you ask what's so funny, someone will reply, "inside joke" or "you had to be there." This is an example of intimate register.

Settings Where This Register Is Used

This register is used primarily in informal, casual settings although it is really dependent on the relationship of the two individuals who are interacting, rather than being restricted to specific settings. Because it is not dependent on signed or spoken lexicon, it can include a "knowing look" passed from one person to another in a setting as formal as a wedding or as informal as sitting in a hot tub.

Vocabulary/Sentence Structure

Because of the common experiential frame, the individuals involved in an intimate exchange are able to communicate without the use of complete sentences and in certain cases, without the use of any language at all.

Fig. 1-5   Intimate Register Exchange

Marie and her 14-year-old daughter Emma are in the car with Marge, an acquaintance, in the back seat. Marge overhears the following interchange:

EMMA: Mom, I've been thinking … .

MARIE: Yeah, I know, but …

EMMA: I think we could if …

MARIE: (gives Emma that look)

EMMA: I'd be willing to go half if …

MARIE: Well, I'll call her and ask …

EMMA: Super! Thanks, Mom

Now, Marge is certain she has heard English, but she has absolutely no idea what has just been said. This is typical of intimate register. Only those who have the shared experiential base can fully comprehend what is being said (or the meaning of certain gestures and nonverbal comments)

Turn–Taking Rules

Turn-taking is rapid, sentences are frequently incomplete, and there is a noticeable absence of specialized jargon or technical language.

Rules For Interaction

Whereas participants in an informal register exchange may finish each other's sentences, individuals engaged in intimate register dialogue seem to read each other's minds when observed by an outsider.

Jan's Gems: The Clothing Analogy

Communication is like getting dressed. A thought or idea is "naked" since it comes into your head devoid of language. However, when we share an idea with another person, we have to dress it up in "clothing" made up of linguistic and paralinguistic[a] elements selected from the speaker's source language "closet."

As the listener takes in the encoded or "clothed" message, s/he analyzes or "undresses" it in order to identify the intent or "naked idea" being expressed. If communication is successful, the message perceived is the same as that sent — including modifications made by the sender in response to the transactional dynamics between speaker and listener in the act of sharing the idea.

In most communication events both participants have a linguistic "closet" or repository where at least one language is stored, including the knowledge of how to complete a complex variety of linguistic acts; such as seeking directions, asking questions, teasing, insulting, inspiring, informing, explaining, evading, etc. The more "clothes" one has in her/ his "closet," the easier it is to produce variations of:

+ *__Register__ — (informal) swimsuits and (formal) tuxedo/cocktail dress; (intimate) underwear and (consultative) business suit*
+ *__Semantics and shadings in meaning__ — not just blue shirts — azure, teal, royal, navy, turquoise, etc.*

The reason one is communicating (speaker goal) and the environment (context) within which the communication is taking place (the status of each individual, the location of the interchange, etc.) determines which "clothing" the speaker will select to "dress" her/his ideas.

Message construction is closely entwined with the cultural norms in which the communication is taking place. In the following chapter, we will look at the influence of culture on message construction and communication.

---

[a].Tone of voice, gestures that accompany an utterance, eye gaze, facial expressions.

CHAPTER REVIEW
Key Points

Communication takes place between two or more people who sometimes share cultural, experiential and linguistic backgrounds, or sometimes they have nothing in common. These similarities and differences influence the nature and success of communication.

Communication is...

✦ Complex and imprecise;
✦ Linked to culture — you can only understand the intended message if you understand the cultural frame of the speaker;
✦ The principle way relationships are formed and maintained;
✦ Made up of constructed messages including linguistic elements (words/signs) and nonverbal elements (facial expressions, gestures, vocal/facial tones, etc.);
✦ Transactional (multi-directional), taking place in an environment shared by two or more people. One's ability to participate in communication is influenced by psychological and physiological noise.

Interpreters must understand the nature of communication and their role as a mediator of communication between two people.

MESSAGES ARE CONSTRUCTED

✦ To convey an idea, ask a question or share information with another person using a combination of speech/signs, affect and nonverbal communicative elements.

✦ Are influenced by where they are, the person with whom they are communicating, the reason (goal) they hope to accomplish, cultural norms and a number of other factors.

✦ Encompass number of features, including:

   ✓ Speaker/Signer Goals which determines words/ phrases chosen, tone of voice, degree of directness, etc.;

   ✓ The Context ... including the people involved (and their status) and the location;

   ✓ The Degree of Directness, clarity, and overt expression of the speaker's intent. Four strategies used to limit the degree of directness are:
- ➤ Equivocation;
- ➤ Euphemisms;
- ➤ Abstractions; and
- ➤ Passive Voice

   ✓ Powerful/Powerless Speech, patterns of speech that make a person seem more or less confident and credible. This is influenced by the culture in which the interaction is taking place.

    Powerless forms include:
- ➤ Hedges
- ➤ Hesitations
- ➤ Intensifiers
- ➤ Polite forms
- ➤ Tag questions
- ➤ Disclaimers

   ✓ Responsible Language through which the speaker takes responsibility for her/his statements, beliefs and feelings.

✓ Linguistic Register determine the levels of formality in a message.

	FROZEN	FORMAL	CONSUL-TATIVE	CASUAL	INTIMATE
TURN-TAKING	None	Limited/controlled	Restrained but active	Fluid; inter-ruptions allowed	Interruption is common
SENTENCE STRUCTURE	Complex; sometimes archaic	Complex; compound	Fully formed	Fragments; some run-ons	Incomplete
VOCABU-LARY	Formal and/or archaic	Formal	Technical jargon	Informal	Some lexicon has personal meanings
VOLUME/SPEED	Large; slower than normal speed	Large; slower than normal speed	Conversa-tional speed and signing space	Relaxed signing space; faster than conversa-tional	Small, truncated; sometime words/signs are not required
TOPICS ALLOWED	Limited	Impersonal	Professional	Personal	Personal

THOUGHT QUESTIONS

1. Name and define five linguistic registers. Identify the three registers most commonly involved when Sign Language interpreters work.

2. Take the idea of moving or relocating and think of vocabulary that is appropriate to discuss this action in each register and in what settings they might occur. Try this exercise with the concepts of urination, death/dying, and missing work or school.

3. What are "paralinguistic" features of communication? Give examples in both English and ASL or French and LSQ.

CD STUDY GUIDE

✦ Meet the authors of our textbook, as well as the experts you will be seeing on the CD Study Guide

✦ The various activities in the guided Chapter 1 Study Guide on CD will allow you to understand the concepts in this chapter more completely and to apply them to your life experience. Work through the Chapter 1 Study Guide on CD, completing all activities, then submit to your instructor or share with your learning partner.

SUGGESTED ACTIVITIES

✦ Prepare a 10-minute presentation on some topic for the class. Tape record your "consultative register" presentation. Then sit down with a friend over dinner and talk about the same topic, recording the "informal register" conversation. Make a list of the things you notice between the two "presentations."

✦ Working in teams, develop a role play of two communication interactions. Have fellow students identify which register was used by noting physical distance, type of language used, sentence structure/ vocabulary selection, etc.

✦ Analyze several ASL video tapes, identifying in each the register, pointing out specific features that mark register variations in ASL.

Endnotes

1. Adler & Towne (1999); Steward (1986); Schutz (1966)
2. Ross & McLaughlin, Eds. (1959); Schachter 1959); McDaniel with Johnson *(1975); Shattuck (1980).
3. Adler & Towne (1999)
4. Moores (1992), p. 23.
5. Burgoon (1994); Manusov (1991); Hall (1969)

Endnotes

1. Adler & Towne (1999); Steward (1986); Schutz (1966)
2. Ross & McLaughlin, Eds. (1959); Schachter 1959); Mc-Daniel with Johnson *(1975); Shattuck (1980).
3. Adler & Towne (1999)
4. Moores (1992), p. 23.
5. Burgoon (1994); Manusov (1991); Hall (1969)
6. Paul (1993); CIT Taskforce (1983) -- included Dennis Cokely, Betty Colonomos, Jan Kanda (Humphrey), Don Renzulli, Ken Rust, Theresa Smith and Sharon Neumann Sholow. For a complete report, see McIntire, Ed. (1984).
7. Shaw (1987)
8. Graha, Papa and Brooks (1992)
9. Barr (1999)
10. Gonzales (2000)
11. Ibid.
12. Shaw (1987)
13. Joos (1967)
14. Shaw (1987)

The Importance of Communication

CHAPTER TWO
The Influence of Culture
on Communication

Communication never happens in a vacuum. The very definition incorporates the concept of an exchange of ideas or information between two or more people. A part of the communication environment is the cultural milieu. Culture frames the entire event including assumptions that will be made and understandings derived by the various participants. Differences in cultural experience contribute to the challenge of effective communication.

DEFINITIONS OF CULTURE

There are literally hundreds of definitions for culture. Understanding the concept is further complicated by the expanded meanings given to the word day-by-day. Culture is enigmatic and largely amorphous — impossible to capture, put into a container, measure, or otherwise get our hands on. The United Nations Educational, Scientific and Cultural Organization (UNESCO) defines culture as "a dynamic value system of learned attitudes with assumptions, conventions, beliefs and rules that permit members of a group to relate to one another and the world."

Tyler, an early anthropologist,[1] defines culture as complex, including: knowledge, beliefs, art, morals, laws, customs and any other capabilities and habits acquired as a member of the culture. In an imaginary culture, that could mean ...

✦ *Knowledge* — how to kill xuipe for meat and clothing;
✦ Beliefs — the wuip has special powers which can help us succeed in our hunt for the xuipe;
✦ *Art* — embedded beads on the forearm or the dyed designs on clothing;

✦ *Morals* — it's okay to help yourself to your neighbor's things, but it is immoral to take another's last hunting knife;

✦ *Laws* — if one takes another's last hunting knife, he or she shall be punished by being sent out on the tundra alone for fourteen nights;

✦ *Customs* — if your brother dies, his wife and children become your responsibility.

Padden and Humphries, Deaf researchers and educators, have defined culture as "a set of learned behaviors of a group of people who have their own language, values, rules of behavior, and traditions."[2] Marie Philip, Deaf researcher and sociologist, has stated that culture can be divided into three subsets of norms and values:[3]

✦ *Material* — including material things such as food, clothing, and other tangible items (e.g., In North American culture, women wear long white satin gowns when getting married and people eat turkey on Thanksgiving);

✦ *Behavioral* — rules for behavior which can be observed, taught and learned (e.g., In North American culture, don't pick your nose in public and do say "excuse me" when you burp or step in front of someone);

✦ *Cognitive* — behavior learned and developed as a child that has a deeper meaning and which is not easily observed or understood (e.g., In Japan, how deeply to bow when greeting another person, how long to sustain a bow and the appropriate eye behaviors that accompany each bow).

Because the cognitive aspects of culture are difficult to observe, one of the first approaches to learning about a culture is by looking at the material aspects and behavioral norms of the members. For discussion in this text, culture will be defined as "a system of meanings and values that shape one's behavior."[4]

THE ROLE OF CULTURE

But why do cultures come into existence? Culture results from a group of people — who have shared experiences, common interests, shared norms of behavior, and shared survival techniques — coming together to form a community. Such a group seeks each other out for social interaction, emotional support and physical safety. In the coming together, a culture is formed so they can act in concert on significant issues.[5] Cultures are made up of many elements, including general beliefs, religious beliefs, myths, values and knowledge.[6]

> Cultural beliefs, such as attitudes toward illness and disability, shape societal thinking. Aspects of culture, such as language, are fluid because they tend not to persist generation after generation. On the other hand, static aspects of culture such as kinship systems, attitudes and beliefs do tend to persist generation after generation.[7]

The culture in which we are reared shapes our concept of who we are; language is the primary instrument of that shaping. Culture defines the meaning and value of one's:

➤ Family and place in it (e.g., birth order);
➤ Gender;
➤ Social experiences;
➤ Economic status;
➤ Educational experiences;
➤ Physical, mental, emotional and spiritual development; and
➤ Temperament or personality type.

Your culture defines who is beautiful or handsome; it will dictate if you are valued because of your gender or physical characteristics. In certain cultures, birth order can dictate one's role in the family, inheritance and even career.

Culture determines simple daily activities such as how people introduce themselves. Most people of European descent will introduce themselves by giving their first name, surname, town and country. However, people from many Asian groups reverse this order of information, identifying their country, town, surname and finally their first name. Many Hindus will begin with their caste, followed by their town and finally their name.[8] These behaviors reflect different cultural values and norms.

Some cultures value independence and personal initiative; they send negative messages — both explicit and silent — about being too dependent. Other cultures value *inter*dependence. Accordingly, they foster loyalty to the group (family, clan, community) and discourage the focus of attention on the individual and his or her accomplishments. In these cultures, it is rarely appropriate for an individual to make a unilateral decision. Rather, they are expected to consult with the family and, depending on the seriousness of the decision, with the extended family.

One group that holds these beliefs is that of American Indians where the extended family plays a critical role.

> ...if you must have a decision on an important matter, expect to wait a few days, weeks or months. The family will want to discuss a decision with the clan (extended family) before giving a final response.[9]

Culture determines if it is more desirable to stand out or to blend in.

> In Japan...everyone seemed to have the same goal — to become like everyone else. The word for "different," I was told, was the same as the word for "wrong"... A common maxim encountered in various

contexts said, "The nail that sticks out must be ham-mered down.[10]

THE RELATIONSHIP OF CULTURE AND LANGUAGE

The relationship between language and culture is so deeply entwined that it makes no sense to talk about one without the other.[11] While culture is a system of meanings and values, language is the primary medium through which culture is communicated and shared with others. Therefore, "culture is always at least a silent participant in any interaction."[12] It is imperative then, that individuals involved in communication recognize and understand their own cultural frame as well as that of those with whom they are communicating .

TWO WORLD VIEWS

In her book *Reading Between the Signs*,[13] Anna Mindess has done a masterful job of laying out two world views into which most cultures fall and describing some of the norms of each. These distinctions are summarized below, but readers are encouraged to read Mindess's text in full. Understanding this base of information is critical for individuals who plan to work as interpreters.

World cultures can be divided into **collectivist** and **individualist** cultures. Approximately 70% of the world's cultures fall into the category of collectivist.[14]

Mainstream North American cultures, for example, typically encourage people to be outspoken and assertive at home, work and school. This includes discussing how they feel about events and people. These characteristics fit *individualist* behaviors.

Let's look at the traditional cultures of the Indigenous peoples In North America, which generally fall into the *collectivist* category. For example, the Zuni of the American Southwest believe that it is much better to listen than to talk. They believe self-control is a great virtue and that feelings are private. According to Epaloose, a Native American anthropologist, "showing feelings is like taking off your clothes in public"[15] and any public expression of either positive or negative emotions would be an embarrassment to both the individual and to his or her family and tribe. He notes:

> Because we don't speak so much, we have both the need and the time to be better at paying attention to what other people say and what they do to show their emotions. This listening can be helpful in school where we care less about competing for a teacher's recognition than in understanding what we are supposed to learn... We may not get the recognition that comes from being good talkers, but in the long run I am confident that our restraint will be rewarded.[16]

It should be noted that there is a great deal of cultural diversity among Native groups in North America. No two groups share identical cultural characteristics, yet the underlying fabric of the traditional norms adheres closely to those of other collectivist cultures.

As indicated in Figure 2-1, there are a number of characteristics in various cultures that can be studied to determine if a culture can be termed collectivist or individualist. Some of those are highlighted over the next several pages.

FIG. 2-1 CULTURAL CHARACTERISTICS Collectivist vs. Individualist	
COLLECTIVIST	*INDIVIDUALIST*
IDENTITY	
Individuals define themselves and others by their group membership; keen awareness of group needs and feelings; individuals are expected to contribute to and take care of the group, even if it means giving up personal plans or goals	Individuals define themselves and others by their immediate personal achievements; feelings are focused on the individual rather than the group; independence is highly valued and individuals are expected to take care of themselves.

FIG. 2-1 CULTURAL CHARACTERISTICS Collectivist vs. Individualist	
COLLECTIVIST	*INDIVIDUALIST*
SHARED KNOWLEDGE	
High degree of shared knowledge and a common history; interpersonal contact is a high priority.	Less expectation of shared knowledge and a common history; interpersonal contact has a lower priority while information gathering has the highest priority.
TIME	
Based on a gut sense of readiness; strong reinforcement for the process and stopping "when done;" normal to take one's time to think, ruminate and fully consider a proposal or idea before responding.	Rude if others arrive late or the meeting is delayed because time is based on the clock and the calendar; strong reinforcement for starting and finishing "on time;" a person is seen as evasive or untrustworthy if they take too long to respond to an idea or if there are frequent long pauses in an interaction.
TRUST & CREDIBILITY	
Based on one's gut sense of the other person's integrity and the role they have played within the group; experience is valued as much as facts.	Based on evidence and hard facts, as well as the logical organization of the information, results and analytical thinking is rewarded
STATUS	
Status is defined by one's connections within the group and to any contributions one's family-group has made to the larger group; accomplishments are ascribed to the group rather than the individual.	Status is defined by one's individual accomplishments and, to a significantly lesser degree, those of immediate family and colleagues; accomplishments result in individual awards and recognition
SPORTS	
Sports are more likely to be team-based, although there are some individual sports	Sports are more likely to be individual-based, even in team sports, individual skill is recognized.
DOING BUSINESS	
Considered rude to get right down to business in a meeting; expected that social connections will be made prior to business — after all, getting to know the other person is the only way to judge her/his character and integrity in the business interaction.	Sense the need to get right down to business in a meeting; frustrated by too much social chit chat; urgency to have facts, figures and research — after all, this is the only way to judge the integrity of a business proposal.

FIG. 2-1 CULTURAL CHARACTERISTICS Collectivist vs. Individualist	
COLLECTIVIST	*INDIVIDUALIST*
GROUP MEMBERSHIP	
Individuals are members of relatively few groups; membership in those groups is long-term and have fairly rigid membership requirements.	Individuals are members of numerous groups and membership requirements are quite flexible; duration of membership in those groups depends on the needs and goals of the individual.
HISTORY	
Great value on the past, history and traditions; reluctance to let go of former events/realities	Focus on the future with new and innovative things; tendency to forget the past and rush through the present.
ACCOMPLISHMENTS	
Major accomplishments are celebrated and lauded as a group accomplishment, even when attained by an individual member. Ideas don't "belong" to the person who brings them forward, therefore no one person would claim credit for an idea; accomplishments are ascribed to and celebrated by the group; loyalty to the group is rewarded.	Individual accomplishments are celebrated and lauded; credit is generally given to the individual. One is defined by his or her words and ideas are seen as the intellectual property of the one who has expressed them publicly; rewards are based on individual merit.
SOCIAL OBLIGATIONS	
Social and civic contributions are expected from all members of the group; members will socialize primarily within the group and will take on civic responsibilities to promote the group's welfare	Social and civic duty is an individual choice; social interactions may be altruistic or they may be used to benefit the individual, achieve personal goals or to show off his or her accomplishments.
CREDIT	
It is dishonorable to accept individual credit for something accomplished without recognizing those who have pioneered the efforts made as well as those members of the group.	Individual accomplishments are rarely considered in light of the efforts that preceded one's own.
PUNISHMENT	
Severe punishment would be banishment from the group — even temporary shunning would be a serious punishment.	Severe punishment is defined as taking away one's individual freedom, goals or personal plans

FIG. 2-1 CULTURAL CHARACTERISTICS Collectivist vs. Individualist	
COLLECTIVIST	*INDIVIDUALIST*
INTERACTIONS	
The context of an event is as important as the event itself; the listener is responsible for the communication; relationships and quality of life are valued.	The thoughts expressed by specific words are more important than the interaction itself; the speaker is responsible for the communication; achievement, results and materialism are valued.
DISCOURSE	
Discourse is often structured to lay a time-ordered (history based) frame upon which new ideas can be proposed.	Discourse typically structured to refer to the present and future with occasional references to the past where essential.

Definition Of Status

Cultures ascribe status to their members in a variety of ways. In many Asian cultures, for example, the status of family is primary and the individual's identity is seen in relation to his or her family. People with cultures based in Pacific Island countries come from a different root, but they have a similar concept that a person's identity is related to his or her role within the group.[17]

Cultural Sense Of Time

One's sense of time is also based on cultural rearing. In many Western cultures, people's lives are often dictated by the clock, appointment books and schedules. Appointments are expected to be kept and people are expected to show up on time. There are also "proper" times for certain activities. For example, in some cultures, tea should be served between 4:00 and 5:00 while dinner is served between 8:00 and 9:00. Being "on time" in some Western cultures means arriving at least 15 minutes early.

Collectivist cultures have a different set of priorities and values related to time. In many cultures, clock-time is not highly valued and the concept of "on time" has little significant meaning. In the Navajo tradition, the present is of extremely high value and, consequently, there is great emphasis on the here and now. Anything that is taking place at the moment supersedes things that have not yet begun. This sometimes leads to missed appointments — not because the appointment is less valued, but simply because the cultural view of time is different.[18]

Beginning sojourners in the Deaf community often comment that "nothing starts on time." If an event is advertised to begin at 6:00 p.m., the planned activities may not actually begin until 6:30, 7:00 or even later. The outsider's view is that things are running late, but the Deaf perspective is that the valuable act of connecting with community members is taking place. This has priority over the clock. This is an example of a classic cultural conflict.

CULTURAL IDENTITY

One's cultural identity influences his or her communication. Cultural identity is complex because of the intricacies of culture and group membership. People are born into a culture of origin — Jewish, Inuit or Ukrainian, for example. They are also identified with one or more categories: male or female, able-bodied or physically disabled, Deaf or hearing, and so on. Over time, individuals may choose to identify with additional groups — religious, recreational, educational, etc.

People vary in terms of how strongly they choose to identify with a group. For some, their culture of birth may be the most salient part of their identity. For others, it is simply incidental. Imagine, for example, an American child of Anglo-Saxon parents who move to Korea when their daughter is two. As the child grows up, she learns Korean and adopts Korean cultural norms side by side with the language, culture, and behavioral norms of her American family. Eventually, she must make decisions that determine which culture will form the heart of her personal identity. This identity will affect her perspective.[19]

Let's listen to the real-life account of Daria Muse, an African American child who lived in South-Central Los Angeles while attending school in a predominately white, middle class suburb. She describes the wide repertoire of behaviors used to juggle her cultural and group affiliations:

> In a roundabout way, I was told from the first day of school that if I wanted to continue my privileged attendance in the hallowed classrooms of Beckford Elementary School, I would have to conform and adapt to their standards. I guess I began to believe all that they said because slowly I began to conform.
>
> ... I began living a double life. At school I was prim and proper in appearance and in speech but during the drive on the school bus from Northridge to South-Central, my other personality emerged. Once I got off the bus, I hardened my face and roughened my speech to show everyone who looked my way that I was not a girl to be messed with.[20]

Let's consider a woman who uses Spanish as her primary form of communication and whose family of origin subscribes to Hispanic cultural norms. She may decide, as her parents did, that Hispanic culture will dictate her beliefs and the norms she will follow. However, she may prefer to identify primarily as a woman or as lesbian, with those associations taking precedence over her ethnicity.

> Culture and group tendencies are dynamic and change over time. They are not the same for all members of the group. Nevertheless, cultural or group tendencies exist ...[21]

THE INFLUENCE OF CULTURAL AFFILIATION ON COMMUNICATION

Communication takes place between people — people who bring with them cultural and group memberships, both visible and invisible. These memberships infuse each individual with expectations regarding roles, behavior, communication, politeness and much more. However, most of us are not consciously aware that we harbor or act upon these invisible expectations, nor are we sufficiently aware of the expectations brought to interpersonal exchanges by members of other cultural groups.

For example, modern day North America has historically been dominated by a white, Anglo-Saxon, male cultural orientation. This frame and its influence have long exerted an invisible influence on our definition of what is acceptable or "right" in the realm of communication. The norm for respectful communication generally includes characteristics such as:

+ Speaking directly to the other individual and calling him or her by name;

+ Making and maintaining fairly consistent eye contact. (Although, if the contact is sustained for too long, it can be construed as a domineering, threatening or as a sexual overture, instead of a gesture of respect);

+ Using an assertive volume of speech — one that can be clearly heard in the environment where the interaction is taking place;

+ Speaking truthfully — indicating agreement or disagreement in a direct and forthright manner.

Based on these mainstream cultural norms, negative judgments are often made about someone who speaks without making eye contact or uses a volume of speech deemed too loud or too soft. Depending on the context, they might be wrongly judged as dishonest, lacking confidence or scheming. However, these norms are being challenged in the multicultural and multilingual world in which we live today. We are beginning to recognize the importance of *not* ascribing a motive or meaning to a behavior solely based on one's own cultural assumptions. Consider the following:

FIG. 2-2 Culturally Ascribed Significance to Communication Behaviors	
SOME CULTURES	OTHER CULTURES
Expect people to stand six-inches apart when addressing each other.	Expect people to stand 3-4 feet apart when addressing each other.
Interpret eye contact as insulting and disrespectful if offered from a younger person to an elder or from one of lesser status to one of greater status.	Interpret eye contact as a basic form of nonverbal respect, regardless of the age or status of the two individuals interacting with each other.
Value relationships and process over task completion.	Value task completion primary, even if it means sacrificing relationship and process.
Believe it is disrespectful to disagree with someone in front of others as there is no polite way to do so; negative feedback or evaluative comments must always be done in private.	Believe it is appropriate (even imperative) to publicly express disagreements with another (in a staff meeting, for example), so long as it is done with political correctness and sensitivity. Failure to share these opinions in an appropriate "public" forum is interpreted as complaining or manipulative.

Interpersonal Communication and Interactions

In the following example, we will look at the impact of cultural differences on interpersonal relationships — specifically, on the marriage between a Japanese man and an American woman. Masato was born, reared and educated in Japan. His single-parent family was of a low socio-economic class. Marie was born, reared and educated in the U.S. in an upper middle-class, two-parent family. They were members of several overlapping groups:

✦ Christians, active in their church;
✦ College-educated young adults;
✦ Interpreters — he, a Japanese/English interpreter; she, an American Sign Language/English interpreter.

Despite these commonalities, significant differences in their cultures and communication norms rise painfully to the surface in their marriage as they act and react unconsciously out of their invisible cultural frames.  Take a look at the challenges faced and misunderstandings that took place in their interactions as husband and wife.

Cultural Conflict Experienced by Masato & Maria
Their expectations about nurturing a child were different. When their young daughter came crying to their bed in the middle of the night, Masato swiftly returned the child to her bed and told her to "be strong" and "grow up." Maria wanted to go to the crying child and comfort her, but Masato forbade it.
Their expectations about personal modesty were different. In the midst of a long trip by car, Maria placed one of her bare feet on the dashboard as she stretched her leg to relieve a cramp in her calf. Masato was startled and offended that his wife would allow her feet to be displayed in such a shameful way. He demanded she put her foot down. Maria had grown up where children and adults went barefoot much of the day and had no concept of negative meanings associated with showing one's feet
Their expectations about turn-taking were different. Maria would sometimes take five to ten minutes to mull over something Masato had said before giving a response. Masato often took three weeks or more, during which time Maria began to despair at the delay.

Over time, Masato began to see his wife as selfish and immature — a woman who spoke too quickly, thought too shallowly, and who over-indulged her children. Maria viewed Masato as sullen and withdrawn, replete with hidden agendas and expectations that she could not decipher, and overly strict with the children. The couple eventually divorced because of "irreconcilable differences," an unfortunate testimony to the significance of cultural differences and the need for people to be aware of and sensitive to the impact of culture on communication and interpersonal interactions.

Business Communication and Interactions

The reality of cultural differences and resulting communication challenges is also experienced in the workplace on a regular basis. Consider the following example involving John, an African American senior sales trainer for a large software company.

CULTURAL CONFLICT AT WORK
John has held his job for eight months and has an outstanding record, both as a sales person and trainer. He is enthusiastic & has a reputation as a real "go-getter." His style in training is assertive and direct and honest. In fact, he takes pride in "telling it like it is" because he believes that people in sales have to be tough to deal with the "real world out there." He also tries to give a lot of positive reinforcement to his trainees, nodding his head affirmatively, giving them a "high five" when they do something well or pointing out their success in front of others
Karen Cho is one of John's trainees. Karen, who is Chinese American, respects John and sees him as a role model. However, Karen is uncomfortable with John's manner. She doesn't like his strong and direct critical feedback. In addition, he touches her to show his support of something she is doing or saying — a soft pat on the back or on the arm — which makes her feel physically threatened. In addition, John sometimes singles Karen out for praise in front of others, which makes her feel extremely uncomfortable.
One day some of the trainees tell John's supervisor, Richard, that they are offended by John's manner, describing him as angry and aggressive. This is done in a large group with all the trainees present. Karen agrees with their comments, but feels it is rude to make such comments in front of others. Two days after this large-group session, Karen goes to see Richard privately to voice her concerns about John's teaching style. Richard interprets Karen's private disclosures with suspicion since she didn't share them with the large group. Karen leaves, feeling dismissed and unheard.
Richard is European-American and has been on the job for approximately 4 months. He has never worked with an African American at John's level of seniority and has not made an effort to get to know John outside of the job.
Upon hearing complaints from the trainees, he calls John in and tells him to tone it down. John walks away from the meeting angry, certain that if he were white, his behavior would be seen as an asset rather than a liability.

Looking at this situation, we can identify several competing cultural values:

Richard

European-Americans usually come from a majority group background that puts them in a position of privilege whether or not it is sought or recognized. This means they:

✦ Often work in settings where a majority of their co-workers come from similar ethnic and cultural backgrounds;

✦ Don't have to worry about negative judgments or threats being made about them based solely on the color of their skin; and

✦ Are — as members of the majority group — most likely unaware of the differences between their own world view and the world views of non-white individuals around them.

John

Many African-Americans come from a culture that generally values a direct communication style, frequently including some physical contact. Further, most black people experience both subtle and blatant racism, including:

✦ Having to repeatedly prove themselves because of the assumption that their employment is a result of affirmative action alone;

✦ Skepticism about the competence of black people in management and senior roles; and

✦ Exclusion from informal networks and social interactions related to upward mobility within companies.

Karen

Karen's membership in Chinese American culture contribute significantly to her actions, feelings and reactions in this situation. Many Asian cultures:

✦ Value modesty and reserve. Physical contact is
largely reserved for physical intimacy;

✦ Are reluctant to complain or express emotions directly as well as a belief that "public" criticism is disrespectful. It is more appropriate for an individual
to go privately to another person to express negative
comments; and

✦ Exhibit a strong work ethic and belief that public
praise is empty and meaningless — after all, workers are expected to "give their all" for the company.

SIGNIFICANCE FOR INTERPRETERS

Effective communication requires that we each identify our
own cultural identity and group membership and understand
how it influences our expectations in communication. Further,
it is incumbent on professional communicators to learn about
the cultural norms and world views
of others in order to avoid insensitive
comments or judgmental reactions
toward those who have a different
cultural frame.

Interpreters are professional communicators. It is their job to
mediate communication between people of *at least* two different languages and cultures and multiple group identities. Interpreters bring to these interactions their own language, culture
and group memberships, all of which influence how the interpreter views the interaction at hand. It is critical for interpreters
to be fully cognizant of the unconscious expectations arising
from these allegiances, and the impact this has on their own
interpersonal communications. Further, interpreters must be
able to effectively identify and properly represent the various
cultural frames and filters that are influencing the communication being interpreted.

Finally, interpreters must be able to identify the cross-cultural dynamics that influence their interactions with fellow professionals in order to identify and reduce the potential for cultural misunderstandings.

CHAPTER REVIEW
Key Points

Communication: Exchange of ideas or information that happens in a culturally influenced communication environment; one must understand the cultural frame of the speaker to fully comprehend the meaning intended.

Culture: Provides a frame or schema for living within a specified group of people; cultures vary in a number of ways (degree of interdependence and independence, gender roles, etc.).

Definitions of Culture:

✦ "Dynamic value system of learned attitudes with assumptions, conventions, beliefs and rules that permit members of a group to relate to one another and the world" (UNESCO).

✦ "A set of learned behaviors of a group of people who have their own language, values, rules of behavior, and traditions." (Padden and Humphries).

✦ Define a community's general beliefs, religious beliefs, myths, values and knowledge (Kohls).

Components of Culture:
✦ A complex whole, including knowledge, beliefs, art, morals, laws, customs and any other capabilities and habits acquired as a member of the culture (Tyler).

✦ Can be divided into three subsets of norms and values — material, behavioral, and cognitive (Philip).

✦ Culture and language are intertwined — language is the primary medium through which culture is communicated; it therefore reflects the norms, values and life style of the cultures using that language.

Two World Views:
✦ **Collectivist:** Seventy percent of world cultures fit into this category, including American Indian/Native cultures.
✦ **Individualist:** American culture fits within this category.

Review Figure 2-1 for a comparative list of norms in these two world views in the areas of shared knowledge, identity, status, trust/credibility, time, doing business, group membership, social obligations, accomplishments, sports, punishment, interactions, history, focus, etc.

Cultural Identity: Refers to the way one's culture of birth influences a person's beliefs and self concept. People are members of multiple groups, some of which subscribe to the norms and beliefs of the culture of birth and some which vary considerably from those norms. Ultimately individuals make choices regarding the culture that will form the heart of their personal identity.

Culture and Communication: Culture dictates expectations regarding roles, behavior, communication norms, politeness, etc. These norms include such things as using attention-getting and attention-maintaining techniques, appropriate eye contact and volume of speech/physical distance when communicating. Understanding a speaker's cultural identity will help the listener uncover the meaning and intention of communication expressed. Figure 2-2 outlines some of those differences.

53

Significance for Interpreters

Interpreters are professional communicators, mediating interactions between people of different language and culture groups. Cultural differences have direct influence on interpersonal communication and interactions in both the personal and professional realm. It is critical for interpreters to be aware of their own cultural beliefs and identity. It is also essential for interpreters to understand different cultural perspectives and to accept those differences in a non-judgmental way. Further, interpreters must be able to identify cross-cultural dynamics that influence interactions and that may cause cultural misunderstandings. They must learn to properly represent the cultural frames and filters that influence the communication being interpreted.

THOUGHT QUESTIONS

1. What is the meaning of culture?
2. How does culture influence behavior?
3. How does culture influence communication?
4. Do interpreters need to know their own culture in order to be a competent interpreter? Why or why not?
5. What cultures, other than Deaf culture, does an interpreter need to understand? How might an interpreter learn about diverse cultures?

CD STUDY GUIDE

✦ The various activities in the guided Chapter 2 Study Guide on CD will allow you to understand the concepts in this chapter more completely and to apply them to your life experience. Work through the Chapter 2 Study Guide on CD, completing all activities, then submit to your instructor or share with your learning partner.

SUGGESTED ACTIVITIES

✦ Conduct a survey to identify the diverse culture groups in your community.

✦ Divide the class into groups, each of which will research and report back on the cultural norms, beliefs and expectations of the culture groups identified in your community.

✦ Invite guest speakers representing diverse cultural groups to your class to share information and insights from their perspectives. Develop a list of questions to ask in advance of the presentation.

✦ View popular movies and identify styles of communication and behaviors that are culturally influenced (e.g.: The Joy Luck Club).

✦ Interview ethnically diverse Deaf people in your community. Ask them about the cultural norms and beliefs of their parents and how that has influenced them to date. Ask them to identify their primary cultural identity.

Endnotes

1. Tyler (1971)

2. Padden and Humphries (1988)

3. Philip (1986b)

4. Lane, P. (1999), p. 5.

5. Schein, (1989)

6. Kohls (1979), p. 119

7. Cheng (1993)

8. Christensen and Delgado (1993)

9. Holland, et al. (1982)

10. Pico Iyer as quoted by Adler and Towne (1992), p. 63.

11. Erting (1990) as quoted by de Garcia in Christensen and Delgado , p. 72

12. Lane, P. (1999), p. 5

13. Mindess, (1999)

14. Ibid.; Lane, P. (1999); Smith (1996)

15. Epaloose as quoted in Adler and Towne (1992), p. 150-151

16. Ibid.

17. Boggs (1985); Handy & Pukui (1972); Akamatsu (1993); Cheng (1993)

18. Epaloose as quoted in Adler and Towne (1992), p. 150-151

19. Lane, P. (1999), p.8

20. Daria Muse as quoted by Adler and Towne (1992), p.40

21. Blank and Slipp (1994), p. 7

CHAPTER THREE
Working in Multicultural Communities

We live in an increasingly multicultural country with a staggering range of diversity.[1] As world citizens and as professionals working in multi-cultural communities, we must become cognizant of the cultural norms, values and traditions of each group to the best  of our ability. Only in this way can we begin to understand the complete cultural context within which communication takes place and meaning is determined.

As stated previously, language cannot be separated from the culture in which it is used. Our ability to understand the meaning of words or signs is based on having an appropriate schema or cultural frame in place. These cultural frames are not universal. Indo-Canadians have a different script for holiday foods and celebration traditions than do Asians and Pacific Islanders. Further, communication can be interpreted on different levels — the literal (denotative) level and the deep structure (connotative) level. "Depending on one's frame of view and the particular context, each word can be interpreted in different ways."[2] It is one thing to hear the words, but another to know what they mean given the speaker's or signer's cultural frame of reference. In the same way, it is one thing to know ASL; it is another thing to know how to use it.

 In some cases, no script exists. People who are not Deaf, for instance, rarely have a script or schema for Deaf clubs or residential schools for the Deaf and many people who are Deaf or hard of hearing have no script or schema for community choirs. The frame held by hearing individuals in Canada and the U.S. includes sounds such as a melodious sonnet, birds singing or a quavering voice. General information is gleaned from sound-based sources. Values develop out of an environment rich with auditory communication sources

— telephone, radio, television, conversations with neighbors, co-workers, and others. Hearing people often inaccurately assume that Deaf and hard of hearing people bring the same experiential and linguistic frame into a variety of settings.

If you want to become an interpreter you must be fluent in two or more languages. Further, you must be knowledgeable of, and comfortable with, the wide variety of cultures that frame the communication and experiences of everybody for whom you interpret. In this chapter, we will look at four minority cultural groups[3] and note some features of those cultures that may impact the work of interpreter.

A Word of Caution: Before beginning this discussion, it is imperative to point out that members of cultural groups are not "cast from a single mold;" there is a great deal of diversity within each group. For example, among Hispanics, there are Dominicans, Colombians, Cubans, Spaniards, Mexicans, Puerto Ricans and a host of others. While they share a common language and some common cultural behaviors and values, they are also quite unique from each other. The same is true for African Americans, Asians, Pacific Islanders and other culture groups.

Further, some members of these communities adhere to the norms and values of their home culture while others pursue cultural duality in an attempt to live with one foot in mainstream society and the other in their familial culture[4] Some individuals are highly assimilated into the mainstream culture; others retain a strong ethnic identity. Still others are alienated from both their ethnic identity and the mainstream culture of the country in which they live[5] For some individuals from cultural minority groups...

...the only explicit knowledge they possess about their ethnic heritage is likely to be limited to stock phrases and food names. They may carry values from their ethnic communities but be unaware of the origins of those values, because these families are often physically integrated into suburban neighborhoods, their lifestyles reflect the ambiance of the neighborhood rather than anything noticeably ethnic.[6]

In spite of these differences, there are some cultural values and beliefs common to each larger ethnic group that can be identified[7] The danger in identifying these commonalities is that they may be misinterpreted as stereotypes.

The comparison of the cultural norms presented below is intended to highlight some significant characteristics interpreters need to be aware of because we live and work in multicultural settings. Readers are reminded that the norms and values of one culture should not be considered more correct or less correct than the norms and values of another cultural group.[8]

INTERPRETING WITH PEOPLE WHO
IDENTIFY PRIMARILY WITH DEAF CULTURE

Individuals who are Deaf or hard of hearing have several choices to make regarding cultural identification and group membership. There is the culture of one's origin, which could be European, African American, Hispanic, Native, or Indo-Canadian, among other possibilities. Some Deaf and hard of hearing individuals become members of Deaf culture and others do not. One person might see himself or herself as a Deaf Indo-Canadian — identifying primarily with Indo-Canadian culture and secondarily with Deaf culture. Another person might see himself or herself as an Indo-Canadian Deaf person — a Deaf person who happens to be Indo-Canadian.

Let's consider a Deaf woman who uses American Sign Language (ASL) as his primary form of communication and who prefers social interactions with others based on Deaf cultural norms as another example. Regardless of his ethnic culture of origin, she may select membership in the Deaf cultural group as her primary identifying factor. On the other hand, another Deaf adult may use ASL as her primary form of communication and prefer Deaf social norms, but she may still choose her membership in the African American culture or a lesbian group to be her primary identifying association.

This section will describe some of the cultural norms for those individuals who choose Deaf as their primary cultural descriptor and some implications for interpreters.

Ninety percent of all Deaf people are born into hearing families. The sense of "connectedness" to these families of origin depends on the degree of communication that has evolved between the hearing family members and the Deaf family member. Among the baby boomer generation and their predecessors, it was common for families to send their children away to residential schools for the Deaf, seeing their children only during holidays and summers. Communication between hearing family members and the Deaf child was usually limited to gestures, some lip-reading and perhaps fingerspelling or home signs.

In recent years, we have seen more programs emerge through which family members learn sign language and Deaf culture. The increased communication has made it possible for Deaf children to learn more about their personal family history and ethnic heritage. Likewise, hearing members of the family are increasingly likely to attend Deaf community events and to communicate with the Deaf family member's friends and peers.

Thus, when interpreting for Deaf children and youth, you can expect to see a variety of family constellations, each with different responses from hearing family members. Some of them communicate effectively with the Deaf family member, often using a combination of ASL, English-like signs, fingerspelling and gestures or home signs. Respecting these bonds and family traditions is important if you want to be an interpreter.

A Culture Based on Sight

The significance of the eyes and the hands in Deaf culture cannot be emphasized strongly enough. That is because everything that aural/oral-based communities do via sound is accomplished via visual and physical channels. This includes getting the attention of another, signaling the telephone or doorbell is ringing, communicating ideas and conveying art forms such as poetry.

In North American hearing culture, the voice is highly valued. People take elocution lessons and public speaking classes. Further, the ability to hear is considered vital. This is not the case among most Deaf people. There is, instead, a great deal of value placed on the eyes and hands. An example of this would be the angry response of many Deaf people when someone shoots a rubber band or throws an eraser across the room. Because of the inherent dangers to the eyes, this behavior is discouraged by the norms of Deaf culture.

Interpreters can demonstrate sensitivity to this value by ensuring there is proper lighting and an appropriate background when interpreting and by wearing solid colors that contrast with the interpreter's skin tone. This helps reduce eyestrain during long interpreting assignments.

Introductions, Greetings and Leave-taking

Like other collectivist cultures, Deaf culture is not typically concerned about clock-time. Meetings are likely to begin 20–40 minutes after the announced starting time.

Upon arrival at a community event, it is important for individuals to "connect" with other group members. At a bare minimum, this means making eye contact and giving a nod of recognition. Preferably, this means greeting each individual — often with a hug — and a brief social interchange. Leave-taking is also protracted, typically requiring 15-30 minutes of "closing comments" as the exiting individuals move toward the door.

The amount of information one must have in order to carry on significant communication is similar to that in other collectivist cultures. This affects introductions and "getting to know you" behavior. Among Deaf people, "knowing" a person generally includes knowing where that person works, where he or she went to school, if members of the person's family are Deaf, and if they share any mutual acquaintances. Through this type of interaction, the Deaf person can also determine the other person's identity and their connection to Deaf culture.

Interpreters must develop culturally appropriate greeting and leave-taking skills. They must also be able to recognize the need for an adequate interpersonal frame to be in place before starting an interpretation or conducting in-depth conversations with Deaf community members. This requires social interaction in the larger community, as well as arriving at appointments early to spend some "getting acquainted" time with the Deaf consumers.

Language of Interaction
The language of interaction among most Deaf people is American Sign Language, as discussed in the following chapter. Most Deaf people use English for written communication. However, for many, mastering written English is a life-long challenge.

Since there is no written form of ASL, group history is passed down from generation to generation in the form of "oral" traditions. Like the many cultures that value oral histories, storytelling is a highly prized art form. The advent of videotape is providing an avenue to record the history and traditions of Deaf people for the first time.

A prerequisite for anyone who hopes to become an interpreter is being competent in ASL, as well as English. This includes becoming familiar with the history of Deaf communities and the oral traditions passed down by master storytellers in the culture.

Communication Norms

Among Deaf people, the most common genre is narrative in nature. Thus visual events are discussed and elaborated upon with a great deal of detail. This is evidenced by the extensive use of role shift and a highly descriptive  classifier system. (*See Chapter Nine for more discussion on this topic.*) You might compare this with the way hearing people discuss auditory events such as music. Such a discussion might include the presence of "pleasant" sounds and the absence of offensive or grating sounds. English even has a way of incorporating sounds of objects into spoken words (buzz, scratchy, screeching, etc.).

Interpreters must become skilled at conveying information in the most visually accessible way. They must also develop comfort with conversation that incorporates graphic visual description, since this is one of the best ways to expand their linguistic and cultural competence.

Attention–getting and Signaling Devices

Because the culture is based on visual rather than auditory signals, the use of visual and physical signals for telephones, fire alarms, alarm clocks, and other such devices is the norm in the Deaf community. This includes flashing lights and vibrating mechanisms.

Attention-getting between people is also based on visual or physical signals. If you are trying to get one person's attention, you might tap him or her on the shoulder or ask a person near by to tap that person on the shoulder. If you are trying to get the attention of a group of people, you might use an arm-waving signal or, in some cases, flash the lights. There are unwritten rules about the appropriate way to flash the lights in different contexts, so hearing people should not use that signal until they know the correct number of times to flash them and the length of time between flashes. Hearing, Deaf, and hard of hearing people share some visual signals such as traffic lights and various signs (rest room, caution, etc.).

It is important for interpreters to develop knowledge and skill in various attention-getting and attention-maintenance devices, which are critical for starting and maintaining personal and interpreted interactions. Further, if you want to be an interpreter you might consider making your home and place of business "Deaf-friendly" by installing a TTY and visual signaling devices.

Eye Contact and Physical Presence
When communicating with a Deaf person in ASL, frequent, sustained eye contact is mandatory. Failing to maintain this norm is interpreted as being bored or disinterested. In mainstream North American hearing culture, this kind of eye contact can be misinterpreted as threatening or sexual, and is therefore avoided.

The nature of a visual culture requires that people be present in the same physical area to communicate. You can't communicate with someone in another room or through the bathroom door when you can't hear. Cultures that are based on sound allow less direct forms of communication, such as speaking without looking at the other person or talking to someone who is not physically present in the room. This is not to say that all members of hearing communities like or accept the norm of calling to someone from another room or talking from behind a newspaper.

Comfort with and skill in using appropriate eye contact is critical for interpreters. Further, you should look at your own communication norms and modify them as appropriate. For example, do you typically talk to people while doing something else (e.g., having a conversation while you are washing dishes)? If so, you should become aware of those habits now and prepare to modify them when interacting with Deaf and hard of hearing individuals.

Reciprocal Signals

 ASL is an interactive language, requiring frequent feedback from the participants in a conversation. Often, this can be as simple as nodding one's head to indicate comprehension, although there is a complex array of more sophisticated and subtle techniques. Collectively, these are known as reciprocal signals. Reciprocal signals are found in some auditory cultures, as well — Japanese, for example. It should be noted that affirmative reciprocal signals are used to indicate comprehension on the part of the listener and should not be misinterpreted as agreeing with what is being said. This can be very confusing for people who are not accustomed to reciprocal signals.

Interpreters need to study this aspect of the language and incorporate them into their interpretation, as well as their personal discourse in ASL.

Emotional Display

Emotions are displayed visually among Deaf people and this visual display of affect is a critical component of communication. In contrast, the visual display of emotions is actively discouraged in mainstream North American hearing culture. Hearing children learn fairly early not to make faces or to gesticulate. Rather, emotions are portrayed vocally, through vocal intonation and volume. This frequently causes misunderstanding between Deaf and hearing people. Hearing people frequently perceive Deaf people as "highly emotional," agitated, or even threatening due to the visual display of emotions that is more intense than what is used in hearing culture.

The fact that we are socialized to sublimate visible emotions by channeling them into our vocal intonation often results in sign language students struggling to incorporate visual emotive affect and facial expression into their signing. If you want to be an interpreter, you need to be aware of your own use of your body and face when communicating emotive information and develop skills in this area.

INTERPRETING WITH
AFRICAN AMERICAN DEAF PEOPLE

The heritage of African Americans is different from the other cultural minorities in North America. For the most part, members of this cultural group are the descendents of former slaves, brought to this country against their will and regarded as the property of a slave owner. While they originally came from various tribes and regions, African Americans today share a cultural base that grows from the common experience of disenfranchisement and oppression. In the eyes of most community members, authentic access and inclusion in the majority culture are still unattainable, as is social justice. Because of this, interpreters may find themselves working with Deaf and hearing members of the African American community who are angry and frustrated, some of whom are politically active in the quest for social justice and therefore may have an additional agenda when communicating with others. If you are a European-American and find yourself feeling personally attacked or blamed for an injustice, remember that the anger is rarely directed at you as an individual, but at the generic majority culture. Similarly, you might encounter Deaf people whose anger about oppression and lack of access is directed at all hearing people.

Family/Community

Although African American culture has been greatly influenced by several hundred years of domination by an extremely individualistic culture, it still retains elements of the collectivist cultures from which it originated. Elders are respected and cared for; the extended family plays an important role in sharing resources, supporting one another and teaching children strategies for survival[9]. A strong sense of cultural history and group identity is passed down through oral traditions in the family and religious institutions[10]. Family members often eat together on a regular basis and hospitality is generally extended to all visitors. Further, community members are expected to display manners and show respect to others when in public[11]. Interpreters working with members of this community would do well to reflect similar values and behaviors.

One note of interest: Hereditary deafness is much less prevalent among African American families than among European-American families[12]. Thus, in settings that involve family members, interpreters can expect primarily hearing parents, siblings, aunts, uncles and grandparents. You will also observe the strong bond of parent-child relationships demonstrated in open expressions of unconditional love.

Spirituality and Religion
Belief in a supreme being is pervasive in this culture and the church plays a central role in African American communities. Church attendance is strongly encouraged, responsibilities of leadership in the church are valued and songs termed "spirituals" are highly prized by all. Families will make any accommodation necessary to be sure their Deaf and hard of hearing children have access to religious training. Interpreters can expect to observe traditional values and discipline based on religious tenets as well as great respect for religious leaders. When interpreting in African American churches, interpreters can expect services that last two to three hours, a significant portion of which will be music, and a unique style of speech (which is actually a cultural art form) when the minister presents the sermon.

Language

When working in settings that reflect African American culture, interpreters may encounter folk tales, proverbs, aphorisms, verbal games and narrative oral poems. These are also valued art forms, handed down from one generation to the next[13]. Further, distinct styles of speech and dialects are used by some individuals, partly as an indication of community membership and unity. While all members of the culture do not use these linguistic variations, they serve as ways to honor and maintain historic and cultural distinctiveness[14] and should be respected by outsiders working with community members. Some understanding of each would be advisable for the individual who interprets African American church services, family reunions, and other events where these styles and dialects may be encountered.

Time/Status

Community norms vary in these areas, frequently reflecting individualist cultural norms. For example, status is often ascribed to the individual who has cars, fur coats and advanced university degrees. However, there has traditionally been some pressure on upwardly mobile community members to remain connected to the larger African American community rather than move away to primarily white churches and/or neighborhoods.

INTERPRETING WITH DEAF HISPANIC PEOPLE

The classification of "Hispanic" includes a very diverse population of people originating from South and Central America, as well as Mexico and Spain. In spite of this diversity, there are some underlying commonalities among the various Hispanic cultures, all of which fit the collectivist categorization.

Deaf and hard of hearing Hispanics often face discrimination within the Deaf community, as well as from members of the majority culture.

Language

They often come from a home that speaks Spanish and practices Hispanic cultural norms. For this reason, the family may not be overly concerned with the Deaf or hard of hearing family member's mastery of English. As the Hispanic population grows in Canada and the U.S., there is an increased likelihood that family members may speak no English or that one may speak some English but not be literate in the language.

Physical Boundaries

Members of most Hispanic cultures are comfortable with physical touch and tend to stand close to each other when speaking. This is partly because Spanish is a soft, low-volume language, which can sound almost like a whisper to people used to using English. Also, Spanish has relatively few plosives (consonants pronounced with a sudden release of breath) which means, as one Hispanic educator has said, "you won't get inadvertently spit on by the speaker when standing close."[15] Interpreters need to expect different physical boundaries when working with members of this culture. They also need to realize that the lack of physical closeness is interpreted by members of the culture as a sign of distance and rejection[16]. They may also need to change their placement in order to hear a Hispanic speaker.

Time

The overall pace of life in Hispanic cultures is unhurried. Priority is placed on maintaining relationships rather than promptness, thus being on time or early is not expected or valued — a difference that interpreters need to be aware of.

Learning Style

Hispanic people generally thrive in a cooperative learning environment rather than in competitive ones[17]. They often flourish in a student-centered, cooperative and hands-on educational setting[18]. This is summarized by one Hispanic woman who said:

"We are taught to listen, not to speak out; to work, not to do our best; to do anything for a friend and to work in a cooperative mode"[19]

When confronted with competitive or critical situations, or when receiving negative feedback, a culturally Hispanic person may "freeze" or be unable to respond.[20] An interpreter's awareness of these aspects will provide insight into common schema and places where cultural mediation may be required to provide access to the intent of the speaker or signer.

Family

Family is the primary cultural structure. Extended family members often live together or near by. Elders are respected and the father is usually seen as an authority figure. Children rarely talk back to parents and teachers are to be respected. Spanish reflects the cultural respect for elders and those in authority by embedding formal linguistic structures to be used when young people address their elders. Interpreters need to be aware of this when providing ASL-to-English interpretation, making certain to include visual indicators of respect toward others in their target language utterances.

Spirituality and Religion

Hispanic countries have a traditional connection with the Roman Catholic Church. Death is viewed as a natural part of life. Although sorrow is felt at the loss of a loved one, time and resources are not spent trying to avoid the inevitable or fearing the unknown because of the religious belief in a life after death. Thus, reasonable efforts are made regarding wellness, but extreme precautions are not the norm. There is generally an acceptance that health problems cannot always be solved. It is important that interpreters be aware of their own schemas and filters to be sure their own beliefs regarding death and illness are not intruding on the beliefs of the Hispanic Deaf individuals and their family members.

INTERPRETING WITH NATIVE[a] DEAF PEOPLE[21]

Current census figures indicate that there are over 1.5 million Native people in the United States and 800,000 in Canada,[22] and these populations are growing dramatically.[23] Consequently, the likelihood of working with Deaf Native individuals or with fellow interpreters who are Native is quite high. Understanding some distinctive cultural features will benefit one's interpersonal and communication skills.

Among the hundreds of Native bands, tribes and nations, no two entities share identical norms and cultural characteristics.[24] Overall, however, Native cultures are collectivist in nature. As a result, the group and group life is of primary value. There is respect for elders, experts and those with spiritual powers. Harmony between people, as well as between people and nature, is also a primary value.

When relocated from their traditional homes to residential schools for the Deaf, Native children suffered the traumatic loss of exposure to their tribal language, traditions, foods, ceremonies and beliefs, as well as daily contact with their highly valued family or band. Further, Native Deaf children have historically faced a great deal of discrimination within the Deaf community because of the majority culture's negative attitudes toward them as a group[25]. As adults, they may distance themselves from their traditional cultural beliefs and values, they may embrace their Native heritage, or they may attempt to remain connected to both.

---

a There are many terms used to refer to members of this group including First Peoples, Indian, American Indian, Native, First Nations, and Aboriginal. Preferred terms differ among various bands and nations. We will use the term "Native" here in an effort to simplify the writing.

71

Let's look at one family from the Navajo Nation. The Ben family is comprised of eleven children, four of whom are Deaf and two of whom are hard of hearing.

> The two oldest Deaf sisters and hard of hearing brother never attended school. They communicate in a unique, complex home sign system. In addition to these home signs, the hard of hearing brother also speaks Navajo. The three of them live in a traditional hogan near their immediate family on the reservation and raise livestock. The sisters also weave rugs and provide child-care for their nieces and nephews.

> The two younger Deaf sisters attended the state school for the Deaf in their state and use ASL, as well as their home sign system to communicate. They live and work in a metropolitan area, socialize primarily in the Deaf community and visit their family several times each year.

> The hard of hearing sister attended both the state school for the Deaf and a mainstreamed school with residential quarters. She is fluent in ASL and in the family home sign system, as well as spoken Navajo and English. She lives and works in the same city as her Deaf sisters and interacts primarily in the Deaf community.

 This family demonstrates the identity and cultural choices made by the Deaf members of one Native family. Different choices have been made because of the values learned from their culture of birth, as well as the individual personalities of each family member. This is clear evidence that each person's choice regarding cultural identity is unique.

Status and Work Ethic

Like most collectivist cultures, traditional Native cultures tend to be non-materialistic. Wealth and status are not viewed in terms of houses, cars, bank accounts or a job with a prestigious title. Status is achieved from supporting and contributing to your family/tribe and sharing what you have with others, not in the amount of things owned[26]. This has a direct impact on the cultural work ethic. Rather than being driven by work, members of the Native culture typically "work to live." That is, doing what is necessary to maintain life, but without the drive to collect, possess, and move up the social ladder.

Communication

Listening and observing are highly valued in many Native cultures. This leads to a decision-making process that is typically lengthy. An interpreter can expect that the Deaf Native consumer might take more time to respond to a question or might defer to their tribe or band before making any decision.

Native people typically place greater emphasis on watching, listening and observing things than on talking about what is going on[27]. Consequently, they may be viewed by members of the majority culture as withdrawn, quiet or even sullen when in fact they are watching, thinking, and learning in order to respond. One Apache man has said, "Watch, be a part, see. Through that you can come to an understanding."[28]

As a result of this emphasis on the visual modality, families often feel quite comfortable in developing and using home signs or formal sign language when there is a Deaf or hard of hearing family member.[29] Therefore, when working with Deaf Natives, interpreters may encounter hearing relatives and community members who either sign or use a highly developed system of home signs.

Family

Interpreters need to recognize the family structure in order to make appropriate interpreting choices and to understand the culture-of-origin context when working with Native Deaf individuals.

Many bands or tribes are matrilineal, tracing one's ancestry through the mother's bloodline, thus the mother, grandmother, and maternal uncle hold significant positions in the family. As a matter of fact, a person's maternal uncle in matrilineal cultures has a more significant role in their life than his or her father.

Regardless of matrilineal or patrilineal patterns, a characteristic common to all Native groups is the valued role of elders and the involvement of extended family members, particularly grandparents.[30] The extended family or band is usually involved when decisions are being made — typical of the collectivist orientation.

Language

Most of Deaf Native people you encounter as a sign language interpreter will probably use ASL. However, it is possible that the language used in their home is a Native language. This is because many Native languages are still in use and there is a growing movement to preserve and teach Native languages to younger members of the band or tribe. This means that when interpreting events involving the family members of a Deaf Native, you may find yourself working with a spoken language interpreter who is fluent in the Native language. You may also encounter family members who switch back and forth between English and their Native language. Interpreters in these settings require advanced process management skills to facilitate the complexities of multilingual communication. This is sometimes more challenging because the Native language interpreter may not be familiar with professional and ethical standards in the field of interpretation.

As mentioned above, certain cultural values and the fact that the syntax of many Native languages are similar to those of American Sign Language, there is a significant likelihood that family members have some way to communicate with their Deaf relative.[31] This can be both positive and negative for the interpreter. If the Deaf family member uses a combination of standard ASL and home signs, the hearing family member may be of great assistance to the interpreter. However, family member(s) who can sign are rarely trained as interpreters and may not trust interpretations that incorporate appropriate linguistic and cultural expansions and reductions.

Time

As described in the previous chapter, the present takes precedence over the future in collectivist cultures and planned events can be superseded by events taking place here and now.[32] If, for example, a doctor's appointment is scheduled for 11:00 a.m. and an out of town guest shows up at the person's house just as s/he is preparing to leave, priority is given to welcoming the guest rather than to the pre-existing appointment. For this reason, an interpreter who is working with members of this cultural group should not be offended if consumers arrive late to appointments or miss them all together. This is not a sign of disrespect, nor does it indicate a lack of interest in the meeting. It is simply a different cultural perspective of time.

Spirituality and Religion

Finally, interpreters may encounter a great deal of spiritual content in the context. Native cultures have a strong spiritual component that reinforces the inter-relatedness of mind, body, and spirit, as well as people with nature.[33] This is important in general, but is of particular import when interpreting in medical settings, as this quote from a Native leader illustrates:

> Man is a three-fold being made up of a body, mind and spirit. Illness affects the mind and spirit as well as the body. Wellness is harmony in body, mind and spirit. Natural unwellness is caused by the violation of a sacred or tribal taboo.[34]

Thus, there is little separation of religion and medical treatment. Healing ceremonies play an important role in the culture and usually involve the extended family and the band or tribe. Rituals connected to various spiritual and healing ceremonies include such practices as waiting a specific number of days following the ceremony before one can bathe, not cutting one's hair, and use of natural and herbal mixtures that may be made into teas or incense. However, the application of these traditional beliefs and practices varies from person to person as noted below:

> The general concepts of Indian spiritual and health beliefs described should not be taken as absolutes for all tribes or Indian individuals. Acculturation levels vary, affecting the degree to which an individual identifies with traditional Indian spiritual health practices.[35]

Children

Native people typically view children as complete, whole persons from a very young age. Thus children are given ample opportunities to explore and learn through experience in patterns that the dominant non-Native culture may view as "permissive."[36]

SUMMARY

As outlined in this chapter, we work in multicultural communities. Mediating between Deaf cultures and hearing culture is a significant part of our work as sign language interpreters, but it is also critical for us to become familiar with the wide range of other cultural practices and beliefs we may encounter.

You should also realize that after all of the classes you take and books you read, culture is a life-long pursuit that is best studied in the laboratory of life. Frequent social interactions with a variety of Deaf and hard of hearing individuals will slowly reveal the keys to cross-cultural understanding.

CHAPTER REVIEW
Key Points

It is important to understand how various cultures define what is expected of and accepted by their members. This chapter has provided a survey of a few of these norms for four cultural groups.

Our ability to understand the meaning of words or signs is based on having an appropriate schema or cultural frame in place. These cultural frames are not universal.

The degree of identification with one's familial culture varies from person to person. Some individuals are highly assimilated into the mainstream culture; others retain a strong ethnic identity. Still others are alienated from both their ethnic identity and the mainstream culture of the country in which they live.

The following chart summarizes some of the norms in four collectivist cultures: Native, Hispanic, African American and Deaf.

	Deaf	African American	Hispanic	Native
Family & Elders	Deaf community "elders" valued; Deaf community often valued as "family"	Elders and church leaders respected; matrilineal	Family is primary cultural structure; elders respected	Elders and extended family (including tribe) valued; some bands matrilineal
Status	Fluent signers, accomplished story tellers, political leaders fighting for Deaf rights	Varied	Varied	Status in sharing resources, not in collecting things
Work Ethic	Mixed — some have N. American values, others see no shame in living off disability payments	Long history of strong work ethic	Historic work ethic marked by relaxed pace	Work is valued to live but not valued simply for the sake getting more

	Deaf	African American	Hispanic	Native
Spirituality	Varies from individual to individual	Church plays a central role in the community	Many are influenced by traditional Catholic values	Strong spiritual component to culture; little separation between medicine and spiritual practice
Decision Making	Often gather information and perspectives from other community members before making a decision	Mixed although family often consulted	Mixed although family often consulted	Slow to make decisions; group consultation required
Geneology	Variety of ethnicities represented; 90% from hearing families; deaf lineage valued	Primarily descendents of former slaves	From Mexico, Central and South America, as well as Spain.	Original people of N. America; many bands matrilineal
Home Language	Usually English although the native language of Deaf individuals is ASL	English although distinctive styles of speech are used to demonstrate group membership and to honor ancestors	May be Spanish or English; very little pressure from family to master English	Native language may be home language
Time	Connecting to the group of greater value than starting an event on time.	Mixed	Unhurried, little value placed on promptness	Current activity takes precedence over planned events

	Deaf	African American	Hispanic	Native
Misc.	Ten percent have Deaf parents and/ or siblings	Small percent have Deaf parents and/ or siblings	Smaller physical zone of comfort, thus speakers stand closer than English speakers	Harmony valued; comfortable with visual/physical communication
Learn-ing Style	Flourish in student centered; cooperative; hands-on settings	Mixed	Flourish in student centered; cooperative; hands-on settings	Watching, thinking, delayed participation

THOUGHT QUESTIONS

1. Identify the various ethnic and cultural groups you are a part of and list the things unique to each of those groups that influence your sense of time, learning style, family constellation, etc.

2. Collect current statistical data regarding the ethnic/cultural make up of the community where you live. Develop a pie chart or graph to represent the population visually.

3. In your own words, summarize five distinct characteristics of Deaf culture. Describe at least two experiences you have had where these values or norms were evident.

4. Discuss the norms of communication when you are one of a few hearing people in a gathering of many Deaf people.

5. Discuss the norms of communication when you are with one or two Deaf people in a large gathering of hearing people.

CD STUDY GUIDE

✦ The various activities in the guided Chapter 3 Study Guide on CD will allow you to understand the concepts in this chapter more completely and to apply them to your life experience. Work through the Chapter 3 Study Guide on CD, completing all activities, then submit to your instructor or share with your learning partner.

SUGGESTED ACTIVITIES

✦ Develop a game to practice communicating by facial expression alone. Ask a Deaf person to join in playing and to give you feedback regarding the clarity of your visual affective communication.

✦ Invite a panel of diverse Deaf people to class to discuss their experiences, norms in their community that are different with different cultural/ethnic Deaf people, and their preferences for working with interpreters.

✦ Interview a Deaf-Blind person to determine norms for attention-getting, turn taking and other behaviors in that group.

✦ Visit a church, temple, mosque or religious center of a group that you are unfamiliar with. Interview a member or leader of that group to get a sense of the groups beliefs and history (where originated, cultural influences, etc.) Report back to your class.

✦ If there are any programs for new immigrants in your community, make a fieldtrip to become familiar with the services and programs available.

Endnotes

1. In 2001, 79% of the population of the U.S. and 86% of the population of Canada are of European extraction (white). By the year 2050, the white population in the U.S. is expected to drop to 60%; the African American population is predicted to expand slightly to about 16%; the population of Hispanics will more than double; and the proportion of Asians/Pacific Islanders will jump as much as 10%. Canada will see similar growth in its non-white population (Kellogg (1993), P. 46

2. Isenhath (1990)
3. According to the New York Times (July 3, 2000) it is no longer valid to refer to members of these groups as minorities because they constitute the majority in many areas. In California, for example, people of color (African Americans, Hispanics and Asians/Pacific islanders) form the majority today and Hispanics will become that state's majority group by 2025. In the twenty-five largest urban school systems in the U.S., the majority of students are ethnic, racial or linguistic minorities.
4. Levine (1977), quoted in Christensen and Delgado, p. 51
5. Kitano & Daniels (1988), quoted in Christensen and Delgado, p. 128
6. Akamatsu (1993), p. 135
7. Forbes (1973); Joe & Miller (1987); Locust (1985), p.151 Hammond & Meiners (1993), p. 143-165.
8. Joe & Miller (1987)
9. Almanac of African American Heritage
10. Boyd-Franklin (1989)
11. Ibid.
12. Schein & Delk (1974)
13. Almanac of African American Heritage (2001)
14. Ibid.
15. Gonzales (2000); Hernandez (1995)
16. Jackson-Maldonado (1992), p.94.
17. Triandis, Marin, Lisansky & Bettancourt (1985(, p 72; Bird, (1990)
18. Boston Globe (1990)
19. Delgado-Gaitan (1987), p. 93
20. Suarez-Orozco (1987); Walker (1987), p. 94
21. In order to be recognized as of Native American in the U.S. one must meet two qualifications: 1) some of your ancestors must have lived in America before its discovery by Europeans; and 2) you must be accepted as an Indian by the legally constituted Indian community where you live. Individual tribes, therefore, have the power to determine if a person can be classed as "native" or not (Dillard, 1983). In Canada, the native population is termed "aboriginal" and is divided into three groups: First Nations, Métis and Inuit.
22. US Bureau of the Census (1983); Statistics Canada (1996)
23. O'Connell (1987), p. 144, quoting the Native American Research and Training Center
24. Hammond & Meiners (1993), p. 146
25. Jickels (1999)
26. Hammond & Meiners (1993), p. 154

27. Dillard (1983); Philips (1983); Sidles, MacAvoy, Bernston & Kuhn, (1987); Trimble (1986)

28. As quoted by Trimble (1986), p. 103.

29. Hammond & Meiners (1993), p. 151; Joe & Miller (1987); Holland 35 al., (1982), p. 121.

30. Ibid

31. Sam Supalla as quoted by Hammond & Meiners (1993),

32. p. 146

33. Hammond & Meiners (1993), p. 151; Joe & Miller, 1987; Holland 35 et.al., (1982), p. 121.

34. Anderson & Fenichel, (1989), p. 153

35. Locust, (1985), p. 153

36. Hammond & Meiners (1993), p. 153

CHAPTER FOUR
Identity and Communication
In the Deaf Community

The Deaf community is culturally and linguistically complex. It includes individuals who were born Deaf and those who have
lost their hearing at some point during their
youth or early adulthood. It does not, however, include people who lose their hearing in
old age. Members of the Deaf community reflect every ethnic and economic background
found in the national fabric. Members also
use a range of labels to identify themselves
and a variety of communication methods.

In this chapter we will define a number of important terms.
These terms reflect the cultural values of those who coined
them. Successful communication requires that we understand
the meaning and implications of these terms from the perspective of those with whom we are communicating.

IDENTITY AND LABELING
The way that one labels or names oneself is significant in all cultures and communities. It reflects
that person's sense of self and his or her place in
the world. Thus, when a woman refers to herself as
a "girl" instead of a "woman," an "Indian" instead
of a "Native American," or a "Chicana" instead of
a "Mexican American," she is telling you a great
deal about her cultural identity and how she views
herself. Similarly, members of the Deaf communi-
ty have several ways to refer to themselves and to each other.
These labels are sometimes significantly different from those
used by hearing (non-deaf) individuals when referring to the
same people.

The Hearing View

For most non-deaf people, deafness refers to the inability to hear or a deficit in hearing. Due to the contemporary expectation for political correctness, hearing people often use the term "hearing impaired" to refer to anyone whose hearing is less than "normal." This term is perceived by hearing people as courteous, respectful and politically correct.

Generally, if any distinction is made by hearing people about the degree of hearing loss someone has, they are likely to refer to a mild, moderate, severe, or profound loss. The term "deaf" is used by hearing people to refer to someone who has anything from a severe to a profound hearing loss. The term "hard of hearing" is used for someone with a mild to moderate hearing loss.

Audiologists, speech language pathologists and other professionals who work with deaf people refer more specifically to someone's decibel loss. They may, for example, describe an individual as having a 60 dB loss in the right ear or a 90 dB loss in both ears.

The Deaf View

The Deaf perspective and the labels used by Deaf people are quite different. Each Deaf person you encounter is a unique individual. Understanding why they prefer to call themselves Deaf, hard of hearing, or hearing impaired is critical to those who hope to work with Deaf people.

While people who can hear stress degree of hearing loss, members of the Deaf population stress developmental experiences such as having other family members who are Deaf, type of schooling, age of onset of deafness and age of exposure to sign language acquisition. Another defining characteristic is attitudinal deafness, which is the degree to which an individual subscribes to the norms and values of Deaf culture, as opposed to those of the majority hearing culture. It is through exchanging this type of information that two Deaf people can ascertain each other's cultural identity and their degree of "sameness" based on common experiences.

From a Deaf perspective, an individual can refer to himself or herself as Deaf while having enough residual hearing to converse on the telephone. Conversely, someone who has a profound hearing loss may refer to himself or herself as hard of hearing. How, you might ask, is that possible?

When people refer to themselves as Deaf, they are usually indicating the presence of a hearing loss (ranging from mild to profound), a preference to socialize with members of the Deaf community and a desire to adhere to Deaf cultural values and norms. When people refer to themselves as hard of hearing, they are usually indicating a hearing loss (ranging from mild to profound) and a preference to identify with hearing cultural norms and values.

Figure 4-1, which follows on several pages, summarizes the various labels and their meanings from a hearing perspective and from a Deaf perspective. *NOTE: Decibel ranges taken from Taylor, 1994.*[a]

---

[a] When the sign for "hard of hearing" is produced with regular accentuation, it carries the above meaning. When signed with modified accentuation, it denotes the degree of affiliation one has with the Deaf community.

FIG. 4-1 LABELS RELATED TO HEARING		
Label	**Meaning To Hearing People**	**Meaning To Deaf People**
MILD hearing loss	26-40 dB loss Able to detect most environmental sounds without amplification.	No specific meaning since cultural identification is much more important than information regarding the ability or inability to hear.
Moderate hearing loss	41-65 dB loss Able to detect most environmental sounds with amplification.	Also, the term "loss" is viewed negatively since many were born deaf or hard of hearing and never "lost" anything.
Severe hearing loss	65-90 dB loss May be able to detect some sounds with amplification.	Again, no specific meaning found since cultural identification is much more important than information regarding the
Profound hearing loss	90 dB loss or above Unable to detect any environmental sounds even with amplifiction.	ability or inability to hear.
Deaf	56 or greater dB loss Severe to profound hearing loss	A label of cultural identification — people may call themselves Deaf if they subscribe to the cultural norms, values, and traditions of the culture, even if their decibel loss is less than severe. When the sign for "Deaf" is produced with regular accentuation, it carries the above meaning. When signed with modified accentuation, it denotes the degree of affiliation one has with the Deaf community.

FIG. 4-1 LABELS RELATED TO HEARING		
Label	Meaning To Hearing People	Meaning To Deaf People
Hearing impaired	Used as a polite form of referring to people of all categories of hearing deficit; widely preferred over the term deaf.	The terms "hearing deficit" and "hearing impaired" are seen as stigmatizing. Therefore, they are viewed as negative labels, focusing on a definition of "normalcy" solely from a non-deaf perspective. The terms "deaf" and "hard of hearing" are viewed as polite forms of referring to deaf people of all categories
Hard of hearing	Mild to moderate hearing loss. Able to detect some environmental sounds with or without amplification.	A cultural identification label — people might call themselves hard of hearing, even if unable to hear anything, if they subscribe to the cultural norms, values and traditions of the hearing majority. Likewise, people who otherwise label themselves as Deaf may describe themselves as hard of hearing when describing their ability to speak, lip-read, or use residual hearing

Hearing Impaired

It should be noted that culturally Deaf individuals view the term "hearing impaired" as negative, stigmatizing, and — since they do not view themselves as impaired — fundamentally inaccurate. They proudly identify themselves as Deaf and prefer that alternate terms be dropped from conventional usage.

Nor is it simply culturally Deaf people who object to the label "hearing impaired." Several chapters of Self Help for the Hard of Hearing (SHHH), a national organization for late-deafened individuals, and provincial chapters of the Canadian Hard of Hearing Association have stated that they do not want the term "hearing impaired" used in reference to them for similar reasons.[1]

As noted in Chapter Three, language and culture cannot be separated. Therefore, understanding the multilingual nature of the Deaf community and language choices made by individual Deaf people will help you understand their cultural identification and group memberships

THE MULTILINGUAL NATURE OF THE DEAF COMMUNITY

Sign language interpreters work with Deaf people who use a variety of sign communication modes. This is sometimes confusing and frustrating! Figure 4-2 demonstrates the spectrum of sign communication you might encounter when interacting with Deaf people in the United States and Anglophone[b] Canada.

The spectrum moves from pure forms of ASL as it has evolved as a natural language to more prescriptive English-based systems such as Seeing Exact English and the Rochester Method. The gradual shading indicates the lack of rigid divisions between the various forms of sign communication. The central portion of the graph indicates the fact that signed representations of English and American Sign Language come together at a mid-point, resulting in a mixing of ASL-based signing and English-based signing. The various mixtures found in this middle ground are referred to as contact varieties, which are discussed in-depth later in this chapter.

---

[b] Anglophone refers to English–speaking, as opposed to French speaking.

FIG 4.2 SIGN COMMUNICATION

American Sign Language	English-based Signs
The naturally occurring visual language of Deaf people in Anglophone North America	Manual representation of English/ Sign Supported Speech (SSS)

Grammatically ASL — *Contact Varieties Mixed Grammars* — *Grammatically English*

Old | Traditional | Modern | Anglicized | Conceptually Accurate Signed English (CASE) | Signed English | Signing Exact English (See²) | Seeing Essential English (See¹) | Rochester Method

Jan Humphrey © 2000
Adapted from Carver, Alcorn & Humphrey © 1995

American Sign Language

Visual-Gestural languages are based on a structured set of linguistic rules in which the communication base is the movement
of the hands, face and body, rather than sound. American Sign
Language (ASL), is a naturally occurring visual-gestural language that adheres to specific linguistic rules. It emerged from
within the Deaf community in the United States (with some
influence from French Sign Language). As a visual-gestural
language, it incorporates facial grammatical markers, physical
affect markers, spatial linguistic information and fingerspelling, as well as a fairly uniform system of signed lexicon. It is
a distinct language with its own grammar and syntax that is
not based on, nor derived from, a spoken language. As a complete and complex language, accepted as the natural language
of the Deaf community, ASL is an integral part of Deaf culture. ASL has historically been mislabeled as "poor English"or
"slang" and has been devalued by the education system.

FIG. 4.3

ASL Varieties

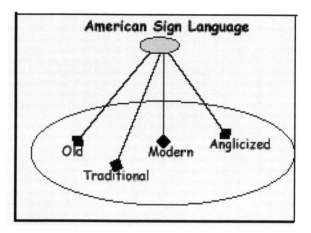

Like all languages, ASL is used by members of a community for the purposes of social interaction, communication of ideas, sharing of emotions, and for the transmission of the group's culture to following generations.[2]

All languages are made up of arbitrary symbols put together according to syntactic, phonological, semantic and pragmatic rules. ASL is no different. Further, as a living language, ASL changes over time to reflect the community of users. This is reflected in Fig. 4-3. Chapter Nine outlines a number of linguistic characteristics of American Sign Language.

While ASL is used by a majority of Deaf people in Canada and the US, it is not the only sign language. In Quebec, most Deaf people use La Langue de Signes Quebecoise, or LSQ. As well, in the far northeastern provinces of Canada, members of the Deaf community use Maritime Sign Language (MSL).[a]

---

[a] Linguists are still analyzing MSL to determine if it is a distinct language or a dialect of ASL.

FIG. 4.4
English-Based Signing (SSS)

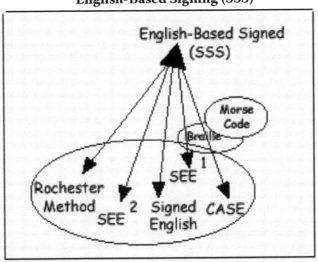

Sign Supported Speech

Sign Supported Speech (SSS) is a broad term used to refer to English-based signing systems which attempt to represent English in a manual/visual form, relying primarily upon the lexicon and syntax of English. All of these systems encourage the simultaneous use of spoken or mouthed English. You might also hear the term Manually Coded English, which is an earlier term for Sign Supported Speech.

There are several forms of manual English in use today, including the Rochester Method, Seeing Essential English (SEE[1]), Signing Exact English (SEE[2]), Signed English (SE) and Conceptually Accurate Signed English (CASE).

Educators have invented a variety of English-based signing systems since the earliest recorded history in North America. The rationale for the evolution of these systems lay in the desire to provide early language stimulation to Deaf children.[3] Ninety-percent of all Deaf children have parents who are not Deaf[4] and who are, therefore, not familiar with or fluent in American Sign Language (ASL). As a result, Deaf children are often not exposed to any accessible language during the critical early language-learning years of their development. Further, even if the parents were fluent in ASL, it was felt that a knowledge of English was still needed to function fully in our society; thus the invention of these coded manual systems of English.[5]

The Rochester Method[c]

The Rochester Method is a system in which each word is finger-spelled with the exception of the word "and", which is signed. This is a very precise manual representation of English. However, because it is slow, cumbersome and visually tiring, the Rochester Method is rarely used today in either the U.S. or in Canada.

Seeing Essential English

Seeing Essential English (SEE[1]) evolved from a 1966 experiment, led by David Anthony, to teach English to mentally retarded Deaf adults in Michigan.[6] This work continued in California with several individuals who embraced the experiment and sought to broaden its application to the education of Deaf children and adults.[7] Anthony explained the system in the following way:

> The major drawback of the American Sign Language has been that it has followed its own syntax and developed its own idioms … Using the American Sign Language as a base, [we] added verb tenses and appropriate endings, noun, adjective, and adverb suffixes and prefixes; and signs for words such as articles for which there have been no signs before …The exciting development is a system of signs that permits us to have one sign for each word, and of the utmost importance, allows us to use the language of signs in the correct patterns of English syntax.[8]

---

[c] Don't let the name fool you. The Rochester Method has been used widely at various points in the history of deaf education outside of Rochester, NY, where it originated.

The resulting system was based on a separate sign or movement for each "word root" (either words or syllables)[9]. In this system, the word "butterfly" is made up of three signs or movements (1but-2er-3fly), one for each syllable. No consideration is given to conceptual accuracy. Thus, the word "carpet" is signed with two movements, the first indicating an automobile ("car") and the second, the action of petting something ("pet"). English grammatical structure is adhered to strictly in SEE^1. Accordingly, signs for prefixes and suffixes have been invented, as have movements to indicate English verb conjugations. Prepositions and English conjunctions are signed. English sequencing and textual formation are followed. According to proponents, the rationale behind the system is to offer Deaf children an opportunity to learn English in a natural, visual form.[d]

The original group of individuals who developed the SEE^1 system eventually split into three main groups due to geographical spread, differences of opinion concerning the application of system, and differences of opinion about the best way to present the signs in written form. The popularity of this system has waned significantly. However, there are still a few pockets in the United States where SEE^1 is used extensively.[e]

Signing Exact English
Signing Exact English (SEE^2), grew out of SEE^1 and was developed primarily by Gustason, Zawalkow, and Pfetzing. SEE2 is based on several principles. One rule is that "English should be signed in a manner that is as consistent as possible with how it is spoken/written."[10] This means that phrases such as 'get the run around,' 'cut it out,' or 'stop horsing around' would be signed as those exact words. Another principle is that "a sign should be translatable to only one English equivalent."[11] Thus, although an

---

[d] Linguistics Of Visual English (LOVE), developed by Dennis Wampler, is another SSS system. It is identical to SEE^1, except that it uses the Stokoe notation system (a type of linguistic shorthand) to convey information concerning how signs are produced whereas SEE^1 uses English glosses.

[e] Richardson, Texas and Davenport, Iowa, for example.

English word such as "run" has numerous meanings and a number of different translations in ASL, a single sign would be used for that word in all sentence constructions. This is based on the "two-out-of-three" rule, wherein each English word is checked against the following criteria: sound, meaning, and spelling. If a word is the same in two out of three criteria, it will be signed the same way in all contexts, regardless of meaning[12].According to Moores,[13] the outcome was that sound and spelling took precedence over meaning.

In this system, the word "consume" would be signed TO EAT, therefore the term "consumer" would be signed, in essence EATER. Thus, the sentence "I am a consumer of interpreter services" would be signed "I am an eater of interpreter services." This, of course, presents a very inappropriate conceptual message. However it meets the two-out-of-three rule and is therefore the sign used within this system.

While no consideration is given to conceptual accuracy, if an ASL sign exists that commonly translates to one English word, it will be used rather than inventing new movements. "Butterfly," for example, is signed by using the ASL sign butterfly. Like SEE[1], this system adheres carefully to English grammatical structure, and incorporates invented signs for prefixes, suffixes, and verb conjugations. In addition to English sequencing and textual formation, English prepositions and conjunctions are signed.

Finally, synonyms are created by adding a fingerspelled letter to the root sign. For example, a "C" handshape is added to the root sign of "make" to produce the concept of "create," a "P" handshape is added to the same root sign for the concept of "produce."

> The word RUN sounds the same and is spelled the same. In SEE[2,] it is therefore signed the same way (to run as in moving your feet fast along the ground) in each of the following sentences.

I will run the marathon.

He will run for the position of Mayor.

I have a run in my nylons.

Signed English
This is a system of signs designed in the early 1980's for use with preschool children. It was based on the argument that an alternative to ASL was necessary for the following reasons:

1. ASL is not used in over 90 percent of the homes of Deaf children enrolled in programs for the Deaf;
2. it is not possible to simultaneously speak English and sign ASL;
3. ASL has no written form; and
4. people in the United States do not readily learn second languages.[14]

Based on this premise, the originators developed a system that denounced the two-out-of-three rule and instead created fourteen "sign markers" which can be added to signs to more accurately represent English. In addition, where no ASL equivalent existed, signs were invented. There are 3,000 entries in the Comprehensive Signed English Dictionary,[15] 1,300 of which the authors made up.[16] In this system, like SEE2, all prepositions, conjunctions, prefixes, suffixes, and verb forms, follow the structure of English rather than ASL.

Conceptually Accurate Signed English
Conceptually Accurate Signed English (CASE) is a term that has evolved primarily among interpreters. This term refers to the use of signs that are selected based on the meaning of the idea being conveyed. Thus, unlike the systems described above, meaning has primary importance and signs are selected to convey the intended concept or meaning. These conceptually accurate signs are produced in English word order and are usually accompanied by inaudible mouthing of the English words. However, certain features of ASL are also incorporated to make

more visual sense. For example, in the sentence "My mom baked a cake and we consumed it in two hours," the word "consumed" means ate rapidly. The sign chosen and the way it is executed would convey both the verb and adverbial meaning.

In the conceptually accurate approach (CASE), a different sign would be used for the word "make" in each of the following sentences in order to show the intended meaning of the word in context.

I will *make* dinner.
Go *make* your bed.
Did you *make* that coat rack?

Bragg[17] refers to this type of signing as the Anglicization of American Sign Language and argues that this is a natural progression in the evolution of ASL. Others believe this is another form of Sign Supported Speech.

CONTACT VARIETIES IN SIGN COMMUNICATION

When two language groups have long, sustained contact with each other there are predictable results. Linguistic variations start to emerge in which words, phrases, grammatical structures and other features of each language are mixed with the other. Some of the processes behind this phenomenon include code switching, code mixing and lexical borrowing.[18]

When linguistic research in ASL began to reveal variations between ASL and English-based signing, it was referred to as Pidgin Sign English (PSE). PSE has been defined as a natural blending of English and ASL which has developed over the years to provide rudimentary communication between Deaf and hearing people.[19] However, several researchers have pointed out that what has been called PSE is not really a true pidgin at all.[20] Cokely,[21] an interpreter, linguist and educator, describes it as a situation in which members of the Deaf community communicate with hearing people in a "foreigner talk" register of ASL and members of the hearing community communicate with

Deaf people in a foreigner talk register of English. The variation along the ASL-English continuum can be accounted for by the dynamic interplay of "foreigner-talk," mutual judgments of each other's proficiency, and learners' attempts to master the target language — whether this is ASL for hearing users or English for Deaf users.

There are some forms of blending English-based signs and ASL that are more English-like in syntax and vocabulary and other forms that are more ASL-like. Some people say this blended form of English and ASL is simply a modern variety of ASL — the Anglicization of ASL as it evolves in a bilingual community.[22] If true, this might explain why some Deaf individuals choose to sign in this blended form on a regular basis. Others say this blended form is simply a less correct form of ASL. Those who subscribe to this opinion state that what is actually occurring is that someone is attempting to sign ASL but they have not yet mastered the more complex elements of the language. This limited mastery of the language results in a combination of English-like and ASL-like characteristics. For information about the features of contact varieties identified to date and areas still requiring research, we recommend "Language Contact in the American Deaf Community."[23]

OTHERS THAT AREN'T ON THE CHART

In the preceding pages, we have discussed the various forms of sign communication that appear in Fig. 4-2. However, there are other forms of communication you may encounter in the Deaf community that you need to be aware of.

Foreign Sign Languages

Each country has its own indigenous sign language used by Deaf people living in that country. As these people relocate to Canada and the United States, they bring with them their indigenous sign languages. You may encounter Mexican Sign

Language, Russian Sign Language, or any number of other foreign sign languages. There are also a variety of fingerspelling systems, most of which are based on the written form of the language in the country of origin.

Not all immigrants will bring a formal sign language with them. In some countries, people who are Deaf are required to speak and use speech reading. They have not been introduced to the sign language of their country. In other countries, people who are Deaf are extremely marginalized and, as a result, have limited access to education or the interaction with other Deaf people. While indigenous visual language will emerge in locations where Deaf people have opportunities to do so (in Deaf families and larger metropolitan areas), isolated individuals do not have an opportunity to learn their native sign language.

Home Signs and Gestures

You may encounter some Deaf people who have never learned a formal sign language, but who manage quite well with home signs.[24] This is a system of pantomime, gestures and manual signals used within the family and with close family friends to support communication and interaction. Home sign systems are usually idiosyncratic, varying from family to family. However, in some native cultures, oral communication is not emphasized for either Deaf or hearing children. In these communities, some very complex home sign systems can emerge.[25]

Minimal Language Skills

Some Deaf individuals have not developed competency or skill in any language — spoken, written or signed. This sometimes occurs because an individual has been educationally or socially deprived and has never had an opportunity to develop language skills. Some Deaf people are educationally deprived due to the reluctance or refusal of their families to send them to school. Often, these individuals stay at home and develop a usable system of home signs but never learn a formal language of any kind. Even if the Deaf child does attend school, educational deprivation may occur if the school system fails to teach the child.

Tragically, Deaf children are sometimes passed from grade to grade without ever developing educational or communicative competence.

The absence of language may also result from a developmental disability that makes the individual unable to learn a language. Typically, people who are linguistically delayed are also behind in their social development because they have not had adequate opportunities to learn societal norms, cultural values, or appropriate ways of interacting with others.

Whatever the reason, people who fit the descriptions above are referred to as having minimal language competency (MLC) or minimal language skills (MLS). Historically, they have also been referred to as "low verbal." This is an obsolete term and should not be used because it is derogatory and negative. Some people prefer the term semi-lingual[26] or high visual orientation (HVO)[27] but these terms are not yet widely accepted.

Techniques to communicate with people who have minimal language skills include gestures, mime, drawings and pictures. However, the communication that takes place in such a situation lacks the precision and specificity of communication that takes place when people use structured, rule-governed languages. Often, the most effective way to approach interactions with MLS clients is the inclusion of a Deaf individual who is skilled in the use and adaptation of visual-gestural communication.[f]

Oral Communication Systems

Some deaf people don't use sign language. Instead, they prefer to speech-read and use their own speech to communicate with others. Speech-reading is a skill involving a combination of deciphering lip, cheek, and throat movements, clarifying gestures[g] and use of contextual clues to determine meaning. Oral

---

[f] Deaf interpreters work with hearing interpreters for a range of reasons, one of which is to support communication when the Deaf individual involved has limited or non-standard ASL skills.

[g] Moving your hands as if swinging a baseball bat, for example, when enunciating.

deaf individuals subscribe to the norms of the hearing majority and rarely interact with culturally Deaf individuals.

Deaf individuals who exclusively use speech and speech-reading to communicate usually function without an interpreter,

particularly in one-to-one situations. However, in some settings it is hard to speech-read due to the distance from the speaker, poor lighting, rapid turn taking, or a variety of other factors.[28] In these settings, some oral deaf individuals use the services of an oral transliterator to silently repeat what is being said in a way that the message can be speech-read.

Some people who use speech-reading use a hand system based on phonetics known as cued speech[i] to support their attempts to perceive spoken language. Cued speech consists of eight hand-shapes for consonants and four positions near the face representing vowels. Combinations of these hand configurations and face placements are used to make visible every syllable being spoken. Cued speech transliterators sometimes work in educational settings.

Deaf-Blind Variations

Finally, there is a population of individuals who are both unable to see (due to visual deterioration, disease of the eye, etc.) or hear. When these characteristics come together, adaptive communication techniques are required[29]. The hearing loss of Deaf-Blind people may range from slightly hard of hearing to profoundly Deaf. The vision may also range from partially sighted to totally blind.

The largest percentage of people who are Deaf-Blind were born Deaf and lost their vision later, typically as a result of Usher's Syndrome. People with Type I Usher's Syndrome are born with a severe-to-profound hearing loss which is often accompanied by balance problems. They typically learn sign language and become members of the Deaf community before losing their

---

[i] Developed by Dr. R. Orin Cornett in 1966.

sight. People with Type II Usher's Syndrome are born with mild to profound hearing loss and typically use speech and speech-reading for communication prior to losing their sight.[30]

The second largest group of people who are Deaf-Blind are those with both visual and hearing loss at birth. This may be due to the mother's illness or exposure to toxic substances that cause neurological damage to the child in-utero. Individuals in this group often have complicating physical conditions including heart problems, respiratory disorders and diabetes. Some people in this category learn sign language; others do not.

One Deaf-Blind advocate has noted that "Deaf-Blindness creates greater dependence on others and unique problems of communication, mobility and orientation that must be solved by using special methods and techniques."[31] There are several ways to communicate with a person who is Deaf-Blind. Those most relevant for sign language interpreters include:

✦ Sign Language
This is effective with individuals who used sign language prior to the deterioration of their vision and who still have some vision remaining. This method usually requires that the signer wear clothing with the greatest contrast to his or her skin color and sign in a space of approximately 8" x 8" square in the middle of the chest. It may also mean positioning oneself a bit closer to or further away from the Deaf-Blind person in order to place yourself in his or her field of vision.

✦ Tactile signs
A number of people who grew up Deaf and later became blind have adapted to "reading" ASL tactilely by placing their hands lightly on top of the hands of the person who is signing to them. This requires the signer to sign in a smaller space than usual and to incorporate information manually that ASL usually embeds visually (such as grammatical and affect markers).

✦ Fingerspelling
Some Deaf-Blind people prefer to have things spelled out in one of several fingerspelling systems. This may mean using the ASL alphabet, the British two-handed alphabet or a system of outlining letters in one's palm.

When communicating with a person who is Deaf-Blind, it is important to be aware of environmental factors -- people moving about, who is speaking to whom, people leaving the room, etc. This information needs to be conveyed to the Deaf-Blind person you are communicating with. If you want to be an interpreter, you need to do additional reading on this subject. Several excellent texts are provided at the end of this chapter.[32] The best place to develop skill and comfort in working with Deaf-Blind is in the Deaf-Blind community itself. Local agencies often provide training for volunteers in guiding and communication techniques.

SUMMARY
If you want to be an interpreter, you must become familiar with the wide range of individuals who are deaf and hard of hearing you are likely to encounter. It is important to respect each individual's choices regarding how they refer to themselves (Deaf, hard of hearing, etc.) As well, it is critical for interpreters to develop a range of communication skills, supporting their ability to work with individuals using ASL, as well as those using contact varieties and English-based signs. Finally, developing communication strategies for working with foreign deaf, minimal language and Deaf-Blind individuals is critical. This often involves working with Deaf interpreters.

CHAPTER REVIEW
Key Points

The meaning of "deafness" varies depending on your schema. Hearing people have one frame and Deaf people have another.

Hearing view of deafness focuses on the ears:

+ Defined as an inability to hear;
+ Viewed as a deficit or an impairment;
+ Connected to specified decibel loss; and
+ Uses terms to indicates the degree of hearing impairment — mild, moderate, severe, or profound.

Deaf view of deafness focuses on community and culture: "Deaf" is a label of pride and solidarity with others who:

+ Have similar experiences;
+ Use a shared form of communication;
+ Subscribe to Deaf cultural values, norms, and traditions; and
+ Viewed as positive, normal, and sometimes inconvenient.

Review Fig. 4-1 that summarizes terms used to describe deafness from each perspective.

The Deaf community is multilingual with members who use linguistically distinct ASL structured communication, as well as those who use English based signs.

There is also a style of signing that is termed "contact variety" which is a blending of the two.

+ **ASL** is a visual-gestural language that incorporates facial grammatical markers, physical affect markers, spatial linguistic information, and fingerspelling, as well as a fairly uniform system of signed lexicon. It is a distinct language with its own grammar and syntax that is not based on, nor derived from, a spoken language.

ASL varieties range from "old" ASL (the language that originally emerged among Deaf people in the US) to "modern" which includes more language borrowings and emerging lexicon. "Anglicized" ASL has more initialized signs and borrows some grammatical structures from English, as well.

✦ **Sign Supported Speech** is a broad category of signing systems that are based on English lexicon and grammatical structures. All of these systems use signs in English word order; several of them include invented "signs" used to convey English grammatical information (such as English-based verb conjugations).

(a) The Rochester Method, in which each letter of the English alphabet is assigned a handshape and all words — with the exception of "and" — are fingerspelled.

(b) Seeing Essential English (SEE1), in which each syllable is given a separate manual movement.

(c) Signing Exact English (SEE2), which is a combination of SEE1, invented initialized signs, and some ASL signs. The "proper" way of signing various words is determined by the "two-out-of-three rule."

(d) Signed English (SE) which combines English grammatical order with ASL signs and some invented initialized sign.

(e) Conceptually Accurate Signed English (CASE) combines English grammatical order with conceptually accurate ASL signs; some initialized signs are used

✦ **Contact Varieties:** Signing that reflects a mixture of structures from ASL and English as a result of prolonged language contact between members of these two different linguistic communities. See also code-switching, code-mixing, and lexical borrowing. Sometimes referred to as Pidgin Signed English. Some people believe this is Anglicized or "modern ASL," while others think this blended form is a linguistically inferior form of ASL.

This chapter contains a fairly complete description of the various English-based signing systems. See Chapter Nine for a more complete discussion of some linguistically unique structures of ASL that create challenges for interpreters.

Foreign Sign Languages

Each country has its own indigenous sign language used by the Deaf people living in that country. You may encounter them when you travel abroad or when Deaf immigrants move to your country. In North America, you will find La Langue des Signes Quebeçoise (LSQ) used in Quebec, Canada and Maritime Sign Language (MSL) used in the Maritime region in Canada. Further, there are a variety of international sign languages used by Deaf people visiting or immigrating to North America.

Home Signs

Home signs are a system of pantomime, gestures and manual signals used within the family and with close family friends to support communication and interaction in the place of a formal sign language.

Minimal Language Skills

Minimal Language Skills (MLS), Minimal Language Competency (MLC) and High Visual Orientation (HVO) are some of the terms used to refer to individuals who have no language skills in any language — spoken, written or signed. This may be due to poor education, developmental disabilities or social/linguistic deprivation. Mime, gestures, drawings and pictures are useful for communication with individuals who have no language base.

Oral Deaf Individuals

Oral deaf individuals do not use sign language and rely on their own speech and speech-reading abilities to communicate with others.

Speech-Reading

Speech-reading is a skill employed by some Deaf and hard of hearing individuals to comprehend spoken communication. It involves a combination of deciphering lip, cheek, and throat movements, clarifying gestures and use of contextual clues to determine meaning. Some oral deaf individuals use oral transliterators to provide a visual reproduction of what is being said in order to lip-read the communication. Others use cued speech, a phonemically-based hand system that uses eight handshapes and four positions to "cue" each syllable spoken.

Deaf-Blind Individuals

Deaf-Blind people have a combination of vision and hearing losses that require adaptive communication techniques. There are a variety of forms of communication, including tactile and "close vision" signing, several forms of fingerspelling, and palm printing, to name just a few.

THOUGHT QUESTIONS

1. Why is it important for an interpreter to know if a client identifies as Deaf, hard of hearing, or oral?

2. Do culturally Deaf individuals view the label hearing impaired more positively than the label hard of hearing or deaf?

3. Describe three types of communication within the category of sign supported speech.

4. When someone gets their hearing tested, the results are presented in an "audiogram" indicating the decibels at which that person can hear in a variety of ranges. Which is more important — the label on an audiogram or the label a person ascribes to her/himself? Why?

5. What is the difference between "deaf" and "Deaf?"

CD STUDY GUIDE

The various activities in the guided Chapter 4 Study Guide on CD will allow you to understand the concepts in this chapter more completely and to apply them to your life experience. Work through the Chapter 4 Study Guide on CD, completing all activities, then submit to your instructor or share with your learning partner.

SUGGESTED ACTIVITIES

✦ The instructor or a guest could demonstrate communication at the various points on the continuum.

✦ Write a descriptive paper on your perception of what the world would be like if Deaf people were the majority and the norms for interaction were Deaf, rather than hearing. What would schools, families, communities, and attitudes be like in such a world?

✦ Interview a variety of Deaf individuals or invite a panel of Deaf people to the class to discuss their view of the world and how they interpret various labels related to hearing and deafness.

✦ Have your hearing tested and discuss the experience with your classmate.

Endnotes

1. Babcock (1992)
2. Baker & Cokely (1980); Wilcox & Wilcox (1997)
3. Stedt & Moores (1990); Gustason (1990); Bornstein (1990)
4. Schein & Delk (1974)

5. Gustason, et. al. (1980)

6. Stedt and Moores (1990)

7. This group of individuals represented a critical diversity: Anthony (deaf of deaf parents), Zawolkow (hearing of deaf parents/certified Sign Language interpreter), Gustason (deaf/educated in public schools), Pfetzing (mother of deaf child/SEE1interpreter) and Wampler (hearing of hearing parents).

8. Anthony, et. al. (1971)

9. Stedt and Moores (1990)

10. Gustason, etal. (1980)

11. Ibid.

12. Ibid.

13. Moores (1977)

14. Bornstein, Hamilton, and Saulnier (1980, 1983)

15. Ibid.

16. Stedt and Moores (1990)

17. Bragg (1989)

18. Di Pietro (1978); Gumperz (1976) Gumperz and Hernandez-Chavez (1971); Poplack (1980); Davis (1989); Lucas and Valli (1989)

19. Woodward (1973b); Woodward & Markowicz (1975); Baker and Cokely (1980)

20. Lucas and Valli (1989)

21. Cokely (1983a)

22. Bragg (1989)

23. Ibid.

24. Dively (1999)

25. Supalla, S. quoted by Hammond and Meiners (1993), p. 154

26. Carter (1995)

27. Neumann-Solow (1991); Savage (1992)

28. Northcott (1984); DiPietro in Garretson (Ed.) (1991)

29. Sauerburger (1995)

30. Ibid., p. 2; Duncan, Prickett, Finkelstein, Vernon & Hollingswoth (1988); Wynne (1987)

31. Robert Smithdas, assistant director of the Helen Keller National Center in the foreword to Sauerburger (1995)

32. A few Deaf-Blind resources: Sauerburger, D. (1993) Independence without sight or sound. New York: American Foundation for the Blind; 0oCommunity-based living options for young adults with deaf-blindness (1987) Sands Point, NY: TAC-Helen Keller National Center; DiPietro, L. (ed.) (1978) Guidelines on interpreting for deaf-blind persons. Washington, DC: Public Service Programs, Gallaudet College; Duncan, E., Prickett, H., Finkelstein, D., Vernon, M., & Hollingsworth, T. (1988) Usher's syndrome: What it is, how to cope, and how to help. Springfield, IL: Charles C. Thomas.

CHAPTER FIVE
Cultural Frames: Schemas, Beneficence and Audism

When entering a situation, people bring with them a schema — a perceptual framework that is based upon their personal experiences and cultural background. Schemas[a] are like scripts. They enable us to make sense of events as they are unfolding and know how to act appropriately.

 For example, we all have a "restaurant schema," based on our experiences in countless restaurants. Based on this schema, we can reasonably expect that a menu will be brought to us, that our water glasses will be refilled periodically, and that we will be presented with a bill at the end of the meal. We also know what is expected of us — we are expected to come appropriately dressed, refrain from entering the kitchen, leave a tip of a certain percent.

We typically use five features or characteristics in forming and organizing our schema.[1]

+ PHYSICAL — classifying individuals based on their appearance, gender, physique, age, etc.;
+ ROLES — we have certain expectations of others-based on their social position (neighbor, doctor, student, etc.);
+ INTERACTIONS — the way people behave in social situations (aloof, friendly, judgmental, etc.) influences our sense of who they are and what we might expect of them;
+ PSYCHOLOGICAL — we group individuals based on our personal psychological assessments of them (curious, nervous, insecure, etc.);

---

[a] The plural of schema is technically schemata but the authors have chosen to use a non-standard form for readability.

✦ MEMBERSHIPS — we also categorize others according to their group affiliation (refugee, Baptist, member of the School Board, female, etc.).

These categorizations are sometimes called constructs and we use them to organize our observations, form impressions, predict what will happen next, determine what is expected of us and generally make sense of interactions with others.

Returning again to the example of the restaurant schema, your role constructs help you predict the actions of the server, cashier, chef, chef's assistant, and your fellow customers. Based on your interaction constructs, you are able to recognize when the personnel are being helpful, friendly, aloof, entertaining or sarcastic. You may also classify people in the restaurant based on their appearance or make psychological judgments about them. Some people in the restaurant may have group memberships you can identify (e.g. Sikh, senior citizen, Rotarian). Sometimes the restaurant itself might be affiliated with membership groups (e.g. a Japanese restaurant, a truck stop, a health food/veggie delicatessen).

Like the restaurant schema, we all have school schema, job schema, friend schema, domestic partner schema and so forth. Individuals can interact appropriately only if they have a frame or schema in place for a particular setting.

Scripts and schemas are useful tools that members of all cultures use to make sense of their world. Of course, members of various cultural groups often have different experiences from which their "scripts" evolve.[2] "We typically select, organize and interpret behavior in ways that fit our pre-existing concepts about people's motives."[3] Many of these notions, or schematic constructs, are transmitted to us through cultural institutions such as religion, schools, and the media.

In addition, all people tend to make generalizations about others based on their schematic constructs. This is logical to a point. However, when our generalizations no longer reflect reality or truth, they lead to stereotyping.[4] Stereotyping is one type of faulty thinking that leads to negative judgments and destructive behaviors resulting in racism, sexism, ageism, and heterosexism. These attitudes lead to individual, group and institutionalized oppression.

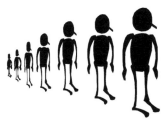

STEREOTYPING, OPPRESSION AND THE DEAF COMMUNITY

Today, individuals who are Deaf are generally viewed as members of a language-culture group. However, this is a fairly recent event. For years, Deaf individuals have been categorized by others as disabled, imperfect human beings because they didn't fit the "normal" schema of "hearing." When we generalize a judgment to the entire group, we have begun stereotyping — prejudging based solely on the basis of group membership.

In the case of Deaf people, members of the majority community have traditionally categorized them as defective, rather than different. This is termed a pathological view and leads to:

✦ Defining deafness as a handicap, a defective or pathological condition; believing the ideal role models for Deaf children are "normal hearing people;"

✦ Spending time and money seeking a "cure;"

✦ Focusing on the use of various devices that enhance auditory perception and/or focus on developing speech (e.g., hearing aids, cochlear implants);

✦ Avoiding use of Sign Language since anything other than English is viewed as inferior; communication which is primarily visual is denigrated;

✦ Supporting only the integrated socialization of Deaf persons with hearing persons, discouraging Deaf-Deaf marriages or socializing primarily with other Deaf people; and

✦ Seeing professionals (e.g., speech therapists, teachers of the Deaf, interpreters) as people who will "fix" the deficits of Deaf people so they can be normalized — after all, they have to live in the hearing world.

These stereotyping attitudes have led to historic, systematic oppression of Deaf people as a group. Unlike individual oppression where one person offends, puts down, or deals unfairly with another individual, group oppression is directed toward all members of a group simply because they are categorized as part of an inferior, undesirable group.[5] Group oppression eventually becomes institutionalized oppression. This means negative attitudes toward the minority or "different" group are transmitted — overtly or covertly — through the institutions of the society: schools, media, medical/mental health professions, etc. This leads to all members of the society sharing a negative categorization of oppressed group members, including members of the oppressed group. This is referred to as internalized oppression. It is extremely difficult to combat discrimination at this level because it results in the denigration of the minority group's language, culture, and of individual personhood[6] so significantly that members of marginalized groups participate in their own oppression (referred to as internalized oppression) as illustrated below.

 Whoopie Goldberg described institutional oppression in her poignant HBO special in the early eighties. She drapes a white towel around her head and lets it stream down her back, referring to it as "my long, luxurious blonde hair."[7]

In the sixties, television programs such as *My Three Sons, Ozzie and Harriet, Donna Reed* and *Leave it to Beaver* allowed black people to study the white world. At the same time, white people saw the black world only through the media caricatures of Amos 'n Andy, Buckwheat and Stymie, and perhaps Rochester on the Jack Benny show. There were a lot of Clairol commercials with beautiful young white women with blonde hair that rippled in the wind like a bleached version of a Greek goddess. A throaty voice-over affirmed that, "Blondes have more fun." But as Whoopie Goldberg observed in her monologue:

> There was no such thing as a blonde Negro. People like me were destined not to have fun. And things in the world seemed to confirm that assumption ... the only people in town with a convertible were white. The only rich people were white. Maybe if we acted white and looked white and thought white, maybe then we could have fun.[8]

North American culture has historically been a white man's culture. Black people couldn't help but learn about white people, while white people went about their lives knowing almost nothing about black people. When no one in the advertisements, movies, magazines or books looks like you, talks like you, dresses and lives in a home like you — you are the member of an oppressed minority group. You will continue to be part of a disempowered group because of the institutional and internalized oppression.

Institutionalized oppression means that the dominant group devalues a marginalized person's sense of personal worth, abilities, intelligence, and right to be different and affirmed in that difference. It means having no power in the very agencies and institutions that impact your life. Let's look at the following description of people who are marginalized by institutional oppression.

> Marginal people are the oppressed, the powerless, and the rejected. They are ethnic minorities, women, the unemployed, the poor, the illiterate, the home-

less, the handicapped, the AIDS-infected, gays, lesbi-
ans and so on. Those who are not part of the institutions
that dominate can be regarded as marginal people.[9]

One may be marginalized by race, gender, economic status,
politics, education, occupation and/or age. Racially, the dominant group in the U.S. and Canada is Caucasian, while people
of color belong to marginalized groups. However, if a person is
poor and unemployed, he or she may be marginalized even if
racially Caucasian. Likewise, a Caucasian woman who belongs
to a highly professional group of people may be marginalized
due to gender discrimination.[10]

Opportunities for self-determination can be extremely limited
or even nonexistent for a marginalized person because they are
denied the right to use their language in educational and business settings. One's way of life — culture, traditions, and beliefs
— are diminished. Access to resources is denied which often
results in discrimination in housing, bank loans, and medical
services. Inevitably, any education provided is inferior and inadequate, effectively blocking the path to political and economic power.[11]

Harlan Lane reviewed professional literature from 1970 -1980[12]
and noted that it confirms the stereotyping and institutionalized oppression that results from pathological thinking (Fig. 5-
1). It reveals the labels ascribed to Deaf individuals by audists.[13]
Audism — like racism or sexism that judges, labels, and limits
individuals on the basis of race or gender — results in a negative
stigma toward individuals who do not hear auditory stimuli.

CHARACTERISTICS OF "BENEFACTORS" (OPPRESSORS)[15]
Most people do not consciously hurt, malign, or oppress others.
In their own minds, the people we will describe below believe
themselves to be benefactors,[16] doing "what is best" for those
"poor folks" (typically referring to individuals who have differ-
ing cultural, economic or group norms). However, members of
the dominant or majority culture react to members of minority

cultures and groups in predictable ways. These types of behaviors are encountered by members of most oppressed minority groups: Indigenous peoples, women, Latinos, people living in poverty, African Americans ... the list could go on and on.

FIG. 5-1 Four Categories Depicting Labels Ascribed to Deaf Individuals in Professional Literature [14]			
SOCIAL	COGNITIVE	BEHAVIORAL	EMOTIONAL
♦ Depends on admiration ♦ Asocial ♦ Childlike ♦ Clannish ♦ Competitive ♦ Weak conscience ♦ Dependent ♦ Disobedient ♦ Irresponsible ♦ Isolated ♦ Morally Undeveloped ♦ Role-rigid ♦ Shy ♦ Submissive ♦ Suggestible ♦ Unsocialized	♦ Poor conceptual thinking ♦ Doubting ♦ Egocentric ♦ Internalized failure ♦ Poor insight ♦ No introspective skills ♦ Poor or no language ♦ Mechanically inept ♦ Naïve ♦ Poor reasoning abilities ♦ Poor self awareness ♦ Shrewd ♦ Unclear thinking ♦ Unaware & unintelligent	♦ Aggressive ♦ Androgynous ♦ Conscientious ♦ Hedonistic ♦ Immature ♦ Impulsive ♦ Lacks initiative ♦ Few interests ♦ Slow motor development ♦ Undeveloped personality ♦ Possessive ♦ Rigid ♦ Shuffling gait ♦ Stubborn ♦ Suspicious ♦ Lacking confidence	♦ Lacks anxiety ♦ Depressed ♦ Emotionally disturbed ♦ Emotionally immature ♦ Lacks empathy ♦ Explosive ♦ easily frustrated ♦ Irritable ♦ Moody ♦ Neurotic ♦ Paranoid ♦ Passionate ♦ Psychotic ♦ Reactions ♦ Serious ♦ Temperamental ♦ Unfeeling

The Reality of Privilege[17]

When you're in the driver's seat, you don't think about conditions in the back seat. You may own a car for two or three years and never even sit in the back seat! Privilege is like that ... when you're born into a privileged class you just take it for granted. Kids who have plenty of food don't think about the fact that they have food. But when you're hungry, it's always on your mind.

WHITE PERSON: I guess I don't think of myself as being privileged. I mean, I've worked hard for what I've got. My grandfather ran a hotel in Colorado. His father (my great-grandfather) built it in the 1800's and that he worked with him from the time he was a boy. Nothing came easy to them but they passed down the skills, resources, economic experience and training from generation to generation.

BLACK RESPONSE: Privilege is like being born tall in a world that revolves around basketball. If you're a seven footer, basketball will come easier than if you're five foot six. Now a seven footer can say, "I had to work hard to become a great basketball player." He's right. But he'd be a fool not to realize he was born with advantages that helped his dream come true. There's no substitute for hard work and you are the beneficiary of generations of hard work, education, opportunity and freedom. But while your grandparents were doing all of that, my great grandparents were forced to till the Mississippi soil and pick cotton until they couldn't straighten their backs. And none of it benefited their children or grandchildren. It all benefited the next generation of white children. So your daddy's hard work and my daddy's hard work didn't bring them equal advantages — not financially or educationally.

Below is a description of some characteristics of "benefactors" drawn primarily from the work of Pablo Freirer[18] and that of Charlotte Baker-Shenk.[19] As you will see from the summation below, "benefactors" are unconsciously motivated by factors related to the maintenance of the status quo and maintenance of power.

Negative View Of The Minority Group

The majority group defines "normalcy" according to their group experience and world view, then impose that view on others. Thus, the majority group establishes the schematic constructs defining how everyone should look, walk, talk, act, react, be educated, work, etc.[20] A minority group member is then stigmatized because s/he does not measure up to those standards.[21] The stigmatized group is marginalized, systematically shut out of opportunities that lead to inclusion and equality.

Reciprocity Of Perspectives

Since the value of right and wrong, good and bad is based on the world view of the majority or power group, members of this group tend to assume that others desire to be like them.[22] European-Americans (white) generally assume Mexican Americans, Native Americans, or African Americans want to walk, talk, dress, and behave like them.

Hearing people assume Deaf people want to become hearing. Thus there is a "fix-it" mentality and millions of dollars are spent on hearing aids, cochlear implants, speech therapy, and so on to "help" them become "normal." In this same way, members of ethnic groups are encouraged to "become white" in their orientation and thinking patterns in order to succeed, and women are encouraged to adopt male behaviors and power politics in order to climb the executive ladder.

Myth Of The Misguided Child[23]

Members of the power group cannot believe a rational person would reject attempts to help them or make them "normal." When this occurs, they assume Deaf people — like children — don't understand what is best for them. With sweeping "benevolence," non-deaf people make decisions that determine the course of the lives of people who are Deaf. There is no place to argue logic, research or experience, for their minds are made up. Thus, audists dictate what is best, including mainstreamed and/or oral education. Sign Supported Speech is sometimes tolerated but American Sign Language, which is too different to be accepted, is demeaned.

Paternalism And Possessive Consciousness[24]

The "benefactor" often takes on a proprietary and caretaker attitude toward members of the oppressed group.[25] There is an intense need on the part of the power group for everything to work out well, yet there is a corresponding lack of trust in the abilities of the minority group to do well on their own. It becomes necessary, then, for the family member who can hear or for the professional who is not Deaf to take charge and to be in control — making decisions for the Deaf person, assuming he or she is unable to do or to learn certain things.

Parents or child-care counselors may assume that Deaf children and youth are unable to develop an internal locus of control. Therefore, they do everything for them: wake them up every morning, set their schedules for them, dole out their money, permit or forbid one student to interact socially with other specific students, and so on, as they deem appropriate. All of these behaviors foster unhealthy dependence in the child and damage his or her self-esteem.

Need for Approval From Marginalized Group Members[26]
"Benefactors" need a "payoff" for their "investment" of time, energy, and concern. They expect and need some expression of appreciation and gratitude from the minority group. If they don't receive it, there is often a sense of victimization and anger — "Oh, what a sucker I've been!" or "Why can't deaf people appreciate what I'm doing for them?"

Numerous authors would explain this phenomena by looking at the dysfunctional dynamics and resultant co-dependent behaviors by members of our society. This topic will be discussed in depth in a later chapter in this text. The same dynamic is referred to as the "rescue triangle."[27]

Resistance To Attempts For Liberation[28]
Finally, the power group is afraid of and angered by any attempts on the part of the marginalized group for liberation, respect or inclusion. The threat of lost power or control will be resisted stringently.[29] Look at the response toward the current liberation and empowerment movement by the Deaf community, including the legitimization of American Sign Language and bilingual-bicultural approaches to teaching Deaf individuals. If you see resistance from hearing parents, teachers, doctors and others you should note this as evidence of this characteristic of "benefactors."

The Reality of Oppression[30]

Most bigots aren't "big racists." They aren't the KKK types, the cross burners, the ones that would call you names, spit on you and beat you up as long as there were at least three of them for every one of you.

Most bigots are nice people — the church-goers, school teachers, police officers, business-people, truck-drivers, mayors and mail carriers. They make the community what it is. They make the wheels turn — the wheels of commerce, the wheels of benevolence, the wheels of oppression and injustice. They are the "little racists."

In the Holocaust, these were the normal people, those who thought of themselves as decent folk. Those who wouldn't kick a Jew to death, but would look the other way when someone else did. It is the normal people who make holocausts happen, the "good folk" who tolerate unspeakable evil.

HOW DOES AUDISM AFFECT DEAF PEOPLE?

The effects of being marginalized are subtle, extremely potent, and long lasting. As an interpreter, it is important that you consider the oppressive impact of audism on the lives of Deaf individuals.

Ambivalence[31]

Due to the psychological consequences of oppression, Deaf individuals often suffer from low self-confidence and feelings of inadequacy. It is common for members of marginalized groups to have both positive and negative feelings about themselves and being deaf. Positive feelings about being Deaf result in increased positive group solidarity cohesiveness, and a sense of identity. Yet some Deaf individuals will refer to themselves in self-deprecating ways, parroting beliefs, attitudes and behaviors expressed by members of the hearing majority group. They doubt their knowledge and abilities, then internalize the stereotypical, stigmatizing opinions that others hold of them.

An Example of Ambivalence[32]

The effect of racism has become self-perpetuating among many minority groups and they believe the myths about themselves. One deaf person may call another "dummy" or one African American may say to another who is acting a bit rowdy in public "stop showin' your color," supporting the myth that deaf people and black people are stupid or incompetent.

Fatalism Or Passivity[33]

Members of marginalized groups often feel powerless to change things. Deaf people often feel there is no value in fighting "the system." Some Deaf individuals you meet will take whatever injustice comes their way with a "go with the flow" attitude, believing there is absolutely nothing they can do to affect change. Cayton,[34] a university professor, describes this dynamic in the following way, "...we are silenced and silence ourselves in the face of the cultural expectation that the speech of others is powerful and privileged."

This attitude is reflected in the failure of limited English-users to register to vote. It is observed in the hesitancy of a Native American to file a lawsuit when discriminated against by his employer. It is evidenced in the decision of the poor, single mother of three to move out on the streets rather than fight an unfair eviction from the landlord of her over-priced slum apartment.

Horizontal Hostility[b]

When one is repeatedly devalued and belittled, greater and greater tension develops between the dominant and minority group members.[35] Since it is unsafe to vent this hostility toward members of the oppressor group, minority group members often turn their anger and frustration on one another. This happens in many ways: barbed comments that constantly put others down; failure to make good on a debt; verbal or physical attacks; and physical violence.

---

[b] Referred to by Freire and by Baker-Shenk as "Horizontal Violence."

One way this is evidenced in the Deaf community is through the "crab theory." For example, if a Deaf person has some type of phenomenal success, members of the Deaf community may join him or her in joy and celebration of the success for a period of time. However, when that individual has received an adequate amount of attention (it is hard to explain how group members know when there has been enough), the group begins to change the subject of conversation, or to ignore the "star." If the achiever insists on holding center stage, group members will begin to make barbed comments and cutting remarks until the individual resumes his or her place as one of the group.[36] This is another form of horizontal hostility. A comparison can be drawn between this phenomena and that of African American children in inner city schools deliberately keeping their grades down to avoid being attacked by their peers.[37]

"Benefactors Are Perfect"[38]

A common characteristic of those so marginalized is the idea that members of the oppressor group are somehow super-beings.[c] They know everything, never make mistakes, always succeed in business, win all of the contests they enter, make straight A's in school, etc. Life is a piece of cake if you are white or male or hearing — or however members of a particular group describe members of the power group. This phenomena is still found among many Deaf individuals who believe that hearing people all have perfect English, never struggle to get jobs or job advancement, and know (or should know) the answers to most any question.

Dependence On The "Benefactor"[39]

Members of a marginalized group, being powerless, are dependent upon members of the power group for certain things which they perceive they are unable to do for themselves.[40] In the case of Deaf individuals, this is exacerbated by the historic "care taking" which has occurred by over-protective parents and/or in

---

[c] Baker-Shenk, 1986, refers to this as "magical thinking."

residential schools where their every physical need was provided — food, shelter, books, admission to special events, etc. As adults, many of these individuals go on to expect society to take care of them. This is acted out in the form of dependence on public funding for rehabilitation and vocational education, living expenses such as social security income for disabled persons, etc. While there is a desire to be independent, there is often a concomitant fear of not being able to make it on one's own in the absence of this type of support.

Since there is also often a belief that hearing people have superior knowledge of the world, there is a deep-seated belief that a Deaf person cannot succeed on his or her own. Perhaps the best way to explain this characteristic is with an example:

> The authors of this text were once talking to a Deaf person about the dream of setting up her own business. She had a dream, she was intelligent and educated. She had a work history of almost seventeen years and was tired of punching a clock and making money for someone else. When we started getting into the specifics of making the dream a reality, our friend responded, "Oh, I would have to have a hearing person as head of the company; I would have to be the assistant."

> This highly capable individual was completely convinced that she could not succeed unless there was a hearing person at the helm of the ship, even though she was the "ideal" person. She was emotionally dependent on a hearing person to make her dream come true, and because she was so caught up in the oppressed-oppressor dynamics, no amount of logic or discussion could change that opinion.

Fear Of Freedom

As angry as oppressed people may be about the injustice discrimination and marginalization they experience, not all are able to embrace the idea of liberation and equality. Freedom is a frightening thought because their own sense of inferiority and emotional dependence on members of the power group for survival often paralyzes them.[41] The shadow of the unknown often haunts oppressed people. Who knows? If we "rock the boat," it may be even worse than what we suffer now.

VIEWING DEAF PEOPLE AS DIFFERENT

In direct opposition to the paternalistic, audist view is the positive belief that Deaf people are members of a distinct cultural group. This belief includes recognition of the fact that there are many characteristics, norms, values, and traditions among Deaf people that are different from those of hearing people. This understanding leads to the view of Deaf individuals as normal, capable human beings who embrace life in a way different from human beings who are not Deaf. When others are seen as different, rather than disabled, a pluralistic, cultural view of that group emerges. This means we are able to:

+ See deafness as a characteristic which distinguishes normal Deaf persons from normal hearing people;
+ Recognize that Deaf people are a linguistic and cultural minority who have experienced oppression due to the audist influence among majority non-deaf groups;
+ Respect, value and support the language and culture of Deaf people; believe the best role models for Deaf children are successful Deaf adults;
+ Emphasize the use of visual communication as a positive, efficient alternative to the auditory channel of communication;
+ View sign language as equal to spoken languages and the most natural communication tool for people who are Deaf;
+ Support the socialization of Deaf persons within the Deaf community (Deaf-Deaf interactions and Deaf-Deaf marriages) and within the larger community; and

✦ Believe the role of interpreter professionals is that of allies working with Deaf people as they seek equal access to the rights, privileges, and opportunities that hearing people enjoy.[42]

These attitudes form the foundation of a "cultural" view of Deaf people. There is respect and support for ASL, Deaf culture, and the personhood of each individual. The self-worth, abilities, intelligence, and right to be different are affirmed and those differences are valued and encouraged. Power is shared and Deaf individuals become liberated, empowered and equal.

It is this view the authors encourage interpreters to explore, understand and embrace. It is important for you to reflect on and identify any attitudes of bigotry you may harbor towards others who are different — and we all have them. At best, we can become "recovering racists, sexists, audists, etc."[43] You must look honestly at any possibility of your need for and use of power. Only by coming face to face with your own prejudices and tendency toward injustice can you properly fulfill the role and responsibility of a non-Deaf person within the Deaf community.

CHAPTER REVIEW
Key Points
Schema: "Scripts" that we learn from life experience which help us predict how to act and how others will act in new, but similar, situations; different from one culture group to the other.

Schematic Constructs: Ways people tend to organize their "scripts", including:

✦ Physical characteristics;
✦ Social roles;

✦ Social interactions;
✦ Psychological characteristics; and
✦ Memberships/associations.
Stereotyping: Pre-judging others based on assumptions that do not reflect reality or truth.

Oppression: The unjust or excessive exercise of power or position that hurts, maligns, or disempowers others.

<u>Types of oppression:</u>

✦ individual
✦ group
✦ institutionalized oppression
Marginalization: The systematic exclusion of minority group members from quality social services, economic opportunities, health care, and meaningful education; the absence of power or "voice."

Audism: An attitude based on pathological thinking resulting in a negative stigma toward anyone who does not hear.

Pathological View of Deaf People: Deaf individuals are viewed as disabled and imperfect needing to be "fixed."

Cultural View of Deaf People: Deaf individuals are normal, capable human beings encountering life in a different — yet acceptable — way, conforming with norms and behaviors based on visual/non-hearing norms.

Characteristics Of "Benefactors" or Oppressors
✦ **Pejorative view of the minority group** — feel that being different than the "ideal" (fat, poor, blind, etc.) is bad;
✦ **Reciprocity of perspectives** — the result of seeing the world from your own frame, thus assuming that members of different groups want to be like your own (results in a "fix-it" mentality);

✦ **Members of group are innocent/childlike** — they are incapable of knowing what is best for them and need others to help make decisions and take care of them;

✦ **Paternalism** — desire to take members of the minority group "under their wing", assuming a "know-it-all" or "take charge" stance;

✦ **Need for approval** — expectation that minority group members should make regular expressions of appreciation and gratitude for all of the help given;

✦ Fear freedom movements — angry reaction when minority group members try to change the power balance.

How Audism Affects Deaf People

✦ **Institutionalized oppression** — subtle, long-term conditioning of the public to view the minority group and its members as "less than;" continues over an extended period of time until the marginalization is normalized and accepted.

✦ **Ambivalence** — mixed negative and positive feelings about oneself based on society's view of being "deficit;"

✦ **Fatalism or passivity** — passively taking whatever happens, sensing that you can do nothing to change things;

✦ **Horizontal violence** — frustration at the disenfranchisement resulting in violence and hostility that members of an oppressed group take out on one another;

✦ **"Benefactors are perfect"** — mistaking privilege for perfection;

✦ **Emotional dependence on the oppressor** — feeling powerless and believing only members of the majority group can change things;

✦ **Fear of freedom** — wanting but simultaneously fearing equality and empowerment.

THOUGHT QUESTIONS

1. Do you think an understanding of the dynamics of oppression will eventually result in greater equality among people? How might that happen? What changes do you hope will result?

2. Can oppressed people be liberated (awarded equality) by the power group or must they liberate themselves?

3. What is culture? Draw on ideas presented by Padden, Philip and Tyler.

4. Explain the similarities and differences between hearing and Deaf cultures.

5. How might an interpreter oppress a Deaf or hearing client?

6. Discuss the relationship of power, status, and oppression.

7. Deaf individuals do not consider themselves disabled, however they benefit from legislation created to end discrimination against disabled people. Does this lead to empowerment and equality or does this further entrench attitudes of paternalism and audism?

8. Identify at least four other groups of people who have experienced institutionalized group oppression. Identify similarities and differences in their experiences and that of Deaf individuals in our country.

CD STUDY GUIDE

The various activities in the guided Chapter 5 Study Guide on CD will allow you to understand the concepts in this chapter more completely and to apply them to your life experience. Work through the Chapter 5 Study Guide on CD, completing all activities, then submit to your instructor or share with your learning partner.

SUGGESTED ACTIVITIES

✦ Invite one or more Deaf community members to talk about the "Gallaudet Revolution" and the impact, if any, on the local Deaf community.

✦ Research the work of advocates in the Deaf community and share with the class.

✦ Class members develop various scenarios within which people would react based on their culture. Invite members of several cultural groups (Deaf, African American, Japanese, hearing White, etc.) to class and ask each to discuss the appropriate response to the scenarios from their world view.

Endnotes

1. Adler & Towne (1992), p. 97-99

2. Wilcox & Wilcox (1985); Alcorn & Humphrey (1988, 1989); Smith (1991)

3. Adler & Towne (1992), p. 100

4. Adapted from Wixtrom (1988)

5. Baker-Shenk (1986)

6. Ibid.

7. Alcorn, p. 140-141

8. Ibid.

9. Jung Young Lee (1995)

10. Ibid. p 32-33

11. Ibid.; Lane, H. (1984)

12. Ibid.

13. Ibid.; Humphries (1977)

14. Lane, H. (1992) p. 36

15. We wish to acknowledge Charlotte Baker-Shenk's work in this area. This entire chapter draws heavily on personal communications with her and her work on this topic. In particular, we have drawn from her 1986 article, Interpreting: The Art of Cross Cultural Mediation.

16. See the Mask of Benevolence by Harlan Lane for an in-depth look at this concept.

17. Alcorn, pp. 317-319

18. Freire (1970); Freire & Vasconcillos (1989)

19. Baker-Shenk (1986)

20. Higgins (1980); Nash & Nash (1981)

21. Goffman (1963)

22. Nash & Nash (1981)

23. Freire (1970); Freire & Vasconcillos (1989); Freire (1973)

24. Ibid.

25. Ibid. Baker-Shenk (1986)

26. Ibid.

27. Karpman (1968)

28. Freire (1970); Freire & Vasconcillos (1989); Freire (1973)

29. Ibid.; Baker-Shenk (1986)

30. Alcorn, P. 128

31. Ibid.; Baker-Shenk (1986)

32. Ibid. p. 140, 141

33. Ibid.

34. Cayton,1991

35. Baker-Shenk (1986); Forestall (1994); Freire & Vasconcillos (1989); Freire (1973)

36. Alcorn & Humphrey (1988, 1989)

37. Carver (1995); Fischgrund, & Akematsu (1993); Fordham, (1988)

38. Freire (1970); Freire & Vasconcillos (1989); Freire (1973)

39. Baker-Shenk, 1986

40. Ibid; Freire,1989; Freire & Vasconcillos,1989; Freire, 1973

41. Ibid.

42. Adapted from Wixtrom (1988)

43. Baker-Shenk (1995)

CHAPTER SIX
Oppression, Power And Interpreters

Deaf people, like other minority groups, have been oppressed throughout history. There have been efforts on the part of various individuals to change the majority view of Deaf people and to gain greater power and equality, but the results have been limited.

LIBERATION MOVEMENT
No one could have predicted, however, the impact of the linguistic community accepting ASL as a legitimate language in the late 20th century. Sociolinguists and anthropologists knew that a new language meant a culture never before studied or recognized. Likewise, for the first time Deaf scholars and researchers were involved in both the linguistic and cultural research that was launched.

Deaf pride emerged and a movement for Deaf liberation began to gather steam as a growing number of Deaf advocates began to speak up, becoming more vocal in their demand for equal rights.[a]

One of the most powerful manifestations of this movement took place at Gallaudet University in 1988. At that time, a number of university staff and faculty, along with individuals throughout the Deaf community in the United States, had asked that priority be given to appointing a Deaf person as the next president of the university. They warned that hiring another hearing president would be like hiring a man as the head of a women's college or a white person as head of an African American institution. In spite of this public pressure, the university chose to appoint a non-signing, hearing woman as president. When the news was announced, the students began a demonstration that captured

---

[a] The Claggett Statement in Appendix A is a sample of one such effort

international attention. The students called their campaign "Deaf President Now" (DPN). They closed down the campus and staged marches on the US capitol. The university finally relented and the first Deaf president was appointed as head of the world's only university for the Deaf.

Since that time, political activism within the international Deaf community has led to greater public awareness, beneficial legislation, favorable court rulings, and some lessening of audist control. One positive outcome has been increased access to employment, medical care, public events and other services by the provision of interpreters.

POWER AND OPPRESSION

We would be remiss, however, if we left the impression that the war has been won. Many of the Deaf individuals you will work with as an interpreter carry with them the scars of ongoing disenfranchisement. There is still a disproportionate number of Deaf people who are unemployed or underemployed. A large number of Deaf adults feel alienated from their families due to strained communication and their sense that family members don't understand life from the perspective of being Deaf — and have no interest in doing so. Daily, Deaf individuals deal with the reality that they are excluded from the "privilege" of the hearing majority. Oppression is "alive and well" in Canada and the US today. After all, oppression is an inevitable result when a "power-over" rather than a "power-with" mindset exists.[1]

HUMOR

Humor is used by minority groups to deal with their day-to-day experiences of disenfranchisement. The humor of marginalized people often incorporates images of turning the tables on the majority group, proving the intelligence, resilience, perseverance and ultimate empowerment of the minority group. Thus, humor is one of the tools used by members of minority groups to fight oppression.

The humor of the Deaf community provides examples of this phenomena. Let's look at a few examples.

DEAF JOKE

Once there were three men sharing a compartment on an extended trip by train. One day, as the hours wore on, the first fellow — who was from Russia — opened a bottle of expensive, top quality Russian vodka. After consuming less than half of the bottle, he opened the window and tossed the bottle of remaining vodka out the window. The second fellow — who was Deaf — was astounded and asked the Russian why he had discarded the expensive flask of vodka. "Oh, there's lots more where that comes from," was the reply.

Later in the day, the third fellow — a Cuban — lit up an expensive, hand-rolled Havana cigar. The aroma carried the sweet fumes of a cigar of truly extraordinary quality. After smoking less than half of the cigar, the Cuban tired of it, opened the window, and tossed the re-mainder out. Once again the Deaf fellow asked why he would do such a thing, adding "what a waste!" The Cuban replied, "Oh, in Cuba there is no shortage of cigars — don't worry."

After reflecting on his experiences of the day, the Deaf fellow orders a sandwich, eats half of it then suddenly stands up, grabs the steward and throws him out the window. When confronted with the shocked faces of the Russian and Cuban passengers, the Deaf fellow confidently replied, "Oh, don't worry. There are plenty of hearing people where I live!"

Here, you see a form of humor that focuses on the minority status of people who are Deaf. Statistically, we know that approximately ten percent of the population has some significant degree of hearing loss, but a small portion of that percentage subscribes to the language and behavioral norms of the community.[2] The idea of turning the tables and disposing of the "excess" is thus humorous to the minority group members, who frequently face the majority community's reluctance to accommodate the needs of Deaf people due to the lack of a critical mass.

This is encountered by Deaf individuals when requesting interpreting services at public events, increased closed-captioning on TV, accessible telecommunication devices in public places, or simply for a store clerk to take the time to write notes so they can get assistance with a purchase. While the passage of legislation has helped alleviate some of these difficulties, the lack of authentic access is a daily frustration for Deaf people.

DEAF JOKE

Deaf people across Canada and the U.S. held a convention and took a vote. It was unanimous — the oppression had become unbearable. They hired a number of space ships and set out en masse to establish a new planet — one that would be based on their cultural norms! After flying for several years, they landed on an uninhabited planet which they named EYEth. Things were great! The language of education, politics and media was ASL. The laws established reflected the cultural norms of the new inhabitants; police, judges, and lawyers were Deaf. Homes and businesses were arranged to maximize visual access. Children were born and things seemed ideal.

Then to the dismay of all, a child was born who could hear! Specialists were brought in and tests conducted, but it seemed nothing could be done to eliminate this unexpected disability. The child was sent to special schools and was required to wear large ear muffs which emitted "white noise" and a mouth piece to prevent inadvertent utterance of spoken words. Still, in the privacy of his home or when he thought no one was looking, the child spoke and reacted to sounds around him. One day, scientists from the EYEth space program contacted the parents with good news. They had discovered a distant planet where there were others like their child. With mixed feelings, the parents sent their son to EARth.

This joke reflects a sarcastic turn of the tables on those who have inflicted years of speech-training, aural amplification, and other audist-based norms on members of the Deaf community. Interestingly, it includes a play on English words (Eyeth and Earth), a phenomena more typical of English jokes than those evolving in ASL.

Here, you have an example of humor that acknowledges the power that interpreters hold.

DEAF JOKE

There was once a miser who lived next door to a Deaf man. One bitterly cold winter, the miser broke down and decided to buy an electric blanket. He put on his boots and heavy coat and went out to the spot in his backyard where he kept his cash box buried. (He didn't believe in banks.) To his dismay, he saw footprints in the snow around the very spot where he had buried his money and when he dug up the box, it was empty. Tracking the footprints, they led straight to his Deaf neighbor. Enraged, he stomped over to his house and pounded on the door. When the Deaf man came to the door, the miser demanded his money, gesturing wildly, but the Deaf man didn't understand him. As much as he hated paying for it, the miser called an interpreter. Together, they went back to the neighbor's house and as the miser once again demanded the return of his money, the interpreter conveyed his words to the Deaf man. As he proclaimed his innocence in Sign Language, the interpreter told the miser what he was saying. Finally, the miser pulled a gun from his jacket and said in frustration, "Listen! You give me the money or you're dead!" Frightened, he quickly signed the location of the money. The interpreter turned, smugly hiding the knowing look on her face, and said to the miser, "He said he doesn't know where your money is and if there's going to be violence here, I'm leaving." With that, she turned and left.

While interpreters are a part of daily life for many Deaf individuals, there is no one who *desires* to conduct their personal and business affairs in the presence of this ancillary third party. There is always a sense of invasion and loss of privacy (and you would probably feel the same way if the tables were turned).

Further, Deaf people experience abuse at the hands of unethical and insensitive members of the interpreting community. On more than one occasion, members of the Deaf community have gone for a job interview, accompanied by an interpreter, only to find later that the interpreter was offered the job! On other occasions, interpreters have inappropriately shared information about a Deaf person that the interpreter had gleaned from his interpreting interactions. Increasing numbers of lawyers are using "consultants" to assist them with information about the language and culture of Deaf people when they are working with a Deaf client, which is a great turn of events. However, there is grave concern that the individuals serving this function are frequently interpreters, rather than members of the Deaf culture and community.

While there are — thankfully — not many interpreters who behave unethically, it only takes one bad one here and there to create an environment of mistrust and suspicion. Jokes such as the ones above grow from experience.

THE IMPACT OF OPPRESSION ON INTERPRETERS

Interpreters are exposed daily to the encounters of the privileged and the disenfranchised — to the conflict of cultures, norms and expectations. The presence of an interpreter ameliorates the lack of access to some degree but in other ways our presence exacerbates the situation.

We see the subtle ways Deaf individuals are excluded, encounter the ignorance of non-initiated hearing people and the arrogance of some educators and medical practitioners who are bent on "fixing" Deaf people. Interpreters work in situations where we see disrespect and denigration of Deaf people on a daily basis[3]. This includes:

✦ Employers who ignore a Deaf employee or dismiss his or her request for minor accommodations;

✦ Parents in denial about their child's deafness drag-
ging the child from doctor to doctor in search of a
miracle; and

✦ Overhearing rude comments made by
patrons in a restaurant who assume that everybody
sitting at the table is unable to hear.

What's worse, these insults and innuendos are typically communicated through us — through our hands, gestures and facial
expression.

Further, we hear Deaf community activists fight against the
closure of state and provincial schools for the deaf, but we accept work in the local school districts where children are being
mainstreamed. We see the plight of qualified Deaf individuals
seeking employment and being overlooked, yet we earn a decent living as interpreters *profiting* from their deafness.

This puts us all in an awkward position. Deaf people know us as
friends and allies in their community yet they struggle at times
to separate us from the majority group of hearing people.

In addition, interpreters are often the target of the backlash of
the oppressed. This manifests itself in:

✦ Frequent comments about ignorant hearing people;

✦ Having to laugh at (and often interpret) jokes that
make fun of interpreters or hearing people in general; and

✦ Interpreting the comments of a Deaf person who is
blaming or criticizing you for something.

When these things happen, we labor to separate out our feelings of hurt at the insult from what we know to be a justified
statement based on the Deaf experience. Further, there is a kind
of "initiation" that we experience as we establish ties in the Deaf
community that involves a certain amount of testing and teasing — with us as the brunt of the joke.

This reality sets up a dilemma for the interpreter. We are generally drawn to the field of interpretation because we care about people, communication and access. Thus, seeing oppression in action day after day stirs up empathy in us that may lead us to feel rage, shame or a sense of helplessness. At the same time, we might feel attacked or defensive when we perceive some of the comments, jokes and insults are indirectly aimed at us.

If you want to be an interpreter, you must be prepared to struggle with conflicting and sometimes confusing feelings regarding your role in relation to the Deaf community. The role of an ally is challenging and living with "one foot in each world" is not an easy task.

Humor as a Tool for Interpreters

A sense of humor will help you in your journey into the culture and community of Deaf people. As a member of the majority hearing culture, it is easy to take offense at jokes aimed at that culture. Don't! Try instead to understand this as a glimpse of an upside-down world in which Deaf people have a chance to gain something from being a member of the minority. Learning to laugh at yourself and your inevitable cultural faux pas is another tool that will help you on your journey.

Comments About Hearing People

It is also important to realize that when you see Deaf individuals talking about "those hearing people" in humorous or critical ways, that they are generally speaking of — the doctor, school administrator, or psychologist, for example. As you learn to act with respect toward the cultural norms of the Deaf community, you become a member of the larger Deaf community. As such, these comments are not referring to you, but to those members of the majority group who have not yet demonstrated awareness of or sensitivity to the needs and norms of the Deaf culture and community.

The Myth of Neutrality[4]
Since the early days when sign language interpreters first began to strive for professional status, there has been an expectation that they be neutral when they work. It has even been said that an interpreter should not *contaminate* an interaction with his or her own emotions or reactions. When you understand the historic and political reality of oppressed people, this makes sense. Deaf consumers need to be free to express their own beliefs, opinions and feelings. They should not have to contend with the opinions or reactions of the interpreter.

However, the neutrality of an interpreter is a myth! It is not possible for emotionally healthy individuals to work with people without experiencing empathy, as well as other feelings. In addition, others in the communication environment will experience feelings about the interpreter as an individual. All of these reactions impact the interaction being interpreted. It is critical that you acknowledge the effect your work is having on you — whether it is the content being conveyed through your hands or voice, the oppressive behavior you witness toward people who are Deaf, or thoughtless comments made to or about you in your presence.

One phenomena interpreters need to be aware of is **vicarious trauma** — trauma that results from observing another person's traumatic experience. In this case, it refers to interpreters who witness so much oppression or abuse that they feel like they themselves have been the victims. Prolonged vicarious trauma can lead to compassion fatigue — a numbing of one's emotions and an inability to interact with others with appropriate empathy. This is most likely to happen when working in serious legal, medical or therapeutic settings for an extended period of time, which you won't be doing until you have several years of interpreting experience under your belt. Nonetheless, you need to develop strategies as a student that will support your emotional wellness as you move into your professional practice. This may include writing in a reflective journal on a regular basis or finding a therapist who can provide coping strategies.

POWER: Implications For Interpreters

When you become an interpreter, you will find yourself in a very powerful position.[5] In many situations, you are the only person in the room who knows what is happening in both languages and cultural frames. Further, as a student of interpretation, you will be developing your own values and belief system related to Deaf people, ASL, Deaf education, interpretation, and other related areas.

Denying that you have power will not resolve the issue. Abdicating your power will be a fruitless effort because the power is inherent in your role and is ascribed to you by the other people involved in the setting. Rather, you must learn how to use the power you have in a wise and prudent manner. It also means coming to grips with your own history with power and oppression.

We are all oppressors to one degree or another. If you want to be an interpreter, you must begin a lifetime practice of reflecting on your attitudes, beliefs, and behaviors to identify any oppressive tendencies and moving forward to change them.

It is also important to avoid the error of early anthropologists who made brief sojourns into foreign territory, observed and interpreted from their own experiential base, and became immediate experts on the customs and traditions of the culture visited. Interpreters are not experts on Deaf culture.

Interpreters are eternal students — inquisitive, observant — and ever humbled by the reality of how much they don't yet understand.

ADVOCATE OR ALLY

Charlotte Baker-Shenk,[6] one of the first to challenge interpreters to consider our role in light of historic oppression, challenges us to seek out what interpreters can do to foster equality by refusing to be a part of systematic, institutional oppression. When they become aware of the cycle of oppression, many well-intentioned hearing people feel obliged to work to end the injustice. A common approach is to become an **advocate** on behalf of Deaf individuals. An advocate is one who speaks out on issues on behalf of others. This role often leads to hearing people becoming the "expert," being invited to speak to the press, a group of employers, or other members of the majority group. The result is that these hearing advocates often take on a leadership role in the fight for equality, stepping into the limelight and unintentionally pushing capable Deaf individuals aside. This is also a subtle form of oppression.

The cycle of oppression can be broken, but interpreters or other hearing people are not the saviors of Deaf people. The role which we can most appropriately play is that of **ally** — one who supports Deaf individuals in their own struggle for liberation. Author Ann Bishop[7] outlines strategies for becoming an ally. A small sampling of her suggestions for those seeking to become allies includes:

✦ Learn about oppression — identify it in your own life and begin a journey toward personal liberation;

✦ Help members of your own group understand oppression;

✦ Recognize that you may be part of the problem — because we grew up in a society surrounded by oppressive attitudes, we easily become oppressors. At the same time, don't waste time or energy on needless guilt trips;

✦ Remember that as a member of the majority group, you cannot see reality as clearly as the oppressed group; listen to and believe Deaf people when they tell you about the discrimination and pain they have experienced and are still experiencing;

✦ Make a list of the invisible privileges you have as a member of the majority group; in this way you begin to break the invisibility of privilege;

✦ Do not take a leadership role; work with and support members of oppressed groups but don't make the mistake of thinking you "know what is good for them;"

✦ Never take public attention or credit for an oppressed group's process of liberation; refuse to act as a spokesperson, even when reporters gravitate to you because they are more comfortable with you;

✦ Do not expect members of the oppressed group to agree on all issues or to welcome you as an ally; and

✦ Develop and maintain friendships with members of oppressed groups outside of your professional involvement with them.

It is important to remember if you are a hearing person that you cannot comprehend the experience of being Deaf, nor should you claim the roots and connectedness that a history of oppression gives to the community.

Baker-Shenk[8] provides an excellent discussion on this subject in her article entitled "The Interpreter: Machine, Advocate or Ally?" We urge you to read her article and to discuss it with your instructor and classmates.

CHAPTER REVIEW
Key Points

There have been many efforts to reduce the discrimination experienced by members of the Deaf community throughout history. Perhaps one of the most significant events on this front was the recognition of ASL as a legitimate language and the concomitant "discovery" of Deaf culture. This led to a sense of pride among members of the Deaf community and a liberation movement that has made significant strides in reducing the oppression of Deaf individuals.

DPN — The Deaf President Now events at Gallaudet University in 1988 were historic and marked the beginning of significant political activism.

The oppression experienced by Deaf people has a life-long effect on them. It also impacts those who work as interpreters. We see the oppression first hand on a regular basis. We are also the target of some backlash from Deaf people toward hearing people.

It is important for interpreters to understand the dynamics of oppression, the responses of Deaf community members to it and strategies to deal with events, actions and feelings that may be triggered. Failing to do so can lead to compassion fatigue and vicarious trauma, both of which can end your career as an interpreter.

✦ Members of minority groups have historically used humor as one way to persevere in the face of discrimination and lack of opportunity. The Deaf community has a rich store of jokes in which the tables are turned on hearing people. If you want to be an interpreter, you must understand the dynamics giving rise to the jokes, why they are humorous from a Deaf perspective, and working through your reactions as a hearing person to them.

✦ Interpreters witness disrespect and the denigration of Deaf people on a daily basis. Further, much of the bigotry is communicated to the Deaf person through the interpreter's hands, face and gestures. If you want to be an interpreter, you must develop strategies to deal with the mixture of feelings that arise as a result of these experiences.

✦ Interpreters are sometimes caught between supporting the Deaf community's political agenda and earning a living. It is critical for interpreters to listen to the Deaf view, reflect on their beliefs and actions in order to search out any oppressive tendencies and make moral and ethical decisions.

✦ Finally, interpreters will endure the stress of interpreting comments that insult hearing people, even the interpreter herself at times, in a way that is as faithful to the intent of the speaker as possible. This requires strategies for support and debriefing in order to deal with the mixture of feelings that will result and thus maintain their mental and emotional health.

Tips for interpreters in this chapter include:

✦ Keep your sense of humor. Laugh at yourself and let "barbed" humor and comments go.

✦ Recognize that comments about ignorant hearing people doesn't include interpreters; those comments are typically aimed at those hearing people who have direct impact on the lives of Deaf people but have made no attempt to learn ASL or understand Deaf culture.

✦ Come to grips with the influence you will have on an interaction as an interpreter and the impact that event will have on you. Interpreter neutrality is a myth!

✦ Recognize and develop strategies to deal with the power inherent in the position of interpreter. A part of that challenge is coming to grips with your own history with oppression and power.

✦ Learning the role of and developing skills as an ally. A number of steps to accomplish this goal were listed.

THOUGHT QUESTIONS

1. Can you think of three other groups of people who have been historically oppressed and have gone through (or are going through) a struggle for liberation? What differences or similarities do you see between these groups and the experiences of the Deaf community.

2. Have you heard other Deaf culture jokes or stories like those in this chapter? Record them and identify the socio-political purpose or goal of the joke.

3. What "initiating" jokes have you encountered or observed when entering the Deaf community? How did you feel about being the target of the joke? How might you handle this situation the next time it occurs?

4. Develop definitions for ally, advocate, disenfranchisement and empowerment. These should be written in your own words — personalized in a way that makes the concepts real for you.

CD STUDY GUIDE

✦ The various activities in the guided Chapter 6 Study Guide on CD will allow you to understand the concepts in this chapter more completely and to apply them to your life experience. Work through the Chapter 6 Study Guide on CD, completing all activities, then submit to your instructor or share with your learning partner.
✦

SUGGESTED ACTIVITIES

✦ Are you a member of an oppressed or disenfranchised group? If so, reflect on the history of that group — perhaps interview your parents or grandparents or older members of that group — to identify similarities and differences between experiences of that group and those of the Deaf community. How is humor used in that group? Are there professionals who are related to that group and experience some of the effects of the disenfranchisement of group members?

✦ Interview two Deaf individuals in your community who remember the DPN protest. Ask how they felt what the event happened and what if any impact did it have on the local Deaf community.

✦ Invite a two or three professional interpreters to class to share their perspective on the impact of the historic oppression of the Deaf community on their personal and professional lives. (TIP: give them a copy of this chapter to read before they come to class so they can be prepared to share)

✦ Research the role of humor in other minority communities. Your instructor might invite one or two Deaf story tellers to class for a Deaf humor day. Whether in person or from other sources, gather samples of jokes or anecdotes then analyze them to see how/if they serve some liberation functions.

Endnotes

1. Bishop (1994)
2. Taylor (1994)
3. To read more on this topic see www.michaelharvey-phd.com
4. Roy (2000)
5. Baker-Shenk (1992)
6. Ibid.
7. Bishop (1994)
8. Baker-Shenk (1992)

CHAPTER SEVEN
The Work of Interpreters

In this chapter, we will define some of the terminology you will encounter when working in the field and discuss several ways to look at the task of interpretation.

BASIC TERMS

Professional interpreters use terms to describe language skills, linguistic fluency, and the people with whom we work. We also have a vocabulary to describe the various tasks an interpreter performs.

Discussing Language Fluency

A person's native or first language is sometimes referred to as one's *mother tongue, native language* or *first language.* Two other common terms used are **A-language** or **L1.** Your A-language or L1 is *usually* the language your parents speak, although this is not always the case.[a1] This is the language in which you are most fluent and are capable of discussing a variety of topics for numerous purposes (social exchanges, to exchange information, etc.). For most people in the United States and Canada their *L1* or *A-language* is English. You are probably comfortable "playing with" or bending the rules of your L1 and you have little, if any, trouble deciphering subtle nuances and degrees of meaning in your mother tongue. While you may speak your A-language with a regional or geographic accent, no one would doubt that you are a native user of the language when listening to you speak or watching you sign.

The terms **L2** or **B-language** refer to your second language, one acquired by living in a country where that language is spoken

---

[a] Ninety percent of all Deaf individuals use a language that is different from that of their parents. When they learn American Sign Language through immersion at an early age, their A–language is ASL while their parent's A–language may be English.

by interacting frequently with people using that language, or by studying the language formally. Typically, you feel fairly comfortable using your L2 or B-language to carry on conversations in a variety of settings on various topics. Jargon particular to a field of study like auto mechanics, linguistics, or nursing, for example, will probably be more difficult in your B-language and you may speak or sign with an accent. As a B-language user, you probably also overlook some of the subtleties and nuances of meaning; further, some forms of humor — particularly playing with the language — may cause you difficulty.

Using your **C-language** is more difficult. You may understand most of what is being expressed to you but have real difficulty responding. Your utterances are heavily accented, you often use improper grammatical structures and make frequent errors when selecting the vocabulary to use. You probably order the words or signs in your C-language according to the grammatical structure of your A-language. The following example demonstrates one person's experience using their C-language.

Example of a C Language

I grew up in Texas and studied Spanish in high school, with friends whose A-language was Spanish. I had some social experiences in Spanish and can understand simple Spanish sentences when they are spoken slowly and when I know the context. When I listen to a Spanish radio station, I can pick out a word here and there but I can't follow the narrative. When it comes to speaking Spanish, I use what we refer to as "Tex-Mex" It varies for each speaker, but might go something like this:

Se llama is Betty Smith. Her brother
es mal, man — muy mal!

One historic challenge facing the field of sign language interpretation has been the attempt of individuals to interpret when one of their working languages is no stronger than a C-language. Interpretation is not possible unless the interpreter has bilingual mastery of two languages, one in which they have native mastery and the second in which they have at least B-language competence.

Discussing The Work of Interpreters

The process of interpreting includes taking a source language message, identifying meaning and speaker intent by analyzing the linguistic and paralinguistic elements of the message, then making a cultural and linguistic transition and producing the message into the target language. This is termed interpretation and is illustrated in Fig. 7-1.

FIG. 7.1 Interpretation

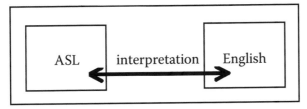

Interpreters convey information between two languages. The **source language (SL)** is the language in which the original message is conveyed. If, for example, a speaker is conveying his or her information in German and the message is being interpreted into Russian, the source language is German. Or, if a Deaf person is signing in ASL and the message is being interpreted into spoken English, the source language is ASL.

The **target language (TL)** is the language into which the original message is interpreted. Thus, an interpreter takes the message expressed in the source language and, after working through a complex mental process,[b]expresses that same message into the

---

[b] These processes are charted in several models that will be discussed in Chapter Ten.

target language. If someone is speaking in French and the message is being interpreted into La Langue des Signes Quebeçoise (LSQ) the target language is LSQ. If a Deaf person is signing in ASL and the message is being interpreted into spoken English, the target language is English.

The TL expression of an interpretation always lags behind the SL utterance because of the time required to take in the SL and make a mental search for meaning. This time is termed **processing time.**

When an interpretation is successful, dynamic equivalence is maintained. This means that the speaker's goals and level of audience involvement is the same for both the audience who received the message in its original form and the audience who received the message through the interpreter.

FIG. 7.2 Transliteration

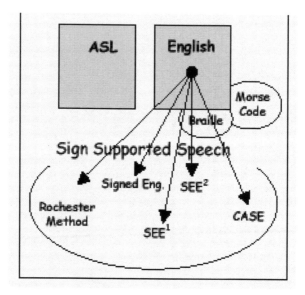

Transliteration is a term that is not used in the field of spoken language interpretation. The most common meaning of "transliteration" is derived from the field of music where the term is used to refer to the transcription of words from one written language into a phonetic form of another language, allowing a singer who doesn't read Italian, for example, to sound out the Italian words by reading them in the transliterated or phonetically based form.

In the field of sign language interpretation, however, transliteration has been redefined to have a different meaning. As illustrated in Fig. 7-2, transliteration refers to the process of taking a message and expressing it in a different form of the *same* language. Thus, if the message is expressed in spoken English and the interpreter expresses it in signed English — a different form of the *same* language — the work being performed is transliteration. While the forms of English vary in **modality** from auditory to visual in transliteration, only one *language* is involved.

Transliteration is inherently easier than interpretation simply because there is no change in languages. Transliteration includes various forms of English-based signing (discussed in Chapter Four). To date, there has been limited research on the mental processes required in transliteration. These factors make transliteration a challenging entity to deal with.

As discussed in Chapter Four, the term *transliteration* is also used when describing the kind of work done when making spoken English visible for an oral Deaf individual (termed **oral transliteration**). The term transliteration is appropriate because there is no change in language, simply the mode of delivery.

Interpreters are sometimes called upon to provide translations. **Translation** refers to the transition of a message from the frozen form of one language into the *frozen* form of another language. Frozen forms include working with texts that are recorded in written, videotaped or audio taped formats. An example of translation by this definition would be taking instructions for a camera which are originally written in Japanese and translating them into English so the product can be sold in Canada and the U.S. Similarly, the Omega Project (a part of Deaf Missions of Iowa[2]) is translating the Bible from its original languages of Greek and Hebrew — both in written form — into American Sign Language on videotape.

Both spoken and sign language interpreters are often called upon to perform **sight translations**. This usually refers to changing a message from a frozen form in one language into spoken or signed form of another language. The translation is done on first sight, without the time normally required to prepare a formal translation. An example of sight translation would be when a Spanish language interpreter in court is asked to "interpret" a legal form to his or her client. The legal form is a frozen form of English. The interpreter would read the form, comprehend the message, identify linguistic and cultural parameters, and produce an equivalent message in spoken Spanish. It is a fairly common experience for a Deaf consumer to seek assistance with print English documents that are noted for complex terms and sentence structure (e.g. legal documents or government notices). While the Deaf consumer will typically ask for someone to "interpret" the letter, an interpreter actually does a sight translation of the written document to make the contents more accessible. Likewise, a hearing person may receive a videotaped letter or a TTY message that they are unable to decipher. An interpreter may be asked to do a *sight translation* of the message into spoken or written English.

Spoken language interpreters generally learn translation prior to learning interpretation, and find a part of their professional employment in the field of translation.[3] In more and more educational programs, sign language interpreter students are taught translation skills prior to interpreting skills because they serve as an effective bridge between learning the language and interpreting between two languages.[4]

Terms For Those Who Do The Work

An **interpreter** is a bilingual-bicultural professional who:

1. Conveys equivalent messages between two languages and cultures; while

2. Being sensitive to the environmental factors which foster or impede the message; and

3. Conducts himself or herself in a professional, ethical manner.

A **transliterator** does exactly the same things, working however between two forms of the same language.

In order to be a competent interpreter or transliterator, you must communicate in a clear, articulate and effective manner. Further, you must possess a certain degree of social skill and grace. Renowned communications experts, Adler and Towne,[5] outline these prerequisite skills below. An interpreter/transliterator must:

+ Have a wide repertoire of cultural and communication behaviors with which to respond to various social interactions;
+ Be able to select the best behavior for a given situation and perform it skillfully;
+ Be able to take others' points of view and analyze a situation in a variety of ways;
+ Be able to monitor their own behavior and revise as appropriate; and
+ Be committed to successful and effective communication.

Obviously, competency in any particular situation varies from one situation to another depending on the setting and people involved. Thus, interpreters must know how to behave in culturally appropriate ways in a range of settings, as well as being skilled in using language to accomplish a variety of interpersonal goals.[6]

Translators perform the work of translation. In the traditional sense, translation is not done in the presence of the people who will read the translation. However, in the field of sign language interpretation translation is more commonly done in the presence of a Deaf person.

Finally, practitioners in our field typically refer to themselves as **interpreters** — even though they may actually be performing the process of translation or transliteration. We will look at this more closely in the next section of this chapter.

LOOKING AT THE WORK OF INTERPRETERS

Interpreters can talk about their work in two different ways:

1. By looking at the output or product of our work and

2. By considering the philosophical frame from which our work flows (one's philosophical frame influences the decisions made by the interpreter).

In this chapter, we look at the output or product of our work, including:

✦ Simultaneous and consecutive interpretation/transliteration,

✦ Sign-to-voice and voice-to-sign interpretation/transliteration,

✦ Types of settings where we work and the number of clients present,

✦ The consumers and clients with whom we work.

Looking at the Output

What do you see when you observe a sign language interpreter at work? Are the source and target languages being produced simultaneously or consecutively? Is the interpreter providing a spoken interpretation or is the interpreter providing a signed interpretation? Below we have discussed five things one can observe when looking at working interpreters. These include:

In terp re ter s l ook
for m eaning

+ The output or product — interpretation, transliteration or oral transliteration;
+ The form of output — simultaneous or consecutive form;
+ The part of the process being performed — sign-to-voice or voice-to-sign;
+ The recipients of the service being provided — the consumers or clients;
+ The location where the work is provided — settings and numbers of clients present.

THE OUTPUT:
Interpretation or Signed/Oral Transliteration

One thing we can observe when looking at an interpreter is the "output" or product. Are we seeing a change of languages or are we seeing a different form of the same language? When observing an interpreter at work, we can observe from the output if he or she is interpreting or transliterating by observing things such as the underlying grammatical structure and overall discourse structure.

THE FORM OF THE OUTPUT:
Simultaneous or Consecutive

Another thing we can observe when looking at an interpreter is the time it takes to render the interpretation. As you know, the term simultaneous means "at the same time," so the phrase **simultaneous interpretation** or **simultaneous transliteration**, refers to the process of interpreting/transliterating into the target language/code at the same time that the source language message is being delivered.

On the other hand, if the speaker completes an idea in the source language and pauses while the interpreter transmits that idea into the target language, then states the next idea in the source language (followed by interpretation), the process is termed **consecutive interpretation**. Consecutive means "in sequence" or "in order." When one is interpreting consecutively, the sequence you will observe is (1) delivery of source language message (or a portion of it), then (2) interpretation/ transliteration into the target language. This is the type of interpretation seen on television when a foreign diplomat makes some spontaneous spoken presentation. The foreign diplomat speaks a portion of his or her message. Then, as the speaker pauses, the interpreter (hopefully!) produces the culturally and linguistically appropriate equivalent into the spoken target language.

The type of sign language interpretation most often seen by the public is simultaneous and for this reason there is sometimes a misperception that this is the norm or the ideal. However, consecutive interpretation is actually much more accurate.[7] Consecutive form is effectively used in all one-on-one and many small group settings. Simultaneous form is only "mandatory" in formal or platform settings.

Although consecutive interpretation is much more accurate, some Deaf individuals prefer that the interpreter begin interpreting the instant the hearing person begins talking. There are a number of factors behind this expectation, including the fact that many Deaf people ...

1. Have had bad experiences with interpreters result-ing in some power issues and a lack of trust;
2. Are not familiar with consecutive form as used by professional interpreters.

One technique that can help reduce the reluctance of consumers in using consecutive form is for the interpreter to incorporate active, interactive nonverbal behaviors (i.e., head nods and other visual cues that comprehension is taking place) indicating the interpreter is taking in the source language utterance. This lets the Deaf client know that the interpreter is "working."

In both simultaneous and consecutive interpretation, the interpreter uses **process time** to analyze the source language utterance, identifying essential elements of meaning and making appropriate cultural and linguistic adjustments, before producing the equivalent message in the target language.

Transliterators generally have less processing time than interpreters because while they are changing the communication mode, they are not changing languages.

By its very nature, consecutive form will always have greater processing time than simultaneous form because one must wait until the source language message (or a portion of it) has been delivered, before beginning the interpretation into the target language.

WORKING WITH DEAF INTERPRETERS
Another situation where you typically see consecutive interpretation is when working with a Deaf Interpreter (DI). In this setting, the hearing interpreter is conveying what is being spoken to the DI who then interprets the message to the Deaf client(s). The very nature of this type of interaction encourages the use of consecutive interpretation.

THE PART OF THE PROCESS BEING PERFORMED:
Sign-to-Voice or Voice-to-Sign
Another way to talk about our work is to notice what specific part of the interpreting process an interpreter is engaged in. When the source language message is produced in ASL, LSQ or a manual form of English, the interpreter/ transliterator is said to be doing **sign-to-voice** work because the signed source language message will be converted into spoken English or

French. The term **voice-to-sign** interpretation refers to working with a spoken language as the source language and a visual language as the target language/code.[c]

Some people contend that sign-to-voice interpreting is the harder part of the process, since reading signs is more challenging than producing signs. This is a common misperception. Actually, if your second language is acquired in an appropriate manner, you should be much stronger working from your second language into your native language.

RECIPIENTS OF THE SERVICE BEING PROVIDED: Consumers, Clients or Customers

We can discuss our work by describing the people who receive our services. We use the terms clients to refer to those for whom we provide an interpretation. Since we work for both Deaf and hearing **consumers, clients,** or **customers,** we can say that we are providing spoken English interpretation/transliteration for the hearing client/consumer or ASL/Signed English interpretation/transliteration for the Deaf consumer.

Historically some people have referred to our work as "interpreting" which has resulted in a focus on the Deaf client(s),  as if only Deaf people benefit from our services. Can you imagine what would happen if the interpreter only performed voice-to-sign interpretation and did not perform sign-to-voice interpretation — especially when the Deaf consumer is sharing information critical to the decision that is being made? Obviously, both Deaf and hearing people depend on interpreting services to conduct their business, so both are our consumers.

THE LOCATION WHERE THE WORK IS PROVIDED: Settings & Numbers of Clients

Sign language interpreters work in a number of settings

---

[c] Outdated terms: "reverse interpreting" for sign–to–voice work and "expressive interpreting" for voice–to–sign work.

so another way we can look at our work is to describe these settings. We frequently describe them in terms that:

✦ Refer to the number of clients present or
✦ Describe the type of interaction that is taking place.
✦ Describe the interpreting "settings"

When using terms that refer to the number of clients present, we say that we are working in:

✦ One-on-one settings;
✦ Small group settings; or
✦ Large group settings.

This is significant because the use of language, the purpose of speakers, the types of appropriate turn-taking, volume, etc., change depending on the type of setting in which we are working. When we describe the types of transaction taking place, we might say job interview, court hearing, mental health counseling, and so forth. Fig. 7-3 on the following pages outlines several types of settings and suggests the types of events within each setting where an interpreter might work with different numbers of clients.

FIG. 7-3 Settings Where Interpreters Work			
SETTING	ONE-ON-ONE	SMALL GROUP	LARGE GROUP
MENTAL HEALTH	Individual counseling or therapy session	Family counseling; group counseling; team meeting in psychiatric hospital to discuss patient	Lecture on mental health issues; large 12-step group; conference with therapists and interpreters to discuss issues of common concern

159

FIG. 7-3 Settings Where Interpreters Work			
SETTING	ONE-ON-ONE	SMALL GROUP	LARGE GROUP
EDUCATION	Parent-teacher conference; student-teacher appointment; student-tutor interaction	Education planning conference (IEP) involving educational team of teacher, principal, resource teacher, counselor & other professionals, parents and parent advocate; graduate seminar; study group; PTA executive board meeting; staff meeting	Lecture to a large class; assembly presentation to student body; PTA meeting; graduation ceremonies; campus-school orientation to large groups of incoming students
RELIGIOUS	Appointment with priest, rabbi, or pastor; pre-marital conference; meeting with funeral director or wedding coordinator	Religious instruction class; committee meetings; Board of Elders or Deacons	Sermon to congregation; wedding; funeral; bar or bat mitzvah
MEDICAL	Office visit and exam; medical consultation	Consultation with family following surgery; hospital staff meeting	Hospital community health education program held weekly in hospital auditorium (seating 300) to discuss various health issues
THEATRE & PERFORMING ARTS	Audition; interview of actor with director; interaction between individual members of the cast	Rehearsal; cast meeting; pre/post-performance discussion group	Theatrical performance; concert

FIG. 7-3 Settings Where Interpreters Work			
SETTING	ONE-ON-ONE	SMALL GROUP	LARGE GROUP
LEGAL	Individual appointment with attorney or judge; interview of a victim or suspect by police personnel	Depositions; direct & cross examination; preparation of witnesses; staff meeting of law firm; meeting with lawyers regarding a case	Opening and closing arguments; instructions to the jury
EMPLOYMENT	Interview with rehabilitation counselor; job interview; employer-employee meeting	Staff meeting; team meeting	Union meeting; annual recognition of employee of the year at large banquet
SOCIAL SERVICES	Interview for application for food stamps or other social service; interview with social worker	12-step meetings (no set agenda/ opportunity for participation by attendees); family meetings; interventions	Conferences and presentations for social workers, members of 12-step groups, etc.

One-on-One

In one-on-one encounters, you typically have one Deaf and one hearing client who are using language in a give-and-take manner. One client will make a comment or ask a question and the second will respond. This continues back and forth until the business at hand is completed and the two depart. In a one-on-one setting, the linguistic register used may be informal or consultative. The exchange may involve general vocabulary or technical jargon. The purpose of the individuals involved varies and can include exchanging or clarifying information, teaching, explaining, or demonstrating. Turn-taking is not generally a problem, since there are two individuals and the shift of communication goes back and forth between the two clients. The purpose of a one-on-one encounter could be to confront, scold, or discipline. If this is the case, there could be a highly emotional interchange resulting in rapid turn-taking, interruptions and emotionally laden language. When beginning your career as an interpreter, we suggest you begin in one-on-one encounters that are not highly emotive. The setting and type of turn-taking lends itself to consecutive form. The pace is manageable and there is ample opportunity to clarify an utterance before producing it into the target language.

Small Groups

This term includes many types of interactions and may involve three to twenty individuals. This could be a group counseling session, a staff meeting, a small classroom or seminar. Typically, there will be more hearing than Deaf clients in such a setting, although this is not always the case. The speech goals are quite varied, including informing, advising, teaching, explaining, and planning, among others. In a small group setting, the turn-taking is usually much more rapid, making interpretation difficult. As in other settings, the interpreter must deal with intake and analysis of the source language utterances and production of a linguistic and cultural equivalent into the target language. In addition, the interpreter in small group settings must indicate who is speaking, convey the emotional overlay of utterances, shift back and forth between sign-to-voice and voice-to-sign interpretation — and do all of this within the constraints of sometimes rapid-fire turn-taking. This is probably one of the most difficult settings in which to interpret, thus more experienced interpreters, rather than beginning level interpreters, are encouraged to work in this type of setting.

Large Group or Platform

As the name indicates, when one interprets in large group setting, there are usually more than 40-50 participants. Due to the size of the audience, the speaker is often required to stand on the platform to be seen and heard. The type of interchange often follows

the rules for high consultative or formal interactions. There is little or no interaction between the speaker and the audience. The language used has more complex syntactic structures and vocabulary. The purpose of the speaker(s) may be to entertain, inform, inspire, or convince. Because of the degree of formality, it is often easier for the interpreter to prepare for a large group or platform presentation. Frequently there is a printed program or agenda that allows the interpreter to identify speakers well in advance. The interpreter may be able to secure a copy of the speech, sermon, textbook or presentation before the event. The speaker may have written a book on the subject that can be obtained by the interpreter or there may be an audio or video-taped recording of a similar presentation by the same speaker that could be used for preparation. Even if this advanced preparation is not possible, the interpreter can sometimes meet with the presenter before the beginning of the presentation, during which time the speaker's goal can be identified, along with a verbal outline of the presentation to come. Because of the opportunity for advanced preparation and the lack of turn-taking, beginning-level interpreters are able to provide interpreting services in some large group settings. However this usually means working from your A-language into your B-language, which can present significant challenge

CHAPTER REVIEW
Key Points

Several terms can be used to discuss a person's language fluency, including:

Rev iew

1. A-language or L1
2. B-language or L2
3. C-language

Less technical terms such as native or first language and mother tongue can also be used. One can only interpret effectively between their first (A-language or L1) and second languages (L2 or B-language).

Interpretation: the result of taking a source language message, identify meaning and speaker intent by analyzing the linguistic and paralinguistic elements of the message, then making a cultural and linguistic transition and producing the message into the target language.

Source language (SL): the language in which the original message is conveyed.

Target language (TL): the language into which the original message is expressed by the interpreter.

Processing Time: the time used by the interpreter to complete the analysis of the source language utterance and to search for cultural and linguistic equivalents before producing an equivalent message in the target language.

Dynamic equivalence: maintaining the speaker's intended interaction with and impact on the audience; when accomplished in an interpretation, the speaker's goals and level of audience involvement is the same for both the audience who received the message in its original form and the audience who received the message through the interpreter.

Transliteration: (as used in the field of sign language interpretation) the result of taking a source language message, identify meaning and speaker intent by analyzing the linguistic and paralinguistic elements of the message, and expressing that in a different form of the same language (e.g. signed English to spoken English).

Translation: changing a message from the frozen form of one language into the frozen form of another language; this is an emerging field for Deaf individuals (e.g. videotaped translations of textbooks, plays and poems).

Sight Translation: changing a message from the frozen form of one language into another signed or spoken language; Deaf individuals hold a fairly common expectation that interpreters will be able to provide this service to them.

Modality: refers to the channel through which a message is expressed, specifically aural/oral or visual/gestural.

Interpreter: one who supports communication between individuals who have different languages; one is often referred to as an interpreter regardless of whether they are providing interpretation or transliteration services.

Discussing the work of interpreters

Simultaneous Form: the process of interpreting/transliterating into the target language/code at the same time the source language message is being delivered; requires shorter processing time; although commonly observed, only mandatory in formal or platform settings.

Consecutive Form: the process of interpreting into the target language after the speaker completes one or more ideas in the source language, pausing while the interpreter transmits that information.

The steps include (1) delivery of source language message (or a portion of it), (2) interpretation into target language, (3) repeating steps #1 and #2.

- ✦ More accurate than simultaneous interpretation
- ✦ Should be used in most one-on-one and small group settings

Sign-To-Voice: working from signed source language into a spoken target language.

Voice-To-Sign: working from spoken target language into a signed source language.

If one's second language is acquired in an appropriate manner, an interpreter should be more competent working from his or her L2 into his or her L1.

Clients or Consumers: the people who use an interpreter's services. Interpreters work for both Deaf and hearing consumers/clients.

Work settings: refers to external factors as a way of describing one's work; includes the number of clients present, the type of interaction taking place, the use of language, the purpose of speakers; dictates appropriate turn-taking, volume of speech/ size of signs, etc.

✦ <u>One-on-One Settings</u>

   ✓ Linguistic register ranges, including informal or consultative;

   ✓ Discourse style may vary from general vocabulary to technical jargon;

   ✓ Goals range from exchanging and/or clarifying information, teaching, explaining, confronting, scolding, or disciplining; may be highly emotional resulting in rapid turn-taking, interruptions and emotionally laden language;

   ✓ Turn-taking generally supports shifting back-and-forth between the two participants; lends itself to consecutive interpreting.

◆ <u>Small Group Settings</u>

✓ Generally involves 3 to 20 individuals (e.g. staff meeting);

✓ Speech goals may include informing, advising, explaining or planning;

✓ Turn-taking is usually rapid; interpreter must indicate who is speaking, convey the emotional overlay of utterances, shift back and forth between sign-to-voice and voice-to-sign interpretation

◆ <u>Large Group Settings</u>

✓ In excess of 20/30 clients — can range up to tens of thousands; the speaker typically stands, may use microphone;

✓ Usually follows the rules for formal interactions — little or no interaction between the speaker and the audience; the language used has complex syntactic structures and vocabulary;

✓ Speaker goal(s) may include entertaining, informing, inspiring, teaching or convincing;

✓ Preparation is possible for many large group events — printed program or agenda which allows the interpreter to identify speakers well in advance or even to secure a copy of the speech, sermon, textbook or presentation in advance.

THOUGHT QUESTIONS

1. Which setting would be best for a beginning interpreter? Why?

2. Is consecutive or simultaneous interpreting more accurate? Why?

3. Give examples of large group or platform settings. Talk about ways an interpreter can prepare for work in such a setting. What physical factors (lighting, etc.) should the interpreter consider? What turn-taking behaviors can be expected? What might the speaker goals be? Can you use consecutive interpretation in this setting?

4. Give examples of one-on-one settings. Talk about ways an interpreter can prepare for work in such a setting. What physical factors (lighting, etc.) should the interpreter consider? What turn-taking behaviors can be expected? What might the speaker goals be? Can you use consecutive interpretation in this setting?

5. Give examples of small group settings. Talk about ways an interpreter can prepare for work in such a setting. What physical factors (lighting, etc.), should the interpreter consider? What turn-taking behaviors can be expected? What might the speaker goals be? Can you use consecutive interpretation in this setting?

6. Compare simultaneous interpretation with consecutive interpretation, explaining the differences, when and why one might use each, etc.

7. Is it true that sign-to-voice interpretation should be an easier task for a sign language interpreter? Why or why not?

CD STUDY GUIDE

✦ The various activities in the guided Chapter 7 Study Guide on CD will allow you to understand the concepts in this chapter more completely and to apply them to your life experience. Work through the Chapter 7 Study Guide on CD, completing all activities, then submit to your instructor or share with your learning partner.

SUGGESTED ACTIVITIES

✦ Observe interpreters at work, making certain to see them in one-on-one, small group and large group settings. Do you see simultaneous or consecutive? Are there variations in placement, size of signs/ volume of speech, etc.? What do you observe in terms of turn-taking? Make notes of your observations and discuss them in class. (Remember, your goal is to learn from observation, not to critique or criticize the work being done!)

✦ Prepare a set of questions for professional practitioners. Then invite a panel of working interpreters to your classroom so you can ask those questions and listen to the range of responses provided.

✦ Go on-line and find at least four web-sites addressing the work of interpreters. Report on your findings in class.

Endnotes

1. Grosjean xe "Grosjean" (1982)
2. For more information contact Deaf Missions of Iowa, RR 2, Box 26, Council Bluff, IA 51501.
3. Spoken language interpreters usually spend more time polishing their translation skills because there is a job market for translators working between languages with written forms. At this point there is not much of a translation market for sign language interpreters, although with the emergence of the bilingual-bicultural approach to Deaf education,

this is becoming a professional area for Deaf translators working with educational texts.

4. Kanda (1984)
5. Adler and Towne (1999), p. 42
6. Ibid, p. 42
7. Russell (2000); Cokely (1985)

CHAPTER EIGHT
How We Approach Our Work

 In Chapter Eight, we looked at the work of interpreters from the output or product. Another way to discuss what we do is to look at the philosophical frame that defines our approach to the task. One's philosophical frame determines the way an interpreter:

✦ Sees his or her clients, their roles and the role of the interpreter;
✦ Views ASL/English and Deaf/hearing norms and rules of interaction; and
✦ Interprets the tenets in the professional Code of Ethics and uses the power inherent in the position of interpreter.

The philosophical frames include the:

✦ Helper philosophy;
✦ Conduit or machine philosophy;
✦ Language facilitation philosophy, and
✦ Bilingual-bicultural philosophy.

HELPER PHILOSOPHY

The Registry of Interpreters for the Deaf (RID) was established in 1964 — the first professional association of sign language interpreters in the world. Prior to its establishment and in the early days of RID's existence, the common approach to delivery of service for interpreters was the philosophical frame. Deaf people were generally viewed as handicapped, limited, and unable to fully manage their personal and business affairs. Thus, it fell to the interpreter to be a care-taker to some extent. It was at this time that the following incident might happen:

The Helper Philosophy in Action

George (Deaf) had an appointment with the doctor last week, so he arranged for his friend's daughter to pick him up and drive him there. When he got in her car, George and Sarah exchanged hugs before starting a running dialogue that continued all the way to the doctor's office. "What's wrong today?" Sarah asked. George, a bit embarrassed, explained he was having a lot of pain with his bowel movements. "Then last week, I realized there was blood in my stool. I'm really scared because I have a friend who died of stomach cancer," he signed. This conversation continued until the nurse called George's name and they moved into the doctor's office." How are you, George?" the doctor asks. As George starts to sign his response, Sarah answers for him, telling the doctor everything she had learned as George looks on helplessly — not even sure of exactly what is being said The doctor, picking up on Sarah's cue starts talking to Sarah about George. When Sarah doesn't have an answer, she briefly summarizes the topic of discussion, asks George a question, then resumes her interaction with the doctor.

Later, while George changes into an examining gown, the doctor turns to Sarah and asks how she learned signs. Sarah gives a 15-minute oration of her background — interspersing the end of the story in the "dead" time while the doctor examines George. As the examination continues, the doctor asks George the name of any medications he is taking. Sarah interrupts and says, "It's in his briefcase in the waiting room," patting George's hand, she continues, "You just sit right there and I'll run get it. Be right back." she says as she leaves the room. On the way home, Sarah signs, "Oh, Mom and Dad were just talking about Mrs. Smith. You know her trouble started exactly the same way. I'm glad you decided to get right over to the doctor. What about your wife? Does she know? I mean, if it is cancer, you need to do a lot of things to get ready for the inevitable." George, not understanding what Sarah means, looks at her with a puzzled expression. She continues, "You need to write up a will and we should probably check your life insurance benefits. I'll call and make those appointments. Did you know if you die in an accident it will pay your wife twice as much as if you die of cancer? Anyway, I just heard about a new medication for stomach cancer. You can only get it on the black market but if you are interested, just let me know and I can hook you up with a guy who brings it over from Mexico."

As seen in this illustration, the interpreter who subscribes to the helper philosophy tends to be overly involved with the clients he or she encounters. This interpreter may move out of the role of interpreting to advise, direct, teach, or cajole Deaf and hearing clients. The attitude behind this behavior is often the belief that Deaf people are incapable of fully understanding or participating in the world around them, due to their limited experiential base or the intolerance of most people. Thus, the need for an interloper. Remember, interpreters in the early days were often volunteers — with no formal training for the role and work of interpreting — whose primary roles were parent, child, teacher, or clergy.

The RID Code of Ethics was developed partially in response to the presence of "helpers" in the field. The founders felt the behavior described above was too typical and that it resulted in inappropriate boundaries and an imbalance of power weighted on the side of hearing people. Further, Deaf professionals were increasingly unwilling to tolerate the paternalistic care-taking attitudes exhibited by the interpreters they encountered. Thus, the emergence of eight principles, known as the Code of Ethics, which were intended to guide the decisions made by interpreters in the field *(see Chapter Twelve for further discussion of ethical guidelines for interpreters).*

MACHINE (CONDUIT) PHILOSOPHY

We were at the far extreme of personal involvement and volunteerism while functioning under the helper philosophy. With the realization that this was inappropriate and oppressive, there was a dramatic swing of the pendulum to the other extreme in an attempt to have no influence on the dynamics or communication taking place. Suddenly the philosophical frame that was accepted as most appropriate for interpreters was the **machine (conduit) philosophy**. This philosophical frame led to an interpretation of the Code of Ethics as a rigid set of rules. Within this philosophical frame interpreters "followed the rules," denying that their presence had an influence on the dynamics and often unaware of the inequity resulting from the history of oppression experienced by Deaf people.[1]

When looking at the work of an interpreter functioning from this philosophical frame, you would also see a "verbatim" transmission of words/signs. Interpreters focused on volume, being sure to sign every word spoken and to speak every sign produced. Unfortunately, consumers often saw a torrent of signs or heard a great number of words — from which it was often difficult to derive meaning. Interpreters took on almost a robotlike role in the communication process, assuming no responsibility for the interaction or communication dynamics taking place between clients.

It was also during this time that interpreters began to describe themselves as equivalent to a telephone wire — simply relaying information from one receiver to another. The following is a scenario captures an interpreter working from a *machine philosophical frame.*

The Machine (Conduit) Philosophy In Action

George (Deaf) had an appointment with the doctor last week, so he arranged for a referral agency to send an interpreter. When he arrived, the interpreter was waiting for him. George identified himself as the Deaf client, asked the interpreter's name and sat down to chat a bit while waiting for the doctor to call them into her office.

"How'd you get involved in interpreting? Your folks Deaf?" George signed. From behind his magazine the interpreter, trying to avoid any unnecessary personal interaction with his client, shook his head negatively and began to read the article in front of him. George didn't know what to think of this behavior. Perhaps this chap was a bit shy but George knew it was to his advantage to be sure they could communicate clearly with each other.

Somewhat nervous that the interpreter might not understand him, George signed, "Let me explain why I'm here.
I've been having a lot of pain with my bowel movements.
Then last week, I realized there was blood in my stool. I'm
pretty scared because I have a friend who died of cancer of
the colon."

The interpreter put down his magazine and signed (while
articulating English words on his lips), "I'm sorry, but you
cannot discuss your medical condition with me in the waiting room. I am not allowed to be a retainer of information.
Think of me as a telephone wire. I just pass along what
you sign to the doctor and sign to you what the doctor is
saying. I am not allowed to have any emotions, feelings, or
personal involvement with my clients." He then looked back
to his magazine.

George is even more anxious now. "Who IS this person?" He
thinks to himself, "Is this a person I can understand? Is this
a person I can trust to convey information accurately? Does
he interact with the Deaf community? Does he understand
who I am as a Deaf man?"

About that time, the nurse calls George's name and they
move into the doctor's office. The interpreter conveys everything that is said into sign language and everything that
is signed into spoken English. After the initial interview, the
doctor moves George to an examining room. While they wait
for George to put on an examination gown, the doctor looks
at the interpreter and asks, "This is fascinating. How did
you learn sign language?" "I'm sorry but I'm not allowed to
engage in personal dialogue while working," is the response
she gets. She feels the sting of anger and embarrassment
at the interpreter's response.

George emerges from the dressing room and the examination begins. At one point, the doctor mumbles something
virtually inaudible to her nurse and the interpreter asks her
to repeat the comment since she couldn't hear it. The doctor
replies, "Oh, it was nothing, just a comment to my nurse."
"No!" The interpreter demands, "I must sign to Mr. S everything that is spoken. PLEASE, what did you say?"

Later in the examination, the doctor asks the interpreter to
hand her the bottle of medication George has indicated is
in his pants pocket. "I'm sorry but that isn't my role," the
interpreter responds matter-of-factly.

This little incident could be taken further, but you get the picture. There was such a pendulum swing to the opposite extreme
of "appropriate" behavior that interpreters became insensitive
to the human dynamics within the interpreting setting. They
became rigid and inflexible. They began, at this time, to refer
to themselves as "professionals," perhaps because they thought
they were displaying the "involved but separate" attitude demonstrated by some hearing professionals. However, in many
ways interpreters became clock-punching, insensitive append-
ages within Deaf and hearing interactions.

COMMUNICATION FACILITATION

In the early to mid-1970s, interpreters became newly aware of
the field of communications and another shift was made in the
philosophical frame away from the machine philosophy to the
communication facilitation philosophy. Within this philosophy the base of ethical decision-making was not significantly
different. However, interpreters became more aware of the need
for appropriate placement, lighting, background, etc. They began to indicate who was speaking since the realization had now
dawned that this was an important component in the communication dynamics taking place.

Interpreters became more aware of the need for proper physical
placement within proximity of the speaker so Deaf clients could
see both the speaker and the interpreter in one visual intake.
Interpreters also learned that appropriate lighting, background,
and absence of visual noise could enhance the conveyance of
information. It was during this period that some interpreters
adopted solid colored smocks contrasting with the tone of their
skin as a "uniform." Finally, the interpreter's personal appearance was analyzed in light of the characteristics that would un-
dergird the professional status of the practitioner. They began

excluding those features that might hamper communication. Beards and mustaches were "outlawed," along with fingernail polish, patterned clothing and most jewelry.

FIG 8.1
Philosophical Shifts in the History of
Sign Language Interpretation in North America

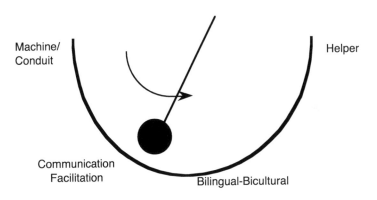

Thus, in the opinion of the authors, when observing the work of an interpreter functioning from a communication facilitator philosophical frame, the output looked much like that of a machine-based interpreter. The focus continued to be on volume (quantity) of signs and words. While interpreters were sensitive to communication dynamics in a physical sense, they were still making ethical and communication decisions that resulted in a lack of equality in terms of access and participation for Deaf consumers. Applied to the scenario above, the interpreter would probably put on a smock before entering the doctor's office and would remove the smock before doing any non-interpreting activities like going to the bathroom. The interpreter would place himself or herself behind the doctor's desk alongside the doctor to facilitate eye contact between the doctor and her patient, whether or not this was a comfortable invasion of the doctor's personal and professional space. While in the examination room, the interpreter might go to great efforts to be sure he or she was "appropriately" placed and to direct an adequate amount of lighting on the area where interpreted communication was taking place.

BILINGUAL–BICULTURAL

Today, interpreters work primarily from a bilingual-bicultural philosophical frame when approaching their work as interpreters. This is a direct result of the recognition of American Sign Language (ASL) as a legitimate language and the accompanying research and validation of Deaf culture.

This **bilingual-bicultural (bi-bi)** philosophy of interpreting has emerged in an effort to hit the mid-point between the two extremes of over-involved (helper) and invisibility (machine). In the bilingual-bicultural philosophy, the interpreters are sensitive to physical communication dynamics, indicate who is speaking, place themselves appropriately, etc. They are also keenly aware of the inherent differences in the languages, cultures, norms for social interaction and schema of the parties using interpreting services. This does not happen by matching word for sign. Effective interpretation requires cultural and linguistic mediation while accomplishing speaker goals and maintaining dynamic equivalence. This requires the use of cultural and linguistic expansions and reductions. Initial research[2] indicates that when interpreters properly mediate the languages and cultures, Deaf individuals receiving the interpreted information are able to demonstrate significantly higher levels of comprehension of the information. This is the reason more and more interpreters today are adopting this philosophical frame.

Let's look at this philosophical approach a bit closer.

Accomplishing Speaker Goal

When communication takes place, the individuals involved have goals in mind they want to accomplish. These goals can include such things as teaching, inspiring, entertaining, counseling or guiding, explaining, requesting, selling and convincing. The speaker uses words to accomplish his or her goal; the signer uses signs. In the bi-bi philosophy, the interpreter knows that these goals are accomplished differently in each language and culture and he or she identifies this goal to help analyze the text and select appropriate target language elements.

Maintaining Dynamic Equivalence

Dynamics refers to the way the people in the interaction react to or engage with the speaker or signer and his or her message. A bilingual-bicultural interpreter will attempt to interpret a message so that those involved in the interpreted communication have the same dynamic response as those not dependent on the interpretation for the information.

Cultural And Linguistic Mediation

Whereas an interpreter functioning from a machine or communication facilitation frame would carefully interpret anything that was said or signed overtly, the bilingual-bicultural interpreter interprets both explicitly stated ideas and information that is conveyed implicitly, if it was necessary for full and meaningful communication. This requires linguistic and cultural adaptations.

+ A *linguistic expansion* involves interpreting implicit information or ideas, as well as the explicit information and ideas, if it is needed to guarantee full communication.
+ A *cultural expansion* involves providing the contextual information needed to make sense out of something that is signed or said to someone with a different schema or experiential base.
+ A *cultural or linguistic reduction* involves reducing the *volume*, and sometimes the *detail*, of information without affecting the meaning intended. This is

sometimes required due to different cultural, social and communication norms and expectations.

Linguistic and cultural adaptations are not made on whim; they are based on one of three reasons:

1. Linguistic need
One language sometimes demands the overt statement of information that is understood but unstated in another language. For example, ASL rarely uses passive voice, so when interpreting an English utterance expressed in passive voice, the interpreter typically changes the statement to active voice. This requires overtly stating the implied actor (if known) or an indefinite pronoun (if the actor is unknown).

2. Cultural need
The culture defines certain behavior as acceptable or unacceptable, necessary or unnecessary. Language reflects these cultural norms. For example, English involves the frequent use of the addressee's name in one-on-one and some small group interactions. ASL uses a different technique to accomplish the same purpose. When interpreting from English to ASL, the frequent inclusion of the addressee's name usually results in misunderstandings which strain the communication dynamics. Thus, the addressee's name should be deleted in the interpretation from English to ASL and a cultural equivalent should be substituted.

3. Difference in experiential frame
The life experience of individuals from different cultures varies vastly. It is sometimes necessary to provide experientially specific information so the recipient can have a schema allowing information to be successfully conveyed and understood. For example, in many areas of Canada it is common for individuals to take off their shoes upon entering another person's home. When an individual interprets to an audience of Americans a message presented by a Canadian who refers to removing their shoes, a bilingual-bicultural interpretation would require briefly providing the information that it is customary to remove the

shoes when entering someone's home. Without doing that, the audience might misunderstand or miss the point of the illustration being given.

A Word of Caution: There is a fine line between expanding or reducing source language elements to provide a cultural and linguistic equivalent and slipping back toward the helper philosophical frame of adding and deleting information to help or protect one's clients. However, if you make your decision to expand (making implicit information explicit) or reduce overtly stated information based on one of the three parameters above, you will be on fairly safe ground.

It should be noted that making these adaptations requires adequate processing time. Consequently, consecutive interpretation is the preferred style of interpretation for one-on-one interactions because it provides extended processing time and results in more accurate language-culture equivalents.[3]

Influence on Ethical Decision-Making

The way an individual operating under the bilingual-bicultural interprets and applies the Code of Ethics is also radically different. From this frame, an interpreter is keenly aware of two features lacking in other philosophical orientations:

1. The reality that they are human beings, not machines; and

2. The power inherent in the position of an interpreter.

This individual believes the Code of Ethics has greater breadth of interpretation and will make ethical decisions based on:

+ The language/culture of the consumers — this means respecting the consumer's choice of language and modality (ASL, English-based signs, mouthed English, etc.);

✦ An understanding of the history of oppression from which Deaf individuals come and the resulting inequities and power imbalance inherent in any Deaf-hearing interaction; and

✦ The fact that the presence of an interpreter in any interaction has an impact on the interpersonal and communication dynamics.

There are times when the client being served will dictate which type of service an interpreter is to use in a situation. If a client indicates that they want "straight English," meaning unprocessed non-conceptual sign-for-word transliteration, the bilingual—bicultural (bi-bi) interpreter has no choice but to respect the linguistic and cultural preference of that individual and move into that form of service delivery. While respecting individual difference, the bi-bi interpreter realizes that due to the inherent inequality of power, the majority of Deaf clients require a complete linguistic and cultural transition if they are to have an opportunity to fully participate in their vocational assessment, medical examination, job training, etc.

Let's see what happens to George at the doctor's office with someone adhering to the bilingual-bicultural philosophy.

The Bilingual–Bicultural Philosophy In Action

George (Deaf) had an appointment with the doctor last week, so he arranged for a referral agency to send an interpreter. When he arrived, the interpreter was waiting for him. George identified himself as the Deaf client, asked the interpreter's name and sat down to chat a bit while waiting for the doctor to call them into her office. Recognizing the cultural norms for greeting and leave-taking behaviors in the Deaf community, Sharon, the interpreter, engages in friendly, casual dialogue with George. "How'd you get involved in interpreting? Your folks Deaf?" George queries. Sharon smiles and begins to recount her story for the one-thousandth time, understanding that George isn't prying or putting her down because she doesn't have Deaf family members. This is part of her identity and will help George "know" (trust) her in the communication exchange to follow.

George starts to recount his medical problems of the past few weeks. Sharon may choose to listen in order to better prepare herself for the job to follow. Or she may cut him off and explain that she prefers that he wait and tell the doctor everything directly — explaining that if he tells her everything now, he might leave out some of the details when they get in to see the doctor. Her demeanor is warm rather than reprimanding and George smiles in acknowledgment.

"Do you think it's cancer?" George asks, "And what about this new black market medication I've heard about?" "I don't know," Sharon responds, "That's why you're here to see the doctor. I'm sure she can answer all of your questions and concerns and I'll stay with you to interpret everything until you know exactly what is going on."

About that time, the nurse calls George's name and they move back to the doctor's office. Sharon, placed in a location that facilitates communication and dressed in a manner appropriate for her role as interpreter, interprets everything, being sure to include the doctor's vocal affect of "attempting to calm" when she signs to George and George's affect of nervousness when she interprets his signs into spoken English. After the initial interview, the doctor moves George to an examining room. While they wait for George to put on an examination gown, the doctor looks at the interpreter and says, "This is fascinating. How did you learn sign language?" Sharon says, "Oh, I took classes at Ohio State," quickly moving as George enters the room and sits on the examination table. She takes a stance of "ready to do business" while being courteous to the physician, her fellow professional.

At one point, the doctor murmurs something virtually inaudible to her nurse and Sharon informs George that the doctor and nurse are conferring, showing by way of facial behaviors that this is normal in a doctor's office. When the doctor asks George the name of any medications he is taking, he can't remember the name. "It's in my briefcase in the waiting room," he signs. The doctor looks to the interpreter, "Could you step outside and hand me his briefcase, please?"

Sharon responds politely, "Perhaps your nurse or reception-
ist could bring it in? That way George won't miss out on any
communication that needs to happen in here."

As you can see, an individual functioning within the bilingual-
bicultural philosophy will interpret the Code of Ethics more
broadly and with greater flexibility than someone adhering to
the machine or communication facilitation philosophy because
the bi-bi interpreter is responsible to mediate culture, as well as
language.[a]

SUMMARY

Briefly, the philosophical frame of interpreters over the past half
century has evolved from helper, machine (conduit), and communication facilitation, to bilingual-bicultural. Because this has
been an evolution, you will find interpreters in North America
who represent all four philosophical frames. The field continues
to emerge and like all professions in their developmental years,
there are a variety of practitioners whose field-based decisions
differ due to divergent philosophical stances.

The authors of this text endorse the bilingual-bicultural philosophy and believe it is broad enough to meet the various linguistic preferences within the diverse Deaf community. While
it may not be the final and perfect philosophical base for the
entire field of sign language interpreting, we believe it is the
most appropriate to date. Our failure to come to grips with the
need for cultural mediation in the past has resulted in less than
equal access for many Deaf individuals who use our services as
interpreters.

---

a.   The Association of Visual Language Interpreters of Canada
(AVLIC) revised their code of ethics to better reflect the role of sign language interpreters as culture mediators. Presentations at RID in 2001 also
addressed this issue.

CHAPTER REVIEW
Key Points

Our work will reflect our beliefs and philosophy about Deaf people and the role of an interpreter.

Helper Philosophical Frame

✦ Views Deaf people as handicapped, limited, unable to fully manage their personal and business affairs; believes that Deaf people are mentally, emotionally, or experientially incapable of fully understanding the world around them.

✦ Views the interpreter as a caretaker whose purpose is to help.

✦ Tends to be overly involved with Deaf and hearing clients, often moving out of the role of interpreter to advise, direct, teach or cajole.

✦ Sees Deaf cultural behaviors as aberrant or immature and views ASL as poor English, reflective of limited education or mental abilities.

Conduit or Machine Philosophy

✦ Interpreters assume no responsibility for the interaction or communication dynamics taking place between clients; assume almost a robot-like role in the communication process.

✦ Viewed by Deaf and hearing clients as rigid and inflexible.

✦ Views Deaf people as needing to learn to take care of themselves; does not recognize a unique Deaf culture or the fact that ASL is a language.

✦ Views English as the only acceptable form of communication.

✦ Confuses quantity (number of words/signs) with quality (linguistic equivalents).

Communication Facilitation Philosophy

✦ Views Deaf individuals as part of the larger handicapped population seeking inclusion in the mainstream.

✦ Views ASL as a useful communication mode for less educated or less intelligent individuals; sees English as superior to ASL.

✦ More aware of the importance of appropriate placement within proximity of the speaker, facilitating visual intake for Deaf clients; aware of the importance of lighting, background, indicating who is speaking, and the absence of visual noise.

✦ Emphasis placed on the interpreter's appearance — beards and mustaches "outlawed," along with fingernail polish, patterned clothing and distracting jewelry.

Bilingual-Bicultural Philosophy

✦ Recognizes Deaf people as members of an oppressed minority; accepts ASL as a language and Deaf culture as that which encompasses the norms, values, and traditions of this community of people.

✦ Views the role of an interpreter as equalizing communication and empowering the Deaf and hearing persons involved.

✦ Continues to be sensitive to physical communication parameters (background, lighting, placement) but is also sensitive to communication dynamics, including the inherent differences in the languages, cultures, norms for social interaction within each culture and the impact of these on understanding the message being communicated.

✦ Defines interpretation broadly, includes the provision of linguistic and cultural equivalents, interpreting implicit information, as well as that overtly stated, and providing the schema to foster comprehension.

Linguistic and Cultural Expansions/Reductions

Manipulating target language output so it contains all of the essential elements of meaning expressed in the source language in such a way as to fit the target language communication norms; decisions regarding expansions and reductions are based on one of three reasons: (a) linguistic need, (b) cultural need, or (c) difference in experiential frame.

THOUGHT QUESTIONS

1. In regard to philosophical frames, which do you see in action most often? How do you know which philosophical frame you are observing? Share some observations and experiences.

2. Which philosophical frame do you think you want to adopt for yourself? Why have you selected that philosophy? What are the strengths and weaknesses of the philosophy you have selected?

3. What is the relationship between the development of the RID Code of Ethics and the helper philosophy?

CD STUDY GUIDE

✦ The various activities in the guided Chapter 8 Study Guide on CD will allow you to understand the concepts in this chapter more completely and to apply them to your life experience. Work through the Chapter 8 Study Guide on CD, completing all activities, then submit to your instructor or share with your learning partner.

SUGGESTED ACTIVITIES

✦ Review early RID documents and publications. Identify items that reflect various philosophical frames discussed in this chapter.

✦ Consider several interpreting situations developed by your instructor. Discuss how an interpreter might act or react in the given scenario, depending on his or her philosophical frame.

✦ Working in groups, develop a list of the pros and cons of each philosophical frame.

✦ Interpreting requires judgment and flexibility. It is possible that one practitioner will shift between various philosophical frames throughout a day or a week of work due to a number of factors. Invite seasoned interpreters to talk about their approach to interpreting.

✦ Interview professional practitioners from other human service fields (e.g. social workers, nurses, child and youth care counselors) to determine if there has been a similar philosophical shift in their fields.

✦ Invite a panel of local professional interpreters to your classroom to discuss the information in this chapter and their approach to interpretation.

Endnotes

1. Baker-Shenk (1992)
2. Singer B, Livingston et. al. (1994)
3. Russell (2000)

CHAPTER NINE
The Challenge of Mediating ASL and English

This chapter will focus on the linguistic differences of English and American Sign Language (ASL) from the perspective of interpretation. ASL is a vehicle that enables signers to communicate their thoughts, ideas, and feelings through a gestural/visual modality, while English is a vehicle that permits speakers to communicate their thoughts, ideas and feelings through a speech/auditory pathway. English and ASL are *not* different expressions of the same language, nor do they share the same grammatical identity or use words/signs in the same way. Unfortunately, the English-based signing systems (discussed in Chapter Four) reinforce this false perception. Further, the pragmatics of each language are different, reflecting the unique cultural frame of each.

The following discussion is not intended to look at ASL and English from a linguistic point of view. Rather, we will delineate some of the characteristics and features of each language that present significant challenges to interpreters as they approach their work.

SPECIFIC LINGUISTIC CONSIDERATIONS
FOR ASL/ENGLISH INTERPRETERS
Modalities
One challenge faced by ASL/English interpreters is the distinct modality in which each language is produced and the different formational characteristics inherent in spoken and signed languages.

The modality used by English is auditory/vocal. English is an orally expressed language that is produced by making a series of sound patterns organized sequentially. The articulation of English requires use of the lips, oral and nasal cavities, tongue, teeth, palate, and vocal folds in the creation of particular sounds, using a controlled emission of air.[1] English also has a written form, which is a graphic representation of the spoken language using a series of alphabetic letters.

English uses speech as the medium of communication, producing approximately five syllables per second or 180 words per minute[2] but listeners do not have to concentrate on the rapid-fire words falling upon their ears in a focused manner to extract meaning.[3] This is due to the fact that English uses **prosody** — the rhythm of speech with pauses and phraseology, as well as certain auditory intonation patterns — to help listeners determine meaning and predict what the speaker will say next. In order to accomplish the required auditory rhythm, English uses a combination of **functional elements** and **content elements** in the formation of utterances. Content words are made up of nouns and verbs. Functional elements include such things as articles (a, the, an), prepositions (on, for, with, to), and conjunctions (and, but, however). Content words supply substance and meaning while functional words serve as a type of "auditory lubrication" fostering comprehension by means of cohesion and transition.[4] It is this combination of content and functional elements that makes English speech flow in a manner that maintains the prosody that fosters comprehension by listeners.

ASL, unlike English, is a spatial, time-oriented language based on visual perception and the visual conveyance of ideas, information, and feeling concepts. ASL is produced by using the hands, wrists, arms, trunk, face and head to convey information.[5] To communicate, one produces a series of rule-governed hand signals (**signs**) with accompanying facial/physical markers (**non-manual signals**). There is no written form of ASL, although most Deaf individuals in North America use the alphabet of English to communicate in written form.

ASL uses movement as the medium of communication. Since the physical articulators of ASL are larger than those used for vocal articulation, ASL takes roughly double the amount of time to produce a single ASL sign compared to the time required for the utterance of a single English word.[6] This is particularly important when considering the significance of receiving information visually, as opposed to auditorily. Unlike the ears, the eyes are operated by muscles that tire with use.

In spite of these differences, ASL transmits information at approximately the same rate as English.[7] How is this possible? ASL has its own visual prosody made up of pauses and phraseology, as well as certain visual intonation patterns to convey utterances composed primarily of content elements in ways that take advantage of the multi-dimensional nature of visual communication.[8] As a visual language, three-dimensional space is used as a conceptual framework within which ASL utterances emerge. The techniques ASL uses to produce comfortable visual articulation — a form of "visual lubrication" — include:

+ Utterances composed primarily of content elements which supply substance and meaning;
+ The restricted use of most functional elements, including articles, interjections (except where used to emphasize or ratify), expletives and conjunctions (except where used to add content);
+ Visual incorporation of the auxiliary verb (to be);
+ Spatial referencing — using the space around a signer to metaphorically establish a person or place as a referent.[9]

This combination of techniques allows ASL articulation to flow in a manner that maintains clarity, fostering comprehension by listeners, allowing a timely delivery of linguistic utterances and avoiding undue visual fatigue.

Implications of Modality for Interpreters

These differences in modalities result in challenges for ASL/ English interpreters.

Deriving Meaning

As mentioned above, each language uses prosody to help participants determine meaning and predict what the speaker/ signer will say next. When an individual is linguistically fluent in the language, these cues make it unnecessary to listen/watch each word/sign in a focused manner to determine meaning. This freedom from sustained, focused concentration provides interpreters with time to:

✦ Analyze the context in which the exchange is happening and the way it influences the communication dynamics;
✦ Analyze the incoming message at a deeper (textual) level; and
✦ Make a switch into the target language without losing meaning or speaker goals.

Interpreters, then, take advantage of these cues to comprehend the incoming message. Likewise, with the stress of listening, analyzing, understanding, searching for equivalence, formulating, producing the interpretation and monitoring the interpretation for accuracy, interpreters must be careful not to rush the target language output. Incorporation of TL prosody  (appropriate pausing, phrasing and intonation patterns) when producing the TL message helps the recipient understand the interpretation.

Dropping Source Language Form

A significant challenge for interpreters is dropping the cultural trappings and linguistic form of the SL utterance prior to making a transition into the TL. Failure to do this results in skewed or unclear communication due to the intrusion of source language/culture features in target language output.[10] Additionally, being able to comprehend and analyze the SL utterance and drop form requires appropriate processing time. It is a challenge for interpreters to resist the urge to hurry and to take the time necessary to extract the meaning and intent from the original utterance then completely reformulate that same meaning and intent into a grammatically correct and culturally appropriate equivalent.

Volume Of Lexical Units/Speed Of Production

Both English and ASL have the ability to convey equivalent kinds and amounts of information in order to meet a wide range of speaker/signer goals. However, because English uses both content and functional elements extensively, and ASL articulates primarily content elements (embedding many of the functional information), interpreters sometimes confuse volume with equivalency. Thus, an interpreter working between English and ASL may find her/himself slipping back toward SL grammatical structure, in order to match the number of words spoken rather than striving for message equivalency, while maintaining the integrity of the TL output. Producing a sign for each English word spoken tires the eyes of the Deaf participants and generally fails to provide equivalent and accessible information. Likewise, abbreviating spoken English to match precisely the ASL signs articulated results in unclear and ungrammatical English sentences. It also misrepresents the linguistic fluency of the Deaf signer.

A second challenge in this area is the speed with which each language can convey information. If a hearing speaker reads a text or speaks from a memorized script, the rate of production is much more rapid than that of spontaneous spoken English. Likewise, if a Deaf presenter reads from a text, the resulting utterance is often stiff and "monotone" in articulation. In both cases, this is problematic for interpreters because the natural prosody — pauses, phraseology, hesitations and redundancies — are lacking. When spoken English is read from a script, the rate of speech is so rapid that there is inadequate time to comprehend, analyze, and interpret the text into ASL. The mono-tone conveyance of a read text into ASL is much more difficult to comprehend and make sense of because the breaks fall at un-natural places and fingerspelled words appear in unusual places violating the generic semantic rules for fingerspelling. Thus, *interpreters work most effectively with spontaneous linguistic expression in both English and ASL.*

Language Identity

English has a written form and ASL has none. The fact that Deaf individuals generally use the English written system has resulted in the misperception that ASL is, in fact, a visual form of Eng-lish, sharing the same grammatical identity and using words/signs in the same way. It is critical that interpreters understand the fallacy of this misperception because they will sometimes need to be able to articulate (for themselves and others) what is involved in interpretation and to defend the choices they are making as they interpret.

Conveying Meaning

As stated earlier, language is used to encode the ideas and thoughts of a signer/speaker so another person can understand what is being communicated. All languages convey information easily. One language is no more specific, ambiguous, descrip-tive, or precise than any other. However, because languages use different grammatical devices to convey information, one may seem to be more straightforward or ambiguous, etc. When we look at English and ASL we see two very different languages us-ing very different, yet equally effective, devices to convey mean-ing. A major challenge faced by ASL/English interpreters, then, is to determine how each language constructs meaning.

One feature that is challenging when working from English into ASL is the frequent use of a single term to convey many concepts. For example, the English word "run" has over thirty definitions. The precise meaning intended in an utterance is determined by looking at the context in which it is used and through connotative analysis. Because of this tendency, English is described as being *indirect*.

FIG. 9-1 Some Meanings of "RUN"	
trip	My son is going to run to the store.
hurry	I have to run.
compete or campaign	She is running for president.
tendency	Diabetes runs in the family.
drive	The drunk ran him down.
unravel	She has a run in her stockings.
movement of a liquid	The creek is running down hill. The child has a runny nose.
stream bed	I'll meet you at the run [used primarily in Appalachian communities].
confined area for animals	I like the house because it has a large dog run.

Other characteristics that promote the indirect or implicit conveyance of information in English include:

✦ Frequent combinations of verbs and prepositions producing new lexical items with meanings different than that of the individual words (e.g., passed out, something's up);

✦ The use of generic terms to represent a wide range of semantic meanings, inviting open-ended interpretation and maintaining generalities (e.g., people say ... , at certain times in history ...);

✦ The use of pronouns that lack a specific referent (e.g., *They* say that being in love is wonderful);

✦ The use of compact lexical items in which one term carries descriptive semantic meaning (e.g., *drugs* carries the semantic meaning of cocaine, marijuana, speed, PCP, etc. or a variety of prescription medications including antibiotics, anti-depressants, pain medications, etc.).

Further, an English presentation or exchange of information tends to deal with the specific issue at hand, avoiding a great deal of elaboration or detail. Thus, unless the speaker is engaged in story-telling, acting, or some special form of discourse, it is likely s/he will not provide the rich variety of detailed and descriptive information required by ASL.

ASL, on the other hand, tends to use explicit lexical items and linguistic constructions that rely heavily on the direct conveyance of information, minimizing the need for participants to identify implied meaning. Like other visual languages, ASL

+ Maintains a strong association to the immediate experience of actual things and events;
+ Tends to be specific, sensory-oriented, succinct; and
+ Requires signers to construct a message with signs based on their effectiveness in communicating semantic meaning through perceptual imagery.[11]

Information is transmitted in signs that reflect explicit and specific meanings. For this reason, ASL is considered *direct.* For example, the sign indicating the concept of "run" can be modified in the way it is produced to portray a variety of types of running — dashing, scampering, running awkwardly, scooting, scurrying — all maintaining the core semantic meaning. ASL would select different signs to convey each of the various meanings that the English word "run" can connote (unravel, function, compete/campaign). ASL typically uses designated semantic representations incorporating specific, descriptive, single-meaning expressions. Fig. 9-2 provides several examples of these differences.

The specific, direct nature of ASL results in utterances that are:

✦ Explicit, not ambiguous;
✦ Reality oriented with semantic precision;
✦ Vivid and highly descriptive.

FIG. 9-2 Indirect vs. Direct Terms	
ENGLISH: Indirect	ASL: Direct
heavy	overweight
'fess up	confess
fill in	substitute
get on with it	proceed
pull your leg	tease
make (a cake)	bake
Someone	my co-worker, the neighbor
call off	cancel
Straighten up	stop missing work (or whatever behavior is inappropriate)
go over	review
get rid of	remove

When the information is available, visual sense is made — whether using ASL or English-based signs — by using specific (direct), rather than generic (indirect) terms.

Visual Conveyance Of Information

ASL uses a variety of devices or techniques to convey information in visually clear and effectively ways. These devices, identified in three different studies in 1994,[12] are found consistently in both ASL utterances used for direct conveyance of information (signer to signer) and in the work of interpreters whose consumers indicated a high level of comprehending essential elements of meaning in an interpreted text. The following discussion describes seven of these techniques, referred to as "expansions." Please note that these descriptions are explanations of certain styles of language use, not a linguistic analysis of the language. While these communication devices are more commonly used in ASL, you may note that English sometimes uses similar techniques to convey information.

The seven expansion techniques include:

✦ Contrasting
✦ Faceting
✦ Reiterating
✦ Role-Shifting/Incorporation of 3-D Information
✦ Noun-Listing/Examples
✦ Couching/Nesting
✦ Describe Then Do

Contrasting

This communication device makes a statement by presenting the negative and positive of the idea. This is, in fact, a type of redundancy that is seen frequently in ASL.

Contrasting is used in these examples, but it would not necessarily be used every time a person was conveying the concept intended. Use of contrasting will be based on the signer's desire to emphasize or reiterate the comment being made or to ensure that the listener understands the point being made.

FIG. 9-3 Examples of Contrasting	
CONCEPT BEING CONVEYED	CONTRASTING TECHNIQUE
I have an old car.	CAR MINE, NEW NOT. CAR OLD!
She is sad.	GIRL HAPPY NOT. SHE (INDEX) SAD!
I'm sick	ME FEEL GOOD, NOT. SICK ME.

Faceting

A "facet" refers to any one of the several parts or possible aspects of something. We think of it most often when describing the faces of a cut gemstone. When applied to ASL, this device refers to the use of two or more signed synonyms when conveying a particular concept.

FIG. 9-4 Examples of Faceting	
CONCEPT BEING CONVEYED	CONTRASTING TECHNIQUE
I'm very happy.	ME HAPPY, SMILE-ON-FACE, SATISFIED
He drove like a maniac!	MAN DRIVE CRAZY — speed, 3-cl (showing squealing around corners), 3-cl (showing changing lanes erratically), b-cl (indicating the bottom of the car hitting the pavement at points)

In the first example, the concept of "very happy" is conveyed by using three direct synonyms, two of which describe the feeling and one of which describes the signer's physical appearance. The description of "driving like a maniac" is conveyed in the use of four descriptive synonyms (three of which involve the use of classifiers). Faceting is used to provide information in a visually clear manner and to give weight to certain ideas or information.

Reiterating

When a sign or sign phrase is repeated within the same short utterance for clarity or emphasis, the technique being used is termed "reiterating."

FIG. 9-5 Examples of Reiterating	
CONCEPT BEING CONVEYED	CONTRASTING TECHNIQUE
I can't go to the party.	CAN'T GO PARTY, CAN'T
I don't want to eat.	DON'T-WANT EAT, DON'T-WANT
I'm not mad.	NOT MAD ME, NOT.

You will note that the signed utterances are short and incorporate English grammatical structure. This may seem to be a contradiction to the concept that ASL uses topic-comment structure. In fact, this type of English grammatical borrowing is fairly common in short utterances of this nature. If fact, the borrowing of English grammatical structure may explain the use of the reiteration device, although research is still incomplete on this premise.

Role-Shifting/Incorporation of 3-D Information

These two techniques are required to convey interactions between two or more people (role-shifting) and to "set the scene" in which an event being discussed took place (3-D information). As noted above, ASL is a "direct" language and uses space to convey a great deal of descriptive and detailed information. Thus, a signer "enters the scene" of an event being conveyed, taking full advantage of the 360° space surrounding the signer. This results in a more image-based, pictorial and dynamic means of using visual communication.

Using **body-agreement** (head, trunk movement; eye indexing and other visual grammatical features), **locatives** and **directional verbs**, the signer literally sets up people and objects according to real space and location. The signer then steps into the role of the individuals involved in the communication exchange being discussed, shifting upper torso from left to right and moving the head/eye gaze higher or lower (depending on the physical set-up as well as the age and status of the person being quoted), s/he becomes the person saying something or reacting to something that has been said — a technique known as role-shifting or character assumption.

The limitation of the written page make it impossible for the authors to provide a description of these two techniques, but they can be observed on a range of ASL videotaped narratives.

Noun-Listing/Examples

This device includes the use of a listing of examples that fit a semantic category after the introduction of a term. This noun-listing (or list of examples) clarifies the use of the term being referenced.[13]

| FIG. 9-6 Examples of Noun-Listing ||
CONCEPT BEING CONVEYED	CONTRASTING TECHNIQUE
Automobile manufacturers	CAR COMPANY (FORD, CHEVY, PONTIAC, ETC.)
Fruit	APPLES, BANANAS, ORANGES, ETC.
Vegetables	TOMATO, CARROTS, BROCCOLI, ETC.
Weapon	GUN, KNIFE, BASEBALL BAT, ETC.

Please note that each noun listing is followed by the sign "et cetera." That is how the *category* is established, referring to the generic category of fruit, vegetables and automobile manufacturers. If the "et cetera" is not included, you are no longer using an expansion technique. Rather, you are giving a specific list of exactly *which* vegetables, fruits and automobile companies are being referring to. This is an important distinction!

| FIG. 9-7 Examples of "Example" Expansions ||
CONCEPT BEING CONVEYED	CONTRASTING TECHNIQUE
I cleaned my house	HOUSE MINE, ME CLEAN ++ SWEEP, MOP, WASH WALLS
Got ready for work	WORK, BATHE, STYLE HAIR, APPLY MAKE UP, DRESS, PAPERS – PUT IN BRIEFCASE

Figure 9-7 demonstrates the technique of expanding via examples, as compared to expansion by noun-listing. Here you will see the term signed first followed by a pause. The signer will then include a list of examples, depending on:

✓ The **reciprocal signals** used by the listener indicating familiarity/clrity (or lack thereof) regarding the central term; or

✓ The signer's goal -- if the goal is to entertain, elaborate or teach, the list of examples will probably follow.

Couching/Nesting

This device is used to provide information in an introductory expansion or "set up" to ensure the listener has the schema or frame required to understand the upcoming discourse.

FIG. 9-8 Examples of Nesting/Couching Expansions	
CONCEPT BEING CONVEYED	CONTRASTING TECHNIQUE
Sewer	YOU KNOW, TOILET FLUSH, WATER SWIRL OUT (down), Metal c-cl (Pipes—Small->Larger Pipes ->) 2h-c-cl (HUGE PIPE) TOILET WATER (RUN-THROUGH) — S-E-W-E-R,
Allergy	MEDICINE-TAKE OR CREAM RUB-ON-SKIN OR FOOD EAT – FINISH – ITCH ALL OVER OR STOMACH UPSET OR HARD BREATH — A-L-L-E-R-G-Y

The decision to use a nesting/couching expansion is based on the listener's schema and background, as well as the signer's decisions regarding the need for clarity.

Describe Then Do

This expansion is made up of two parts: first, the signer states what s/he will do/say from a narrator position; and second, via a role-shift, the signer does/says what was described from the position of the person/thing doing the action.

FIG. 9-9 Examples of Describe Then Do Expansions	
CONCEPT BEING CONVEYED	CONTRASTING TECHNIQUE
I'll call the police	POLICE, CALL WILL; (r-s) 1-cl (WALK ACROSS ROOM) TELEPHONE, PUT ON TTY, POLICE CALL, TYPE++
I have to clean the house	HOUSE, CLEAN MUST; (R-S) SWEEP++, MOP++, VACUUM++

The first part of this technique sometimes happens so quickly that it is difficult to see it in action.

Implications For Interpreters

The central focus of our work as interpreters is to convey communication of equivalent meaning between people who are linguistically and culturally different. Thus, working between a language that might be described (for the purposes of interpreting) as indirect/non-elaborative and one that might be described as direct/elaborative has numerous implications for our work.

Degree Of Detail

English users sometimes get restless when someone takes a long time getting to the point of what they want to say. When Deaf individuals take time to develop the scene, identify the participants, and provide the action in a highly descriptive way (incorporating several expansion devices), it is imperative that interpreters develop techniques to truncate the amount of detail in linguistically and culturally appropriate ways. This would include selecting English terms that are more generic and compact in semantic meaning (saying, "I had a morning you wouldn't believe!" when seeing a detailed listing of frustrating events being signed, for example).

The following is a sample of an ASL discourse. It was originally produced in ASL and we have used English to convey the content, not attempting to make a full cultural or linguistic adaptation in the English representation. In the sample below, which contains several of the expansion techniques outlined above, the Deaf individual is telling someone about a phone call received from her/his mother.

Sample ASL Discourse

This morning — about 6:00 a.m. — I was sound asleep (sawing logs - out like a light!). As I slowly woke up (eyes not wanting to open), I realized the phone was ringing (light flash, flash, flash). It rang numerous times as I got out of bed, and dragged myself (sleepy-eyed and stumbling over things on the way) to the phone. It was my mom who lives in Indiana (about 1750 miles from here). She said, "Hello. Did I wake you?" (as if she didn't know there was a two-hour

203

time difference). I responded gruffly, "Of course!" (What a stupid question!) "What's wrong?"

She said, "I just wanted to let you know that I have to cancel my trip to your place. Yesterday your aunt was working in the garden (role-shift: hoeing, pulling weeds, etc.). After weeding the vegetables, she stood up and evidently tripped on a garden rake that had been left prongs-up on the sidewalk and broke her right hip. (role-shift: standing up, not seeing rake prongs -- tripping, sailing through the air with a panicked look on the face, landing on right hip with a look of great pain). I called an ambulance (role-shift: dialing 911, put telephone receiver on TTY and — typing — asking them to come). The ambulance arrived, put her on stretcher and took her to the hospital.

At the hospital, the doctor looked her over, sent for x-rays and discovered her hip is broken (not cracked – broken). It's not a simple break — it's a bad one. The bone is shattered; her thigh is black and blue (role-shift: indicate painful walking, sitting, etc.); so I will have to cancel my trip and won't be able to come for that visit we planned."

The presence of details, expansions, and role-shift comments (direct address) in the example above *could* be found in an English conveyance of this event (depending on a number of factors), but it is not *that* common. ASL, however, typically *requires* this degree of information in order to be linguistically correct. In telling this story, a few of the details might have been omitted, but there will generally be a higher number of details in an ASL rendition than in an English version of the same event.

Note the number of places where a signer would use classifiers, directional verbs and locatives. By the time you have taken in the information presented in ASL, the listener would probably have a visual and kinesthetic sense of what things looked like, how they were set up in relationship to each other, the feelings and behaviors of individuals or groups involved in the incident being reported, and the movement and responses of any significant objects involved in the incident.

An English speaker might convey the same information in the following way:

Sample English Discourse

I was really irritated when my Mom called me early this morning until I found out she was calling to let me know she won't be able to come for a visit tomorrow as planned. It seems my aunt was working in the garden yesterday when she fell and broke her hip. It's a bad one, so Mom is going to have to stay with her.

In this example, after stating the main point — Mom isn't coming tomorrow — the speaker could have chosen to give no further details. If choosing to give details, s/he would generally only provide those directly related to the primary point regarding Mom's canceled trip. Yet the absence of copious contextual information prevents a Deaf listener from comprehending the point being communicated. The result will either be confusion and miscommunication or an interruption followed by a request for clarifying information.

Degree Of First-Person Address

Fluent users of English rely heavily on the use of third person address. This means talking about what a person said without directly quoting her/him (e.g., He walked up to me and shook his finger in my face and told me where I could go). Competesnt users of ASL typically use first person address to convey similar information. If an interpreter is working from English into ASL and maintains the English form of direct address rather than shifting into first person address, the topic under discussion will often become unclear to the ASL participant. Likewise, when working from ASL into English, interpreters must remember to change the frequent first person depiction into third person address. Failing to make this accommodation for language/culture differences results in the Deaf participant being misrepresented as child-like to the hearing participant.

When working from English into ASL, an interpreter needs to use frequent role-shifts, in which the interpreter will identify the person speaking, make a slight body shift to the left or right and "become" that person. For example in the ASL discourse sample, the signer took on the role of Mom when she was speaking and "became" the aunt when describing her fall. Likewise, when working from ASL to English, the interpreter will need to substitute the frequent use of first person address with third person address.

Implicit And Explicit Meaning

Interpreters are generally expected to convey meaning across languages. This means going beyond the form of the source language text, identifying the deep structure meaning, finding equivalence in the target language and making the interpretation. When English uses multiple-meaning words and phrases (e.g., *make* an outline of your presentation), the interpreter needs to drop the form and sign the meaning (e.g., *write* an outline of your presentation). Likewise, when English combines verbs with prepositions to form new lexical items (e.g., make an *outline* of your presentation), the interpreter drops the form (out — as in outside; line — as in a long thin mark) and signs the meaning.

Similarly, interpreters need to know how to use generic terms with non-specific referents in both English and ASL (e.g., there are *certain times* in a person's life when ..., or *they say* being in love is wonderful) and where it is clear in the subtext what the referent is, providing that specific information in the ASL interpretation. When hearing a compact lexical item in English (e.g., drugs), the interpreter needs to convert that to an appropriate noun listing in ASL and when seeing a noun listing in ASL, the interpreter needs to convert that to a compact lexical item in English.

FIG. 9-10 Vague Terms vs. Specific Terms		
General	Specific	More Specific
They	The owners	John's parents who own the café
Person	Relative	His cousin
Things	Office things	Paper, pencils
At times	Twice per month	1st and 3rd Tuesday of each month
Someone	A woman	A small woman with red hair

English deals comfortably with the "general" words, but when interpreted into ASL the "specific" or "more specific" terms would be used when contextual information clearly implies or refers to them. Fig. 9-10 provides examples of general to specific to more specific.

Word Order/Grammatical Structure
Both English and ASL use form and linear sequential patterning in their grammatical structure. This is reflected by the fact that a signer/speaker can produce only one lexical ASL/English unit at a time. However, both languages mingle linear articulation with concurrent expression of other linguistic information.

English uses vocal intonation, auditory stress patterns, and grammatical redundancy to accomplish this. ASL also has visual intonation (termed modulation), patterns of stress, and grammatical redundancy. In addition, ASL capitalizes on features of visual intake to convey multiple pieces of information simultaneously.

Word Order
English requires fairly strict adherence to word order in the aspect of grammatical structure. For example, a verb does not typically serve as the subject of a sentence (Run me fast). However, in some areas, English is fairly flexible. A conditional phrase, for instance, can either precede or follow the consequence (*if it rains*, I'll call or I'll call *if it rains*).

In the past, some linguists have described ASL as being "free-form" and thereby having flexible grammatical structure. In fact, like other languages, ASL is fairly rigid in some areas and flexible in others. An adjective, for example, can come before or after the noun it is modifying (e.g., white car or CAR WHITE). There seems to be no rigid rule in the language regarding noun-adjective order. The same is true of verb-adverb combinations. Sometimes, in fact, the adverbial information is conveyed in a modified production of the verb. In other cases, however, an adverb may be signed (e.g., slowly, carefully, etc.) and there seems to be no rigid rule stating that the adverb, when signed, must follow or precede the verb it is modifying. However, conditional phrases must precede the consequence in ASL.

FIG. 9-11 Examples of Reiterating
Conditional in primary position: *If it rains tomorrow*, class will be canceled.
Conditional in secondary position: Class will be canceled tomorrow *if it rains*.
If this utterance were signed with the conditional in secondary position, it would result in confusion and misunderstanding.

Failure to place a condition in the initial or primary placement within your ASL sentence construction will inevitably result in confusion and miscommunication, not to mention a non-grammatical form in ASL. In addition to sentence position, such statements require the use of a sustained brow raise throughout the conditional portion of the utterance, followed by a pause prior to stating the consequence.

Grammatical Structure

Both English and ASL use subject-verb-object grammatical structure, however the *primary* sentence structure of ASL is a topicalized form. For this reason, ASL is termed a topic-prone language. Interpreters whose first language is English must be aware of how the topic is formed in ASL and how it must be translated into English.

Topicalized structures in ASL are arranged so that the person, place or subject that is the focus of the comment is in first or primary position in an utterance, accompanied by the brow raise, followed by a pause, then a comment or question related to the topic.[14] In the English sentence, "I like ice cream," the subject is "I;" however the subject being discussed is ice cream therefore ice cream is the topic of the utterance. Although the same concept in ASL *could* follow S-V-O form,[a] it could also be topicalized to read ICE CREAM, I LIKE! (with the accompanying non-verbal grammatical markers and pausing as described above). Asking another person if s/he likes ice cream using a topicalized structure would be ICE CREAM, YOU LIKE?

There is sometimes a series of topics and sub-topics leading to the comment or question.[15] The topic or subject is determined by the signer and is context-specific, based on the discussion or questions under consideration and the listener's response to each sub-topic. For example, the English sentence, "My dad works on the 7th floor of the UN Building in New York City," could be signed as described in Fig. 9-12.

FIG. 9-12 Example of ASL Topic-Comment Structure with a Series of Sub-Topics	
TOPIC:	New York City
SUBTOPIC:	The United Nations Building
SUBTOPIC	7th Floor
COMMENT	My Dad works there

Implications Of Word-Order/ Grammatical Structure For Interpreters

The differences here require interpreters to constantly monitor the integrity of output in the target language. This means they must take time, not only to receive and analyze the source language utterance, but also to produce the TL in grammatically correct form. It is easy for interpreters whose first language is

---

[a] According to Valli & Lucas (1992) sentences that have transitive verbs are more likely to use the subject in the primary position.

English to slip into their native language grammatical structure, particularly in the presence of an emotionally charged environment, a complex or difficult text, rapid source language production or a topic that is unfamiliar to the interpreter. This is even more challenging when working in one-on-one or small group interactions where the source language changes rapidly between ASL and English.

Time/Tense Markers

All languages have techniques to communicate the concept of past, present, and future. O'Dea[16] explains that English expresses time through a complex inflectional system where the tense of a verb, as well as syntactic markers, indicate when an action takes place. This system includes the conjugation of each verb used (walkED, walkS, walkING) to mark past, present, or future tense.

While English frequently structures a text according to the sequence of real (chronological) time, this inflectional system makes it possible for a speaker to "jump time frames" and still be clearly understood. In Fig. 9-13, the time shifts from (1) tomorrow, (2) yesterday, and (3) back to today (this morning).

FIG. 9-13 Examples of English Time-Markers
My friend *went* to the store *yesterday*. After she got there, she *decided* to buy some goodies for the party. Lots of our friends *will be* there. *Are* you *coming?*
Here, the verbs to-go and to-decide are conjugated in English, indicating past tense (went, decided); a sudden shift is made to future tense (will be, are coming) with no indication as to when the party will be. The English speaker, however, would have no difficulty following this shift in time/tense.

Unlike English, ASL uses syntactic markers to indicate the tense or time frame of an utterance. The time marker must be signed early in an utterance, and that time marker will indicate the time frame of all following verbs until a new time marker is noted. Let's look at the same utterance as produced in ASL.

FIG. 9-14 Examples of ASL Tense/Time-Markers
yesterday — friend-mine — store go — LOOK AROUND, PUT THINGS IN BASKET — THINK, AH! tomorrow PARTY — BUY FOOD, ETC. WILL LATER PARTY ' FRIENDS MANY-COME-TO. YOU COME?

In the ASL example, the use of the time marker *yesterday* results in a past-tense conjugation of the verb *go*; the use of the time marker *tomorrow* shifts the verb tense to future, although it is clear this was stated yesterday about a future event. *Later* refers to the concept of later today, which is also a future tense form. In this example, *"will"* is not a time marker. It serves as an affirmation — meaning the party *shall* take place.

ASL typically works within a frame of chronological sequencing. In other words, a signer will convey an event by discussing the first thing that happened and continue relaying events in the order they actually took place. This seems to occur because ASL, as a visual language, ties time to the present communication event.[17] Although ASL has techniques that allow one to violate this structural rule, clear communication is supported when it is followed.

In the example in Figure 9-14, note that the ASL states:

1. what happened yesterday
    -- looked around store
    -- put things in basket
2. what will happen tomorrow
    -- party
    -- many friends come

thus following things in exact real-time sequence
— unlike an English speaker who could move comfortably from past-to-present-to-future and back to past.

Implications Of Time/Tense Markers For Interpreters

It is critical for ASL/English interpreters to monitor their target language output to be sure the interpretation includes the tense/time marking norms in each language. Failure to do so will often result in confusion and miscommunication.

Negation/Affirmation

English adds words or phrases in order to indicate negation and affirmation. This generally requires the addition of a specific negative or positive term to the verb.

FIG. 9-15 Examples of Reiterating
Negation: I will not go. I can't drive after dark. She would never do that.
Affirmation: She'll go. I can drive to the meeting. Sure, that's fine.

The same can be said for ASL. Separate lexical items can be used to show affirmation or negation, but they are not required. This information can be conveyed simply with the addition of non-manual markers (NMM) that convey linguistic information in ASL — the head nodding up and down indicating "yes" or shaking side-to-side "no" — as the comment is signed.

FIG. 9-16 Examples of ASL Negation/Affirmation	
Negation (embedded)	negative head shake go-to (index) me
Negation (added)	neg. head shake GO-TO (index) won't me
Affirmation (embedded)	pos. head nod me go-to (index) will
Affirmation (added)	pos. head nod me go-to (index) will
All of these examples encompass the fact that the signer will or will not go and where the signer will or will not go, all within the execution of one to two signs (depending on if "me" is understood or signed) and the non-manual marker used.	

This is another way ASL takes advantage of the ability to convey simultaneous information in the visual-spatial modality. A specific negating or affirming sign may be added to a comment in ASL, overtly indicating the negation or affirmation, but in that case, the non-manual marker described above must also be incorporated. Failure to incorporate the proper non-manual marker will result in an incomplete or inaccurate conveyance of information.

Within informal and consultative registers, the incorporation of the non-manual marker to negate/affirm an utterance can stand alone. However, high consultative and formal registers of ASL require that the negation/affirmation be signed, in addition to the requisite non-manual marker.

FIG. 9-17 Sample of Confusing English Non-Verbal Head Movements with ASL Negation	
English	head shaking slowly side-to-side Whew! That's nice!
Interpretation	head shaking slowly side-to-side WOW! FINE-wg
In this example, the interpreter has carried the hearing nonverbal form of positive emphatic meaning into the interpretation, resulting in negating the statement!	

Implications Of Negation/Affirmation For Interpreters

This area of linguistic difference is not extremely difficult or challenging for interpreters so long as they have fluency in both languages. It is sometimes problematic when interpreters unconsciously use certain non-deaf forms of nonverbal emphasis when signing affirmative ASL statements. For example, when looking at new cars in the dealer's showroom, an English speaker might say, "Whew! Look at that car!" while slowly shaking her/his head from side-to-side to indicate positive emphatic meaning. When this nonverbal head movement is applied to ASL sentences, it looks like a negation, thus the interpretation says the opposite of what the source language utterance meant.

Voice

The "voice" of an utterance indicates the relation of the subject to the verb. "Passive voice" in English includes some form of the verb "to be" with the main verb in past participle form. In the sentence "The house was built by Bob," the verb "was built" conforms with this rule. Further, the subject has been moved into a "by-phrase" so even though this is considered a passive voice construction, it poses no challenge for an interpreter because the actor is clearly identified. In the sentence "The car was wrecked," the verb "was wrecked" conforms with the required verb rule. However, there is no "by-phrase," thus the person or thing causing the car to be wrecked is not identified. Note additional examples in Fig. 9-18 where we cannot tell from the structure of the sentences *who* shot the president, *who* turned off the light at the wrong place, or *what* broke the window because these sentences are written in the passive voice.

FIG. 9-18 Examples of Passive Voice in English
The president was shot.
It was turned off at the wrong place.
The window was broken.

English uses passive voice fairly often, especially at upper consultative and formal registers. This sentence form is more ambiguous than active construction and is an example of using indirect referencing in English.

ASL, on the other hand, is based primarily on active voice. In most ASL constructions, the actor must be identified or the information will be misconstrued to mean that the recipient of the action was, in fact, the actor. If someone signed "The president was shot," without making the appropriate linguistic adaptation into active voice (PRESIDENT, SHOT FINISH), the information conveyed would be that the president her/himself shot someone or something! Of course, this statement would be wrong, as it conveys an incorrect message which is also ungrammatical in ASL.

Researchers have consistently noted that ASL does not use passive voice. This is still an area of research, because ASL does use passive-like constructions on occasion.[b] For example, the sentence "The baseball game was canceled" can be signed without indicating who will cancel the game, but this is not a preferred or common type of sentence construction. Fig. 9-19 shows the degree of clarity in certain ASL constructions where passive voice is attempted. In samples one and two, the result is an ungrammatical form in ASL and holds misinformation.

| FIG. 9-19 Passive Voice Samples ||
English Example	Meaning In ASL When Signed Maintaining Form
My house was robbed.	house-mine[t], steal *makes no sense*
The boy was murdered.	boy (index) [t], kill finish *The boy killed someone.*
The car was wrecked.	car[t], wreck finish *The car crashed.*

English users sometimes select passive voice in order to be vague. ASL users can likewise use certain constructions in order to be vague. This sometimes includes an indefinite actor, including such lexical items as SOMEONE, PERSON, and SOMEWHERE. The area of passive voice in ASL is being researched as we go to press.

Implications Of Voice For Interpreters

As interpreters analyze an incoming message, they must be aware of the voice of the linguistic constructions and have strategies at hand to effectively convey the meaning accurately in the TL. Typically, passive English forms are transformed into

---

[b] As this book went to press, we could find nothing in print saying that ASL does, in fact, use passive voice constructions but you should stay abreast with ongoing ASL research in this area.

active voice in ASL. Analysis of the message requires that the interpreter identify the goal of the signer/ speaker as well. If the speaker/signer is using passive voice in order to be deliberately vague, it is not appropriate for the interpreter to make the message perfectly clear and unambiguous. An example of this is found when working in mental health settings. A counselor may deliberately ask a question in a vague and general way in order to see what information comes up from a general question. In such a case, an equivalent lack of specificity needs to be present in the target language interpretation. However, where the goal is to be clear and passive voice is used in English SL, it is incumbent on the interpreter to make a complete linguistic transition into ASL, including changing the form from passive into active voice.

Noun/Verb Modifiers

The authors have chosen the term "noun/verb modifiers" to describe how English and ASL deal with describing:

+ The relationship of a person/place/thing to another person/place/thing;
+ What a person/place/thing looks like;
+ How a person/place/thing moves.

Relationship Of A Person/Place/ Thing To Another Person/Place/Thing

English uses prepositions and prepositional phrases to describe the relationship of one noun to another noun. For example, in the sentence "the cat is under the table," the preposition *under* lets the listener know the relationship of the cat to the table. English uses prepositions extensively. As a matter of fact, almost any complex or compound English sentence you can invent will have at least two prepositional phrases to indicate the relationship of a noun to a noun.

FIG. 9-20 Examples of Prepositions in English
There are three prepositional phrases in the relatively simple sentence which follows:
I went *(1) to the store (2) with my friend* to *(3)* buy a present *(4) for my Mom's birthday.*

ASL uses several constructions to show such relationships. Prepositions are sometimes signed for emphasis or clarity. However, ASL generally uses *classifiers*[18] to indicate the relationship of one noun to another. Classifiers are a specific set of signs that serve identifiable functions. In ASL, a classifier generally cannot be used until the noun it is representing has been signed. Any relationship that requires a prepositional phrase in English can be clearly communicated by the manipulation of classifiers representing two or more nouns.

FIG. 9-21 Example Of Classifiers In ASL
TABLE (index) CAT cl-table/cat
(indicating cat *under* table)
TABLE (index) BOOK cl-table/book
(indicating book *on* table3)

Supalla, a Deaf linguist, has noted that classifiers can be divided into two categories: real-world and abstract. Those classifiers which take on life-size proportions and the actions perform are termed "real-world" classifiers. Those that are less iconic or take on a reduced proportion in size as they describe the object or action taking place are "abstract" classifiers. Fluent signers will avoid staying solely with abstract or solely with real world classifiers. They will move back and forth between the two in the telling of an event.

FIG. 9-22 Example Of Directional Verbs In ASL
sister (index)   book
directional verb indicating relationship of actor and recipient to book
you -- give -- to

ASL also uses a category of verbs, known as directional verbs, to incorporate the actor (noun) and the recipient of an action (noun) as a way of describing the relationship of one noun to another.

Description of A Person/Place/Thing

In describing a noun, English uses adjectives. The greater the description, the longer the string of adjectives required. English also uses vocal intonation to modify the spoken adjective(s), supplying additional descriptive information.

ASL describes nouns in two ways: by using separate signs that provide descriptive information and by using classifiers. For example, in Fig. 9-23, the adjective "beautiful" and the color "red" would probably be signed. The rest of the descriptives would be conveyed by way of a special set of classifiers called SASSes — size and shape specifiers.[1]

FIG. 9-23 Example Of Adjectives In English

It was a $_1$gorgeous, $_2$sexy, $_3$beaded, $_4$hand-embroidered, $_5$red gown!

SASSes are used to describe a wide variety of nouns — people, objects, patterns, animals, you name it! Further, SASSes are a prime example of the descriptive visual nature of ASL. This combination of adjective signs and classifiers could be used to convey information such as "he had a *grizzled* beard, *bleary* eyes, and his *tongue hung out of the side of his mouth*." SASSes would be used to convey information such as "the evening gown was *frilly along the neckline*, had *scallops on the bottom of the skirt* and a *minute wavy pattern in the sleeves*."

We have not provided an ASL example here because the richness of SASSes cannot be duplicated in the limitations of two-dimensional paper and pen.

Describing Action

When English users seek to describe *how* something moves or how something is done, they typically use adverbs and adverbial phrases. An adverb or adverbial phrase immediately precedes or follows the verb in an utterance.

FIG . 9-24 English Adverbs/Adverbial Phrases

Example of Adverbs

She *slowly* consumed the food, then *quietly* slipped out of the room and *rapidly* fell asleep.

Example of Adverbial Phrase

He worked *as quickly as possible*

ASL has adverbs which are single lexical items, however more frequently this information is provided in the verb itself together with specific facial markers.

FIG. 9-25 ASL Adverbial Information

She *slowly* consumed the food, then *quietly* slipped out of the room and *rapidly* fell asleep.

This sentence would be signed to show adverbial information by using ASL morphology as follows:

1) Signing the verb «to-eat» in a slow, deliberate manner;
2) Using a person-classifier to indicate an individual slowly moving to her feet then inconspicuously moving toward the exit; and
3) A combination of role-shift, facial features, eye movements and a specific sign which semantically means to practically «pass out» at the moment you put your head down.

Implications Of Noun/Verb Modifiers For Interpreters

The ways English and ASL modify nouns and verbs are often a challenge for interpreters, primarily in the area of dropping source language form. When working from English into ASL, interpreters need to monitor themselves. If they are frequently signing prepositions, adjectives and adverbs this may indicate source language intrusion and a lack of complete linguistic transition. The interpreter can then modify her/his output, increasing the use of classifiers and using adjectives and adverb signs for specific, limited purposes.

Another challenge for interpreters comes when working from ASL into English. When taking in an utterance, rich with descriptive information (via classifiers), interpreters often find they are lacking English vocabulary to adequately convey what is being described. They will sometimes fall back to " ... a big black thing with a little thing-a-ma-jig hanging off over there ... " When the interpreter is aware this is happening, s/he can modify her/his output, using greater precision in their choice of target language terminology (... a large, flat black object with a small rectangular fixture attached on the left hand side ...). Continually striving for full fluency in ASL should increase the interpreting skills needed when working between English and ASL.

Affect Markers

Although some visual affect markers are permitted in mainstream hearing culture, the emotive part of most messages is found primarily in invisible vocal intonations within English utterances, particularly at consultative and formal registers. You've probably had an experience like this. You and a friend walk into a bookstore or restaurant and you spot your ex-spouse or former boss. You may say to your friend, "I can't believe *he* is here!" — using vocal intonation on the word he to indicate a positive or negative feeling. While saying this, your expressionless face belies that you are communicating anything related to strong feelings. This is typical in English and is considered appropriate social behavior among most people who can hear.

Due to the nature of ASL, everything significant that needs to be communicated must be visible — including affect. Thus, affect is generally conveyed through modifications in the way signs are produced and in observable body and facial markers.

These affect markers may be used alone to convey emotive information or they may be accompanied by a sign or a series of signs. It is imperative that the facial affect markers be clearly produced and that they accompany any information conveyed — even when the affect is minimal. Note the facial affect markers of a Deaf person in the situation described below in Fig. 9-26.

FIG. 9-26 Example Of ASL Affect Markers When The Feeling Is Negative/Positive
negative nose twitch or visible negative facial marker
R-O-N   (index)
positive eye movement or visible positive facial marker
R-O-N   (index)

Implications Of Affect Markers For Interpreters

In the mainstream society of Canada and the U.S., it is considered impolite to "make faces." Thus children are taught from a very young age not to stare, point, or gape, much less duplicate another person's characteristics or behaviors. Because of the visual display of affect in ASL, signers are sometimes viewed negatively by hearing people who are unaware that facial affect markers are a mandatory part of ASL communication. This is exacerbated when the high degree of direct address and resultant role-shifting in ASL frequently requires that the interpreter take on the behaviors and feelings of multiple characters.

Interpreters need to recognize these differences, but they should not allow the target language output to be diminished in clarity or essential affective information as a result. The absence of visual affect markers in ASL results in a monotone-type of presentation which fails to captivate an audience and is often not true to the intent of the speaker.

Jan's Gems

I'll never forget being called to the emergency room of a hospital late one night to interpret for a Deaf individual who had been found on the floor of his apartment after three days of no food or water, unable to move due to a back injury. He was suffering from intense pain, as well as dehydration. When the doctor examined the Deaf man, saying "Does this hurt?" I saw the pain in his eyes, the tension in his body in response to the poking and prodding. Assuming the doctor saw the same thing, I said in a calm voice -- devoid of emotion -- "Yes, that hurts ... hurts ... Yes, that hurts too." Upon completing the examination, the doctor gave the Deaf person a prescription and told him to go home. I realized in an instant that my failure to incorporate this man's pain in my vocal intonation and selection of vocabulary had given this doctor an inaccurate picture of what the Deaf individual was trying to convey. It was a lesson I will never forget.

Another challenge arising for interpreters when working from ASL into English is incorporating the affect being conveyed in effective and culturally appropriate ways. This includes conveying information that may be conveyed only by affect markers, but which clearly contain information.

Numbering Systems

With its grammatical structure, English is able to convey all numeric information, with only two numbering systems — ordinal and cardinal. In other words, any time you say something in English which has numeric information you will either use the form one, two, three, four, etc. or first, second, third, fourth, etc.

ASL, on the other hand, has a complex system of numbers requiring different number forms for various topic areas. In its grammatical system, there is a different type of numeric system used for clock-time, counting, people-height, building-height, room-measurements, sports-scores, etc. Research is incomplete, but we know of approximately 27 numbering systems at this time.

Implications Of Numbering Systems for Interpreters

Failure to learn and properly use the various numeric systems in ASL is guaranteed to result in miscommunication. It is imperative that interpreting students learn these systems and that interpreters perfect their ability to read and produce each numbering system accurately.

Pronouns

Generally speaking, English uses specific pronouns for third person singular. When you hear the pronoun "she/her", you know the

speaker is referring to a female. Likewise, the pronoun "he/him" refers to a male and the pronoun "it" generally refers to an inanimate object. English also tends to use number-neutral pronouns. This means that when you hear the word "we," "they," or "them," you do not know how many people or things form the group. Because of the way English works, this does not hinder a listener from comprehending the message of a text.

ASL, on the other hand, generally uses number-specific, gender-neutral pronouns. When signing "we," "they," or "them," the sign often incorporates the number of people or things being referred to (e.g., we-two; they-five). This is a part of the direct or specific nature of ASL. When signing the personal pronoun s/he, an index is used which is devoid of information regarding the gender of the referent. Due to the grammatical structure of ASL, gender-neutral pronouns do not skew one's ability to understand what is being conveyed.

Implications of Pronouns For Interpreters

ASL prefers number-specificity, thus when working from English to ASL, an interpreter must actively seek other textual clues to determine which, if any, number-specific pronoun can be used in the target language. Some texts can be conveyed without this specificity, but others become confusing and unclear without this pronoun form.

While ASL does not demand gender-specificity, an interpreter can generally ferret out information to assist her/him in identifying the gender of the referent. However, there are two constructions that do not provide this information, creating a challenge for interpreters. This happens if the person being referred to is initially identified in one of the following ways:

✦ As "my boss," "my friend" or some other gender-neutral term;

✦ Using a sign name without having the name spelled, thus depriving the audience from knowing the gender of the referent.

Both of these situations wreak havoc for the ASL-to-English interpreter. S/he can say "my neighbor" or "this individual" a few times, but English requires that after naming the referent once or twice, a pronoun must be used. This often requires the interpreter to interrupt the Deaf speaker and ask, "man or woman?"

CHAPTER REVIEW
Key Points

Figure 9-27 summarizes a few areas in which the differences between English and ASL result in significant challenges to interpreters. Remember, this is a partial listing intended as a review and to stimulate your understanding of the challenges in mediating languages. The authors remind you that in order to become an interpreter, you must be fully bilingual — fluent in both your native language and one other language (e.g., spoken English and ASL or French and LSQ). As an interpreter or interpreting student you should study the linguistics of your working languages.

Fig. 9-27 Linguistic Differences That Challenge Inerpreters		
English	ASL	Challenge
MODALITY Auditory/vocal modality requires use of content and functional elements to create proper rhythm	MODALITY Visual/spatial modality fosters use of spatial referencing and restricts use of functional elements -- utterances made up primarily of content elements	1. deriving meaning 2. dropping source language form 3. managing the volume of lexical units and the speed of source language delivey
GRAMMATICAL STRUCTURE subject-verb-object (SVO) linear rather than simultaneous	GRAMMATICAL STRUCTURE topic-prone; imbedded information allows for greater degree of simultaneous conveyance of information	1. producing target language that is grammatically correct -- avoiding source language intrusions 2. conditionals in ASL must precede consequence
TIME/TENSE MARKERS Verbs change forms (conjugated) to mark present, past or future tense (walk, walkING, walkS, walkED)	TIME/TENSE MARKERS Time marker comes early in the utterance and conugates all following verbs until a new time marker is noted	1. producing target language that appropriately conveys time 2. recognizing time markers in ASL when working from ASL into English
NEGATION/ AFFIRMATION Adds a word to indicate affirmation or negation (ex: I will NOT go) Affirmation is usually embedded in the verb, although a lexical item may be added for emphasis or clarity	NEGATION/ AFFIRMATION Signer adds a non-manual marker (head nodding "yes" or shaking "no") as the utterance is signed. In formal register, the non-manual marker must be accompanied with a signed affirmation/ negation, optional in consultative and informal registers	1. incorporation of proper variations of negation/affirmation re: informal-consultative vs. high consultative-formal registers 2. avoidance of non-Deaf form of head shaking from side-to-side when making an emphatic statement -- looks like negation in ASL

Fig. 9-27 Linguistic Differences That Challenge Inerpreters

English	ASL	Challenge
DETERMINING MEANING Described as indirect due to the common use of implicit conveyance of information -- requires listener to extrapolate meaning by identifying implicit and explicit units of meaning * multiple meaning words * new lexical items made by combining verbs with prepositions *use of generic terms which represent a wide range of se mantic meanings * pronouns can be used with implied referent * use of compact lexical items which carry descriptive semantic meaning	DETERMINING MEANING Described as direct due to the common use of unambiguous, explicit lexical items minimizing need for participants to identify implied units of meaning * few, if any multiple meaning lexical items * maintains strong association to im mediate event * specific sensory orientation * signs are based on effectiveness in communicating semantic meaning through perceptual imagery	1. degree of detail -- mastering expansion and reduction techniques as appropriate for the direct and indirect nature of each language 2. use of first or third person address as appropriate for each language, including appropriate use of role-shifting in ASL 3. identifying implicit and explicit units of meaning in the source language and converting information into appropriate implicit and explicit units of meaning in the target language
AFFFECT MARKERS generally conveyed via words with appropriate vocal inflection	AFFECT MARKERS generally conveyed visually via facial markers and sign modulations, although affect signs may be signed with accompanying facial marker	1. learning to work publicly with a language whose visual qualities (particularly role shifting and visual affect) may have negative response 2. incorporating visual affect/informational units from visual into spoken language forms

226

Fig. 9-27 Linguistic Differences
That Challenge Inerpreters

English	ASL	Challenge
NOUN/VERB MODIFIER describing relationship of noun to another noun: uses prepositions	NOUN/VERB MODIFIER describing relationship of noun to another noun: (a) uses classifiers although prepositions are sometimes signed for emphasis (b) some verbs (known as directional verbs) incorporate the actor and the recipient of the action because of the way the verb moves through space	1. when working from English into ASL, using classifiers and other language appropriate strategies to convey information, thus avoiding source language intrusion 2. when working from ASL into English, having an adequate English vocabulary to translate SASSes and other classifier-rooted utteranes with equivalent meaning and clarity
description of a noun: adjectives are added -- usually preceding the noun	description of a noun: (a) classifiers known as size and shape specifiers (SASSes) (b) sometimes signed adjectives are used in combination with SASSes	
describing how something moves: adverbs are added to the verb	describing how something moves: adverbs sometimes signed but more frequently conveys this information by modifying the way the verb is produced and by using specific non-manual markers which indicate adverbial information	

227

Fig. 9-27 Linguistic Differences
That Challenge Inerpreters

English	ASL	Challenge
PRONOUNS gender-specific number-neutral	PRONOUNS number-specific gender-neutral	1. providing number specificity when working from English into ASL where possible 2. providing gender specificity when working from ASL into English where the referent is set up with no notation of gender (eg: my friend; the neighbor)
NUMBERS two numbering systems: cardinal and ordinal	NUMBERS multiple numbering systems for various topic areas	mastering reading and using the various systems appropriately in ASL
VOICE passive voice is used frequently, particularly in upper-consultative and formal registers	VOICE uses primarily active voice	when working from English into ASL, identifying passive voice constructions in English and making proper transition to active voice in ASL

The Nature of English

✦ Orally expressed language based on the linear sequencing of vocalized sound patterns.

✦ Can produce approximately 5 syllables per second (180 words per minute).

✦ Requires a certain rhythm of speech to foster comprehension, including pausing/phrasing and intonation patterns.

✦ Requires the listener to determine meaning based on both explicit and implicit information.

Sentence construction

✦ The primary grammatical structure is subject-verb-object (SVO).

Indirect

✦ Tends to use multiple-meaning lexical items; and

✦ Lexical items and indirect address foster non-elaborative and ambiguous ways of conveying information.

Time/tense markers
+ Conjugated verbs indicate the tense of the verb in each sentence.
+ Elaborate verb tense system allows incidents to be told without following real-time sequencing.

Negation/Affirmation
+ The addition of words or phrases is used to affirm or negate the verb or verb phrase.
+ Vocal intonation sometimes used to indicate affirmation or negation.

Voice
+ Comfortably uses both passive and active voice constructions.
+ Passive voice is more frequently used at high-consultative and formal registers.

Prepositions and prepositional phrases — used to provide information regarding the relationship of a noun to another noun.

Adjectives — used to describe a noun

Adverbs and adverbial phrases — used to describe verbs.

Affect markers
+ Conveyed through modifications in the way words are produced and in the selection of lexical items.
+ Facial and body-based affect markers are sometimes used but are restricted to lower registers.

Conditionals
+ Used frequently.
+ Marked by vocal intonation and a specific group of lexical items (e.g., if/then).
+ The "if" portion of a conditional statement may either precede or follow the consequence.

Numbers -- two systems:
+ Cardinal — used to denote quantity (4, 42, etc.)
+ Ordinal — used to denote order (1st, 14th, etc.)

Pronouns
+ Generally gender-specific in third person singular (she/her — he/him).
+ Generally number-neutral (we, they — no indication of how many people make up the group).

The Nature of ASL
+ spatial, temporal-oriented language based on visual perception and conveyance of ideas, information and feelings;.
+ takes twice the amount of time to produce a single ASL sign as compared to speaking a single English word due to physical articulation, however, the same information can be transmitted in the same amount of time.

Sentence construction

+ topic-prone.
+ takes advantage of the multi-dimensional nature of visual communication (by using space, movement and the simultaneity of visual intake) to convey information.

Direct

+ strong association to the reality of actual things/events.
+ uses lexical items that are specific in nature, avoiding multiple-meaning and ambiguous terms and constructions.
+ uses a series of expansion techniques to formulate information.

Time/tense markers

+ the tense must be stated prior to the verb in an utterance and modifies all subsequent verbs.
+ information usually ordered according to real-time (sequential) sequencing,

Negation/Affirmation

+ can be articulated with separate lexical items but is typically marked with a head shake or head nod simultaneous to the utterance of the verb or verb phrase.

Voice

+ primarily based on active voice, although has the ability to make passive voice constructions in certain instances.

Classifiers — a special set of signs used to provide information regarding: (a) relationship of a noun to another noun, (b) description of a noun, (c) description of how something moves.

Real world classifiers — take on life-size proportions and sometimes look a bit like a reduced form of mime when being produced.

Abstract classifiers — smaller than life-size; their shape and movement is less iconic than real-world classifiers.

Affect markers

+ visual
+ conveyed through modifications in the way signs are produced, specific facial markers, as well as specific body movement and agreement markers.

Conditionals

+ marked by a sustained brow raise and head shift,
+ precede the result.

Numbers — multiple systems used for various topic areas (e.g. clock time, people height, counting, etc.)

Pronouns — generally gender-neutral and number-specific.

THOUGHT QUESTIONS

1. ASL has no written form. Is this unique among the world languages?

2. Valli and Lucas (1992) note several characteristics of languages. Select a language you know well and provide examples of how it does each of the following:

    ✦ Can be manipulated to create an unlimited number of sentences and new messages;
    ✦ Has ways of showing how the symbols used to express the language are related to each other;
    ✦ Changes and expands across time;
    ✦ Can be used in an unrestricted number of settings (medical, religious, educational, etc.) to express both spontaneous and prepared ideas for a variety of purposes (to make a statement, execute a command, make a request, etc.);
    ✦ Can be used to refer to the past, the future, and other non-immediate situations;
    ✦ Can be used to both send and receive messages in an interactive format;
    ✦ Has geographical, gender, register and other variants.

3. Identify the functional and content elements in the following sentences:

    ✦ Get two pancakes with all of the trimmings for only $2.99 any morning between 6 - 9 a.m. at the IHOP nearest you.
    ✦ I bought this radio in here last week and yesterday I found this ad for the same thing at a lesser price.
    ✦ I can't believe he had the nerve to come here and demand that I give him back the bracelet he gave me for my birthday last year!

4. Develop a chart depicting the various meanings of the English word "made/make" like that in Fig. 9-1.

5. Explain the meaning of conditional phrases and discuss how they are used in ASL and in English.

6. Define Size and Shape Classifiers. Select an ASL video and identify the SASSes used.

7. Define the concept of passive voice. Look through the daily paper and find examples of passive voice.

SUGGESTED ACTIVITIES

✦ Have the instructor or a guest model the various examples from the chapter.

✦ Working in teams, prepare a text in passive voice and an equivalent text in active voice.

✦ Watch videotapes of interpreters working with various texts and identify examples where the language is changed appropriately between source and target utterances.

✦ Watch a videotape of a narrative in ASL and identify examples of the various features of ASL discussed in the chapter.

✦ Watch a videotape or listen to an audio tape of an English narrative and identify examples of the various features discussed in the chapter

ENDNOTES

1. Wilentz (1968)
2. Isenhath (1990)
3. Baker & Cokely (1980)
4. Friedman (1976); Baker (1977); Bellugi & Fischer (1972); Grosjean (1977)
5. Klima & Bellugi (1979)
6. Friedman, (1976); Klima & Bellugi (1979); Isenhath (1990)
7. Ibid.
8. Cokely (1985)
9. Isenhath (1990)
10. Lawrence (1994); Livingston, et. al. (1994); Singer (1994)
11. Klima and Bellugi (1979) analyzed similar structures as a form of compounding in ASL
12. Baker & Cokely (1980); Valli and Lucas (1992); Liddell (1990)
13. Colonomos (1983)
14. Odea (1995)
15. Friedman (1975)
16. It should be noted that classifiers are not unique to ASL or other sign languages. Several spoken languages also have classifier systems, including Swahili and Navajo.
17. Baker & Cokely (1980)
18. Colonomos (1983); Alcorn & Kanda (1989); Bienvenu & Colonomos (1989)

CHAPTER TEN
The Process of Interpreting

In this chapter, we will introduce several models that seek to outline the steps in the process of interpretation. This is being provided so that the seemingly "invisible" area in which interpreters work will become more transparent.

PROCESS MODELS

The task of taking source language utterances and transmitting them into the target language requires the same mental tasks and processes no matter where the work takes place. It is the same process whether one is interpreting between spoken languages or signed languages.

An interpreter is required to analyze linguistically complex SL utterances as quickly and efficiently as possible.[1] Roberts[2] notes that this includes the "ability to understand the source language in all of its nuances and the ability to express oneself correctly, fluently, clearly and with poise in the target language." One of the greatest challenges in the journey toward becoming an interpreter is discovering and understanding the steps required to convey equivalent messages between two distinct, separate languages and cultures while maintaining dynamic equivalence.

Several models; have been proposed in the fields of both spoken and sign language interpretation. While each model is unique, they all attempt to portray the largely invisible cognitive processes required to take an utterance from one language-culture and render a culturally and linguistically equivalent utterance in the target language. Some of the models are substantiated by formal data collection and research; they are detailed and scientific in nature. Others are based on the application and interpretation of emerging field research and each developer's experience as an interpreter and interpreter-educator.

233

A partial list of models includes:

1. Gerver — 1976[3]
2. Ingram — 1977[4]
3. Moser-Mercer — 1978[5]
4. Seleskovitch — 1978[6]
5. Colonomos — 1980, 1983, 1984, 1987[7]
6. Cokely — 1985, 1992[8]
7. Kitano — 1993[9]
8. Pradis — 1994[10]

The basic components of all of these models are similar

✦ While maintaining awareness of environmental factors,[a] the interpreter takes in the source language utterance;
✦ Lexical and semantic units are grouped into workable units or "chunks" (in a process referred to as a "segmentation"[11]) and held until the interpreter has enough input to make sense or find meaning in what is being said/signed;
✦ The "chunk" is analyzed to identify the speaker's intent, the goal s/he seeks to accomplish, explicit[b] and implied[c] ideas, and the multitude of contextual factors that "color" or influence the meaning of the source language utterance in that particular situation;
✦ The conscious and deliberate discarding of source language lexical units and communication behaviors;

---

[a] Includes those present in the interaction, the relationship and status of each participant, where the interaction is taking place, etc.
[b] Clearly stated or distinctly set forth so that there is no doubt as the meaning of a message or statement.
[c] Information or ideas that are insinuated, suggested or hinted at; a claim or truth that follows from other claims or truths.

✦ A mental note is made of the schema and experiential frame brought by both hearing and Deaf
consumers and a search is made for equivalents of
cultural norms, as well as cultural overlays of meaning;

✦ A search is made of the target language to identify
lexical/semantic units and communication behaviors that can be used to produce an utterance in
the target language conveying equivalent meaning,
while maintaining the communication dynamics;

✦ After a momentary review of the selected items, the
interpretation is expressed in the target language;
and

✦ The interpreter monitors internal and external feedback[d] to check for errors or needed corrections[12].

The drawback of all of these models is their inability to illustrate
the simultaneity of the process and the multi-tasking required
of the interpreter. All of this is happening with lightening speed,
in a dynamic transactional environment where message revi-
sion is inherent. The reality of this phenomena is absent from
the static, linear representations of process models proposed to
date.

THE PROCESS OF INTERPRETING: A CLOSER LOOK

The following is an attempt to describe the social, cognitive
and linguistic tasks of an interpreter. Like the models above,
this description is not able to make evident the dynamic and
overlapping nature of the various decisions and analytical processes taking place. We have attempted, however, to address the
process from a holistic perspective, including the challenge of
managing the overall process. We have identified five steps, all of
which take place in the midst of continual assessment of con-

---

[d] Internal monitor refers to the interpreter's own sense of the accuracy
of the interpretation; external monitor refers to cues gleaned from client
responses that indicate the clarity of the interpretation.

textual factors and interpersonal dynamics, as well as monitoring both the process and the output.

The five steps of the interpreting process are:

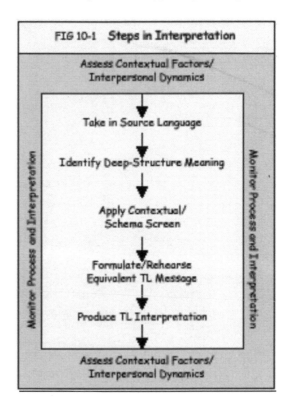

1. Take in source language;
2. Identify deep structure meaning;
3. Apply contextual/schema screen;
4. Formulate/rehearse target language utterance;
5. Produce interpretation.

STEP ONE: Take in Source Language

One of the biggest mistakes interpreters make is that they start the interpretation after the first few words/signs have been delivered — before having a sense of what is being said/signed. As a result, the interpretation typically incorporates source

FIG 10-1 Steps in Interpretation

Assess Contextual Factors/
Interpersonal Dynamics

Take in Source Language

Identify Deep-Structure Meaning

Apply Contextual/
Schema Screen

Formulate/Rehearse
Equivalent TL Message

Produce TL Interpretation

Assess Contextual Factors/
Interpersonal Dynamics

Monitor Process and Interpretation

Monitor Process and Interpretation

language form in violation of target language grammatical and textual norms.[e]

By rushing the process, the interpreter places the participants' goal of clear communication in jeopardy.

True comprehension is only possible when the listener remains focused on the SL message until s/he is able to make sense of the incoming text. Thus the first step in the interpreting process is perceiving and temporarily storing the incoming source language utterance. As the interpreter, you must not allow yourself to be pressured into starting the target language rendition too quickly.

Physical Requirements
In order to take in the source language, one must be *physically able to hear* (in the case of spoken source language) and *see* (in the case of signed source language). The bimodal nature of ASL/English interpretation requires the interpreter to move back and forth between auditory/oral channels and visual/gestural channels. This is physically tiring. An interpreter must also develop the *mental and physical endurance required to focus and sustain attending skills.*

Cognitive Competence
Momentary inability to hear/see can be overcome by a process of mentally "filling in the blanks"[f] by using clues from the overall context, the information immediately preceding and following the point where the interruption occurred, and by drawing on her/his cumulative world experience. In addition, an interpreter must have the *ability to store, connect, retrieve and process information quickly* in order to take in, comprehend and store the SL units of meaning effectively.

e External processing takes place when an interpreter starts interpreting before s/he understands the incoming message, then begins clarifying and correcting the initial interpretation within the body of the interpretation itself. This is confusing and stressful for consumers and should be avoided.

f Referred to as cloze skills.

Linguistic and Cultural Requirements

Seeing/hearing the source language must be complemented with bilingual-bicultural competence.[13] This includes familiarity with a range of registers in each language and understanding how speakers/signers accomplish various goals in culturally appropriate ways.

Each language has prescribed **reciprocal signals**[14] — certain eye behaviors, head nods, verbal utterances (e.g. right, uh-huh) to indicate that one is attending and comprehending (or not comprehending) the messages being received. Interpreters need to be familiar with these reciprocal signals and be able to apply them appropriately in each language-culture. The failure of an interpreter to incorporate these reciprocal signals into their "listening" behaviors while taking in the source language may halt the flow of the utterance and/or negatively impact the communication dynamics.

Social Competence

The interpreting process takes place primarily in the head of the interpreter. However, as the interpreter you cannot forget that you are working with *people* — Deaf and hearing consumers. Developing social skills and cultural finesse to support effective interpersonal interactions is crucial.

Cultures define certain social/interpersonal behaviors as respectful and appropriate to encourage and sustain interactions between individuals, small groups, etc. Interpreters must be able to demonstrate social competence in both languages-cultures in order to appropriately interact in a variety of interpersonal settings. This competence includes greeting and leave taking skills, forms of polite speech, etc.

STEP TWO: Analyze Deep Structure Meaning

An interpreter is required to analyze the surface structure of source language texts. This answers such questions as:

238

+ What are the overt speaker/signer goals?
+ What linguistic register is being used?
+ What ideas are clearly declared?
+ What affective information is being overtly conveyed?
+ What structural properties (e.g. grammatical and discourse structures, humor, metaphors, etc.) have been used by the speaker/signer?
+ What are the stated or overt relationships between participants? (e.g. power differentiation of employer/employee or parent/child)

However, the secret to creating a target language interpretation that is linguistically and culturally equivalent is discovering the meaning that lies in the deeper structure of the source language utterance.[9] In other words, an interpreter must look at the meaning found in both the explicitly stated, as well as the implied propositions. The search for deep structure meaning can be found in the answers to such questions as:

+ Is the register being used consistent with the setting and the evident relationship between the participants? If not, what might be causing this dissonance?
+ What implied emotional (affective) overlays are present and how do they impact the meaning?[15]
+ What nonverbal or paralinguistic features accompany the utterance? Do they support, contradict or otherwise change the stated ideas?
+ Can you identify additional or emerging speaker/ signer goals based on information gleaned from deep structure analysis?
+ What kind of response does the speaker/signer seem to be expecting from the recipient(s) of their utterances?

---

[9] Referred to as cognitive processing skills by Patri, 2000.

✦ What is the goal or purpose that is causing the speaker/signer to use the grammatical and discourse structures, humor, metaphors, etc. selected?

✦ What is the observed and emerging relationship between participants?

This sounds like an overwhelming, even impossible task! But in reality, you do this every day when you listen to your parents, friends, and teachers. We may not consciously be aware of each unit of meaning (propositions) in an utterance, the emotive overlay (feelings), linguistic register, textual organization or grammatical structure. But in our day-to-day interactions, we consider what the other person is communicating — directly and indirectly, explicitly or through implication, in speech/ signs as well as through nonverbal behaviors — in an effort to get a sense of who the other person is and what they are *really* saying.

An interpreter, like all other effective communicators, is looking for the sense, essence or gestalt of the SL text.[16] Uncovering the deep structure meaning will reveal this.

Identifying deep structure meaning requires certain cognitive competencies. It requires *thinking* one's way through the communication, seeing clearly the *meaning intended* as you *synthesize what is being said*, relating each comment to other comments and filtering all that is said through your own life experience.[17]

Cognitive Competence
In order for a language to exist and be learnable by persons from a variety of cultures, words must have definite uses and designated concepts. *Thinking* requires the exercise of mental faculties in order to form ideas and make conclusions, "starting with what is known or assumed and advancing to a definite conclusion through the inferences drawn."[18] Good thinking can be identified because it is logical and results in "clarity, precision,

specificity, accuracy, relevance, consistency, depth, completeness, and balance."[19]

Thus, deep structure analysis requires higher order thinking, including critical listening and thinking skills. *Listening critically* means to attend to the SL utterance in order to maximize our understanding of what an individual means when speaking/signing. This is essential because not all speakers/signers present their questions, ideas, and information in clearly articulated ways. Ideas are sometimes obscured, implied, vague or hinted at. In addition, statements are frequently framed by a number of assumptions regarding the listener's cohort membership, schema and cultural background.

Critical thinking skills refers to the ability to break the whole into its parts, to examine in detail, to look more deeply into a text and determine its nature.[20] This includes the ability to rapidly scrutinize the incoming text to determine its features, recognizing and making accurate connections between new ideas and previous information, to tighten up our understanding, and sharpen our insight into the meaning of the message. It also means listening for nuances, ambiguities and making a continual effort to be clear and precise in language usage. This is done by engaging in disciplined reasoning, inferring[h] and deducing in order to extract the message carried "below the words/signs" or "between the lines" as well as the information explicitly stated.

Discovering deep structure meaning also requires the interpreter to be aware of her/his own beliefs and biases,[i] setting them aside, suspending judgment and entering the task of interpretation with the goal of understanding and analyzing the goal(s) and perspective of those involved in the interaction. Another part of listening and thinking critically is being aware of any

---

[h] The act of using critical thinking to draw a conclusion that something is so in light of other information being true.

[i] Bias: a mental leaning or inclination because of one's point of view; one notices some things rather than others, emphasizes some points rather than others and thinks in one direction rather than others.

cultural assumptions[21] embedded in or framing the source language text. This is critical because cultural assumptions influence one's point of view, values, beliefs and practices.

Richard Paul suggests we ask ourselves if we are clear about several things when attempting to critically analyze a text, including:

✦ The purpose/goal of this interaction and each participant involved.
✦ The topic, problem or question being discussed.
✦ Your own point of view or frame of reference, as well as the views and frames of reference of the participants.
✦ Our assumptions about the comments being made, as well as the reasons or evidence upon which the statements are based.
✦ Any unstated emotion detected through tone of voice/signs, choice of words, and
✦ physical behaviors. Further, ask yourself if these unstated feelings match those that are stated (if any). If not, how is the meaning changed by this embedded emotive overlay?
✦ Any additional ideas or information that are implied when looking at the *whole* utterance. If you identify some, ask yourself why this information isn't being stated overtly.

✦ The reaction the source language-culture signer/speaker seems to expect from the recipient.
✦ Any contradiction or variance in the register being used, why this is happening and if it influences the message in any way.
✦ The purpose of any humor being used.
✦ Our inferences and line of reasoning as well as the implications and consequences that follow from our reasoning.

Finally, getting beneath the words/signs to understand the message itself requires rational control of your own beliefs, values and inferences, making a commitment to analyze and evaluate the statements of others based on reason and evidence. It means questioning when it is rational to question and to believe when it is rational to believe.[22] Our goal in interpretation is to accurately identify deep structure meaning in the context of the participants' personal experiences (schema), perspectives, point of view or philosophy.

Linguistic and Cultural Requirements

In order to analyze deep structure meaning, one must be fluent enough in each language to recognize unstated but clearly implied information. This means being linguistically and culturally able to recognize various rhetorical structures (personal anecdote, formal presentation, negotiation, etc.) and use that knowledge to identify speaker/signer goals, as well as to predict the logical path the speaker will follow in accomplishing those goals. An interpreter must be able to recognize a range of euphemisms, nuances, subtleties, innuendo, insinuation, indirect suggestions, metaphors and shades of meaning that might occur in the spoken/signed communication, as well as accompanying culture-based nonverbal signals.[23]

STEP THREE: Apply Contextual/Schema Screen

At a later phase in the interpreting process, the interpreter must determine how the original message can be presented in the target language and culture in order to maintain all of the units of meaning (proposi-tions), the affect (feelings), appropriate linguistic register and textual organization. Many of these decisions are based on the application of the contextual/schema screen.

As stated previously, communication does not take place in a vacuum. Critical to comprehending the meaning of spoken/signed and nonverbal communication is understanding contextual factors and interpersonal dynamics. This requires verification of any cohort, schematic and contextual factors influencing the individuals involved in the interaction.

Cohort Groups

This concept refers to "a group of people who, because they were born within a few years of each other, experience many of the same historical and social conditions."[24] In other words, people born in the same era are exposed to similar ideas, prevailing assumptions, critical public events, technologies and popular trends.

These experiences influence the beliefs of cohort members regarding such things as work, job security, independence and innumerable other life-shaping concepts. The presence of individuals from different cohort groups may signal the interpreter that there is a need for cultural expansions in the interpretation to support access to the messages being delivered.

FIG 10-2 COHORT DIFFERENCES		
When asked to share some favorite games, toys, forms of entertainment and historic events from their childhood, the responses of members of different cohort groups will vary.		
1930-1945	1950-1965	1970-1985
Shirley Temple dolls	Barbie dolls	Cabbage patch dolls
Radio	Phonographs and reel-to-reel tapes	8-track and cassette tapes
Tommy Dorsey	The Beatles	Michael Jackson
Great depression and World War II	Assassination of JFK and MLK	Nixon resigns; Hostages taken in Iran
Racial segregation	Civil rights movement	Multiculturalism and diversity
1st commercial airlines	Sputnik space race; 1st walk on the moon	Challenger explodes
Urbanization	Consumerism	Technology

Schema

When two people come together to share ideas or information, the similarity or difference in their backgrounds and experiences have a dramatic impact on the ease or difficulty of communication. If they come from similar experiential backgrounds, they have a common "schema" and there will be relatively few misunderstandings. However, the life experience of individuals from different language-culture groups varies vastly. The more different their backgrounds and experiences, the more challenging it is to ensure clear communication.

When the experiential frame of the individuals communicating is different, it is sometimes necessary for the interpreter to frame the message with cultural expansions. This gives the recipient a schema, allowing the information to be successfully conveyed and understood.

FIG. 10-3 EXAMPLE OF A DIFFERENT SCHEMA
A white, middle-class suburban school teacher went into the inner city as a substitute teacher one Spring. One of her activities involved describing objects and letting the children guess the object she was describing. As she described a rabbit (thinking about the Easter bunny, etc.), the children's eyes grew bigger and a look of terror came over some of the children. Later the substitute teacher learned that the only thing the children could imagine to fit the description was the large rats that ran loose in the poverty housing project, biting and sometimes killing babies and young children

Contextual Factors

Even before entering an interpreting environment, an interpreter is expected to *predict* ... who will be involved, what relationship might exist between the participants, where will the interaction take place, and other factors that will comprise the context in which the interaction will take place. These predictions should guide the interpreter's *preparation* for the interpretation, seeking such information as:

✦ The overall goal of the participants in the interaction;

✦ The similarities/differences in background and experience of the parties involved; and

✦ The level of formality in the setting and in the language used.

Other contextual factors that should be noted include:

✦ Who is here? Why are they here? What is the relationship between the parties present?

✦ What nonverbal interactions and reactions are taking place and what do they mean?

✦ Where is this interaction taking place? What are the norms and protocol common to this setting? Are the participants conforming to those norms? If not, why not?

STEP FOUR: Formulate/Rehearse Equivalent Message

Once the deep structure meaning of the source language message has been identified, an interpreter begins to consider how to convey the intended meaning in the target language/ culture in such a way that it will have the same dynamic impact[j] on the recipients of the message. At this stage of the process, the interpreter makes cultural and linguistic choices — planning, formulating and reviewing elements to be used in expressing equivalent meaning. More time will be spent at this stage when dealing with complex tests, consumers using non-standard linguistic forms and when the interpreter is a relatively new practitioner.

Linguistic Competence

In order to accomplish this task, one must have mastery of a sufficient store of lexicon, a range of registers, semantic finesse, comprehension and ability to use discourse formulation and discourse markers in order to make visual/auditory sense.

---

[j] For example, if the speaker/signer's goal is to confound, the interpretation should not be so precise as to undermine that goal. Dynamic equivalence means that consumers of the interpreted message should have the same sense of the speaker/signer as that of consumers of the direct message.

Assess Contextual Factors/Interpersonal Dynamics

Throughout the interpreted interaction, the interpreter
is constantly assessing contextual factors, interpersonal
dynamics and their impact.

* The relationship between the people involved

* Formal and informal power structures represented

* Similarities/differences in background/experiences
  of the parties involved

* The level of formality in the setting and language used

* Emotional overlay of interaction

Assess Contextual Factors/Interpersonal Dynamics

From the moment the interpretation begins, the interpret er
monitors the overall process and interpretation. This includes
such activities as:

* Verifying comprehension and asking for clarification
  as needed

* Slowing the process to allow movement between simultaneous and consecutive forms

* Checking for and correcting errors in output

* Verifying comprehension of consumers

Cultural Requirements

Further, interpreters must know the parameters of the target
culture that define appropriate ways to express various goals,
how to engage in turn taking, and how to incorporate various
emotional overlays.

STEP FIVE: Produce Target Language Interpretation

This is the point where the interpretation becomes
audible/visible to the participants for whom interpretation is being provided. This goal is to produce
an interpretation that is linguistically correct, culturally appropriate, that sounds natural and comfortable and

that contains all of the units of meaning carried in the original utterance.

Linguistic And Cultural Adaptations[k]

To achieve equivalent meaning, an interpreter must mediate the source language-culture with 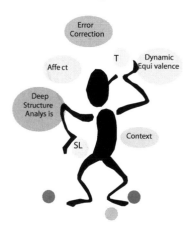 the target language-culture. As discussed in Chapter Eight, this requires the use of linguistic and cultural adaptations, termed expansions and reductions. Decisions about when and how to make cultural adaptations requires the interpreter to know the speaker/signer's goal(s) and have a sense of the experiential frame of each participant. If expansions are made where participants have a common experiential frame, they are sometimes offended — feeling like you are "talking down" to them. However, our failure to come to grips with the need for cultural mediation in the past has resulted in less than equal access for many Deaf individuals who use our services as interpreters.

Communication never happens in isolation. The very definition of communication incorporates the concept of an *exchange* of ideas or information between two or more entities. A part of the communication environment is the cultural milieu. Culture frames the entire event including assumptions that will be made and understandings derived by the various participants. These differences in cultural experience often contribute to miscommunication between individuals.

If my goal as an interpreter is to make a linguistic and cultural equivalent, I must be aware of these differences in the languages with which I work and I must adjust the stated/unstated presentation of propositions appropriately

[k]See Chapter Nine for a discussion of required expansions in ASL.

PROCESS MULTI-TASKING AND MONITORING

While the interpreter is engaging in the steps of the interpreting process outlined above, s/he is simultaneously monitoring the significant aspects of the interaction. This includes such things as:

✦ Confirming comprehension/asking for clarification;
✦ Slowing the process to allow for movement between simultaneous and consecutive modes;
✦ Checking for and correcting errors in output;
✦ Verifying consumer comprehension; and
✦ Verifying maintenance of interpersonal dynamics.

Contextual Scan

An interpreter needs to be constantly scanning the environment in order to note a variety of contextual factors. This includes such things as:

✦ Scanning the visual and auditory environment
— Can the consumers see/hear me? If not, can I resolve the problem?
✦ Noting any changes in the participants present
— Did someone enter or leave the room? Do I see evidence of any impact of that change on the participants in the interaction?
✦ Noting emotional overlay and reactions — What is the evolving emotional environment of this exchange?

Overall Monitoring Process

Monitoring and managing the overall interpreting process refers to the kinds of things an interpreter must do in addition to the mental process of interpretation to ensure accuracy of interpretation and maintenance of dynamics between participants. Interpreters are required to monitor their work — *in process*, as well as after the fact. Monitoring your work *in process* means mentally "observing" your target language-culture output, as well as watching consumers for signals that they are, or are not, understanding the interpretation.

This includes such monitoring activities as verifying the:

+ Quality and accuracy of the messages being conveyed;
+ Effectiveness of the overall process of communication; and
+ Identification and maintenance of dynamic equivalence between participants.

It also means having techniques for making corrections in culture/language appropriate and non-intrusive ways. The interpreter must have strategies to seek clarification or to slow down the interaction in order to have time to process the message and produce it into an equivalent utterance in the target language.

Asking for Clarification

You should not start interpreting until you understand what is being signed/said. This means holding the interpretation until you have a sense of what is being said/signed and asking consumers for clarification if you are unclear or uncertain about any aspect of what has been communicated. The need for clarification sometimes exists because of a missed lexical item and uncertainty regarding how the point being made fits with what has preceded it.

Use of First Person

Interpreters are generally trained to use first person when interpreting. In other words, the interpreter says/signs "me" or "I" when the consumer refers to her/himself. This works in most settings and Deaf consumers are familiar with this practice.

However, there are times when the interpreter should use third person rather than first person. This technique is particularly helpful when there is a need to incorporate the sense of who is responsible for the utterance being delivered. For example, in an educational setting, the teacher in class may be angry with the Deaf student and in the midst of bawling her out for something she has done. If the interpreter notices that the student is confused — uncertain as to WHO is doing the bawling out, the interpreter would point at the teacher and say, "He is saying ..." in order to clarify who is speaking.

Third person address is also used to clarify communication when there are multiple consumers in the setting. In a setting with more than three people, pointing to indicate who is talking and saying "she is asking," "he is answering," etc. clarifies the turn-taking and overall flow of communication.

Making the decision of using first person or third person is part of managing the process.

Working With Uninitiated Consumers

Dealing with uninitiated consumers is part of managing the process and the way it is handled often has significant impact on the interpersonal dynamics that emerge. Self-advocacy skills are required.

In spite of increasing public awareness, some people still do not understand an interpreter's role or what the interpreter needs to perform her/his job maximally. This is sometimes the result of having worked with untrained friends and family members who have functioned as "interpreters", as well as myths and attitudes that guide the actions and reactions of non-deaf individuals when they interact with people who are Deaf, Deaf-Blind or hard of hearing.

It may be necessary for the interpreter or the Deaf consumer to "brief" parties about the "do's and don'ts" of working with an interpreter. For example, an interpreter may have to tactfully, but insistently, explain to an x-ray technician that the Deaf client cannot hear through the partition as s/he shouts, "take a breath — hold it — now breathe." Thus, interpreters must be able to predict their needs prior to entering interpreted settings and effectively and professionally communicate those needs to others.

Working With Rehearsed and/or Read Texts

There are some times when a speaker/signer is presenting the same block of information over and over. This could be because the presenter is reading their presentation from a print text or teleprompter. It could also be due to the fact that the speaker has made a particular presentation so many times that it is basically a memorized text. This is problematic for interpreters because the natural prosody[I] is lost, resulting in inadequate time to comprehend, analyze, and interpret the text into the target language. This requires use of a particular set of management skills and will vary depending on the context in which the message is being articulated.

Using Consecutive Form

Being able to comprehend and analyze source language utterances and drop form requires adequate processing time. It is essential for interpreters to take the time necessary to do a good job, rather than rushing the process. An interpreter working between English and ASL may find her/himself slipping back toward source language grammatical structure, in order to match the volume of lexical items rather than striving for message equivalency. However, we know that the longer the processing time the less interpreting errors are made.[25]

It is important to remember that producing a multitude of signs to match English volume tires the eyes of the Deaf participants and generally fails to provide equivalent and accessible information. Further, truncating spoken English to match ASL, in which functional elements are sparsely used, results in unclear and ungrammatical English sentences and misrepresents the linguistic fluency of the Deaf signer.

[I] The natural rhythm of stress, intonation, pauses, phraseology, hesitations and redundancies.

For these reasons, we strongly urge the use of consecutive interpretation in one-on-one settings. It allows the interpreter to fully comprehend an utterance, drop form and execute a grammatically correct target language interpretation.

CHAPTER REVIEW
Key Points

In this chapter, we have given you an overview of the cognitive, interpersonal and monitoring processes involved when engaged in the act of interpretation.

Several interpreting models were identified, all with the same drawback: they are unable to demonstrate the simultaneity of the task and the multi-tasking required of the interpreter. The basic components of various interpreting models include:

- ✦ Intake of the source language utterance while maintaining awareness of environmental factors
- ✦ Grouping lexical and semantic units into workable units and holding them until there is enough input to make sense;
- ✦ Identify the speaker's intent/goals as well as explicit and implied ideas while assessing all contextual factors;
- ✦ The conscious and deliberate discarding of source language lexical units and communication behaviors;
- ✦ Identify the schema and experiential frame of participants, making a search for cultural equivalents where necessary;
- ✦ Search for target language elements that can be used to produce equivalent meaning and maintain communication dynamics;
- ✦ Review then express interpretation; and
- ✦ Monitors internal and external feedback to identify needed corrections

A Step-by-Step Look at the Process
1. Take in Source Language

Physical Requirements:
+ Be able to see/hear incoming utterance
+ Physical and mental endurance required to focus and sustain attending skills
+ Patience to wait — not to rush the process

Cognitive Competence:
+ Cloze skills in ASL and English
+ Ability to extract meaning from linguistic forms quickly and discard SL "dressing"
+ Ability to store, connect, and retrieve quickly

Linguistic and Cultural Requirements:
+ Bilingual competence — familiar with range of registers in each language
+ Bicultural competence — know how speakers accomplish various goals in culturally appropriate ways
+ Proper use of turn-taking, turn-retaining and reciprocal signals in each language/culture

Social Competence:
+ Social skills and cultural finesse to support effective interpersonal interactions in a variety of settings

2. Analyze Deep Structure Meaning

Cognitive Competence:
+ Ability to think critically — with clarity, precision, specificity, accuracy, relevance, consistency, depth, completeness and balance (according to Richard Paul)

✦ Includes critical listing skills in order to identify the speaker's *meaning/intent* — identifying assumptions the speaker may have regarding the listener's cohort memberships, schema and cultural background

✦ Also includes critical thinking skills — breaking the whole into parts, examining the detail, identifying new ideas/information and connections made to previous information in order to decipher any nuances and ambiguities present

✦ Requires disciplined reasoning, inferring and deducing in order to extract the message from the form of words/signs used to carry the message

✦ Interpreter must be aware of her/his own beliefs and biases in order to set them aside and truly reposition oneself to comprehend what is being said from the speaker's position

Linguistic and Cultural Requirements:

✦ Able to recognize various rhetorical structures in each language and use that knowledge to identify the speaker's goals and predict the logical path a speaker will use to accomplish those goals

✦ Able to recognize euphemisms, nuances, subtleties, innuendo, insinuation, indirect suggestions, metaphors and shades of meaning and to accurately comprehend the meaning intended and purpose for using these structures

✦ Adept at reading culture-based nonverbal signals that often accompany SL utterances

3. Apply Contextual/Schema Screen

Cohort Groups:

✦ Able to identify cohort membership by various participants that may be coloring or shaping original meaning and how it is being expressed

✦ Able to retain this information for TL formulation (in the event a cultural expansion is required for equivalence)

Schema:
  ✦ Ability to deduce similarities and differences in participant background and experiences that may be influencing the communication and interpersonal dynamics

Contextual Factors:
  ✦ Ability to predict contextual factors one may encounter and use these predictions to guide preparation prior to entering the interpreted event
  ✦ Adept at modifying predictions as needed and to use emerging contextual information to analyze how context is influencing message delivery

4. Formulate/Rehearse Equivalent Message

Linguistic Competence:
  ✦ Bilingual finesse, including mastery of wide range of lexicon, registers and discourse formulation

Cultural Competence:
  ➤ Bicultural expertise — able to appropriately express a variety of goals, engage in turn-taking, turn-maintaining, incorporation of emotional overlays, etc.

Linguistic and Cultural Adaptations:
  ✦ Able to use bicultural expertise in the construction of TL messages that compliment speaker goals and maintain dynamic equivalence
  ✦ Able to consistently make TL selections that clearly express intended information and speaker goals

Process Multi-tasking and Monitoring

Interpreters must be able to manage a variety of tasks while working the interpreting process outlined above, including:

> ➤ Confirming comprehension/asking for clarification;
> ➤ Slowing the process to allow for movement between simultaneous and consecutive modes;
> ➤ Checking for and correcting errors in output;
> ➤ Verifying consumer comprehension; and
> ➤ Verifying maintenance of interpersonal dynamics.

In addition, the interpreter must be assessing contextual factors, interpersonal dynamics and overall process management. Tasks here include:

✦ Working with rehearsed and/or read tests
✦ Working with uninitiated consumers
✦ When to use first person
✦ How to ask for clarification
✦ When to use consecutive, as opposed to simultaneous, form

THOUGHT QUESTIONS

1. Define schema from a personal perspective by identifying some elements of your own values, beliefs and assumptions.

2. Identify elements common to your own cohort group, similar to those found in Fig. 10-2. How might these experiences in your background differ from:

a) a 50-year old woman from Iran?
b) a Deaf man in his 80's?
c) a fellow student from a different ethnic and cultural group?

3. What significance does schema (including cohort group membership) have for interpreters?

4. What similarities and differences are there between interpretation between spoken languages and those experienced by sign language interpreters?

CD STUDY GUIDE

✦ The various activities in the guided Chapter 10 Study Guide on CD will allow you to understand the concepts in this chapter more completely and to apply them to your life experience. Work through the Chapter 10 Study Guide on CD, completing all activities, then submit to your instructor or share with your learning partner.

SUGGESTED ACTIVITIES

✦ Have different teams of students research the interpreter models mentioned in the chapter and share their findings with the class (Gerver, Ingram, Moser-Mercer, Cokely, Colonomos, Seleskovitch, Kitano, Pradis).

✦ Divide into groups of 3-4 students and construct your own "interpreting model" using construction paper, pictures from magazines, and other materials.

Endnotes

1. Patri (2000)
2. Roberts (1992)
3. Reviewed in Moser (1997)
4. Domingues and Ingram (1977)
5. Reviewed in Moser (1997)
6. Seleskovitch (1978)
7. Colonomos (1980, 1983, 1984, 1987, 1988)
8. Cokely (1985, 1992)
9. Reviewed in Moser (1997)
10. Ibid.
11. Kelly (1979)
12. Colonomos (1980, 1983, 1984, 1987, 1988)
13. Ibid.; Roberts (1992); Cokely (1985, 1992)
14. For more information see *ASL Faces: Reciprocal Signals, Affect Faces and Non-Manual Markers* by HMB Productions contact hmbprod@aol. com or Sign Enhancers.
15. Referred to as meta-notative qualities, contextual force, etc. in Isham (1986)
16. Seleskovitch (1991)
17. Paul (1993)
18. Ibid.
19. Ibid.
20. Ibid.
21. Ibid.
22. Ibid.
23. Shaboltz & Seyler, Eds. (1982)
24. Berger, Kathleen Stassen (1998)
25. Russell, D (2003, 2005); Alexiva (1991), Mikkelson (1995), Cokely (1985, 1992)

CHAPTER ELEVEN
The History and Professionalization
Of Interpreting

In this chapter, we present an overview of the history and advancement of interpreting as a profession. We will look at both the Registry of Interpreters for the Deaf (RID) and the Association of Visual Language Interpreters of Canada (AVLIC). Each organization is discussed in some depth, including their organizational meetings, some information regarding the constitution, bylaws, and officers of each, their respective certification systems, as well as some current issues facing each organization. This will be followed by a brief look at spoken language interpreters, interpreter education and significant legislation related to professional interpreters.

This information is fairly detailed for two reasons:

1. You will be a more responsible practitioner if you understand the historical evolution of our professional organizations and,
2. It will prepare you for one part of the written certification test administered by both organizations.

If you are studying for certification, you may choose to read only the information that is applicable to the organization whose test you will be taking.

HOW IT ALL BEGAN

Sign language interpreters have probably been around since the first deaf/signing cave person needed desperately to communicate something of substance to a hearing/speaking cave person. They probably grabbed a family member who could hear, talk and sign to serve as an intermediary.

The earliest record of sign language interpreters in Canada and the United States shows that they tended to:

1. Have Deaf parents or siblings,
2. Be teachers of the Deaf, or
3. Be members of the clergy.[1]

This is logical since there were no sign language classes or interpreter preparation programs prior to the late 1950's and early 1960's. Being paid for interpreting was unheard of in those early times and interpreters were not called upon very often.

The interpreting scene prior to 1964 was so vastly different from that which exists today that it is a strain on the imagination to contemplate it ... we did not work as interpreters, but rather volunteered our services as our schedules permitted. If we received any compensation it was freely given and happily accepted, but not expected.[2] Thus out of the goodness of their hearts, or obligation to family members, these individuals interpreted for an occasional medical appointment, wedding, funeral or such. Their services were deemed adequate at that period in our history.

The 1960s and '70s were revolutionary in many ways. It was an era of hippies, rock music, civil rights, women's lib and the war in Vietnam. It was also a time of increased social conscience, leading to attempts to include some minority groups who had been disenfranchised from the dream of equality. It was also a critical time in the field of sign language interpreting.

THE ESTABLISHMENT OF THE REGISTRY OF INTERPRETERS FOR THE DEAF (RID)[a]

One of the first times sign language interpreters from across the U.S. met was when they came to interpret for a national meeting held at Ball State Teacher's College (now Ball State University)

[a] Readers should check the RID web page for the most current revisions to all RID-related information (http://www.rid.org)

 Muncie, Indiana, June 14-17, 1964. The inter-
preters hired to work at that meeting agreed to
stay in Muncie for an additional day to discuss
the increased demand for interpreters and the
need to develop a list or registry of those who
were qualified to interpret nationally.[3] Edgar Lowell and Ralph
Hoag, prominent educators of the day, proposed the establishment of a national organization for sign language interpreters.
From that meeting the *National Registry of Professional Interpreters and Translators for the Deaf* was born. The name was
changed to the *Registry of Interpreters for the Deaf* the following
year when a constitution and bylaws were adopted and a code
of ethics drafted. With financial support from the Rehabilitation Services Administration, a national office was established,
a registry was printed, and investigation into testing and certification was begun.[4] The organization was incorporated in 1972.
Sign language interpreters from throughout the U.S., Canada,
Europe, Australia, and New Zealand joined RID — the first
such organization in the world.

The founders of RID were primarily people with Deaf family
members, teachers of the Deaf and clergy involved in Deaf ministries. This beginning has given rise to many issues we face today within the profession, including:

✦ The historic tendency of interpreters to take on a
"helper" role and how this role blocked the empowerment of Deaf community members.[b]
✦ The place of "non-native" interpreters (those who
have no Deaf family members); and
✦ Issues specific to those with Deaf family members.

Even the name of the organization has been the topic of
much deliberation since we now realize that the phrase
"for the Deaf" can be interpreted as being paternalis-

[b] Chapter Eight has a complete discussion of the philosophical shift from
helper, through machine and language facilitation, to the bilingual–bicultural philosophical approach.

tic or oppressive. Further, we do not interpret only "for the deaf," we also interpret for hearing clients and consumers.

When asked about this controversy, Lillian Beard — one of the founding members of RID — replied, "I can't believe there is such a debate about changing our name. When we decided upon the name, I was so proud of the acronym — RID — after all, having professional interpreters would hopefully *rid* the world of barriers for Deaf people!"[5]

Today, practitioners in the field commonly refer to themselves as sign language interpreters, visual language interpreters, or ASL/English interpreters rather than interpreters *for the deaf*.

The original purposes of RID included:

✦ Publishing a registry of interpreters;
✦ Investigating evaluation and certification systems; and,
✦ Informing the public about interpreting services.

Today, the *goal* of RID is to promote the profession of interpreting and transliterating American Sign Language and English, and their *mission* is to provide international, national, regional, state and local forums and an organizational structure for the continued growth and development of the profession of interpretation and transliteration of American Sign Language and English. RID is committed to increasing the number of interpreters, ensuring that they are qualified to practice and that they practice in accordance with professional standards. They accomplish this by:

✦ Providing training for new interpreters through the professional development committee and for professional interpreters through the Certification Maintenance Program;
✦ Continues testing and certification of interpreters through a National Testing System; and

✦ Supporting self-regulation like that found in other professional bodies through the Ethical Practices System.

RID is a member-run organization — members vote on organizational business biennially and on certain issues by mail ballot. Membership categories include:

1. Certified — limited to those individuals who hold any type of certification;
2. Associate — for those individuals who are working as interpreters but who are not yet certified;
3. Supporting — for individuals who are supportive of the goals of the organizations but who are not interpreters;
4. Student — for individuals enrolled full time in an interpreter education program; and
5. Organizational — for organizations, agencies, schools, and companies who wish to demonstrate support of the organization.

Every two years the members elect a board composed of Immediate-Past President, President, Vice President, Secretary-Treasurer, Member-At-Large, and one Regional Representative for each geographic region.[6]

Further, the structure of RID allows for affiliate chapters. Generally, there is one affiliate chapter per state although there are exceptions to that rule. All affiliate chapters must have "Registry of Interpreters for the Deaf" in the name of their organization,[7] must develop a set of by-laws which are compatible with those of the national organization, and must submit annual financial information to the national RID office to maintain recognized status.

There are many benefits to RID membership including:

✦ An automatic subscription to the monthly newsletter *RID VIEWS*;
✦ Reduced rates on purchases of RID publications;
✦ Opportunities to subscribe to health, life, disability, and malpractice insurance at group rates;
✦ The ability to participate in certification at membership rates;
✦ Networking with peer professionals;
✦ Access to many professional development opportunities;
✦ Access to consultation, direction, and advice from organizational leaders;
✦ A strong advocate as RID responds to local, regional and national professional issues upon request; and finally
✦ The benefit of increased national awareness of interpreting as RID serves as a "national voice" for sign language interpreters and participates in numerous Federal and State governmental meetings with various national organizations.

The Establishment of the Association of Visual Language Interpreters Of Canada (AVLIC)[c]

The evolution of sign language interpreting in Canada followed many of the same lines as those in the United States. Those involved in sign language interpreting were primarily individuals who had Deaf family members, hearing individuals who had developed friendships with Deaf individuals, or graduates of some type of formal interpreter education. There had been a gradual shift away from the "helper/friend/counselor" concept of the interpreter role toward that

---

[c] Readers should check the AVLIC web page for the most current revisions to all AVLIC-related information (http://www.avlic.ca)

of a "trained professional." With this shift, greater numbers of consumers were demanding quality, professional interpreting services. By the early 1970's, many sign language interpreters throughout Canada were members of RID and several affiliate chapters of RID were established. The Manitoba Registry of Interpreters for the Deaf (MRID) and the Alberta Chapter of the Registry of Interpreters for the Deaf (ACRID) were incorporated provincially in 1976 and 1977 respectively.

However, RID did not meet the needs of Canadian interpreters who longed for a professional association in Canada to help them improve their skills, establish standards for professional interpreters and through which Canadian interpreters could affiliate as professionals reflecting the needs unique to Canada.[8] In 1979 an inaugural conference was held in Ottawa to consider the feasibility of such a move with financial support from the National Department of Health and Welfare, the Canadian Hearing Society, the Canadian Association of the Deaf, the Western Institute for the Deaf and the Canadian Coordinating Council on Deafness. An organizational meeting was held in Winnipeg in November, 1979 and the Association of Visual Language Interpreters of Canada (AVLIC) was born. The involvement of both the Deaf and interpreting communities in the birth of the organization is a model of community consultation and collaboration which AVLIC has sought to maintain in all of its affairs to date.[9]

The founders of AVLIC were in the luxurious position of being able to learn from the trials and errors of RID, its sister organization. The name "Visual Language Interpreters" was adopted with great care by organizational founders.[10] Aware of the challenges encountered by RID regarding its name, Canadian interpreters decided not to include consumers in the organizational name. At the same time, they wanted a name that was broad enough to include those practitioners who provided oral and signed transliteration, as well as sign language interpretation. In addition, the Canadian organization needed a name that would include a greater variety of working languages, including French and LSQ.[11] The organizational name was adopted with the understanding that the term "visual language" includes languages and communication modes based on the use of sight. This term includes American Sign Language (ASL), La Langue des Signes Quebeçoise (LSQ), English-based sign systems, speech-reading and elements of gesture. It should be noted, however, that some controversy has arisen because the term "visual language" is not always understood to mean sign language by members of the Deaf community. Further, the name reflects only one of the languages interpreters work with.[12] Further, Deaf-Blind consumers have registered concern that it does not incorporate tactile interpreting.[13]

AVLIC has been a member-run organization from its inception in which members vote on organizational business biennially. AVLIC has three membership categories:

1. Active — which includes working interpreters, persons involved in interpreter education, or involved in the development of sign language programs or associations;
2. Supporting — for individuals who support the aims of the association; and
3. Chapter — for Provincial or regional organizations of sign language interpreters whose aims and objectives are parallel to those of AVLIC.

Only active members are allowed to vote on organizational issues.

AVLIC was established to accomplish several purposes, including:

1. Provide a professional milieu in which the nurturing of positive growth can take place;
2. Promote networking;
3. Develop personal knowledge, skills and ethical behavior, and
4. Advance the profession in general.

A basic premise of AVLIC's approach to these tasks is the active involvement and frequent consultation with the Canadian Association of the Deaf and the Canadian Cultural Society of the Deaf on all major issues.

The goals of AVLIC include:

1. Promoting standardization and uniform quality of interpreting services;
2. Providing an open forum for discussion of issues pertinent to visual language interpreters and consumer groups;
3. Advocating and providing for professional development opportunities;
4. Implementing and coordinating accreditation of Visual Language Interpreters; and
5. Encouraging the development of programs designed to facilitate the education and training of potential interpreters.

The AVLIC Board of Directors is composed of officers and committee coordinators. All individuals hold office for two years following their election or appointment. The nine-member Executive Board includes:

1. Past President
2. President
3. 2-Vice Presidents
4. Secretary
5. Treasurer
6. Evaluations Committee Chair
7. 2-members-at-large.[14]

There are many benefits to AVLIC membership including:

✦ An automatic subscription to the association bilingual newsletter *AVLIC NEWS* which is published quarterly;

+ The opportunity to participate in certification at membership rates;
+ Networking with peer professionals;
+ Discounts on national and provincial conferences;
+ Access to many professional development opportunities;
+ National dispute resolution process;
+ Consultation, direction and advice from organizational leaders;
+ Advocacy from Board members in response to issues raised by members; and
+ Increased national awareness regarding sign language interpreters at provincial and federal levels as AVLIC participates in committees and task forces.

Certification of Sign Language Interpreters

Evaluation of interpreters takes place on many levels:

+ As interpreting students in school when tested by teachers;
+ By prospective employers when applying for a job and in some cases when seeking a pay raise;
+ By certain governmental agencies (such as the State Commission for the Deaf or Medical Interpreting Services) to determine if an individual has entry-level competencies.

Certification of interpreters, on the other hand, is currently offered by two national interpreter organizations in North America: the Registry of Interpreters for the Deaf (RID) and the Association of Visual Language Interpreters of Canada (AVLIC).

RID Certification

One of the most formidable goals established by the founders of RID was the establishment of a national testing and certification system to verify the skills, ethics and professional behavior of

interpreters. The following is a discussion of the original certificates offered by RID from 1972 - 1988, 1989 and the current certificates introduced
in 2001. It is important to
be familiar with the various
certificates outlined below
because you will encounter
individuals who hold both
older and more recent certificates.

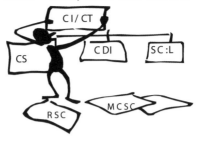

RID CERTIFICATION 1972–1989
Sign Language Certification

RID evaluation of sign language interpreters began in 1972. The
process included a live interview in front of a panel of five people
(interpreters and Deaf community members) and demonstration of two interpreting samples (ASL-to-English and English-
to-ASL), as well as two transliterating samples (English-based
signs-to-spoken English and spoken English-to-English-based
signs). Successful completion of all components of the evaluation with 75% or greater accuracy, resulted in the award of a
Comprehensive Skills Certificate (CSC). Successful completion
of the interview portion with 75% or greater accuracy and all
performance components of the evaluation with 60-74% accuracy, merited the award of an *Interpreting Certificate/Translit-
erating Certificate (IC/TC)*. If an individual completed the interview portion with 75% or greater accuracy and only one of
the performance areas (interpretation or transliteration) with
60% or greater accuracy, s/he was awarded either an *Interpreting Certificate (IC)* or a *Transliterating Certificate (TC)*.

Deaf individuals could become certified by successfully completing the interview and the two sign-to-English portions of
the evaluation, modified to accept a signed paraphrase of the
source signed message, with 75% accuracy or above. They were
awarded a *Reverse Skills Certificate (RSC)*. All evaluation results

were somewhat diagnostic in that the applicant was told which skill areas were stronger and which were weaker.

Certificates expired after five-years unless the holder:

1. Took a second evaluation, or
2. Successfully completed a specialist certificate.

An interpreter was considered "fully certified" if s/he held either a CSC (hearing) or an RSC (Deaf). A person was considered "partially certified" if s/he held an IC, TC, or an IC/TC.

A revised testing system was implemented in 1989 and several significant changes were made. The live interview and performance assessment was eliminated and replaced with a two-stage exam including a written test and a video taped skills demonstration.

Hearing applicants took a multiple-choice test composed of 150 questions. The written exam was offered two times per year at Regional Testing Centers. Applicants had to get 98 out of the 150 questions correct to pass the test.

When an applicant passed the written test, s/he became a candidate for certification and could take the skills test for transliteration, interpretation or both. Each performance test was made up of three segments:

1. A sign-to-voice segment requiring the candidate to simultaneously interpret a text into spoken English;
2. A voice-to-sign segment in which the interpreter simultaneously interprets (for the CI exam) or transliterates (for the CT exam) a spoken English lecture; and
3. An interactive segment in which the candidate interprets (for the CI exam) or transliterates (for the CT exam) for a life-like interactive scenario involving a hearing and a Deaf client.

Successful performance on the skills exam led to the Certificate of Interpretation (CI) or the Certificate of Transliteration (CT). A person was considered "fully certfied" if s/he held both the CI and CT.

Oral Transliteration (OIC:C)

From 1979 to 1983, RID awarded certification for oral transliteration (termed oral interpretation at that point in our history). The testing format was identical to that of sign language interpreting certification. However, the performance segments included:[15]

1. Paraphrasing and transliterating a spoken message to a Deaf or hard-of-hearing person depending on speech reading; and
2. Demonstrating the ability to lip-read a Deaf or hard of hearing person using non-auditory speech and mouth movements.[16]

Successful completion of all components of the evaluation with 75% accuracy or above, resulted in the award of an *Oral Interpreter Certificate: Comprehensive (OIC:C)*. Partial certificates were awarded if applicants passed the interview with 75% or greater accuracy but only scored 60-74% accuracy in the skills portion (*Oral Interpreter Certificate: Spoken-to-Visible (OIC:S/ V and Oral Interpreter Certificate: Visible-to-Spoken (OIC:V/S)*. Deaf individuals could become orally certified by successfully completing the interview and the visible-to-spoken portions of the evaluation.

Like the sign language certificates, oral transliterating certificates expired after five years unless the holder took a second evaluation or successfully completed another specialist certificate.

Specialist Certificates

In addition to the certificates defined above, individuals who held a generalist certificate (*CI, CT, CI-CT, RSC or CSC*) could seek "specialist certificates." Those certificates (offered by RID between 1975 and 1978) included:

1. Specialist Certificate: Legal (SC:L)

2. Specialist Certificate: Performing Arts (SC:PA)

3. Masters Comprehensive Skills Certificate (MCSC)

A person holding one of these certificates completed specialized training and demonstrated a satisfactory level of performance in the specialty area tested.

CURRENT GENERALIST CERTIFICATION (2001–present)
Generalist Sign Language Certification: Deaf

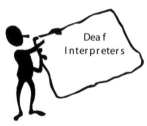

Beginning in 2001 a new examination was introduced by RID for those individuals who are Deaf or hard of hearing seeking certification as a Deaf interpreter. The Deaf interpreter certification exam (Certified Deaf Interpreter — CDI) tests one's knowledge of Deaf interpreting and professionalism, as well as the ability to:

1. Interpret simultaneously from English to ASL;
2. Interpret consecutively in an interaction between a Deaf and hearing person;
3. Interpret from print English to ASL; and
4. Mirror information accurately (for Deaf-Blind or relay interpreting settings).

The written exam for the CDI is given on the same dates and at the same locations as the other certification written exams.

The institution of this test is an exciting addition to the "traditional" interpreting exams. For example, in the knowledge test applicants view signed questions and several possible answers from a compact disc on a computer monitor. Responses may be given in either ASL or written on an answer sheet (the test taker may select the format most comfortable for them). This is also the first time the skills actually used by Deaf interpreters have been tested.

The CDI replaced all existing Reverse Skills Certificates (RSC) and Certified Deaf Interpreter-Provisional (CDI-P) certificates effective 2003.

Generalist Sign Language Certification: Hearing

The National Interpreter Certification (NIC) was developed by an NAD-RID joint taskforce and is administered by the RID National Testing System. Like previous certifications, the NIC has a two-step process: the written exam and the performance exam, both of which are based on the following ten competencies:

✦ Ability to assess interpreting situations to determine if one is qualified to interpret in that assignment;
✦ Preparation for assignments, including determining logistics and the purpose of the interaction for all parties involved;
✦ Maintaining competence in the field of interpreting;
✦ Applying the Code of Ethics to interpreting situations
✦ Demonstration of awareness and sensitivity to diverse groups;
✦ Ability to facilitate communication via the interpreting process;
✦ Apply appropriate communication mode and linguistic register;

✦ Construct equivalent discourse in the target language while monitoring message comprehension and feedback to modify interpretation accordingly;
✦ Use ASL proficiently;
✦ Use English proficiently.

The written exam is administered on the first Saturday of June and December each year. In addition, the written exam can be taken throughout the year in a computer-administered setting, Test takers are given a maximum of 3-hours to complete the 150 question exam.

An individual who passes the written exam becomes a *"candidate for certification"* and will be allowed to take the NIC performance test at any time over the following five years.

The performance portion of the NIC testing process is comprised of two parts: the professionalism interview and the skills exam. In the interview portion, candidates are given five signed ethical questions based on typical situtions an interpreter might confront. Test takers may select the interviewer from five options. Questions are presented both in sign and in print English. Responses are to be provided in sign language, either with or without voice. Answers are graded on the content of the ethical responses, *not* on the candidate's signing skills.The grading rubric for the interview can be found on the RID website.

There are five interpreting scenarios in the skills portion of the exam, some involving interactive interpreting (sign-to-voice and voice-to-sign), others requiring only voice-to-sign or sign-to-voice. Each scenario provides an introduction to the speaker(s)/signer(s) and audience members, as well as some prep materials for the interpreter to consider before beginning the interpretation.

Candidates for Certification are given the option of taking the interview first or the skills portion first.

Three levels of certification are awarded, each of which represents professional-level certification and all are eligible to take any specialist certificates offered by RID.

✦ **NIC** - demonstrating professional-level ethics, as well as standard interpreting and transliterating skills;

✦ **NIC-Advanced** -- demonstrating professional-level ethics and advanced interpreting and transliterating skills;

✦ **NIC-Masters** -- demonstrating advanced professional-level ethics, as well as advanced interpreting and transliterating skills.

EDUCATIONAL REQUIREMENTS. Effective June 30, 2008, candidates for certification applying for the performance portion of the certification exam will have to meet minimum educational prerequisites. In 2008, all hearing applicants must have the minimum of an AA degree in order to take the performance portio of any RID certification. Beginning 2012, hearing applicants must have a BA degree and deaf applicants must have an AA degree. By 2016, all applicants must hold a Bachelor's degree.

Oral Transliteration (OTC) This examination tests one's ability to transliterate for a variety of oral deaf individuals in a variety of settings. Skills required include:

1. Conveying a spoken English transliteration that is accessible to someone using speech reading strategies;
2. Voicing over an oral deaf individual as s/he speaks audibly; and
3. Facilitating an interactive setting involving an oral deaf person.

This exam is set up like the generalist tests with a written exam followed by a skills demonstration. The written exam is made up of 125 multiple-choice questions in six content areas. The content areas include:

1. History of oral education and the oral deaf community (12%)
2. Language and Communication (8%)
3. Speech Production (12%)
4. Transliteration (31%)
5. Speech reading (20%)
6. Professional issues (17%)

Applicants must get a score of 89 to pass. The written exam must be passed before one is eligible to take the skills exam.

 SPECIALIST CERTIFICATE: Legal (SC:L) If an individual wants to be certified as a legal interpreter, s/he must either currently possess a valid legal interpreting certificate issued prior to 1987 or satisfy all of the following eligibility criteria in at least one category area:

✦ Category #1: Possess valid NIC, CSC, CI and CT, or MCSC; hold a Bachelor's degree in any field or an Associate of Arts degree in interpreting; evidence of five years of interpreting experience (post RID certification) including documentation of at least 50 hours of legal interpreting or mentorship and 30 hours of formal legal training.

✦ Category #2: Possess valid NIC, CSC, CI and CT, or MCSC; hold an Associate of Arts degree in any field; evidence of five years of interpreting experience (post RID certification) including documentation of at least 75 hours of legal interpreting or mentorship and 50 hours of formal legal training.

✦ Category #3: Possess valid NIC, CSC, CI and CT, or MCSC; evidence of five years of interpreting experience (post RID certification) including documentation of at least 100 hours of legal interpreting or mentorship and 70 hours of formal legal training.
✦ Category #4: Hold valid CDI or Provisional SC:L.

This certificate, like others offered by RID, includes both a written and performance exam. The written exam is made up of 100 multiple-choice questions; applicants must get at least 77 answers correct to pass. The topic areas covered in the written exam include:

1. Language
2. Judicial system
3. Team interpreting
4. Professional issues

Successful completion of the written test qualifies an individual to take a four-segment skills test based on the following legal settings:

1. Miranda warning
2. A courtroom scene (criminal trial)
3. Qualifying an interpreter[d]
4. Jury instructions

AVLIC Certification[17]

The Association of Visual Language Interpreters began to investigate the development of a national certification system almost immediately after incorporating and maintained frequent consultation from the Canadian Association of the Deaf and the Canadian Cultural Society of the Deaf throughout. The ten-year development of the Canadian Evaluation System (CES) reflected the changing body of knowledge available regarding psycholinguistic standards, test domains and trends in the field. The

---

[d] A formal process of determining if an interpreter is deemed "qualified" to provide interpretation for a particular court process.

CES is a result of AVLIC's long-standing commitment to the standardization of interpreter qualifications in Canada.

Adopted by AVLIC members in 1988, the CES test was first administered in 1990. The test was revised in 2004 to reflect member feedback and developments in the field. The goal of the CES is to accredit interpreters who can demonstrate message equivalent interpretation between American Sign Language and English.

Only ASL/English interpretation is tested. This is done because the committee who developed the test determined that:

1. The components and skills specific to transliteration have not been researched or clearly defined, therefore it is not currently feasible to test transliteration; and
2. Interpretation forms the foundation for transliteration, thus individuals providing transliteration must demonstrate an understanding of Deaf culture and be able to function in ASL.

There are four phases to AVLIC certification:

✦ PHASE ONE: Written Test of Knowledge (WTK)
The written test of knowledge (WTK) includes 75 multiple choice questions regarding the history and organization of AVLIC-related organizations, the field of sign language interpreting, and language and culture. Test takers must score at least 70% to pass the WTK.

This test is offered two times per year (June and November) in a variety of centers and is proctored by an individual appointed by the national AVLIC office. Candidates are allowed two hours in which to complete the test. Applicants are required to hold active membership status.

The WTK is made up of 75 multiple choice questions in three categories: AVLIC and related organizations; interpreting; and culture and language. Applicants must correctly answer at least 70 questions.[e]

If an individual passes the WTK, s/he is qualified to take the test of interpretation (TOI). If the member allows her/his membership to lapse, their WTK is automatically invalidated and the member will have to re-write the exam when seeking certification so it is important to maintain active membership status. It should also be noted that passing the WTK does not constitute "partial certification." In the AVLIC system, an individual is only able to claim certification status after taking and passing the TOI

✦ PHASE TWO: Preparation
This phase is to assist test takers by providing a foundation for the Test of Interpretation (TOI). There are two mandetory workshops, both focusing on discourse analysis. One focuses on interpreting narratives and the other focuses on interpreting interactive interviews. The workshop exercises are fashioned after the actual Test of Interpretation.

Prerequisite to the workshops is completion of pre-readings and a pre-workshop taping session that is used for evaluation of ASL and message equivalence using a rating system of "0" - not demonstrated; "1" inconsistently demonstrated, and "2" consistently demonstrated. The components being measured are similar to the criteria used in the TOI. The interpreted sample is returned to candidates

---

[e] The current WTK was implemented in November 1999. Members who passed the previous version must take and pass the TOI no later than December 2004 in order to avoid being required to rewrite the WTK.

on workshop weekend with feedback, but is not intended to be an in-depth diagnostic assessment.

✦ PHASE THREE: Test of Interpretation
After completing phase two, candidates may apply for the Test of Interpretation (TOI) which verifies whether an individual is at or above the standard in terms of message equivalence interpretation between English and ASL.

The test includes several samples of dialogue and narrative discourse, typical of that encountered by working interpreters in "generalist" settings. Prior to the test date, candidates will receive outlines for the scenarios they will interpret on the test. They will also be able to view warm up video materials via password protected web streaming.

The test reflects the kind of work a generalist would be ex-

pected to handle and contains Deaf consumers reflecting diversity of language including various ASL contact varieties and English-like signing.

The candidate's performance is videotaped. Candidates have the option of also submitting a video recording of narrative and interactive interview (maximum of 15-min. in length) that can be considered by raters as supplemental evidence of a successful interpretation, however, these samples will only be viewed by the Message Equivalency raters when the work on the TOI is considered borderline.

✦ PHASE FOUR: Certification Maintenance
An individual who achieves the national standard of interpretation will be awarded an American Sign Language/English Certificate of Interpretation (COI). The certificate remains in effect so long as the member adheres to the AVLIC Code of Ethics and maintains annual active membership with fees paid in full. In addition, documentation must be submitted

by current COI interpreters annually. This phase will be in full operation in 2010 (approximately). .

Educational Interpreter Performance Assessment (EIPA)

This tool is a dioagniostioc instrument developed for use with educational interpreters working with children and young adults. It looks at transliteration (including a range of English signing systems) and interpretation and proviodes diagnostic feedback to test takers. Further, it can be geared to look at interpreting samples at various grade levels, using samples from natural working environments. One might be awarded a proficiency level of 1-5, along with professional development recommendations, In 2006, the RID Board of Directors voted to recognize inividuals holding EIPA Level 3 or greater as certified interpreters. As this book goes to press, there is a great deal of debate among RID members regarding this decision.

A Look At The Field Of
Spoken Language Interpretation

The field of spoken language interpretation evolved in a very different way than the field of sign language interpretation. From the beginning, professional spoken language interpreters have been involved primarily in international political events beginning with the Paris Peace Conference in 1919, following World War I. Those early practitioners were not trained to work as interpreters. They were experienced civil servants, journalists, and diplomats with fluency in four or more languages, and probably had the ability to comprehend several more, who were suddenly thrust into international politics.[18]

The normal process during those early days was consecutive interpretation but as the field grew and progressed, technology made simultaneous interpreting possible. The first headphone system was developed during the late 1920's.[19] This system enabled interpreters to provide spoken language interpretation to individuals in the audience in a variety of languages without auditory interference to the participants. The system was first used in 1931 at the League of Nations Assembly. It was im-

283

proved and was a regular part of the Nuremberg trials following World War II. Later, the addition of a soundproof booth at the rear or to the side of the meeting room enhanced the interpreters' ability to concentrate on their task without visual, physical, or auditory interference. At the same time this reduced the auditory distraction to those people seated in the vicinity of spoken language interpreters. This is the system that is found today at the United Nations and multi-lingual conferences.

In the late 1970's and during the '80s, as international trade increased, spoken language interpreters found themselves involved more and more in business interactions. In recent years, spoken language interpreters have entered into community interpreting settings — going into medical, legal, and social service settings.

Today, individuals who want to become spoken language interpreters, usually get a Bachelor's degree in one of the languages with which they will work — German, for example. Then they are required to live in the country of that language for two years before returning to get a master's degree in interpreting. Spoken language interpreters also work almost exclusively from their second language into their first or native language.

There is some formal testing and certification of spoken language interpreters, beginning in 1978 when the Court Interpreters Act was passed by the U.S. federal government requiring that all non-English speaking litigants in federal court proceedings be provided with certified interpreters.

The Emergence Of Sign Language Interpreter Education Programs

When legislative and political initiatives first began to appear in the early 1960's mandating the presence of interpreters for Deaf people in certain settings, individuals were drafted from among those who had been serving as informal, voluntary interpreters. Because their numbers did not meet the need, educational programs sprang up. Initially these were funded under the auspices of the federal government and later through vocational and community college programs.

At that time, the profession was faced with a dilemma. In order to train interpreters, students had to learn ASL. Sign language had never been taught formally, partly because there had never been a demand to teach it and partly because of the myth that hearing people couldn't learn sign language. Since American Sign Language had not yet been identified as an authentic language, signs were seen as an iconic and an idiosyncratic "slang". Sign classes throughout 1960-1970 consisted of students memorizing lists of English words with parallel "signs" for each word.

Further, no one knew how to teach interpreting. We simply knew we needed more interpreters. Most of the early interpreter educators were interpreters themselves but virtually none had any academic preparation to teach adults or to develop curricula prior to entering a classroom for the first time. The first courses for potential interpreters ranged from two to six weeks in length and primarily offered students an opportunity to learn more signs for "advanced" English words — medical terms, sexual signs, etc., rather than learning how to interpret, per se. Feedback given to students who attempted to interpret a text was essentially a list of the words the student had signed incorrectly.

A number of certified interpreters today came out of this chaotic period — not so much because the educational programs provided what they needed, but because they had the determination to stick with it through the hard-knocks school of frustration, doing the best they could. They were frequently given encouragement from members of the Deaf community who encouraged them, helping them learn the cultural "ropes" and upgrade their skills.

In the early 1970's, the U.S. government granted funds to six institutions[20] with the challenge of providing interpreter education throughout the country. These programs pioneered what we currently know as interpreter education. They offered some full and part-time academic programs. In most cases, their students were individuals who already knew sign language and who wanted to develop their interpreting skills. Unfortunately, because no one had done formal research on interpreting to determine the component parts of the task, the "successful" educational experience was rare.

A Revolution In Interpreter Education

In 1965, William Stokoe published his seminal text, *A Dictionary of American Sign Language on Linguistic Principles* which eventually led to the formal recognition of American Sign Language as a fully rule-governed language. This discovery and related research has had a far-reaching impact on interpreting and interpreter education. It was reasoned that if ASL was indeed a language, Deaf people must therefore have a unique culture. If Deaf people had their own language and culture, it stood to reason that an individual seeking to become an interpreter would need to be fluent in that language and knowledgeable of the culture in order to effectively work with members of the Deaf community. From there, the reasoning went, if interpreters were working with a language/culture group, they may, in fact, have something in common with spoken language interpreters. Thus began a revolution in the field of sign language interpretation and sign language interpreter education.

As more was learned about the process of interpreting, the amount of time required to teach American Sign Language and the complexity of needed interpreter skills, interpreter education moved from short-term courses (3- to-6 months) to two and four-year degree programs.[21] It is anticipated that in the near future — like those who go into spoken language interpreting — one who wishes to become a sign language interpreter will need to earn a bachelor's degree in American Sign Language (ASL) and a master's degree in interpretation.[22]

Legislative Initiatives

The field of both spoken and sign language interpretation has been significantly influenced by federal legislation in the United States. This is true because these various pieces of legislation have mandated states, federal agencies, and local entities receiving federal money to provide services to Deaf and hard-of-hearing individuals. In some cases, these services were mandated as a result of broadened inclusion referred to as "access." While Canada does not have similar federal legislation, they have likewise benefited from the U.S. legislation since it set a standard to guide provincial and federal standards.

Important federal initiatives are presented in chronological order in Fig. 11-1 on this and the following pages

FIG. 11-1 Significant Legislative Initiatives		
1965	PL 89-333 The Vocational Rehabilitation Act of 1965	Identified sign language interpreting as a service for Deaf clients of vocational rehabilitation for the first time, marking the beginning of paid interpreting opportunities for sign language interpreters in the U.S.
1973	PL 93-112 Rehab Act of 1973 Section 501(employment practices of the fed government) Section 503 (fed contractors) Section 504 (recipients of federal assistance)	Defines "handicapped individuals" and their rights. Mandates fully accessible rehabilitation services to members of all disability groups. This means that agencies and institutions receiving federal funds must be accessible — post secondary institutions, business, criminal legal proceedings, and medical settings, etc. have to provide sign language interpreters and other forms of access accommodation.

FIG. 11-1 Significant Legislative Initiatives		
1975	PL 94-142 .Education for All Handicapped Children Act[23]	Requires that disabled children be educated in the "least restrictive environment." This has led to the widespread integration of disabled children within regular classrooms and has resulted in a proliferation of interpreting jobs within elementary and secondary schools.
1978	PL 95-539 The Court Interpreters Act of 1978	Mandates the use of only certified interpreters when non-English speaking litigants are involved in Federal court.
1978	PL 95-602 Rehabilitation Amendments of 1978	Sec. 101 — mandates the use of personnel trained in the use of the client's native language or mode of communication. Sec. 304 provides money that currently funds 12 federal interpreter education centers.
1991	Americans with Disabilities Act	Applies the concept of "equal access" to the private business sector. ADA requires businesses of a certain minimum size to provide interpreters to Deaf employees, TTYs, etc.

There is currently a move toward gaining state/provincial regulation of sign language interpreters and oral transliterators. The need for such regulation is a "result" of the Americans With Disabilities Act (ADA) which caused the demand for interpreting services to soar to unprecedented heights."[24] It is also being fueled by members of the Deaf community and parents of Deaf children and youth who are demanding minimum standards for interpreters in mainstream educational settings. According to Hall,[25] states have responded by passing legislation that either recognizes existing interpreter standards/certifications such as RID or by assigning the authority of testing and licensing interpreters to a state board or agency.

CHAPTER REVIEW
Key Points
Early interpreters generally worked on a volunteer basis and tended to:

1. Have Deaf parents or siblings;
2. Be teachers of the Deaf; or
3. Be members of the clergy.

Spoken language interpreting — first looked upon as a profession at the Paris Peace Conference in 1919, following World War I.

Early practitioners were experienced civil servants, journalists, and diplomats with fluency in four or more languages who were suddenly thrust into international politics.

Interpreter education for spoken language interpreters generally requires a Bachelor's degree in the language(s) they are specializing in, living two years in the country of those language(s), then completing a Master's degree in interpretation and translation.

Visual language interpreters generally complete formal education ranging from 2-year Diplomas and Associate of Arts degrees, although Bachelor's and Master's degrees in ASL/English interpretation are becoming more common.

Comparing Spoken and Sign Language Interpreters
The process of interpreting is the same regardless of whether one is working with spoken languages or signed languages or a combination of spoken/signed languages.

Spoken language interpreters have a much shorter history of testing, certification and professional associations than sign language interpreters.

In addition to the difference in educational preparation, spoken language interpreters also work almost exclusively in settings where their L2 is the source language and the target language is their L1. Sign language interpreters, on the other hand, work as much or more from their first into their second language. Spoken language interpreters are generally paid better than sign language interpreters, possibly because their clients have always been viewed as coming from a language-culture group whereas sign language clients have historically been labeled as handicapped or disabled rather than as a language-culture group.

Legislation: The field of spoken and sign language interpretation has been significantly influenced by federal legislation in the United States. See the chart to review key laws.

Registry Of Interpreters For The Deaf (RID)
Established — 1964 at Ball State Teacher's College.

Certification
RID uses a three-arm approach to cetification, including (a) The National Testing System (NTS), (b) Certification Maintenance Program (CMP); and (c) the Ethical Practices System (EPS).

RID certification 1972–1989
Deaf Interpreters:
Reverse Skills Certificate (RSC) — awarded to Deaf individuals who successfully completed the interview and the two sign-to-voice portions of the evaluation with 75% accuracy or above.

Hearing Interpreters:
+ **Comprehensive Skills Certificate (CSC)** — awarded upon successful completion of all segments at a 75% level of accuracy. Partial Certification was awarded when a person earned scored 75% on the interview portion and 60-74% on all performance components. In that event, they could earn only one certificate (IC or TC) if that was the only portion of the test passed at a high enough level or both

the IC and TC.

✦ **Oral Interpreter Certificate: Comprehensive (OIC:C)** — required an interview plus four performance segments with 75% or more. In this test, candidates demonstrate ability to paraphrase and transliterate a spoken English message as well as the ability to speech-read an oral deaf adult and present the message in spoken English This certificate was offered 1979-1983.

✦ **Speciality Certificates** -- Between 1975-1978, specialty certificates were awarded, including the Specalist Certificate: Legal (SC:L) and performing arts (SC:PA).

RID certification 1988 – 2000
Hearing Interpreters

✦ **Certificate of Interpretation (CI) and Certificate of Transliteration (CT)**. After passing the written exam, the candidate has 5 years to take the performance exam. There were two performance exams -- one for interpretation and another for transliteration. An interpreter could be partially certified (CI or CT) or fully certified (CI and CT). This test will be phased out in December 2008. After that date, only the NIC will be offered.

RID certification 2000 – present
Hearing Interpreters:

✦ **NAD-RID National Interpreting Certificate (NIC)**

Part one — written test on 10 competency areas. After passing the written exam, the candidate has 5 years to take the performance exam which includes two parts: professionalism interview and skills exam. Successful candidates may be awarded:

✓ NIC

✓ NIC-Advanced

✓ NIC-Masters

All three categiorioes are considered fully certified since they measure professional competence in interpretation, transliteration and professionalism.

✦ Certificate of Oral Transliteration (OTC)

✓ written exam in six content areas

✓ skills exam

Deaf Interpreters:
✦ Certificated Deaf Interpreter (CDI)
Part one — written test on knowledge of Deaf interpreting and professionalism. After passing the written exam, the candidate has 5 years to take the skills exam covering:

✓ Interpret simultaneously from English to ASL

✓ Interpret consecutively in an interaction between a Deaf and hearing person

✓ Interpret from print English to ASL

✓ Mirror information accurately (e.g. Deaf-blind or relay interpreting settings.

Current specialist RID certification
Specialist Certificate: Legal (SC:L)
Exam includes written and skills component. Applicant must either hold valid legal interpreting certificate issued prior to 1987 or satisfy all criteria in at least one qualifying category:

✓ **Category #1:** (a) possess valid NIC, CSC, CI and CT, or MCSC; (b) hold a BA or BS in any field or an AA in interpreting; (c) 5 years of interpreting experience (post RID certification): (d) at least 50 hours of legal interpreting/mentoring and 30 hours of formal legal training.

✓ **Category #2**: (a) Possess valid NIC, CSC, CI and CT, or MCSC; (b) AA in any field; (c) 5 years of interpreting experience (post RID certification); (d) at least 75 hours of legal interpreting/mentoring and 50 hours of formal legal training.

✓ **Category #3**: (a) Possess valid NIC, CSC, CI and CT, or MCSC; (b) five years of interpreting experience (post basic certification); (c) at least 100 hours of legal interpreting/ mentoring and 70 hours of formal legal training.

✓ **Category #4**: Hold valid Provisional SC;L

Association Of Visual Language Interpreters Of Canada (AVLIC)

Established — November, 1979 in Winnipeg, Manitoba.

"Visual Language" includes languages and communication modes based on the use of sight, including American Sign Language (ASL), La Langue des Signes Quebeçoise (LSQ), sign systems, speech-reading and elements of gesture.

Certification

✦ Implemented in 1990, revised in 2003

✦ Only tests ASL/English interpretation

✦ **PHASE ONE: WTK** — written test of knowledge includes questions regarding:

✓ History and organization of AVLIC and related organizations;

✓ The field of sign language interpreting, language and culture.

✦ **PHASE TWO: Preparation**

✓ Participate in two required preparation workshops

✓ Study prep material

✦ **PHASE THREE: Test of Interpretation (TOI)**
When an individual completes Phase Two, they are qualified to take the test of interpretation (TOI) which is scored in three domains:

✓ ASL as a target language;

✓ English as a target language;

✓ Message equivalency

✦ **PHASE FOUR: Certification Maintenance**

✓ Maintain membership

✓ Adhere to Code of Professional Conduct

✓ Submit annual documentation of professional development activities

THOUGHT QUESTIONS

1. Describe the history and evolution of RID and AVLIC. In what ways are the two organizations similar? Different?

2. Discuss the general certification process of RID. In what ways are the two organizations similar? Different?

3. Explain the concept of specialist certification. What specialist certifications are/have been available? Do you think specialization is beneficial to the field, considering the shortage of interpreters?

4. How is the field of spoken language interpretation similar to that of sign language interpretation? How are they different?

5. Do interpreters work only for the Deaf client present in a communication event? Primarily for the Deaf client?

6. Why is it important for an interpreter to receive feedback?

7. Compare and contrast the interpreters who pioneered the field and those in the field today.

8. Is it beneficial for interpreters in the U.S. to know about interpreter organizations and certification in Canada and for interpreters in Canada to know about interpreter organizations and certification in the U.S.? Why or why not?

CD STUDY GUIDE

✦ The various activities in the guided Chapter 11 Study Guide on CD will allow you to understand the concepts in this chapter more completely and to apply them to your life experience. Work through the Chapter 11 Study Guide on CD, completing all activities, then submit to your instructor or share with your learning partner.

SUGGESTED ACTIVITIES

✦ Develop a directory of organizations in your area which are involved with Deaf people or interpreters.

✦ Invite a panel of spoken and sign language interpreters to the class to discuss their experiences and answer questions.

✦ Attend a meeting of the local chapter of RID or AVLIC. Make notes on topics of current concern to the local chapter. Interview one or two members about their opinions on the topic and make a presentation to the class.

✦ Volunteer to work on a committee of the local AVLIC chapter. Reflect on your experiences and write a paper about the advantages of involvement in the professional association.

Endnotes

1. Groce (1985); Frishberg (1986); Domingue and Ingram (1977)

2. Fant (1990)

3. Beard (1976, 1989, 2001)

4. Frishberg (1986)

5. Beard (1976, 1989, 2001)

6. A region may consist of one or more states/provinces. The by-laws dictate that regions must be divided in such a way that there are approximately an equal number of votes per region.

7. An exception is made for the Texas Society of Interpreters for the Deaf (TSID) because they were established prior to RID.

8. Letourneau (1987)

9. Russell & Malcolm (1991)

10. Letourneau (1993)

11. It should be noted that in its 2001 Annual General Meeting, members of AVLIC voted to stop providing organizational material in French/LSQ and to suspend work on the French/LSQ certification exam. This decision was a bilateral decision made due to the financial condition of both AVLIC and the Quebec chapter of AVLIC.

12. Evans (1993)

13. Russell & Malcolm (1991)
14. The structure of the AVLIC Board was changed in 1998, effective at the 2002 annual general meeting.
15. Frishberg (1986)
16. Frishberg (1986), p. 99
17. AVLIC Webpage, "Evaluations," July 11, 2001
18. Frishberg (1986)
19. Ibid.
20. Those institutions included: California State University, Northridge; Gallaudet College; New York University; St. Paul Technical Vocational Institute; Seattle Central Community College; and the University of Tennessee, Knoxville.
21. Frishberg (1986); Kanda (1987)
22. McIntire (1984); Kanda (, 1987)
23. There is a great deal of controversy about the impact of this legislation on Deaf children. Many Deaf organizations and advocates are fighting to define mainstreaming as the most restrictive environment for many Deaf children due to the significance of the communication barriers they encounter in mainstream settings.
24. Hall "State Regulation of Interpreters: Critical Issues and Model legislation" RID Policy Paper.
25. Ibid.

CHAPTER TWELVE
Principles of Professional Practice

This chapter introduces the concept of ethical and professional behavior as it relates to the practice of sign language interpretation. This is a critical topic and it should be noted that this chapter merely serves as an introduction and overview. If you want to be an interpreter, you should take additional courses in which to assess 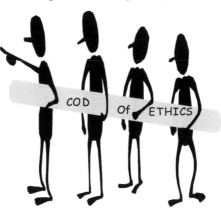 and develop your ability to think critically and reviewing **meta-ethical principles** and the codes of conduct set out by other professions.[a]

Further, as a professional practitioner, you will find there are no easy or simplistic answers and your sense of appropriate responses will grow and change with your experience. You will need to participate in on-going dialogue with your colleagues as you encounter complex and multi-layered situations on a daily basis.

WHAT DISTINGUISHES PROFESSIONALS?

When a used car salesman tells you, "*This* is the car for you," or the sales clerk in the store says, "That dress is *perfect* for you!" you are fully aware that they are motivated primarily by self-interest. After all, they will gain a commission if you buy their product. As business people, they are keenly aware that the profit margin is the value driving the marketplace in which they work. But when a doctor tells you, "You need this surgery," or an

---

[a] There are several resources available to you, including Decisions? Decisions! by Dr. Jan Humphrey, one of the authors of this text.

interpreter coordinator says, "You need six interpreters for this job," you assume that recommendation stems from that individual's professional judgment based on what is best for you. Professionals like the doctor or interpreter distinguish themselves from individuals in business or in a trade because professionals subscribe to a higher standard of behavior than that motivated purely by profit or self-interest.

If you look up the roots of these terms you will find that in ancient times, a *trades person* literally trod the ground, selling wares from place to place. *Professionals*, on the  other hand, distinguished themselves by holding their clients interests paramount thus *professing* values higher than those of the profit-based market place.

A renowned ethicist[1] notes that a profession is distinguished by three essential features:

1. A profession has a *special monopoly* over the right to provide a particular service through licensure or certification;
2. A profession has a *defined (limited) scope of practice* and *a related body of knowledge*. Whereas a business can shift from selling shoes to selling crystal figurines, a teacher cannot suddenly start practicing medicine and call herself a doctor; and
3. Professionals adhere to a clearly articulated *set of values or code of ethics.*

 By definition, the public expects professionals to be trustworthy individuals. The attorney, doctor, minister, teacher, counselor and interpreter are all expected to know how to do their work, to come to the task prepared, and to be worthy of the trust placed in them by their clients, patients, parishioners or students. Professionals are expected to deal with sensitive information in a discrete manner and they are expected to avoid emotional involvement that might work to the detriment of their clientele. Further, most professionals work in the privacy of their office or in settings where no one will question the decisions being made. It is critical, then, that a professional have an internalized moral base and sense of ethics.

Sadly, we are reminded everyday that this is not always the case. In the media there is a constant clamor of allegations and denials regarding tax evasion, corruption, fraud, influence peddling, sexual impropriety, inside trading, and drug abuse that raises disturbing questions about our clergy, our neighbors, our teachers and our government leaders. As a result, the subject of ethics has emerged as one of the most fundamental issues confronting our society today.

WHAT ARE ETHICS?

What, then, are *ethics*? Senator Orin Hatch has compared the attempt to define ethics to "trying to nail Jell-O on a tree." Some define ethics as *standards, morals, rules of conduct, or a state of goodness.*[2] Others define ethics as *the study of human conduct in light of moral principles.*[3]

In this text, we will define **ethics** as *behavioral standards — a set of principles that defines what is judged appropriate or inappropriate, right or wrong.*[b] Over the years, most professions have developed guidelines defining appropriate professional conduct. In the medical profession, this is known as the Hippocratic Oath. In most other professions, these guidelines are referred to as a Code of Ethics.

If you want to be an interpreter, it is not enough for you to memorize the RID or AVLIC Code of Ethics or to emblazon

---

[b] Like Blair Ewing (Ethics in Education), the authors reject the idea of "moral relativism" which states that there is no right or wrong, or ultimate moral base. This belief defies the need for a set of professional ethics or the base upon which codes of ethics are founded.

the code on your business card or professional attire. Another writer in this area says professionals need to have "strong personal moral and ethical judgment that translates into principled professional conduct."[4] Thus, it is necessary for you to integrate your professional code of ethical conduct into your daily decisions, actions, and interactions as an interpreter.

GUIDELINES FOR PROFESSIONAL CONDUCT

Professional associations commonly develop guidelines for professional conduct, referred to as a Code of Ethics. They develop codes of ethical behavior for a number of reasons, including:

1. Educating members of the profession regarding what is appropriate and inappropriate behavior;
2. Fostering the development of professional goals and norms;
3. Deterring inappropriate and immoral conduct;
4. Disciplining offenders;
5. Providing information to the market regarding what is acceptable practice by members of the said profession; and
6. Protecting the public from unethical practitioners.[5]

For these reasons, AVLIC and RID have developed guidelines for professional behavior, articulating the standards that define what is judged appropriate conduct in the field of sign language interpretation. Professionals must function in the "real world," where business judgments, like ethical and human relations issues, often have no easy answers.[6] Our code of professional conduct provides guidelines to assist us as we make, review and evaluate professional decisions. A code of conduct also fosters a standard of behavior so consumers know what they can expect when similar situations arise, regardless of who the interpreter may be. Lou Fant[7], renowned interpreter and pioneer in the field, notes that standards of conduct elicit trust from consumers toward interpreters because they know that "we will always act morally in out dealings with them." Finally, the RID and AVLIC ethical codes lead to actions that empower others. Let's look at the two codes in light of the discussion above.

NAD-RID CODE OF PROFESSIONAL CONDUCT

1. Interpreters adhere to standards of confidential communication.
2. Interpreters possess the professional skills and knowledge required for the specific interpreting situation.
3. Interpreters conduct themselves in a manner appropriate to the specific interpreting situation.
4. Interpreters demonstrate respect for consumers.
5. Interpreters demonstrate respect for colleagues, interns and students of the profession.
6. Interpreters maintain ethical business practices.
7. Interpreters engage in professional development.

Adopted July 2005

The guiding principles behind the NAD-RID Code of Professional Conduct include the concepts of:

+ confidentiality
+ linguistic and professional competence
+ impartiality
+ professional growth and development
+ ethical business practices, and
+ the rights of participants in interpreted situations to informed choice

The underlying metaethical principle is that the interpreter will do no harm. It is therefore the responsibility of every interpreter to exercise judgment and critical thinking, applying lessons learned in practical experience to reflect on past actions in the practice of the profession.

The tenets of this Code of Professional Conduct are to be viewed holistically and as guiding principles for professional behavior. Because of the breadth of these tenents there is no need for a separate code for each area of interpeting.The full document can be found in Appendix B.

AVLIC developed their current Code of Ethics and Guidelines for Professional Conduct by first identifying the values upon which its standards of conduct are based, then fleshing out their expectations a bit more clearly. They also state the purpose of the Code of Ethics. Note the preamble and values below.

AVLIC CODE OF ETHICS

The purpose of the Code of Ethics is to provide guidance for interpreters, and in so doing, to ensure quality of service for all persons involved. Adherence to the following tenets are essential for maintaining national standards; professional discretion must be exercised at all times.

The Association of Visual Language Interpreters of Canada (AVLIC) expects its members to maintain high standards of professional conduct in their capacity and identity as an interpreter. Members are required to abide by the Code of Ethics and follow the Guidelines for Professional Conduct as a condition of membership in the organization.

This document articulates ethical principles, values, and standards of conduct to guide all members of AVLIC in their pursuit of professional practice. It is intended to provide direction to interpreters for ethical and professional decision-making in their day-to-day work. The Code of Ethics and Guidelines for Professional Conduct is the mechanism by which the public is protected in the delivery of service.

VALUES UNDERLYING THE CODE OF ETHICS & GUIDELINES FOR PROFESSIONAL CONDUCT

AVLIC values:
1. PROFESSIONAL ACCOUNTABILITY: Accepting responsibility for professional decisions and actions.
2. PROFESSIONAL COMPETENCE: Committing to provide quality professional service throughout one's practice.

3. NON-DISCRIMINATION: Approaching professional service with respect and cultural sensitivity.
4. INTEGRITY IN PROFESSIONAL RELATIONSHIPS: Dealing honestly and fairly with consumers and colleagues
5. INTEGRITY IN BUSINESS PRACTICES: Dealing honestly and ethically in all business practices

Members are to understand that each of these core values and accompanying sections are to be considered when making ethical and professional decisions in their capacity and identity as an interpreter. These values are of equal weight and importance.

What follows are several pages spelling out standards of conduct in each of the five value domains. (The full document is located in Appendix C).

Both Codes of Ethics identify competent, professional behavior that dictate what the field has defined as professional, ethical and moral. Finally, the codes assume that practitioners are able to apply critical thinking skills and good decision-making skills as they come to a reasoned decision regarding their professional conduct, even when working under difficult or stressful conditions.

INTERPRETATION OF THE CODE

There are several precepts within which we can fit all the specific tenets of the RID and AVLIC codes of ethics. We have provided these below with an expansion regarding the interpretation and application of the specific ethical codes.

Empowerment Of The Client

Individual ethics involve behaving in a way that demonstrates genuine concern for the well-being of others. Professional ethics involves behaving in a way that leads to actions and agendas that empower others.[8] This is done by vesting control in the hands of our consumers.

Accurate Conveyance Of Information

Information is power.[9] If we do our job well as interpreters — conveying the spirit and intent of the speaker while making it accessible in the client's preferred language or mode (complete with linguistic and cultural adaptations if required) — they will be able to fully participate in the event being interpreted. This is liberating and empowering. As professionals, we will only accept assignments for which we are qualified and able to do; we will prepare for assignments in order to analyze the speaker's goal/intent rapidly and accurately. We will also be sensitive to cross-cultural communication dynamics, in order to make appropriate cultural transitions and to insure our clients have access to the spirit and intent of the message.

Confidentiality

Professionals enter into a trust relationship with their clients. Because of that relationship, we disrobe in front of our physician, we bare our souls to our psychiatrist, say confession to our priest, and otherwise make ourselves vulnerable. We do that knowing our physical, emotional, or spiritual problems will not be the topic of someone's dinner conversation. Further, we know that if we encounter our physician, psychiatrist, or priest at a social function, there won't even be a facial expression that will "give us away" to others in the room.

If that relationship is violated, professional ethical standards are violated. As professionals, we realize that the failure to guard all interpreting and quasi-interpreting information closely will rob our clients of the power to control personal and professional information.

As sign language interpreters, we are even more sensitive to the need for confidentiality due to the close-knit nature of the Deaf community in which it only takes a minimum of information to identify the parties involved in an interpreted situation.

There are several situations in which it is necessary and appropriate for us to discuss the specifics of an assignment with a professional colleague. When this is the case, we are expected to be ethically responsible, using great discretion in sharing only information that is critical to the effective functioning of the professional team in order to provide the highest quality of service to the clients involved.

Purchase Of Services

Clients are invested with power when they are able to select the professional whose services they will purchase. As a professional, it is my responsibility to respect the preferences of the client with regarding to which interpreter they prefer, to set appropriate fees for my services in a fair, market-appropriate manner and to convey that information to a prospective client before accepting an assignment. If our fees are not paid on time, we will be discreet regarding attempts to secure payment. While there are some occasions when it is appropriate for professionals to donate or volunteer their services, it is critical to remember that being indebted to another with no way to reciprocate is demeaning to one's personhood and self-respect. We will therefore be judicious when determining if it is appropriate for me to donate my professional services on a case-by-case basis.

Professional Distance

Empowering clients requires that I demonstrate respect toward my clients. As interpreters, we do not impose our opinions, advice, sense of values, or preferred form of communication on our clients. By accepting only those interpreting jobs that we are qualified to do, we reflect respect for the client and make it possible for the client to obtain the services of an appropriate interpreter for the job.

As professionals, we realize that if we are too involved with a client emotionally, our concern for her/his well-being may cause us to behave in a way that does not lead to her/his authentic empowerment. For example, if an interpreter is too close

307

emotionally to her clients, it may be impossible for either of them to terminate the services if the interpreter's skills are not up to par or the interpreter feels unqualified to work in the setting. Therefore, we will refrain from interpreting in settings where the involvement of family members, good friends or close professional associates affects the quality of service we provide and/or the professional decisions we make.

Professional Competence

As we wait in the engineer's office and peruse the diplomas, awards and professional certificates on the wall, we are doing so primarily out of curiosity — not because we are unsure if the weight bearing walls of the building the engineer is designing for us will support the roof. A consumer of professional services expects that by virtue of being in practice, the practitioner is competent to provide the service offered. It is therefore incumbent on the professional to be competent to practice in her/his given field.

This involves knowing one's own limits — physically, emotionally, experientially, linguistically, culturally, and in every other area. If a job demands that an interpreter work in a cramped space and he is claustrophobic, he is not competent to do the job in that setting. If the complexities of an interaction require the knowledge and skills of a highly experienced individual, and an interpreter has just graduated from school, she is not competent to do the job. If an interpreter is unable to understand what the client is saying, either because of the specialized jargon being used, his/her style of signing/speaking, or because of the interpreter's limited linguistic abilities in general, he is not competent to do the job.

Professionals "profess" that the client's interest or well-being is paramount. *One of the most honorable and professional actions one can take is to know her/his limitations and to decline a job s/he is not able to do well.*

Competence is defined by the AVLIC Code of Ethics to mean being:

- ✦ Linguistically capable to determine the intent and spirit of a speaker and being able to express that intent and spirit in an equivalent manner in the target language and culture;
- ✦ Flexible enough to adjust communication methods so that services can be provided in the client's preferred language or mode;
- ✦ Cognizant of the task and of my own capabilities so I can determine if I am able to function professionally and competently, given the specific assignment (client, setting, topic of interaction, type of skills required, etc.);
- ✦ Committed to continuing my professional development to expand my competence and to be better able to serve my clientele.

Competence also means working as certified practitioners and members of the professional association(s). *Professional certification provides evidence of our competence and professionalism.* When people practice without the appropriate education, supervision, and certification, the number of horror stories begins to escalate because the quality of service that is available to consumers is placed at risk.[10]

Promote The Profession

Professions normally require advanced education and supervised internship before being allowed to become a practitioner. In the evolution of the profession of sign language interpreting, this is becoming the norm. It is incumbent on professional practitioners to encourage and mentor new interpreters as well as to maintain their own skills and knowledge by participating in regular, on-going professional development.

As a professional, I will be an active member of my professional association, I will actively seek to upgrade my educational background, and I will engage in regular, on-going professional development activities. I will constantly endeavor to further the development of my decision-making skills, my judgment and common sense, and my interpreting skills and knowledge.

I will advocate on behalf of the profession and my professional colleagues. This includes consideration of colleagues who earn their living as contract interpreters when I determine if it is appropriate to donate my services. It means working with my professional peers to insure more humane working conditions, the assignment of multiple interpreters where length or difficulty of assignments make it necessary, equitable pay, and the opportunity to properly prepare for assignments.

Finally, I will treat other interpreters with professional respect. I will provide encouragement and support to my peers and to those entering the field. I will not engage in character assassination or idle gossip; if I have a concern, I will approach my colleague and deal with her/him directly. I will refrain from unprofessional or unethical behavior and I will urge my colleagues to do the same. I will comply with the standards for ethical behavior set out by my professional association.

LEARNING TO MAKE ETHICAL DECISIONS

Ethical decision-making requires **critical thinking**. This requires that you look at a question or issue from a variety of view points — with an open mind to as many feasible options or perspectives to a given situation as possible. Further, thinking critically expects me to evaluate each option for possible consequences, and to select the best available option based on the facts that are known or can be ascertained.[11] Critical thinking skills include:

✦ Determining if the information received is reliable;
✦ Determining if decisions made are consistent with professional codes of ethics;
✦ Understanding how the Code of Ethics may conflict with your own individual or family value structures;
✦ Testing new ideas and solutions;
✦ Comparing new ideas and solutions with standard (accepted) responses to those decisions;
✦ Integrating the information learned with acceptable norms of professional behavior.

As an interpreter, you will find yourself in many situations that require you to make a decision, to plan a response, or to take some action. As an interpreter (or a critical thinker in any arena), be careful not to settle for the first acceptable solution that comes to mind. Jumping to the first correct option might prevent you from discovering even better options.

If you find that you are unable to make appropriate, ethical decisions on a consistent basis, the problem may be due to:

✦ Lack of clarity regarding the expectations of your client or employer;
✦ Unavoidable intervening factors such as conflict among client demands, employer demands, the Code of Ethics, and one's own morally and ethically guided principles;
✦ Ignorance or naiveté; or
✦ A lack of concern about or unawareness of long-range or short-range consequences.

FACT:
As an interpreter, you will encounter delicate and potentially frustrating situations where you must make decisions.

FACT:
Demands on interpreters are intricate, sometimes difficult to meet, and sometimes contradictory.

FACT:

There is rarely a *single right* answer.

FACT:

Interpreters don't always have time to research the "correct" or "appropriate" or "ethically responsible" answer(s) demanded on the job and in the field. You must do the best you can, learn from successes and errors and move forward.

FACT:

You are human — you will make some mistakes and some poor choices.

FACT:

It takes time to develop professional discretion and judgment. Be patient with yourself.

PRACTICING THE PRINCIPLES

In all areas of your life where you can anticipate decisions that will need to be made, it is best if you rehearse those situations in advance so you have several alternative responses readily available to you. It is also critical you realize that with a few exceptions, there is rarely a single correct response. In the typical situation you will encounter, there may be three, four, five, or more options available to you. Given the setting, the clients, and numerous other contextual factors, you will select the one response that you feel is most appropriate. At some point after making your decision, you should reflect on and evaluate the appropriateness of your decision. Let's try it:

> **SITUATION:** You are on vacation in an isolated rural community. Your family and friends in that area know you have been studying sign language interpretation and when a Deaf man is taken to the emergency room at the hospital where your aunt works, she calls and asks you to come interpret.

Step One – List Options

Take a minute and write down every possible response option available to you. No response is too ridiculous to be recorded.

Let's compare lists. Did you include the following?

1. Say yes and go right down.
2. Say no and insist that your aunt call another interpreter in town.
3. Panic and hang up on your aunt. When she calls back, don't answer.
4. Launch into a 15-minute explanation of the complexities of sign language interpretation, the Code of Ethics, etc.
5. Ask your significant other for her/his advice then do whatever s/he suggests.
6. Tell your aunt that since it is an emergency, you will come, but that it is imperative that she continue to call around town until she can find a qualified interpreter to come do the job.

Add your ideas to this list, then move to step two.

Step Two – Identify The Consequences Of Each Option

Now go back to your original list. Take each option you listed to its probable consequence. For example, if you say yes and go to the hospital, what might happen? We have done the same for our options listed above.

1. Say yes and go right down .

   a) Everything could work out great — I become the heroine/hero of the day and I am written up in the local newspaper.
   b) The Deaf accident victim may be bloody and since I don't do well around blood, I may pass out. Communication is not provided to the Deaf accident victim and now the medical personnel must deal with me!

313

c) I may do "okay" — nothing to brag about but we manage. I get my first medical interpreting experience, learned some things to do and not to do next time.

d) I may do a really bad job — misinterpreting what the Deaf accident victim signs, missing the meaning of some of the complex medical terminology. I realize I'm over my head and ask for the medical personnel to call someone else but they are busy and say things are fine. I feel horrible.

e) I may do "okay" and this experience may help me decide that I want to go on for advanced training in medical interpreting.

f) I may be sued for malpractice or negligence when it is determined that complications developed as a result of my misinterpretation.

g) I may be featured in the local newspaper as the outstanding person of the week.

2. Say no and insist that your aunt call another interpreter in town.

a) That may be fine. The hospital has other interpreters on call — your aunt just thought of you first.

b) There may not be another interpreter for a 300-mile radius.

c) Your aunt doesn't know of any other interpreters or how to contact them and neither does anyone else at the hospital.

d) Your aunt gets mad, calls you an academic snob and hangs up the phone.

Try these next four on your own:

✦ Panic and hang up on your aunt. When she calls back, don't answer.

✦ Launch into a 15-minute explanation of the complexities of sign language interpretation, the Code of
Ethics, etc.

✦ Ask your significant other for her/his advice then do
whatever s/he suggests.

✦ Tell your aunt that since it is an emergency, you will
come but that it is imperative that she continue to
call around town until she can find a qualified interpreter to come do the job.

Continue this exercise on the other options you recorded, then
go to step three.

Step Three - Collect/Review Facts

Having identified all possible response options and all foresee-
able consequences, it is now necessary to rank your options.
This is not possible unless you possess all the information necessary.

For example, knowing that there are five other interpreters in
town (two of whom are certified) or knowing that there are no
other interpreters within a 300-mile radius will eliminate some
options and consequences. Likewise, knowing that your aunt
has jumped to the conclusion that this accident victim is Deaf

because he is wearing a hearing aid and in fact the
individual functions well with speech and residual hearing (he doesn't even know sign language)
would influence how you rank options and consequences.

Because we want you to develop your critical thinking skills, you should first list all possible options,
then identify all possible consequences for each
option before doing this third step. If you start limiting your options during these classroom exercises, you may
hamper the development of critical decision-making skills.
When you begin to apply these skills to real-life situations, the

order will shift slightly. For purposes of this exercise, here are some facts for you to consider

1. The population of the town is 180,000; there are approximately 80 Deaf people living in the town.

2. There is one other person in town who interprets at the local church and occasionally for medical and legal situations. She has never received "formal" interpreter education, but she has lived in this town all of her life and knows all 80 Deaf community members very well.

3. As an interpreting student, you have completed 600-hours of ASL instruction, three interpreting courses, and 50 fieldwork hours to date. You never signed or interacted with Deaf people before the beginning of your interpreter education experience, two years ago.

4. Before entering the interpreter education program, you worked 12-years as a registered nurse.

"Create" a few more "facts" of your own at this time.

Step Four – Review Consequences
You may need to eliminate some and add others now that you have all the facts.

Step Five – Review Options
You may need to eliminate some options and add others now that you have all of the facts. If you add some, develop all possible consequences for that new option.

There may be times when behaving "ethically," according to the Code of Ethics, conflicts with your personal moral code or family values. It is essential that you become aware of these areas of conflict and deal with them before you enter the field as a practitioner. Such a conflict may result in your need to turn down certain types of work (due to client, setting, content, etc.), or you may decide you need to consider some line of work other than interpreting because the conflict is too significant and pervasive to allow you to conform to the ethical standards in the profession. Thus, you may eliminate or modify some options based on a conflict with your personal moral code.

Step Six – Rank Options

Given all the options and possible consequences, being cognizant of the Code of Ethics, determine which option you think is first, second, and third most appropriate to act on.

Step Seven – Act

Now take the action that you selected as the first ranked option.

For educational purposes, your teacher will give you several additional situations, guide you through steps one through six, then lead you through a role play of each situation at this point. There are several challenges here, including rapid recovery when things don't go as predicted. You may need to drop back to one of your other options; you may need to rethink and come up with other options and consequences as the events unfold.

Step Eight – Review Action

Review your decision and the results, taking into account what worked and what didn't. Consider other options, unexpected consequences, etc.

REMEMBER: You *will* stumble and fall — "To err is human." You are learning how to apply a professional Code of Ethics to a complex, multi-dimensional experience while you manipulate two languages (at least one of which may be fairly new to you) and in the midst of the "chemistry" of often intense interpersonal interactions. Give yourself time; just remember that to grow, you must learn from the mistakes you make. Katherine Hepburn once said, "It's O.K. if you fall on your face — at least you are still moving forward!"

The only time a mistake is "bad" is when you keep making the same one. So long as you keep making new mistakes, you are progressing. As you begin your field work and later enter the field of sign language interpreting, it is imperative that you review the decisions you have made on a regular basis in order to note the mistakes made and the lessons learned.

You can do this by mentally reviewing your day, but we suggest you try the use of a journal.

Step Nine - Record For Reference

By taking the time to write down your experiences, reflections, and evaluations you have a record of your professional growth and development. Further, journal writing is a proven method for stress reduction. The life of interpreters is stressful and you need to develop habits now that will assist you in dealing with stress in a positive, healthy way.

THE FOUNDATION OF ETHICS: Knowing Yourself

Ethical behavior grows out of a strong moral sense, the ability to think critically and the courage to choose to do the right thing. Our level of moral development and ability to consciously make good decisions, then, is a cornerstone of becoming an ethical person (See Appendix D). However, research indicates that only 20% of our decisions are based on conscious cognition. Most of our other decisions and behaviors, however, are motivated by unconscious factors stemming from a life time of experiences.[12]

The experiences we have gone through on our way to adulthood determine our self-concept.[13] Many of us come to adulthood with characteristics such as:[14]

+ Low self-esteem, not liking yourself, feeling ashamed of yourself;

- ✦ Covering up or compensating for your poor self-concept by being:

  - ✓ a perfectionist

  - ✓ caretaking, controlling

  - ✓ judgmental toward others (often reflected in gossip)

  - ✓ super responsible or super irresponsible;

- ✦ Needing the approval of others; being a "people pleaser" or a chameleon — changing what you believe, based on the group you are with at the time;
- ✦ Trying to solve others' problems; be a caretaker;
- ✦ Being unable to act assertively or to stand up for yourself by acting assertively

If you want to be an interpreter, it is time to deal honestly with who you are and how you got to be that person. What do you believe? Why do you act, react, and feel as you do? The failure to deal with these issues will probably result in your attempt to apply the Code of Ethics in a dogmatic, black-and-white manner or to become enmeshed with your clients, taking on inappropriate responsibility for them and getting overly involved in their lives. Either of these responses are detrimental to you as an interpreter, to your clients/consumers, and to the field as a whole.

SUPPORT GROUPS AND MENTORS

As you enter the field of sign language interpreting, it is important that you get the kind of guidance and support needed "out in the real world," particularly in relation to making difficult ethical decisions. You will encounter many situations armed with limited experience; you will not be fully equipped to exercise discretion, judgment, or to make appropriate decisions in all settings. In addition, you will become increasingly aware of personal/professional habits and behaviors that are self-defeating and that there is a need for accountability and support.

We suggest that you get involved with a support group made up of professional peers. A support group should be small enough that everyone has time to share (no more than four or five individuals); its members should be committed to confidentiality, growth, and honesty. A support group must be a place where you can take risks. If everyone is "wet behind the ears" you may not be able to glean some of the insight needed, so it should be made up of working interpreters with various lengths of experience. The local chapter of AVLIC or RID may already have support groups established that you can join. However, there may not be an established support group, so you may also wish to form your own.

Another source of support you may want to take advantage of is mentoring or "twinning." Mentoring is a primary pathway to competency in most professions. In this type of arrangement, a more experienced interpreter "adopts" a less experienced interpreter, showing them the ropes, introducing them to the Deaf and interpreting communities, and serving as a sounding board to review and evaluate the less experienced interpreter's professional behavior, decision-making, and quality of interpretation or transliteration. The local chapter of RID or AVLIC may have a mentoring system in place. However, it is more typical for a less experienced interpreter to approach someone s/he wants to learn from in a mentor relationship and ask if the more experienced interpreter would be willing to become her/his mentor.

CHAPTER REVIEW
Key Points

Professionals...
+ Hold their client's interests paramount.
+ Have a special monopoly through licensure or certification.
+ Have a defined (limited) scope of practice.
+ Adhere to a clearly articulated set of values or code of ethics.
+ Are supposed to be trustworthy individuals who know how to do their work, come to the task prepared, and are worthy of the trust placed in them.
+ Are expected to deal with sensitive information in a discrete manner.
+ Are expected to avoid inappropriate emotional involvement.
+ Work unsupervised and are expected to have an internalized moral base and sense of ethics.

Codes of Ethics and Guidelines for Professional Conduct
+ Found in a variety of professions.
+ Grow out of meta-ethical principles that are common within a culture/community.
+ Are a set of behavioral standards or principles that define what is deemed appropriate in a particular professional field.
+ Require practitioners to have a well-developed sense of self and critical thinking skills.

GOALS of professional codes of ethical behavior are to:
+ Educate members regarding what is appropriate and inappropriate behavior;

+ Foster the development of professional goals and norms;
+ Deter inappropriate and immoral conduct;
+ Discipline offenders;
+ Provide information to the market regarding what is acceptable practice by members of the said profession; and
+ Protect the public from unethical practitioners.

VALUES undergirding the AVLIC and RID Codes of Ethics, include those stated in the AVLIC preamble, as well as:

+ The right of all people to be treated fairly and with respect;
+ Respect of individual privacy;
+ The right of all individuals to take charge of their personal and business affairs without the imposition of a third party's opinion, values, or judgment distorting or influencing the communication or interaction;
+ The right of all individuals to communicate freely in the language/mode most comfortable to them;
+ The right of all individuals to know what a service will cost in advance of the provision of that service;
+ The belief that professional practitioners can learn and that good judgment and decision-making will be the result of experience and education;
+ A belief in the value of life-long learning and professional development.

Steps in critical thinking and decision-making:

+ Write down every possible option available.
+ Identify all possible consequences of each option.
+ Collect and review the facts.
+ Review the consequences in light of these facts.
+ Review the options.

♦ Rank options.
♦ Act.
♦ Review action.
♦ Log what you learned for future reference.

Sources of Support and Professional Growth
Support Groups — a small group of professional peers committed to confidentiality, growth, and honesty.

Mentoring or Twinning — an arrangement in which a more experienced interpreter "adopts" a less experienced interpreter, showing her the ropes, introducing her to the Deaf and interpreting communities, and serving as a sounding board to review and evaluate the less-experienced interpreter's professional behavior, decision-making, and quality of interpretation or transliteration.

THOUGHT QUESTIONS
1. What distinguishes "professionals" from other business persons?

2. Contact a number of professional organizations in your area (medical, legal, educational, etc.) and ask for copies of their professional Codes of Ethics. Compare them with the AVLIC and RID codes.

3. Develop three role situation cards like those you worked on in this chapter. Bring them to class and practice the decision-making and critical thinking skills tasks.

4. Does the information regarding dysfunctional backgrounds and co-dependent behaviors fit with the information about making ethical decisions? If yes, how? If no, what relevance does that information have for this chapter? For an individual who seeks to become an interpreter?

CD STUDY GUIDE

✦ The various activities in the guided Chapter 12 Study Guide on CD will allow you to understand the concepts in this chapter more completely and to apply them to your life experience. Work through the Chapter 12 Study Guide on CD, completing all activities, then submit to your instructor or share with your learning partner.

SUGGESTED ACTIVITIES

✦ Invite a panel of working interpreters to speak about the challenge of making ethical decisions.
✦ Invite other professionals to speak about the challenge of making ethical decisions.
✦ Gather a variety of Codes of Ethics from different fields and compare them with the RID and AVLIC codes.
✦ Observe interpreters at work and record events where ethical decision-making was required.

Endnotes

1. Stromberg (1990)
2. Seymour (1990)
3. Hill (1990)
4. McCuen (1983)
5. Stromburg (1990)
6. Waggoner (1990)
7. Fant (1990)
8. Hill (1990)
9. Lane 1988)
10. Seymour (1990)
11. Waggoner (1990)
12. Minirth, et. al. (1990)
13. Mellody (1990); Kristberg (1985); Woititz (1985); Beattie (1987)
14. Bradshaw (1990)

CHAPTER THIRTEEN
Where Interpreters Work

In this chapter, we will address some of the special considerations one must bear in mind when interpreting in particular settings. The task of interpreting is virtually the same process in each setting, but this distinction helps us focus on the unique considerations of each. In each of the following settings, we will consider:

✦ Standard qualifications needed to work in a given setting.

✦ Working conditions and pay for services.

✦ Supervision, evaluation, and opportunities for professional development.

✦ Protocol and specialized considerations.

We will consider educational, religious, medical, social service and legal settings in this chapter.

INTERPRETING IN EDUCATIONAL SETTINGS

A majority of graduates from interpreter preparation programs will work in an educational setting. These can be divided into preschool, elementary, secondary, and post-secondary environments. Post-secondary settings can further be divided into adult education or upgrading courses, vocational training, and academic settings from college through university graduate-level courses. Due to legislation and shifting social attitudes, there has been a dramatic increase in the number of Deaf individuals integrated into various educational settings.

In addition to maintaining grade-appropriate academic progress, the goal of integrated education is for Deaf students to become *independent, empowered, and integrated* with Deaf and hearing peers while developing a healthy sense of themselves as Deaf individuals. Ideally, this includes exposure to and an understanding of Deaf history and heritage, the culture of Deaf people, and exposure to the rich linguistic tradition of American Sign Language. Unfortunately, many mainstreamed educational settings have failed to meet or include these goals. This may be due, in part, to the instructional and support personnel hired, including the interpreters.

It has been the practice in many school districts to hire a teacher's aide when a Deaf or hard of hearing student is added to a regular classroom. In many cases, these aides:

+ Assist the teacher in the classroom;
+ Tutor the Deaf student, and
+ Interpret.

This practice is laden with problems. Because teacher's aides are considered unskilled labor, the salary paid and education/training required is minimal. Further, the presence of a Deaf child does not justify the hiring of an aide in place of an interpreter. Unlike some disabled students, Deaf children can open doors, handle books, and go to the bathroom independently. Hiring an aide fosters the perception that deafness is a defect. It also lets the school district maintain the appearance of optimal support services for main-streamed students while using unqualified personnel.

Deaf and hard of hearing students require the services of a interpreter to maximize access, integration, equality, and empowerment for everyone in this setting. The role of an interpreter will vary dramatically depending on whether s/he is working with children, youth or adults.

Standard Qualifications
In educational settings, standards vary dramatically from place to place. Some schools require that interpreters be certified; others hire anybody who can fingerspell or who has a great uncle who was Deaf. This attitude threatens the authentic access to

education expected by family, community and the Deaf or hard of hearing students themselves.

Historically, school personnel have put the least skilled, most inexperienced interpreters with young children who have least mastery of the language. We believe this is a very poor choice. Young Deaf children often enter the educational system with un-der-developed or non-existent linguistic abilities due to the lack of accessible communication in their home environment. The interpreter is often the only language model a child encounters in a mainstreamed educational setting. Unqualified interpreters in the classroom result in continued language deprivation and academic stagnation for the young child.

Fluency in sign language and flexibility in working with chil-dren-to-adult signing ranges should be required. After all, edu-cation is one's key to economic and social independence. Chil-dren, youth and adults have a right to an education including interpreters who can truly make the education provided acces-sible.

Minimally, interpreters in this setting should be graduates of an interpreter education program with some course work in child development and education. Ideally, interpreters in educational settings should hold interpreter certification and a Bachelor's degree. This would generally insure that the individual hired can perform the interpreting/transliterating tasks required, has experience with formal education himself, and has knowledge of, and training in, education. Further, job interviews should re-quire a demonstration of communication and interpreting skill with Deaf individuals on the screening panel.

Two Models
Albuquerque, New Mexico , is a model of an elementary and secondary educational setting. This school district has es-tablished a clear standard, requiring RID certification and a Bachelor's degree for educational interpreters. It guarantees a minimal academic experience from which the interpreter can

draw as s/he interprets. It also certifies a minimal linguistic and interpreting ability.[a]

The University of California, Berkeley is a model of a post-secondary educational setting. They require all interpreters to be RID certified. Any classes that exceed 50-minutes are teamed by two interpreters. There is a full-time coordinator who provides supervision, evaluation, professional development to the interpreting staff, as well as advocacy on behalf of the interpreting staff.

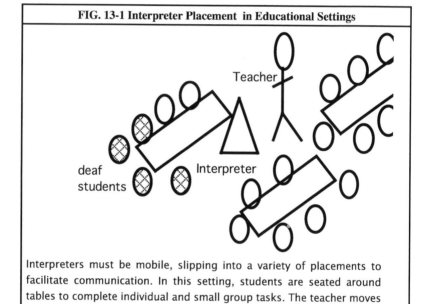

FIG. 13-1 Interpreter Placement in Educational Settings

Interpreters must be mobile, slipping into a variety of placements to facilitate communication. In this setting, students are seated around tables to complete individual and small group tasks. The teacher moves around the room checking on student progress and, at times, making comments to all of the students.

Role Delineation

The variety of job descriptions in preschool through secondary settings demonstrates the lack of clear role delineation. An interpreter may be hired as a "communication aide," "teaching assistant," "program assistant," "tutor," or a number of other titles.

---

[a] For more information, see Wilcox, Schroeder, and Martinez (1990)

This mixture of titles results in a variety of pay scales and union affiliations, and raises some significant ethical concerns.

Basically, interpreters in educational settings:

+ Are *primarily* responsible for providing communication access in the wide range of instructional activities within an educational program — this includes guidance and counseling sessions, student parliament meetings, extracurricular activities, tutorials, parent/student meetings, field trips, and student assemblies;

+ Should not impinge on the teacher's authority including teaching, student discipline, parent contacts and referrals (some of these tasks may, however, be performed by an interpreter at the direction and under the supervision of the teacher).

It should be noted that the specific responsibilities of an interpreter vary depending on the age and level of sophistication of the students they work with.[1] A five-year-old, for example, cannot distinguish between a teacher and an interpreter — all she sees is a "big person." As such, an interpreter working with young students must perform a broader range of duties than the interpreter working for a high school student or an adult student.

Working Conditions
Working conditions vary significantly from one city and school district or college to the next. In one situation known to the authors, a single interpreter moves between three different grades to interpret for one or more children in each grade. This means she is in grade one from 8–10 a.m., runs to grade four to interpret from 10:00 – 12:00. She is expected to supervise the playground three days a week from 12-1 p.m., then to interpret in a grade six class from 1-3 p.m. which marks the end of the school

day. She gets no scheduled breaks, no prep time, and no time to consult with teachers regarding lessons. These are unacceptable working conditions.

Interpreters working in all levels of educational settings need to have regular breaks plus a lunch period. They should be paid for one prep period, just like the teachers, allowing them to preview textbooks, films, and other lesson materials and to consult with classroom teachers as needed. When interpreting college courses, preparation time is often more critical at the beginning of a semester or quarter than it might be near the end of a course. Prep time should be negotiated depending on the nature of the course and style of instruction.

Further, interpreters must be given adequate breaks or be provided a team interpreter in order to avoid repetitive strain injury (AKA over-use syndrome). Traditionally, administrators have justified the assignment of two interpreters to a class on the basis of time, however this is not a good yardstick. An assignment may need to be teamed on the basis of:

✦ Difficulty of content — interpreting for a two-hour typing lab is quite different than interpreting for a one-hour lecture in criminology;
✦ Instructional strategies used — lecture is more strenuous than independent work, for example, and extensive use of small groups is more difficult than a moderately paced large group question and answer session;
✦ Classroom environment — interpreting for a theater class can be more exhausting due to the size of space, amount of physical activity required, and environmental noise than a sedate, acoustically sound classroom.

It should be noted that rotating interpreters in and out of a class — interpreter A works the first 30 minutes of a class, then leaves to do another class as interpreter B comes in to do the next 30 minutes of the class — is *not* authentic teaming. Teamed interpreting means there is continuity in, and support between, the members of the interpreting team throughout the class.

Additionally, educational institutions should have a system of substitute interpreters in place in the event the regular interpreter is ill or has a family emergency. The current practice in many schools is to simply count the student's attendance but leave them without an interpreter for the day. Sometimes, a school will bring in a family member to "interpret" for the day or ask someone to sit beside the Deaf student and write notes for them. On an emergency one-time-only basis, this may be excusable but it should not be the standard of practice.

Pay For Services

Interpreters in public school settings have the luxury of a steady paycheck, regular hours, and in some cases, additional medical and insurance benefits and "school" holidays. Some interpreters in post-secondary settings are on "staff" and have similar guarantees. Because of this security, they are often paid less per hour than contract interpreters.

Most interpreters in post-secondary settings, however, work on a contract basis. They secure contracts on a semester-by-semester basis and if a student drops a class in the midst of a semester, the interpreting contract will be terminated.

It is therefore necessary for interpreters in these settings to negotiate contracts that protect their ability to earn a living. They need to be sure that contracts include:

✦ A cancellation policy, i.e. if a student withdraws, the interpreter will be paid the equivalent of two-weeks or one month of their contract, giving the interpreter time to look for other work during the time committed to the initial contract;

✦ A pay rate that takes into consideration any special training or qualifications the interpreter may hold that are pertinent to this particular class or client and therefore make that interpreter more valuable in the assignment;

✦ Amenities including a parking pass and access to the library, audio-visual equipment, and computers needed to prepare for classes, loaned copies of textbooks for each class being interpreted;

✦ Paid time for preparation and to meet out of class with the student, the teacher, etc.;

✦ Pay for in-class, as well as related out-of-class work (group projects, field trips, etc.);

✦ Mileage between multi-campus sites; and

✦ Agreement regarding employment of team interpreters where appropriate.

Pay rates vary widely from school district to school district, a fact that may be tied to the lack of clear role delineation and the absence of minimal educational and skills standards. When classified as a teacher's aide or special education assistant, interpreters are often paid only slightly more than minimum wage. The pay scale of an institution should tie pay level with an interpreter's educational background, years of experience and certification. However, this is not always the case. Contract interpreters in post-secondary settings are almost always below that fee scale commanded by community interpreters in private practice.

It can be reasoned that the critical shortage of interpreters in educational settings is partly due to the lack of adequate pay and appropriate working conditions. However, if qualifications required truly reflected those needed to do the job adequately, interpreters in educational settings should be certified and hold at least a bachelor's degree. If this were the case, it seems logical that their salary and benefits would parallel those of entry-level teachers who are also required to hold a bachelor's degree and teacher certification.

Supervision and Evaluation

Most educational institutions providing interpreters for Deaf and hard of hearing students do not have personnel who can adequately supervise and evaluate the interpreting/transliterating performance of their employees. Oh, there might be some kind of evaluation process, but they are usually based on a spoken-English interview and observation of the interpreter by someone who doesn't even know sign language.

In these cases, consideration is rarely given to accuracy of interpretation, linguistic capability, or other interpreting-specific data. As a result, some incompetent interpreters stay in the classroom, providing an inadequate level of service with serious consequences to the children, youth and adults seeking an education. Other interpreters, sensing keenly the need for contact with interpreting colleagues and opportunities for professional feedback and growth, leave the area of education.

We suggest that educational institutions/districts contract with an outside individual who would perform meaningful evaluations for the interpreters they employ on a regular basis. A report could be generated and given to the school, as well as the individual interpreter, noting areas of successful work, patterns and/or areas needing improvement, and suggested professional development activities.

Opportunities For Professional Development

While interpreters are required to attend regular professional development days in their local school district, the content is infrequently pertinent to interpreter upgrading. We suggest that the school or university provide diagnostic services to the interpreters they employ (if the school doesn't have personnel

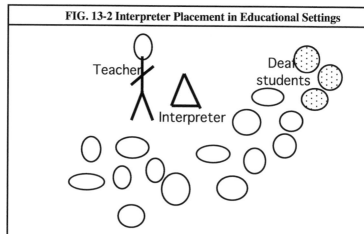

FIG. 13-2 Interpreter Placement in Educational Settings

Teacher

Deaf students

Interpreter

When the instructor stays, primarily, at the front of the room, the Interpreter usually sits to the side and slightly to the front of the teacher. This allows students to see the interpreter and teacher in one visual frame. Some Deaf students prefer to sit to one side or the other (rather then in the middle), so they can easily locate and identify other students who are asking questions or making comments.

qualified to perform the diagnostic assignments, this can be contracted out as discussed above). Based on the areas of weakness identified, the school should pay for at least two opportunities for professional development per year. This could happen during regularly scheduled professional development days or it could be in the form of paying for interpreters to attend appropriate upgrading activities that are provided through the local RID/AVLIC chapter or nearby program of interpreter preparation.

In-service days activities could be opened up so interpreters from throughout a region could attend, thus providing the interpreters from across the district or college who rarely see each other an opportunity to come together and develop a sense of professionalism and collegiality.

Some schools pay the membership of their interpreters in the national and local chapters of RID/AVLIC. Others assist interpreters with registration and travel costs to attend regional or national professional meetings. This demonstrates genuine commitment to the development of school employees and eventually the quality of support they provide to students.

Ethical Considerations

An interpreter in a K-12 educational setting is most effective when he serves as part of an educational team. In such a team, the educational goals for each individual child are discussed, thus the interpreter can better understand the goal and purpose of various educational assignments and communication events. In the educational team, discussions are held regarding the student's academic placement, her/his intellectual abilities, social skills, etc. While the interpreter is not a trained teacher (and thus cannot comment regarding intellectual or academic abilities), he is fully capable of commenting on the interpreting process, the student's language preference, language skills and the appropriateness of interpreting services within a  particular educational placement. Further, the interpreter can use team meetings to educate others in the educational setting about the interpreting process, needed working conditions and preparatory information in order to do the job appropriately, and other pertinent factors.

An Ethical Conflict of Boundaries?

One challenge arising in educational settings is the establishment of appropriate boundaries between the interpreter and the hearing, Deaf and hard of hearing students — especially when working with the same student(s) over extended periods of time or with students who are close in age to the age of the interpreter. An individual, for example, may interpret for a child through several years of school or in an intensive educational program five to six days per week all day long. We encourage interpreters and school personnel to consider rotating interpreters at least every other year to avoid some of the issues related to working with the same child/youth over too long a period of time. Some rural districts have set up agreements to move interpreters between districts to meet this need.

In another instance, a twenty-year old interpreter may be assigned to interpret for students who are age nineteen to twenty. This kind of assignment should be avoided if possible simply because there are so many individuals involved who are still learning how to set personal and professional boundaries. If it cannot be avoided, the interpreter will have to work diligently to establish boundaries by dressing consistently in an adult, professional manner, avoiding casual out-of-class contact with students, etc.

An Ethical Conflict of Role?

A significant problem can arise if the teacher and others in the setting expect the interpreter to serve as a member of the educational team while the interpreter approaches the task from a narrow, "neutral" definition of her job. Such an interpreter would probably make it known loud and clear that she is "just an interpreter" who cannot engage in dialogue with the teacher or educational team about the student or the work she does.

There are many experienced practitioners in the field who believe a narrow interpretation of an interpreter's role and ethical boundaries is detrimental in K-12 educational settings (and depending on the individual student, in other educational settings as well). As the interpreter, you will often be the only person on the educational team who knows how the student best processes information (ASL vs. English-based signs), attends, and engages in informal interactions with other students (Deaf and hearing) in the class. Thus, the interpreter can and should participate in these meetings so long as she focuses comments on interpretation and related linguistic and cultural challenges.

An Ethical Conflict of Confidentiality?

Some interpreters are concerned about the kind of dialogue that takes place during educational planning meetings and in one-on-one interactions with members of the educational team. It is an issue one should be concerned about; it is an area demanding professional discernment. It is *not* appropriate to engage in idle gossip or chatter about a student — or for that matter, teachers, administrators or others in the setting. It is not appropriate to label a child or to share comments that go beyond the scope of your practice as an interpreter.

This can be challenging in educational settings because you may observe other professionals engaging in this kind of behavior. You may even see other interpreters do it. Interpreters must constantly reflect on the ethical and professional decisions involved to confirm they are conducting themselves in appropriate ways and to change their behavior if they believe professionalism has been compromised.

Deaf Community view Of Mainstream Educational Settings And Interpreters Working There

The issue of mainstreaming young Deaf children is quite controversial within the Deaf community. Many leaders believe that mainstreaming has a negative effect on the academic achievement of Deaf children due to an impoverished linguistic environment and a reduction in self-esteem and development of leadership skills due to the increased isolation of Deaf children from each other. Whereas interpreters generally encounter appreciation and affirmation from members of the Deaf community, those in mainstreamed elementary educational settings may encounter negative responses from members of the Deaf community as a result of working in this setting. Some interpreters have chosen to stand in solidarity with the Deaf community on this issue by refusing to work in certain educational settings.

INTERPRETING IN EMPLOYMENT–RELATED SETTINGS

Employment-related settings include situations at various stages of employment. These include such events as:

- ✦ The job interview;
- ✦ Orientation of a new employee to the company facilities, regulations and policies;
- ✦ On-the-job training of a new employee, an intern, or a probationary hire;

✦ Union or staff meetings to discuss special topics, or
general sharing of work-related information;
✦ Employer-employee interactions (e.g., reprimands,
performance evaluations, employee complaint to
supervisor); and
✦ Office events such as holiday parties, recognition
ceremonies, or a farewell reception.

Because of this variety of settings, we cannot make simplistic generalizations regarding interpreting in employment-related settings.

Knowledge And Skills
Deaf individuals have experienced discrimination in the job
market in North America since the industrial revolution. It is
critical for an interpreter to maintain access to all communication in employment-related settings that support equalization
of interpersonal interactions.

Interpreters must be adequately prepared before entering an
employment-related setting in order to properly support the interactions being interpreted. This means becoming familiar with
the protocol, equipment, specialized terminology, and types of
work performed in the unique situation at hand (equivalent to
buying "work clothes" for your linguistic closet).

It also means being keenly aware of the "culture" of each workplace entered. This is critical because so much of the information-sharing and power-brokering is done in informal channels
— through the jokes, over lunch, etc. Failure on the part of the
interpreter to recognize these subtle sociolinguistic events may
actually contribute to the exclusion, rather than inclusion, of
the Deaf or hard of hearing employees. For this reason, it is
recommended that interpreters be especially tuned into cultural adjustments that may be needed in the interpretation.

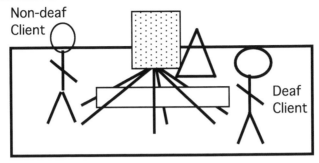

FIG. 13-3 Interpreter Placement in One-to-One I nteractions In a Small Space with Equipment Present

Non-deaf Client

Deaf Client

One-to-One Interaction
Around Equipment in Small Space

When interpreting in employment-related settings, an interpreter may need to work in a small space where a large piece of equipment takes up most of the room. Interpreter placement in this type of setting is challenging. The interpreter should position her/himself where s/he can be seen by the Deaf client and heard by the hearing client, staying clear of the equipment to avoid injury.

Standard Qualifications

There is no standard regarding the qualifications one must have prior to interpreting in employment-related settings. This is often detrimental to all involved since an employer will often locate an employee who has minimal sign skills and assume this employee can adequately interpret for a current or prospective Deaf employee. It is thus suggested that an interpreter should minimally be a graduate of an interpreter education program and preferably hold interpreter certification prior to interpreting in job-related settings.

Supervision And Evaluation

In those companies with large numbers of Deaf employees, you will sometimes find a full-time interpreter on the staff. It is not common, however, for companies to employ someone knowledgeable about the interpreting process or the languages and cultures of Deaf and hearing people who can provide appropriate supervision and evaluation for interpreters. An interpreter working in this setting will generally have no supervision or evaluation. However, when the interpreted event calls for a team of interpreters, these professional colleagues may agree to provide feedback to one another.

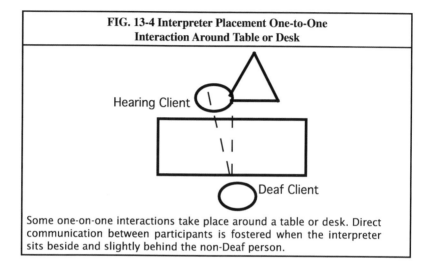

FIG. 13-4 Interpreter Placement One-to-One Interaction Around Table or Desk

Hearing Client

Deaf Client

Some one-on-one interactions take place around a table or desk. Direct communication between participants is fostered when the interpreter sits beside and slightly behind the non-Deaf person.

Pay For Services

Employment-related interpreting is usually done by freelance interpreters. Pay will vary depending on local market norms, as well as the individual interpreter's level of education and certification and years of experience. If interpreters are required for a lengthy assignment, such as on-the-job-training or a day-long orientation, they may charge a day rate rather than by the hour. Typically, however, interpreters are paid by the hour in employment-related settings.

Working Conditions

Working conditions are usually less than optimal. After all, an interpreter may be walking into an auto mechanic shop, an employer's cluttered office, on the floor of the meat slaughtering plant, or in an orientation to safety procedures for underwater welding. Since we don't want interpreter needs to become an excuse for refusing to hire Deaf individuals, interpreters in these settings learn to do the best they can within the situations they find. Some basic questions should be asked when called to work in these settings. Will the conference with the employee take place in an office or on the floor of the plant? If in the plant, what attire do the workers usually wear — hard hats, steel toed shoes, goggles? If special gear is required, request that a hat, pair of goggles, lab jacket (or whatever) be provided when you arrive.

Discretion must be used in selecting the attire you will wear to such a setting, especially when you realize that you will be in an automobile factory in the morning and interpreting for formal union negotiations (suit and tie required) in the afternoon! Flexibility is the key.

INTERPRETING IN RELIGIOUS SETTINGS

Religious settings can include a wide variety of events. Four categories of events that occur frequently include liturgical services, funerals, weddings and special events (e.g., baptisms, bat/bar mitzvah). It is essential that the interpreter contact members of the religious group for whom she is interpreting in advance of an event because signs vary dramatically from group to group.

For example, the way of signing "baptism" in a Baptist setting (where the term refers to a youth or adult being immersed below the surface of water) is very different from the way of signing "baptism" in a Catholic setting (where the term usually refers to sprinkling water on an infant). Another example is the term used to refer to the holy book of religious teachings for various religious bodies. For the Christian, the name is the Bible, for the Buddhist, it is The Path to Enlightenment, the Torah and the Talmud for someone from the Jewish community, and the Koran for the Muslim. The signs used to refer to each of these documents vary depending on the beliefs and teachings surrounding each religious group. It is critical, then for interpreters not only to be familiar with how certain terms are signed in each, but the basic teachings, as well.

FIG. 13-5 Interpreter Placement In Typical" One-On-One Settings	
Sign Language Interpreter	When working in a one-on-one situation, placement of participants and interpreter should allow the Deaf client to see the hearing individual while keeping the interpreter in sight, as well. Strategies should be used to encourage rapport between the hearing andDeaf individuals, rather than the interpreter.
Hearing Client	If the Deaf client prefers oral communication s/he will not usually employ the services of an oral transliterator for a one-on-one interaction
Deaf Client	If the client is Deaf Blind, the interpreter's placement will vary depending on the type of visual impairment, preferred mode of communication and other factors.

Standard Qualifications

Qualifications are not generally established in religious settings, although an interpreter who subscribes to the beliefs of the particular religious body is usually preferred. Entry-level interpreters often work in religious settings. This may be because of the lack of standards in this setting and a general lack of understanding on the part of parishioners regarding the challenge faced when interpreting in these settings.

Special Considerations

While the text for songs, sermons, prayers, etc. can often be obtained in advance of an event to help the interpreter prepare, the register including ritualistic and/or poetic use of language found in many religious settings make interpreting particularly challenging. Preparation for work in religious settings is essential — not optional.

The text for most funerals, weddings, and baptisms is standard in each religious sect; copies can be obtained well in advance. An interpreter can even attend several weddings performed by

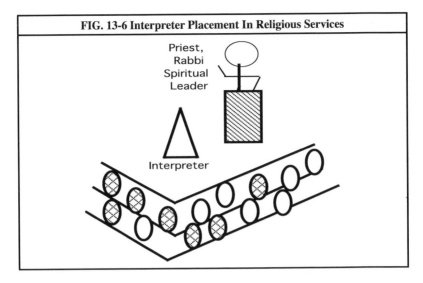

FIG. 13-6 Interpreter Placement In Religious Services

the minister or masses led by the priest in order to familiar-
ize himself with the ritual, rhythm, speaker style and language
used prior to the in terpreting assignment. In some cases, the
entire homily or sermon can be obtained prior to a service. In
all cases, the words for music and scriptures to be read can be
obtained prior to an event. Prayers, songs, or other spoken,
sung, or chanted texts in different languages present a particular challenge to an interpreter in these settings. Depending on
the Deaf participants, the choices available to the interpreter
include providing:

✦ A full linguistic and cultural equivalent from the
   spoken language into ASL; and
✦ A transliteration into an English-based representation of the source language. If, for example, the
   reading is in Hebrew, an interpreter might provide a
   fingerspelled phonetic representation of the source
   language.

Thus, you must know your audience as well as the source language text well enough that you can provide the interpretation
or transliteration requested and/or appropriate.

Ethical Considerations

Interpreters need to consider several areas of potential conflict prior to interpreting in a religious setting. If you subscribe to a particular set of beliefs and feel strongly about them, interpreting effectively in any setting where different or opposing beliefs are espoused may be challenging. The same can be true when the interpreter believes strongly in the teachings or beliefs being presented and there are Deaf visitors or inquirers present.

The temptation to edit material or add one's own opinions/judgments is powerful. Inappropriate behaviors/responses can occur in such subtle ways, the interpreter may not even realize s/he is doing something unprofessional. Before interpreting in a religious setting  be sure you can put your own beliefs and convictions aside so you can properly convey the spirit and intent of the speaker(s).

Role Delineation

Unfortunately, the interpreter's role in religious settings often gets mixed with that of spiritual leader, director of religious ministries, counselor and guide. This is seen particularly in those settings where a member of a congregation or religious sect volunteers to provide interpreter services. Here we would offer a word of caution: Let the minister serve as spiritual guide and counselor — as an interpreter, you are not trained in theology or in moral advisement.

Pay For Services

Religious organizations often depend on volunteers to staff activities and organizational positions. It is not surprising, then, that they also expect interpreters to volunteer their services to the church, temple or mosque when required. Further, the lack of awareness about the process of interpretation leads to the misperception that a single interpreter is adequate to handle the interpreting needs for a single event — even when that event involves complex and difficult texts or long hours.

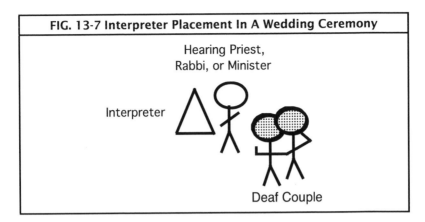

FIG. 13-7 Interpreter Placement In A Wedding Ceremony

Hearing Priest, Rabbi, or Minister

Interpreter

Deaf Couple

If you attend a particular religious group and are approached by someone asking you to interpret weekly services on a volunteer basis, you may feel you should agree because this is the kind of contribution all members of this group typically offer. Obviously, this is a decision you will have to make based on the consideration of a variety of factors.

We would encourage you to remember that if the minister, rabbi, pianist, cantor or song leader receives remuneration, it is appropriate for you to negotiate either a fair wage or an honorarium for the service you provide. In fact, paying the interpreter can be a benefit to the religious organization. Deaf congregants can expect (demand) a minimum level of expertise, regular and timely attendance, appropriate preparation for the work and an interpreter who behaves ethically. These points are important since it is hard to reprimand a volunteer. Further, the religious group would be in a position to hire a substitute in your absence if payment is part of the regular arrangement.

When asked to interpret in religious settings, you should tactfully negotiate your fees and appropriate working conditions. For example, in certain settings you will need a team interpreter, regular breaks, the text at least one week in advance, etc. If you want to donate the money received back to the religious community later, you can still do so.

Supervision And Professional Development

Interpreters in religious settings rarely receive regular supervision, evaluation or opportunities for professional development. Sometimes another interpreter in this setting — often one who has been around for a number of years — will informally provide evaluation or feedback. This can be quite rewarding or frustrating, depending on whether the informal mentor has had any recent training or professional development her/himself.

Some religious groups have workshops, upgrading opportunities, and even organizations established specifically to meet the needs of interpreters working in their ranks. These are beneficial because they often give insights into specific terminology and texts — particularly if taught by individuals who have stayed current with professional, as well as religious, practices and knowledge.

WORKING WITH DEAF INTERPRETERS

You will encounter a number of interpreting assignments where you should be working with a Deaf Interpreter (DI). The settings can range from medical, to legal or psychiatric -- or any other setting where we provide interpreting services. The decision about working with hearing interpreters only or working in a deaf-hearing interpreting team will be based on the communication needs of the deaf client(s).

Standard Qualifications

Both the Deaf and hearing interpreters should be trained and qualified to work in the specific setting where this type of service is being provided. Don't make the mistake iof assuming that just because a person is deaf, s/he is qualified to work as a deaf interpreter.

Special Considerations

A DI is used when the communication needs of the deaf consumer makes it necessary. It might be that the deaf consumer has developmental delays or mental health issues, is a recent immigrant to the country and is unfamiliar with standard ASL, never mastered standard ASL for some reason. The DI is trained to use pantomime, ASL with extreme expansions, drawing pictures, acting out things, etc. to hopefully communicate with the deaf consumer.

Ethical Considerations

Both the Deaf and hearing interpreters are bound by the professional Code of Ethics and guidelines for professional behavior. This is especially important because the Deaf consumer may be reluctant to have a member of the Deaf community participate in the event for fear of loss of confidentiality.

Role Delineation

It is important to set up clear role delineation -- the hearing interpreter is interpreting to/for the Deaf Interpreter The DI is interpreting between the deaf consumer and the hearing interpreter. While working, each interpreter monitors the other in the event of an error, but the hearing interpreter should not by-pass the DI's interpretation and voice interpret for the deaf client directly.

As well, the interpreting team needs to discuss how introductions will take place in order to maintain the appearance of equality between the interpreters on the team. It is common for the DI to introduce him/hersef to the deaf client while the hearing interpreter introduces her/himself to the hearing client, each explaining how the process will work while making the introductions. It is also important for the interpreting team to enter together, thus avoiding inadvertant connections from forming between the hearing customer and the hearing interpreter.

Pay For Services

Both the Deaf and hearing interpreters should be paid for their services at regular interpreter rates. This should be negotiated when setting up the job.

Supervision and Professional Development
You will find minimal, if any, supervision when working with a DI. It is encumbent on interpreters to seek out workshops and other training opportunities where the skills for deaf-hearing teams can be developed.

INTERPRETING IN MEDICAL SETTINGS

Medical settings can be divided into medical appointments and laboratory/hospital procedures. Medical appointments may take place in a neighborhood clinic, at the office of a private physician, in a campus infirmary or in a hospital-based medical center. Hospital settings vary from emergency room procedures to routine tests and surgical/post-surgical events. In all of these settings, the interpreter often meets the clients for the first time upon entering the medical setting. While the Deaf client has probably used an interpreter's services somewhere before, in a medical setting s/he may be nervous, worried, or in pain and this will affect communication.

The behavior of the medical personnel encountered will be influenced by a number of factors, including the number of patients waiting to be seen, the level of stress and tension due to the nature of the illness or emergency at hand, and a variety of other factors. It may also be influenced by the presence of a sign language interpreter — possibly a totally new experience for this particular doctor, nurse or lab technician.

Placement
This is definitely one setting in which the "ideal" placement (beside and slightly behind the hearing speaker) is virtually impossible. In some settings, you can arrange yourself and stay in one location throughout the interaction. However, medical examination rooms are small and crowded with equipment; nurses and medical technicians are often crowded into the room along with the doctor and patient. Depending on the type of exami-

nation or procedure, the patient may be face-up or face-down on the table, s/he may be required to walk about the room (on one or both feet), or to alternately breathe deeply and hold her/his breath. When interpreting for a medical examination, it is necessary for the interpreter to be highly mobile in order to constantly reposition her/himself, thus insuring that the Deaf client can see the visual communication in this variety of physical positions while the interpreter maintains respect for the client's physical privacy.

Protocol

Interpreters are fortunate because they are often able to draw some cues from the other professionals in a setting regarding how to act, what to wear and other factors. This is true in the medical setting. When the doctor or nurse hands a patient a gown with instructions to strip, the doctor or nurse then leave the room to allow the patient to change clothes in privacy. As an interpreter, you should pick up on this clue and be right behind the medical professionals as they exit the room.

Role Delineation

A professional demeanor and self-advocacy skills are needed by interpreters in medical settings because the medical personnel encountered will not typically understand an interpreter's role or how to make best use of having an interpreter present. As a result, you must be able to predict what your needs will be in the up-coming situation and effectively and professionally communicate your needs to the medical personnel.

For example, it may be necessary for you to "brief" the nursing staff on the floor where the Deaf patient is staying so they know to call the interpreter when communication needs arise. You may have to tactfully, but insistently, explain to an x-ray technician the fact that the Deaf client cannot hear through the partition as she shouts, "take a breath — hold it — now breathe."

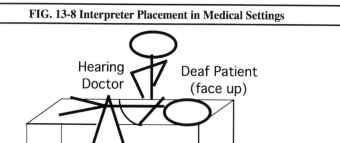

FIG. 13-8 Interpreter Placement in Medical Settings

Hearing Doctor

Deaf Patient (face up)

Interpreter

An interpreter's position will vary in medical settings depending on the constraints of the room, the type of examination being done and the equipment needed by the medical personnel.

If the patient is on the table, face up, the interpreter will often place her/himself across the table from the doctor. In this way, the doctor can move about freely as s/he conducts the medical examination, without tripping over the interpreter.

Special Knowledge And Skills

When interpreting in medical settings, it is necessary for the interpreter to be familiar with a variety of medical terms, procedures and protocol. For example, a relatively simple question like, "Are you taking any medications?" must be understood to include medications that are taken orally, injected, inhaled, or applied to the skin. The interpretation of a question about "allergies" may need to be accompanied by the variety of reactions one might experience if allergic to a substance (wheezing, itching, watery eyes, skin rash, headache, etc.). An interpreter should be aware of the fact that when interpreting for x-rays, he should ask for a lead apron to protect himself from the radiation.

An interpreter in medical settings should be aware of the stages of various procedures and the relative importance of communication at each of those stages. For example, when a Deaf person is going into surgery, it is helpful to the patient if the interpreter is able to go into the surgical suite until the patient is fully anesthetized. If these arrangements are made, the interpreter must understand the necessity of scrubbing up and putting on surgical garb. She should also know how to advocate for removal of the mouth covering at that early, non-invasive stage of surgery. Whether or not the interpreter is able to convince the medical staff of her need to go into surgery, she must be able to advocate for her to be allowed into the recovery room. It is at that stage in the process that communication is critical. Recovery room nurses go through a number of communication steps (calling the patient by name, asking the patient what day it is or where they are, etc.) in order to determine if the patient is coming out from under the anesthetic properly. Lack of communication at this stage could be deadly to the patient. It is certainly beneficial if the interpreter is able to stay with the patient once he has been sent back to the floor. However, this is a less critical stage and if family is nearby, they can provide the minimal communication necessary at this phase of the process.

Pay For Services

Payment and fees in medical settings vary from city to city and region to region. In the U.S., hospitals are required by law to provide interpreters for Deaf patients. The same is true in Canada because of a Supreme Court ruling in 1997; however, there are different levels of awareness and implementation of these requirements from rural to urban settings. In some states, the State Commission for the Deaf provides payment for interpreters in medical settings. In other areas, an agency has subcontracted with hospitals and health maintenance organizations to provide all interpreting services. You need to know the system that applies in your area when starting to work in medical settings.

Supervision and Professional Development

In those situations where an agency has subcontracted with health facilities, there may be some sporadic supervision and evaluation. In other situations, there is no supervision or evaluation provided either by the health care facility or the professional interpreter association.

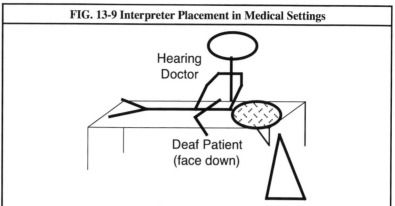

FIG. 13-9 Interpreter Placement in Medical Settings

Hearing Doctor

Deaf Patient (face down)

If the patient is face-down on the table, the interpreter will probably sit or squat at the patient's head so s/he can see the interpreted communication. If the doctor is doing a rectal , prostate or other exam in a sensitive area, the interpreter should be near the patient's head, maintaining eye contact with the patient.

Professional development is primarily available through professional interpreter workshops, continuing education opportunities, and skills upgrading seminars sponsored by interpreter education programs. Whereas medical personnel are required by law to maintain their knowledge and skills, at this time there are no requirements for professional development or maintenance in order to work as an interpreter in medical settings.[b]

Standard Qualifications

There are no standard qualifications that one must satisfy prior to working as an interpreter in medical settings. It is informally held that one should be certified prior to interpreting in most medical settings. However, uncertified interpreters are frequently found working in these settings.

---

[b] RID certified interpreters are required to provide evidence of continuing education beyond certification to maintain their credential, but there is no requirement stating that a certain number of upgrading hours must be in the area of medical interpreting, or any other specialized area of work.

Medical interpreting is critical; inaccurate communication can be life threatening. The authors of this text recommend specialized training for those of you who seek to specialize in medical interpreting, such as that offered at the College of St. Catherine's in Minnesota.[c]

Some communities require interpreters to complete special training or to take and pass some type of skills screening in order to be qualified to work in medical settings. The authors applaud those communities and we urge interpreters working in medical settings to take classes and workshops specific to terminology, protocol, and ASL-English interpretation in this specialized area.

Further, it is anticipated that a specialist certificate for interpreting in medical settings may be considered by our professional associations at some point in the future.

It should be noted that we are beginning to see Deaf and hard of hearing doctors, dentists, chiropractors and other medical personnel. This provides Deaf and hard of hearing individuals with the choice of using an interpreter in certain settings or going to a practitioner with whom they can communicate directly.

INTERPRETING IN LEGAL SETTINGS

Legal settings can be divided into attorney—client appointments, police interactions, and courtroom proceedings. Attorney-client appointments may take place in a legal aid clinic, at the office of an attorney, in the hallway of the courthouse, or in a conference room at the city or county jail.

Settings involving the police vary from police-victim, police-suspect, and police-witness interviews. These interactions can take place in a variety of locations, including at the police department, in the jail, or at a person's home or business.

---

[c] BA in Interpreting with specializations in Medical, Educational and Deaf–Blind interpretation (601 25th Ave. So, Minneapolis, MN 55454).

Courtroom proceedings involve civil, criminal and administrative hearings. They may involve adults or juveniles. The Deaf person(s) involved in a case may be the plaintiff, the defendant, the victim, the witness, a member of the jury, or a family member of the plaintiff, defendant, victim or witness. There are several Deaf attorneys in general practice in both Canada and the U.S. and one Deaf judge (that the authors know of). They generally have a full-time personal interpreter or use real-time captioning so it is doubtful that you will walk into a situation where your Deaf client is the attorney or judge.

In all of these settings, the interpreter may encounter a client she has met in the Deaf community, but it is just as likely the interpreter may never have seen these particular clients before entering the legal setting. While the Deaf client has probably used an interpreter's services somewhere before, in this setting they may be nervous, worried, or frightened. These factors may negatively affect the clarity of communication. Further, the legal personnel behave according to a particular role and reflect a protocol that is frequently misunderstood by the lay person. Most legal personnel have no experience working with an interpreter.

Placement and Protocol
In many legal settings, the interpreter can arrange herself beside and slightly behind the hearing speaker. However, this is not always possible. In the courtroom, there is rapid turn-taking between multiple speakers and protocol dictates that no one sit or stand in certain areas (e.g., in the "well" — the area in front of the judge's bench). Certain arrangements in jail also present a challenge for placement — communicating through a slit in the solid door of a holding cell, for example, is virtually impossible. When interpreting in legal settings, the interpreter must be highly skilled, familiar with the judicial system and legal language, aware of and sensitive to the unique protocol in each of the legal settings encountered, able to appropriately articulate

working condition needs as an interpreter and to qualify her/himself before members of the court.

Interpreters can gather some cues regarding protocol from the other professionals in the setting. For example, when courtroom personnel stand as the judge enters, the interpreter should follow suit. When police or attorneys act with caution around a suspect, the interpreter should do likewise.

As in other settings, professionalism and self-advocacy skills are needed by an interpreter in legal settings. This means you must be able to predict what your needs will be in each situation and you must be able to effectively communicate your needs to the legal personnel. It may be necessary for you to "brief" the judge in a particular case regarding the need for multiple teams of interpreters or the involvement of a Deaf interpreter in order to most effectively meet the needs of the clients involved. You may have to tactfully explain to an attorney or police officer that when s/he moves between you and the Deaf client/suspect, communication ceases because you can't see each other.

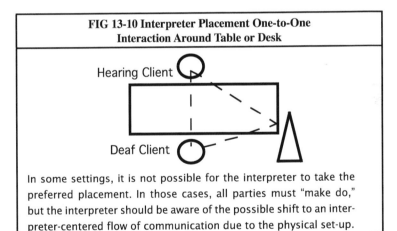

FIG 13-10 Interpreter Placement One-to-One Interaction Around Table or Desk

Hearing Client

Deaf Client

In some settings, it is not possible for the interpreter to take the preferred placement. In those cases, all parties must "make do," but the interpreter should be aware of the possible shift to an interpreter-centered flow of communication due to the physical set-up.

Standard Qualifications

Clear, accurate communication in legal settings is critical; inaccurate communication can endanger the life and liberty of those involved. In 1991, RID adopted a competency-based curriculum which an interpreter must master prior to taking the test for legal certification. Interpreters should complete special training in the legal system, legal terminology, and skills development specific to legal language and interactions. Further, we urge only those with legal certification to work in legal settings. At this time, only RID offers certification for interpreters in this specialist area;

Pay For Services & Working Conditions

Fees for interpreting in legal settings varies in different geographical locations and depending on the system that may be in place. In some rural communities, there is no formal system in place for the employment of interpreters in legal settings. Each interpreter is an independent contractor, setting his own fees. He must independently bill the attorney, the police department or the court. The opportunity for legal work is sporadic. On the other hand, in Los Angeles, California the Superior Court has a full-time interpreter coordinator who works with over 60 different languages. This court has a set pay rate of pay for a half-day and for a full day of courtroom interpreting. Interpreters are required to hold legal certification in order to work for the court. Interpreters complete a time sheet, submit it bi-monthly, and receive payment in a timely fashion. Because of the entrenchment of this system, most private interpreting agencies in this area and attorneys who contract individually with interpreters for depositions, attorney-client appointments, etc., pay "court rates." Sign language interpreters have a considerable amount of work in Los Angeles due to the large Deaf population, the regular inclusion of Deaf jurors within the jury system, and the adversarial nature of interactions in California.

Supervision And Professional Development

These factors will vary depending on the size of the community being served, the multi-lingual/multi-ethnic nature of the area, and the level of services being provided to other language groups by the local legal system. In larger communities, excellent supervision and evaluation may be provided along with regular professional development opportunities for both sign and spoken language interpreters. In other areas, one agency or individual may serve an entire region as "the" legal interpreter with no structured arrangement for evaluation, supervision, or professional development opportunities.

Ethical Considerations

Interpreters in the judicial system encounter unique ethical challenges and a multitude of ethical questions on a daily basis. Dialogue and consultation with other individuals who work as sign language interpreters in this specialist area is critical to maintain one's mental health and to glean the kinds of support required to work as a competent and professional practitioner.

An Ethical Conflict Regarding Confidentiality?

Professional consultation is the standard of practice in all professional fields. Doctors and therapists talk to other doctors and therapists regarding treatment options and responses of a specific patient. Ministers consult with one another regarding the spiritual welfare of a parishioner and lawyers discuss cases and clients with one another. All of this is done in the professional plane, with clear expectations that such dialogue is shared in strictest confidence. They consult as a way to hold themselves accountable to their profession regarding the decisions being made, to brainstorm options and to glean support from colleagues about the work being done. Interpreters — especially interpreters in specialist settings — only hurt themselves and their consumers by denying themselves access to this type of collegial consultation and support.

Certainly caution should be used and only those details mandatory to gather the ideas, options and support needed should be shared. Further, it would be wise to reconfirm the confidentiality of the dialogue before it begins. But having taken these precautions, it is highly advisable for interpreters in legal settings to confer with fellow professionals when necessary — and doing so within the constraints spelled out above *does not constitute violation of confidentiality.* Rather, it is an indication of credible professional practice.

Ethical Concern: Familiarity With A Case With Multiple Deaf Individuals Involved

It is best for a Deaf litigant to have one interpreter (or team of interpreters, depending on complexity and length of hearing) for courtroom proceedings and a separate interpreter for client-attorney interactions. The interpreter working for the court should refrain from interpreting for the defense and prosecuting attorneys as they prepare their witnesses. Taking these precautions is wise because it avoids contamination of the interpreter who may observe a difference between what a witness prepares to testify and what is actually said on the witness stand that may inadvertently influence the interpretation. In the same manner, an interpreter who has been involved in the police interrogation of a victim, witness, or perpetrator should refrain from interpreting for that individual if the matter goes to trial.

If there is only one interpreter in a 400-mile radius, it may be necessary for the court to import interpreters at different phases of the judicial process. These decisions must be entered into carefully and the legally certified interpreter should be cognizant of all these factors since s/he is often the person who must convince judicial personnel of the legal system's need to "import" interpreters for special circumstances.

An Ethical Conflict Regarding Role?

There has been a great deal of discussion of late regarding the appropriateness of an interpreter making a complete linguistic and cultural transition between English and ASL in legal settings, which boils down to a difference in philosophical frame among practitioners. Some say that when interpreting the Miranda Warning, for example, it is *never* appropriate for the interpreter to make linguistic and cultural expansions. Others say it is unethical to fail to make these transitions and thus ensure that the Deaf or hard of hearing person involved comprehends the meaning of the statements being conveyed.

As an interpreter working in legal settings, you will have to question each decision made and be prepared to defend that choice should it be challenged by a lawyer, judge or fellow interpreter. The authors of this text believe that you can only function as an ethical practitioner if you make the event taking place and the language being used transparent to the participants for whom you are interpreting, supporting authentic inclusion of all parties involved.

An Ethical Conflict Regarding Qualifications?

One question legal interpreters must ask themselves is whether they are truly qualified to work in the legal situation at hand. Given the significant linguistic and cultural differences between a monolingual/monocultural Deaf individual and the legal system, ensconced in archaic language and extremely formal protocol, serious consideration should always be given to the use of Deaf interpreters in legal settings. Some believe that only with the involvement of Deaf interpreters do Deaf and hard of hearing individuals have full access to legal events.

INTERPRETING IN MENTAL HEALTH AND PSYCHIATRIC SETTINGS

Mental health and psychiatric settings can be divided into psychiatric testing and evaluation, outpatient therapy sessions and inpatient psychiatric treatment. Therapy and psychiatric treatment can be further divided into various types, such as art therapy, occupational therapy, individual and group therapy sessions, etc.

Special Knowledge And Skills

The challenge in all of these settings lies in the fact that psychologists, counselors, and psychiatrists use *language* as a key to identifying mental health as opposed to unhealthy mental and psychiatric behaviors. Further, the language they primarily use is English. For this reason, it is imperative that an interpreter in these settings work closely with the therapist, insuring that her presence and role of communication facilitator enhances rather than impedes the dynamics. Further, this is another setting where use of deaf interpreters should be seriously considered in an effort to ensure cross cultural communications with clarity and certainty.

Interpreters sometimes work with in-patient clients. The fact that an individual is a patient in a psychiatric ward sometimes means he is a danger to himself or others. For this reason, the interpreter may have to pass through a series of locked steel doors or ride on elevators that require a key to operate. In some cases, a "pass" must be secured and worn by the interpreter to distinguish her from patients in the setting.

If you find yourself in such a setting, be alert to others in the environment. Always be aware of the location of exits or security guards in the event someone near you becomes aggressive or violent. Further, inquire about appropriate attire to wear into such an institution. You will often find that interpreters, as well as other staff working in the setting, are required to wear informal attire in to neutralize the environment as much as possible for the patients.

Psychiatric evaluations are generally based on written English and hearing norms. They are written in such a way that the meaning and goal of the question is often quite obscure. We recommend that psychiatric evaluations and testing be performed *only* with a trained Deaf interpreter or with a Deaf advocate present since misinterpretations of questions and answers have repeatedly led to the misdiagnosis of the Deaf individuals involved.

Standard Qualifications

Communication in mental health settings is critical; inaccurate communication can be life threatening. The complexities of interpreting in mental health settings require that interpreters be certified and particularly skilled in the use of ASL, adept at cross-cultural behaviors, and have special training in the vocabulary, therapist-patient dynamics, and protocol prior to working in mental health and psychiatric settings. In addition, interpreters should be emotionally stable themselves, be able to establish clear and appropriate boundaries and have access to their own therapist in the event something in the interpreted event triggers something in them. Since interpreting in these settings can be quite stressful, the interpreter needs to have a support system in place to maintain her/his own mental health, including interpreting colleagues with whom to debrief appropriate issues and questions that may arise.

Protocol
Professionals in mental health and psychiatric interpreting frequently engage in critical incident debriefings. This is a time when the professionals discuss what is happening with the client, with themselves, and the dynamics including their own feelings and reactions to what is taking place. Communication taking place in a debriefing session is confidential and is often critical for the success of future sessions. Interpreters should engage in brief sessions with the therapist before and after a counseling session in order to identify the therapist's goals, clarify any communication concerns, and to be sure the therapist is feeling comfortable.

Other Considerations
Other features of interpreting in mental health and psychiatric settings are similar to those delineated under interpreting in medical and legal settings above.

Interpreting For Conferences
Interpreting in certain religious, educa-tional, medical, and performing arts settings involve platform interpreting. Interpreting for conferences is a specialized type of platform interpreting. A conference usually takes place over

several days and presentations follow a unifying theme. Papers and speakers are frequently available in advance of the presentation; this allows interpreters to more fully prepare for the task.

At conferences, specialized terminology will usually be used, reflecting the technology under discussion or the professional field represented. In addition to the platform interpreting found in plenary or major presentations, conferences often have multiple breakout groups, an exhibit hall which sometimes requires escort interpreters, receptions, banquets, and other activities.

Pay for Services
When interpreting at a conference, there are often full and part-time interpreting positions. Full-time interpreters are provided a day rate, often ranging from $300 - $550 per day, while part-time interpreters are paid an hourly rate. Depending on the conference, travel, lodging and expenses may also be paid to interpreters.

Supervision And Evaluation
More and more, organizations are employing interpreter coordinators to hire and schedule interpreters at conferences. These coordinators provide on-sight supervision to the interpreting teams and in some situations, are able to give evaluative feedback to individual interpreters.

Working Conditions
Conference interpreters usually work long days and thus teams of interpreters as well as regular breaks are required. In some instances, an interpreter lounge is required, providing interpreters with a location near the conference center where a tired interpreter can grab something to eat and put his feet up for a few minutes. More and more large conferences arrange to have a massage therapist available to interpreters for short-term, immediate shoulder-arm-hand massages, as well as hot wax machines and other services to help interpreters make it through the long days without suffering physical damage.

FIG. 13-11 Interpreter Placement In Conferences[d]

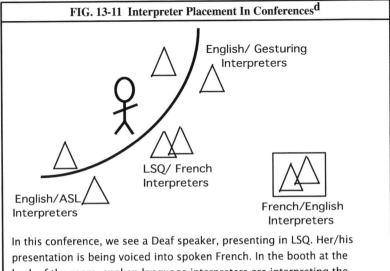

English/ Gesturing Interpreters

LSQ/ French Interpreters

English/ASL Interpreters

French/English Interpreters

In this conference, we see a Deaf speaker, presenting in LSQ. Her/his presentation is being voiced into spoken French. In the booth at the back of the room, spoken language interpreters are interpreting the French into spoken English, which is being projected into the conference room via an infrared system. The platform interpreters are receiving spoken English on their headsets and conveying the presentation into ASL and Gestuno. Note that all interpreter positions are teamed.

Special Considerations

A sign language interpreter working at a conference may encounter an array of other interpreting professionals and equipment rarely found in other settings. If multiple spoken languages are being used at the conference, one will frequently find an infrared or FM speaker system that allows audience members who have a special headset to hear the spoken language interpretation. If the speaker is rendering her address in a language in which the sign language interpreter is not fluent, the sign language interpreter will have to interpret from the feed received over the headset. In Canada, conference interpreters typically work with spoken English, spoken French, ASL and LSQ.

---

d Gestuno is a system of signs and gestures used for international deaf events.

Additionally, it is common to provide multiple visual language services at large conferences. One may see transliteration, interpretation, oral transmission, tactile (Deaf-Blind) and an international gestural system — all at the same time!

Professional and Ethical Considerations

Fewer ethical questions may arise in a conference setting than in community interpreting settings. One area to note is respect for the documents provided interpreters in order for them to prepare for a presentation. It is not ethical of an individual to take ownership of someone's unpublished presentation or copies of overheads used. Once the presentation is over, interpreters should return these papers to the presenter or to the interpreter coordinator.

At national and international conferences, it is quite likely that you will be working with interpreters with whom you are unfamiliar. One professional issue is setting up positive working relationships with these colleagues, including how to divide the work and cues indicating when you need a feed from your partner.

INTERPRETING IN THEATRICAL OR PERFORMING ARTS SETTINGS

Examples of theatrical or performing arts settings include dramatic performances and musical concerts. These, too, are specialized forms of platform interpreting. Interpreters can be found at Broadway and off-Broadway performances, and at a variety of Renaissance Fairs throughout North America, at dramatic and musical performances sponsored by national parks, community theaters, and college/university performing arts programs.

Musical Concerts

Interpretation of musical performances often requires numerous hours of rehearsal. Music, after all, is an art form of hearing cultures, and interpreting art forms across cultures is particularly challenging. The interpreter needs copies of the lyrics for all songs and adequate time to analyze the message of each song in order to provide an equivalent rendition of the song in an artistic and rhythmic manner. If possible, the interpreter should memorize the words of the various songs although he can also use copies of the words on a music stand to refer to in a concert where numerous pieces of music will be used.

One of the characteristics of musical performances is the inclusion of instrumental refrains; an interpreter will need to make decisions regarding what to do when the saxophone player performs a five minute solo. Some interpreters choose some physical movement in synchronization with the rhythm of the music; others simply turn their gaze and body to give visual focus on the soloist.

Preparation for a musical concert can be more successful if the interpreter works with a CD or audio tape recording of the musical artist(s) singing the songs. You may also get a pass to attend one or more of the artist's concerts provided prior to the interpreted performance.

Theatrical Performances

There are several placement and role options available when interpreting in theatrical and performing arts settings. Interpreters may simply be placed at the front of the stage and provide an interpretation of the dialogue. They may be placed in "zones," in which each practitioner interprets the dialogue being delivered by actors anytime they enter that interpreter's zone. Interpreters may also be requested to provide shadow interpreting. In this style of theatrical interpretation, the interpreter actually becomes "a part of the show," dressing in costume, moving in a large, dramatic signing space, physically portraying the character(s) she is shadowing. In this arrangement, the interpreter is sometimes dressed in black, literally moving as if she were that actor's shadow.

There are pros and cons to each of these options. Standing stationary in an off stage location is the least desirable because Deaf theater goers must literally choose to watch the interpretation or the action on stage.  This arrangement makes it difficult for Deaf audience members to follow the actions, shift of characters, and dialogue.

The "zone" method violates the norms of visual communication, requiring a shift of interpreters right in the middle of a line if the actor moves out of one zone and into another. Thus the "character" portrayed loses consistency due to the fact that each character could be interpreted by three different interpreters — complete with variation in interpreting style. However, Deaf audience members are able to see the action on the stage with this technique. A modified zone approach involves two interpreters, placed on the stage, who shift their placement from stage left to stage right and back at predetermined points in the play, in order to enable Deaf audience members to follow the action and dialogue.

The advantage to having interpreters shadow the actors, is the close visual proximity of the interpreter to the actor. Here the Deaf patron doesn't need to make a decision about who to watch because he can watch both the interpreter and the actor at the same time. In the best of cases, the Deaf patron mentally superimposes the interpreter onto the actor, and forgets that the actor does not sign. However, because spoken performances follow auditory turn-taking behaviors, Deaf audience members watching shadow interpreters often have difficulty locating who is speaking when there is rapid turn-taking.

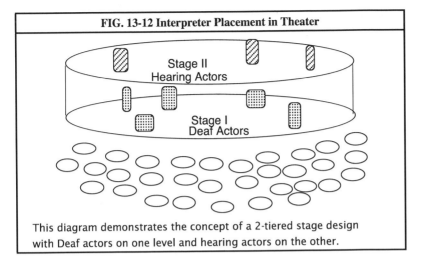

FIG. 13-12 Interpreter Placement in Theater

Stage II
Hearing Actors

Stage I
Deaf Actors

This diagram demonstrates the concept of a 2-tiered stage design with Deaf actors on one level and hearing actors on the other.

Two of the most effective approaches to providing access to dramatic performances involve the use of Deaf actors rather than, or in addition to, interpreters. The first (rarely used to date) is a double stage approach. In this approach, there are literally two stages — one over the other — with a cast of hearing actors speaking lines on one stage and Deaf actors signing lines on the second stage In the second approach, the actors are Deaf and there is an accompanying dramatic voice interpretation for each Deaf character. In some theaters, the dramatic voice is provided via infrared or FM systems, requiring hearing audience members to wear special headsets.

If the shadowing technique is used, interpreters are an integral part of the performance and must attend all rehearsals and performances. Interpreters are costumed and actually develop as the characters' alter egos. Here, interpreters take on similar physical characteristics and motivation as the actors, and are acknowledged by them onstage. They carry objects, dance, participate in set changes, and any other tasks that are performed by actors (including, sometimes, acting other roles).

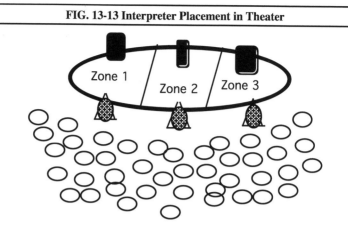

FIG. 13-13 Interpreter Placement in Theater

Zone 1   Zone 2   Zone 3

This diagram demonstrates the concept of zone interpreting for theatrical presentations. As actors move about on the stage, the interpreter in zone 1 interprets all dialogue occurring in her/his zone. As the actor(s) move into zone 2 or 3, those zone interpreters pick up the interpretation. This allows Deaf audience members to follow the action on stage more closely. Interpreters may be standing on the floor, seated in a visually appropriate location in each zone, or elevated slightly above each zone.

Productions sometimes mix shadow interpreting with the zoned set up. In this instance, interpreters are placed somewhere on the set and remain there for a period of time. In a scene that requires a great deal of quick movement on the part of the actors, this type of staging reduces the amount of cluttered movement and protects sight lines for Deaf audience members.

Standard Qualifications

There are no standard qualifications. It is beneficial for an interpreter working in this setting to have a background in music or theater. If you find yourself working in this setting frequently, we advise you to take a course or two in dramatic arts, character development, and script analysis, as well as stage directions. A person with musical training will be more apt to identify the rhythm and type of music being performed; they may then be able to make more equivalent interpreting choices. Further, Deaf actors, stage managers and directors (as well as audience members) recommend that theatrical interpreters have train-ing in acting or performance art, be physically able to move and interact with actors on the stage, and possess the highest level of signing and translation skills.

Pay For Services

This will vary depending on a number of conditions. When oth-ers in the theatrical or performing arts setting are being paid union wages, the interpreter would be well advised to charge a fee in line with those union wages. In fact, interpreters may be required to join one of the performing arts unions in order to work in a given venue. In situations like a community theatre, everybody is volunteering their time and the expectation may be that interpreters will volunteer their time as well. If this is a paid opportunity, be sure to calculate the time spent for transla-tion and rehearsals.

Supervision And Evaluation

There is typically no supervision or evaluation for interpreters in performing arts settings. Usually, colleagues will work together to provide one another with feedback regarding techniques that are effective, accuracy of message analysis and the like.

Special Considerations

When interpreting for plays and dramatic performances, the interpreter must obtain and study the script. An interpreter's involvement in rehearsals is critical since the director will often choose to include the interpreter in the blocking[e] directions for the play, insuring proper lighting on the interpreter and main-taining sight lines for all audience members. In this way, ev-erybody becomes accustomed to having an interpreter on stage and comfortably move around the stage together. Further, by participating in rehearsals, the interpreter will gain insight into the character development of each actor and be more accurate in portraying the personalities of various characters in the play.

[e] "Blocking" is the process of planning each movement of an actor on the stage, including entrances, exits, movement across the stage, and interac-tions with other actors.

Stage performances are unique in their use of lighting for dramatic and thematic purposes, as well as to enhance the visibility of the performers. When interpreters work in this setting, the lighting is so strong that it is common for them to use stage makeup in order for the grammatical facial markers to be visible to the audience. If the interpreter doesn't know how to use stage makeup properly, s/he should contact the makeup artist in advance of the performance and request her/his services.

Clothing should be selected that compliments the attire of the performers. As noted above, the interpreter is often costumed but where this is not the case, the interpreter should consult with the director to identify the style and color of clothing that best blends with the apparel of the actors. Avoid sleeves that blouse or dangle as this will become a visual distraction.

One word of caution: Take note of the background flats or curtains. The color of the interpreter's attire should be different from the color of the backdrop, otherwise, the interpreter's body may blend into

the background and the audience will see only a face and two arms — very disconcerting! Finally, we suggest that the interpreter(s) engage the services of one or two Deaf consumers in advance of a performing arts event and, with the assistance of the lighting director and stage manager, a) identify the color(s) most comfortable to the Deaf consumer's eyes, and, b) identify the placement most appropriate for the production and most comfortable for Deaf audience members.

Working Conditions

Because interpreting in these settings is relatively new, an interpreter in this setting will often need to advocate on behalf of themselves to obtain necessary working conditions. This includes obtaining scripts and words to music well in advance, payment for rehearsal and preparation time, securing appropriate lighting to ensure visibility of the interpreter, payment to Deaf consultants for advisement regarding placement, lighting, etc. and contracting with an adequate number of interpreters depending on the length of performance and number of characters being portrayed.

Ethical Considerations

In some situations, the performers interact with the interpreter in a way that is not considered appropriate in other settings. This is perfectly acceptable in these settings. As a matter of fact, if the interpreter insists on "staying in role," failing to respond to and interact with the performer, s/he is more obtrusive to the audience.

Interpreters can go overboard; however, remember that you are there to compliment the performers and to support authentic access for Deaf and hard of hearing audience members. You are not there to entertain or draw the spotlight away from the actors and singers.

INTERPRETING IN SOCIAL SERVICE SETTINGS

The term "social service settings" is broad and difficult to define in a succinct way. These settings include events such as applying for welfare assistance, interactions with child welfare authorities (e.g., food stamps, aid to dependent children, child protective services), matters heard at a Board of Tenant Relations, and even 12-step meetings (Alcoholics Anonymous, Workaholics Anonymous, etc.). Deaf individuals entering social service settings usually have greater difficulty with access because there are few laws that mandate the provision of interpreters in these settings. Further, most of these settings involve very personal matters so the ability to trust the interpreter's ethics and confidentiality is just as important as accuracy in communication.

Special Considerations

Interpreters in social service settings must be familiar with any terminology unique to each setting. Welfare agencies have their own lingo when it comes to talking about types and evidence of income, living arrangements between partners, income assistance, etc. Twelve-step programs use unique concepts such as "higher power," "clean and sober," and "dry drunk vs. a recovering alcoholic." This requires interpreters to prepare by reading some 12-Step literature, reading literature published by the particular social service agency or otherwise familiarizing her/himself with setting-specific terminology.

Working Conditions

Working conditions for social service settings are usually not ideal. You will often work in crowded, noisy areas with numerous employees and Deaf/hearing individuals who are present to pursue some type of service. There are also often children present who may be a source of visual, as well as auditory, distractions. You must be flexible with placement since the desk around which the parties gather is often in very small offices and it is hard to get even an additional chair into the setting, without regard to getting it behind the desk near the worker who is asking questions.

It is common for individuals attending 12-step meetings to smoke — sometimes in the room during the meeting taking place. The eyes tire more rapidly in a smoke-filled room, thus you may need to insist on a team situation for such settings. If you have a problem with smoke-filled rooms, you may have to decline a request to interpret if there will be smokers in the room.

INTERPRETING FOR VIDEO RELAY AND VIDEO REMOTE

A new and exciting area of interpreting involves settings where the interpreter is interacting with the Deaf client remotely via video phone or video conferencing equipment. The technological evolution makes this an exciting and frequently changing venue in which to work.

Video relay interpreting refers to situations where Deaf individuals are making telephone calls to non-deaf individuals. Rather than use traditional relay services involving the use of TTYs, the Deaf caller dials into a service center staffed by a number of *video interpreters (VI's)* equipped with computers and telephone lines. The Deaf caller, who appears on the video monitor, is greeted by the VI and provides the VI with the phone number of the person they are trying to call. The VI places the call, providing a signed interpretation of what the hearing person says and voice interpretation to the hearing person of what the Deaf caller is signing. Video relay interpreting is funded and regulated by the federal government. Interpreters are trained and employed by private companies, each of which has developed its own technology and approach to service delivery.

One condition of video relay interpreting is that the Deaf individual and the hearing person s/he is communicating with cannot be physically in the same location since that does not replicate telephone access. If an employee needs an interpreter for a staff meeting or a doctor needs an interpreter for an appointment with a Deaf patient, they are not able to use video relay as a way to bring a virtual interpreter into that event. Instead, a number of companies provide *video remote interpreting* services to meet this need. Video remote interpreting provides an interpreter via video conferencing equipment who is able to see the Deaf individual and hear the doctor, teacher, or employer. The interpreter provides sign interpretation for everything that is spoken and voice interpretation for everything that is signed. One of the most frequent users of video remote interpreting services are colleges and universities located in communities where they are unable to secure qualified interpreters for Deaf students.

Standard Qualifications

This is such a new area of employment that standards are still being debated. As this book goes to print, the standards vary somewhat from video relay company to video relay company. It is recommended that interpreters be certified with a range of interpreting experience beyond certification. This is true because of the complexity of content and range of callers one must deal with, as well as the lack of ability to prep for video relay interpreting jobs. In addition, interpreters must complete initial and on-going training in the use of the ever changing technology they are required to operate while interpreting.

Pay for Service

Pay for service is determined by each company or agency typically based on the interpreter's certification, years of experience, and special qualifications. This is a highly competetive area of employment so pay range and benefits are typically better than that of other agencies in each geographic area.

Working Conditions

The evolution of video interpreting is having a profound impact on the field of sign language interpreting. Video relay is similar to doing freelance work -- a range of consumers, various types of calls and call content, but with the convenience of having regular breaks and being able to go to one location rather than driving all over the community.

There are some emerging concerns regarding working conditions, including:

1. The possibility of eye strain working under artificial lights and focusing all day on a video monitor;
2. Possible physical strain given the modified smaller signing space required by camera placement;
3. The need for other VI's to team in the event of long calls, heavy content or highly emotional content.

Supervision Supervision and mentorship varies from company to company. It is recommended that a supervisor always be available to support video interpreters in their work and to provide on-going evaluative feedback.

INTERPRETING IN PERSONAL SETTINGS

This caegory covers a wide range of events including family reunions, birthday and wedding anniversary parties, family "encounters", confrontations with neighbors, purchasing a car, furniture or other major item, etc. Of all the settings for interpreting, these are the least predictable.

Role Delineation and Special Considerations

In some experiences in such settings, the interpreter's role and responsibility are fairly clear (e.g. when a Deaf person goes to purchase a car and asks an interpreter to accompany him). Interpreting information regarding the price and specifications of the new car and of a trade-in are not too demanding. However, when the pressured sales pitch kicks in, the interpreter may have difficulty striking an appropriate balance of language/culture mediation.

Pay for Service

Pay will depend on who is setting up the interpreting service. Many interpreters charge less when the Deaf client is paying for the service, while charging their standard rate when hired by a company or agency. Interpreting students and recent graduates often gain hands-on interpreting experience by volunteering in personal settings. Some professional interpreters will provide services pro bono in these settings and others barter for services.

Working Conditions, Supervision

Settings, working conditions and such will vary from situation to situation. There is no form of supervision or evalution in such settings.

An interpreter working in personal settings must have a clear sense of boundaries, problem ownership, role, and responsibilities. The lines can easily become blurred in these situations. Such an interpreter must be mature, emotionally healthy, and must be able to reflect on her work in order to determine if different behaviors should be used the next time she is in such a situation.

Skills and Special Considerations

An interpreter going into personal settings must be aware of the anticipated interaction and any specialized terminology related to that event. If purchasing a home, for example, an interpreter should know the meaning of escrow, title deed, and other real estate terms. If interpreting for a family event, she should learn the names of family members and any sign names that have been established. The interpreter must also be able to deal with a variety of emotions which might come up in such settings and be able to accurately interpret these affects into both signed and spoken interpretations.

Many interpreters have been told it is not appropriate to eat when interpreting an event where food is served. This makes sense. It is virtually impossible to eat while interpreting between Deaf and hearing individuals sharing a table at a banquet or wedding reception. However, the interpreter's refusal to take a plate is sometimes offensive to the cultural norms of the hearing host of the event. In these settings, it is more socially appropriate to accept a plate of food, even if you only take one or two bites.

INTERPRETING IN A TEAM

Working as a member of an interpreting team is likely to occur in many of the settings we have dicussed in this chapter. When working as part of a team, it is important to remember that the two or three of you are working to construct a single interpretation. Team members are not there to compete, but to support and encourage each other toward best practice.

Assigning a team of interpreters will depend on a number of factors, including

+ LENGTH OF ASSIGNMENT
Typically, jobs that extend longer than 50-minutes are teamed in order to avoid mental exhaustion and

thus maintain the integrity of the message, as well as to prevent physical damage to the interpreter. There are times, however, when the interpreter is not interpreting non-stop. A gym class, for example, or a lab where the deaf client is primarily engaged in other work and there is no lecture going on. In this setting, one interpreter might work for 2-3 hours alone.

✦ DENSITY OR COMPLEXITY OF CONTENT
The more complex the content being interpreter, the greater the likelihood a team of interpreters will be required. This builds in a level of quality control since the interpreter in the "off" position should be supporting the working interpreter and monitoring her/his work.

✦ SIZE OF ROOM
There are times when the room in which an event is taking place prohibits deaf participants from seeing the interpreter. This could be because of pillars in the middle of the room or the sheer distance from the back of the room to the stage. In such a situation, interpreters may be placed throughout the room, giving participants a choice of where to focus their visual intake.

✦ PRESENCE OF INDIVIDUALS WHO REQUIRE TACTILE OR CLOSE VISION INTERPRETATION
When members of an audience include Deaf-Blind individuals, multiple interpreting teams are required to ensure communication access. Deaf-Blind relay interpreters are often Deaf Interpreters, although hearing interpreters sometimes fill this role.

ROLE DELINEATION
It is the responsibility of both interpreters to prepare for the interpreting assignment -- reading the textbook or presentation in advance, researching the topic on the computer, etc. It

is also the responsibility of both interpreters to arrive prior to start time, introduce themselves to the consumers, confirm the physical set up with the deaf consumers, etc.

The "off" interpreter is expected to support and back up the "working" interpreter throughout the job. S/he should remain in the room, attending to the information being conveyed, ensuring that the team interpreter is managing the job effectively. This is not the time to be checking your pager for messages, going outside for a smoke, or reading the newspaper. You are being paid to work for the full appointment, not just the half where you are in the "hot seat."

PLACEMENT

Historically, interpreting teams have placed themselves where one interpreter is in front of the deaf customer(s) and the other is slightly off to the side. In this way, the 'off" interpreter could feed the "working" inerpreter signs if s/he missed something, keep time so interpreters know when to switch, and make notes for the working team member.

Another way of approaching placement is to have both team members sit side-by-side in front of the deaf client. The "off" interpreter still keeps the time and makes nots, indicating to the team member when it is time to switch roles. However, this placement avoids the distracting movement of having interpreters move back and forth, changing chairs every 20-minutes, It allows a voice feed, softly in the ear of the working interpreter, rather than a signed feed. It also makes it possible for the "off" interpreter to take over a small chunk of interpretation if the "working" interpreter is having difficulty, without drawing undue attention to the interpreters. Some teams who work in this formation "split the task" of interpreting, with one interpreter doing sign-to-voice for 20-minutes and the other doing voice-to-sign for 20 minutes. They then exchange roles. This is particularly effective with a highly participatory deaf individual, allowing interruptions and overlapping speech.

CHAPTER REVIEW

Key Points

This chapter reviews a variety of settings where interpreters work, including standard qualifications, special considerations, pay, supervision, and a number of other factors.

Religious Settings generally involves four types of events: religious services, funerals, weddings, and special events. Specific signs vary from church to church to reflect their unique theology.

- ✦ <u>Standard Qualifications</u>: none; some preference for an interpreter of the same faith/belief.
- ✦ <u>Special Considerations</u>: heavy use of formal and frozen register and art forms.
- ✦ <u>Ethical Considerations</u>: conveying religious content without letting one's own belief system interfere; separation of interpreter role and spiritual guide and counselor.
- ✦ <u>Placement</u>: varies.
- ✦ <u>Pay for Services</u>: varies, depending on the situation.
- ✦ <u>Supervision, evaluation & professional development</u>: infrequent.

Educational Settings includes preschool, elementary, secondary, and post-secondary environments. The role and responsibilities of an interpreter varies depending on specific setting.

- ✦ <u>Standard Qualifications</u>: vary widely; recommend minimally of graduation from of an interpreter education program — preferably interpreter certification and a Bachelor's degree.
- ✦ <u>Working Considerations</u>: pay should include preparation time as well as time actually worked in classroom; should include adequate breaks and a team interpreter in order to avoid over-use syndrome.

✦ <u>Ethical Considerations</u>: role more broadly defined with younger children and more narrow with older students; the interpreter is a member of the educational team; a danger of becoming too familiar with one's student and her/his family if working with same student year after year.

✦ <u>Role Delineation</u>: the primary function is providing communication access *in the wide range of instructional activities* within an educational program which *lead to independence, empowerment, and integration*; must not impinge on the teacher's authority or role in the classroom.

✦ <u>Placement</u>: varies depending on specific setting.

✦ Pay for Services: varies, depending on the setting, qualifications, certification, education and multiple-role job descriptions

✦ <u>Supervision, evaluation & professional development</u>: rare — usually no school personnel qualified to evaluate interpreters; some schools provide registration and travel costs for interpreters to attend workshops and conferences.

✦ <u>Deaf community view of this setting</u>: highly controversial; many Deaf community leaders believe that due to an impoverished linguistic environment, mainstreaming has a negative effect on the academic achievement, self-esteem and leadership skills of Deaf children.

Working with a Deaf Interpreter. You should work with a Deaf Interpreter (DI) when the deaf customer's communication is affected by special circumstances. This might include having a physical or mental development issue, being unfamiliar with standard ASL, or otherwise using non-standard ASL.

✦ <u>Role Delineation</u>: both the DI and the hearing interpreters are professional practitioners in this setting

✦ <u>Special Knowledge and Skills</u>: special training and practice are required to do an effective job working in a deaf-hearing interpreting team.

✦ <u>Pay for Services</u>: varies from city to city and region to region; payment should be the same for both interpreters

✦ <u>Opportunities for Professional Development</u>: primarily available through professional interpreter workshops, continuing education opportunities, and skills-upgrading seminars.

Interpreting in Medical Settings can be divided into medical appointments and laboratory/hospital procedures.

✦ <u>Role Delineation</u>: medical staff often doesn't understand interpreter's role or what s/he needs to perform her/his job maximally.

✦ <u>Special Knowledge and Skills</u>: interpreter must be familiar with a variety of medical terms, procedures, and protocol.

✦ <u>Pay for Services</u>: varies from city to city and region to region; payment is often higher for medical settings than for other, less "hazardous", settings.

✦ <u>Opportunities for Professional Development</u>: primarily available through professional interpreter workshops, continuing education opportunities, and skills-upgrading seminars.

✦ <u>Standard Qualifications</u>: no standard; recommended certification prior to interpreting in medical settings, due to the fact that inaccurate communication can be life threatening.

Legal Settings   includes attorney-client appointments, police interactions, and courtroom proceedings; courtroom proceedings involve civil, criminal, and administrative hearings. Clients may be adults or juveniles in the role of plaintiff, defendant, victim, witness, a member of the jury, or a family member of a plaintiff, defendant, victim or witness.

- ✦ Standard Qualifications: most states and provinces require that interpreters be certified because inaccurate communication can endanger the life and liberty of those involved.
- ✦ Pay for Services & Working Conditions: higher fees are generally charged due to level of expertise required.
- ✦ Supervision/Evaluation and Professional Development: influenced by the size and multi-lingual/multi-ethnic nature of the community
- ✦ Ethical Concerns: familiarity with a case and multiple Deaf individuals involved is of concern; Deaf litigant should have one interpreter for courtroom proceedings and a separate interpreter for client-attorney interactions. It is not considered appropriate for an interpreter who has been involved in police interrogation of a victim, witness, or perpetrator to interpret for that individual during the trial. Different interpreters should be used for each side in contested matters.

Mental Health and Psychiatric Settings can be divided into psychiatric testing and evaluation, outpatient group or individual therapy sessions, inpatient group or individual therapy sessions.

- ✦ Special Knowledge and Skills: imperative that an interpreter in these settings work closely with the therapist, insuring that the interpreter's presence doesn't shift communication and interpersonal dynamics; interpreters must be alert to insure personal safety, particularly with in-patient settings; psychiatric evaluations and testing should be performed only with a relay interpreter or a Deaf advocate since misinterpretations of questions and answers have repeatedly led to misdiagnosis.

✦ Standard Qualifications: should be certified.
✦ Pay for Services & Working Conditions: higher fees are generally charged due to level of expertise required.

Interpreting for Conferences is a specialized type of platform interpreting; usually takes place over several days with a unifying theme; papers and speakers are usually available in advance; specialized terminology is usually used.

✦ Pay for Services: may be paid an hourly or day rate; travel, lodging and expenses may also be paid to interpreters.
✦ Supervision and Evaluation: not common but *may* have an interpreter coordinator to provide minimal on-sight supervision in addition to setting up schedule.
✦ Working Conditions: usually work long days, thus requiring regular breaks and teams of interpreters; interpreters need a location near the conference center where a tired interpreter may eat and rest.
✦ Special Considerations: may be multiple visual and spoken languages and an array of technology and equipment with which or around which the interpreter must work.

Theatrical or performing arts interpreter often becomes "a part of the show," dressing in costume, moving in a large, dramatic signing space, physically portraying a variety of characters or personifying the rhythm of music; the performers sometimes interact with the interpreter in a way that is not considered appropriate in other settings.

✦ Standard Qualifications: none
✦ Pay for Services: Varies.

✦ Supervision and Evaluation: rare.

✦ Special Considerations: theatrical and/or musical training is of great value; attending rehearsals and translating the script required; lighting is essential and requires work with the stage manager in advance; clothing should compliment costumes.

✦ Placement: complex and specialized including single interpreter, placed to one side of the stage; "Shadowing;" "Zone;" and a combination of fixed and zone interpreting. May use Deaf actors rather than, or in addition to, interpreters.

✦ Working Conditions: must obtain scripts and music well in advance, secure payment for rehearsal and preparation time, appropriate lighting and contract with an adequate number of interpreters.

Interpreting in Employment-Related Settings involves job interviews; new employee orientation; on-the-job training; union or staff meetings; employer-employee interactions and office events.

✦ Standard Qualifications: minimally — graduate of an interpreter education program, preferably certified.

✦ Special Knowledge and Skills: must be sensitive to cultural adjustments needed in employment-related settings, as well as the specialized terminology, protocol, and technology unique to each field.

✦ Supervision and Evaluation: rare

✦ Pay for Services: varies.

✦ Working Conditions: usually less than optimal requiring interpreters to be flexible. Special equipment may be required for some settings.

Interpreting in Social Service Settings includes welfare applications, interactions with child welfare authorities, matters heard at a Board of Tenant Relations, 12-step meetings, etc..

- Standard Qualifications: minimally a mature, emotionally stable graduate of an interpreter education program with knowledge of special terminology which might arise.
- Pay for Services: varies
- Supervision and Evaluation: none
- Special Knowledge and Skills: should be familiar with terminology unique to the setting.
- Working Conditions: poor, often crowded, noisy, and sometimes smoke-filled.

Personal Settings covers family reunions, family "encounters", confrontations with neighbors, personal purchase, etc.; highly unpredictable and potentially emotional.

- Special Considerations: flexibility of role, variety of emotional overlays, need for boundaries, knowledge of problem ownership, and clear sense of role and responsibilities.
- Working Conditions: unpredictable.
- Supervision & Evaluation: none
- Pay: will vary; may be on a barter arrangement.

Interpreting in An Interpreting Team This involves a team of 2 or more interpreters working together to interpret a single text or presentation.,

- Used when
  - text is dense or complex
  - the presentation is longer than 50-minutes and the interpretation is continuous
  - the room is too large to allow all deaf participants to see the interpreter at the front of the room
  - there are participants using tactile or close vision interpretation

✦ <u>Placement</u>: can be such that one interpreter is in front of the deaf clients while the "off" interpreter sits off to the side; an increasingly popular and effective placement has both interpreters sitting side-by-side, sometimes splitting the sign-to-voice and voice-to-sign tasks.

✦ <u>Role of the "off" Interpreter</u>: to be present and attending to the working interpreter, providing any support appropriate to maximize the best interpretation the two of your can construct together.

THOUGHT QUESTIONS

1. What similarities do you see in each of these varied settings? What areas are clearly different in each setting?

2. Given your personal values, what ethical challenges might you encounter if you were an interpreter in the settings listed in this chapter?

3. Discuss the relationship between assertiveness and the way you interact with clients and other interpreters on the job.

4. What problems are created by the lack of standards regarding interpreter qualifications in many of the settings outlined in the text?

CD STUDY GUIDE

✦ The various activities in the guided Chapter 13 Study Guide on CD will allow you to understand the concepts in this chapter more completely and to apply them to your life experience. Work through the Chapter 13 Study Guide on CD, completing all activities, then submit to your instructor or share with your learning partner.

SUGGESTED ACTIVITIES

✦ Observe several different interpreters in at least 5 of the settings discussed in this chapter. Make notes on your observations and discuss them in class.

✦ Interview 3 experienced interpreters, each of whom may specialize in different settings. Ask them questions regarding pay, supervision, placement, and other factors discussed in this chapter to compare the textbook with your geographical area.

✦ If you are studying interpreting in a large city, make arrangements for students to observe nursing students, dental students, medical students, etc., and to practice interpreter placement in these mock settings.

Endnotes

1. Stuckless, etal. (1988)

CHAPTER FOURTEEN
Basic Business Practices

THE JOB MARKET

It has been determined that nine-to-twelve full-time interpreters are needed to meet bare minimal interpreting needs of an area with 1,000 Deaf residents.[1] Even with annual graduates from educational programs throughout the US and Canada, there continues to be a critical shortage of sign language interpreters in metropolitan, suburban and rural areas.

The demand for interpreters is driven primarily by legislative initiatives and court decisions mandating greater access for Deaf and hard of hearing individuals to education, employment and a wide range of community services.

Opportunities to Work: Urban vs. Rural

There are generally more job opportunities in large, metropolitan areas than in rural communities. This is true because:

✦ Deaf people tend to congregate in metropolitan areas because educational, employment and social opportunities are greater in these locations;

✦ There are typically more services to support the needs of Deaf individuals in metropolitan areas, including interpreting agencies, doctors, lawyers and therapists familiar with Deaf people, etc.; and

✦ The economic base in urban areas is usually larger and more able to support the employment of Deaf people.

That is not to say Deaf people shun rural areas. Some return to their rural home communities; others are drawn by the access to skiing, hiking, and other outdoor work and enjoyment. However, it is estimated that the Deaf population in the metropolitan areas of Los Angeles is 25,000. In Toronto it is 15,000. In Dallas, Texas, it is 13,000. Compare that to smaller towns such as Amarillo, Texas, which has a Deaf population of 300, Thunder Bay (in Canada) which has 75, and Twin Falls, Idaho, with 65 and you can understand why the opportunities for work in larger communities exists. Thus, depending on where you live, the prospects for employment in the field of sign language interpreting are quite good or quite dismal.

Areas of Employment

The majority of sign language interpreters are employed in one or more of the following areas: education, employment, medical, legal or social services. There are also opportunities for employment with state/provincial and federal governments. In addition, there are numerous part-time opportunities for employment in the performing arts — musical performances, theater, folk festivals, travel documentaries and tours — and for various church and temple services and programs.

Most Common Types Of Employment

At this time, most full-time interpreting jobs are found in two settings:

✦ As a "staff interpreter" in interpreter agencies; and
✦ In mainstreamed classrooms ranging from K-12 and into a variety of post-secondary settings.

These are also the two places where an interpreter is most likely to get benefits including sick leave, paid vacation, extended health insurance and paid professional development. The emergence of full-time interpreting jobs is relatively new, beginning in the mid-eighties, and has had one negative result among sign language interpreters: a frightening surge in the rate of repetitive motion injuries. As a result, "full-time" has been defined as being 30 to 40 hours per week, depending on the setting, with no more than 20-22 hours of actual interpreting within that 30-to-40 hours time span.[2]

Interpreters in Private Practice

A number of sign language interpreters prefer to work as independent contractors rather than working full-time for a school or interpreting agency. As self-employed practitioners, these interpreters are insured of a great deal of variety. They rarely work for the same client two days in a row. They are constantly going into new environments, and they have full control over their schedules. It is possible to work as a full-time, self-employed interpreter and make enough money to support yourself. Four certified interpreters in private practice with whom we spoke, with an average of 15 years interpreting experience, indicated annual incomes from $32,000 in Austin, Texas, $48,000 in New York City, $35,000 in St. Paul, Minnesota, and $52,000 in Los Angeles, California.

However, freelance interpreting is not a particularly lucrative area for a beginning-level interpreter. It takes some time to:

✦ Develop your skills to the level that you can handle the variety of clients and situations encountered by freelance interpreters with the limited prep common to this area of work;

✦ Develop a pool of Deaf and hearing clientele; and

✦ Allow the Deaf community to know you well enough for an appropriate level of comfort and trust to develop.

PAY RATES

Interpreter pay rates are as varied as the number of interpreter jobs on any given day. The pay tends to reflect the geographical area of employment. Further, there are several ways in which interpreters can assess fees for service. Some interpreters charge by the hour, some by the job, some based on an initial "call out" fee followed by an hourly rate, others by the full or half-day.

Call out, Hourly, Half-day and Day Rates

If you are living in an area where the cost of living is high and you are being paid by the hour, the rate of pay might range from $30.00 - $75.00 per hour. If you are living in a rural, low cost of living area, you may be paid $12.00 to $30.00 per hour.

When working freelance jobs, interpreters typically charge a minimum of two-hours. Some interpreters charge a "call out" fee plus an hourly fee. In this event, your first hour might be $50.00 with each additional hour costing $25.00.[3] Since the concept of a "call out" fee is somewhat new, let us elaborate. Freelance interpreter, Cheryl Palmer, notes that as an interpreter in private practice charging an hourly rate (even with a two-hour minimum), she was losing money on jobs of two-hours or less. Not wanting to increase her hourly rate (fearing she might price herself out of the market), she opted for establishing a base "call out" fee. This basically increases one's pay for a one or two-hour assignment, negates the need for stating a two-hour minimum, and makes it possible to cover the cost of doing business while making a small profit.

If you are working one job for more than three hours, you may prefer to negotiate half-day and day-rates. In some communities for example, legal interpreters are paid $130 for a half day and $198 for a full day of work. If you are a salaried interpreter, you may make $25,000 - $58,000 per year.[a]

Supply and demand also have some influence on how much one can charge for her/his services. If there is a scarcity of interpreters in a particular area and more than one employer who is desperate to have services, one employer may outbid the other to "win" the interpreter for her/his need.

It is important to remember that interpreting is a human service occupation. Like nursing, teaching and similar professions you will not become wealthy working as an interpreter. You will,

---

[a] All figures are based on actual pay rates and salaries as reflected in personal conversations with 25 interpreters across North America.

however, store up riches in the satisfaction of a job well done and in seeing authentic empowerment and inclusion of Deaf and hard of hearing people.

THE COST OF DOING BUSINESS

There are many variables in determining your rate of pay. As stated above, the cost of living in a geographic area is one factor.

Other critical factors include the level of education attained by the interpreter, the amount of interpreting experience and the type of certification. Interpreters working as contract or freelance interpreters should take the cost of doing business into consideration when setting fees. Things to remember in that calculate include the cost of:

+ Transportation — auto registration, auto insurance, depreciation of the car, gas, oil, toll fees, parking or expenses related to public transit;

+ Office expenses — stationary, envelopes, postage, business cards, telephone, fax, cell phone, email, computer hardware and software, office rent, office supplies;

+ Taxes, retirement fund, disability insurance — these are all required for the private practice interpreter;

+ Billing/booking time — you must make calls to confirm jobs, complete and mail invoices, etc., but when you are in the office doing that, you are not working (i.e. earning money) so the cost of this time needs to be figured into the cost of doing business;

+ Business clothing — any shoes, safety gear or clothing used exclusively when working in the role of an interpreter;

+ Insurance — personal health, business and malpractice; and

✦ <u>Public relations</u> — this includes the cost of mailing out promotional materials such as a calendar with your name and number on it, the cost of ads in Deaf community newsletters and special program books, etc.

In addition, contract or self-employed interpreters must plan for those weeks (months?) when business is light, because their income will be reduced as a result. They will also want to build in both professional development and holiday accounts to avoid burn out and to stay current with the field.

PREPARING TO DO BUSINESS

In addition to skills and knowledge related to interpretation, you need to develop business skills related to the work you will be doing. This will include:

1. Development of résumés;
2. Skills in writing business letters;
3. Basic bookkeeping and techniques for developing invoices and collecting money owed to you;
4. Schedule maintenance, booking appointments at appropriate intervals, calling to confirm, etc.; and
5. Development of business policies.

Resumé Writing

Learning to write resumés is something that can be developed through interpreter education courses, adult school courses, or with assistance from staff at various support and employment centers. There are various formats, but the basic information does not vary much. It should include your name, address and a contact telephone number, education and work experience (related to interpreting) and professional affiliations.

If you are an entry-level interpreter, don't forget to include your fieldwork and practicum experiences as part of your "work" experience. Potential employers are less interested in the fact that you have been *paid* for your work than they are in the variety of settings where you have worked and the fact that your work was satisfactory to the persons who supervised you.

Writing Business Letters

This is another skill you should develop, either in interpreter education courses, a business writing course, or a continuing education course. Letter format and content will vary depending on the goal of the letter. Generally, you want to be courteous without being wordy. A business letter rarely exceeds one page.

Basic Bookkeeping

This includes techniques for tracking the work you have done, developing invoices and collecting the money owed to you. It also involves keeping receipts and records in order to file your taxes promptly and accurately. Some interpreters prefer to hire a bookkeeping service, but most find their business is small enough that they can handle this aspect of the business themselves. Invoices need to have some basic information:

- ✦ Date the invoice is being sent;
- ✦ Your name (or company name) with street and email addresses, along with telephone/fax numbers;
- ✦ Name and address of the individual to whom you are sending the invoice;
- ✦ Contact person's name;
- ✦ Date the work was provided;
- ✦ Type of work provided;
- ✦ Time spent doing the job, rate of pay, and the amount due.

In addition, there should be a statement of any policies you have in place, such as "payable upon receipt" or "penalty added after 30-days." There are a number of fairly simple computer programs available which link invoices, bookkeeping, and tax records.

Schedule Maintenance

This involves learning how much time to leave between appointments to insure that you have enough time to get to the second and third jobs while considering the possibility that some appointments may not start on time or may run overtime. Some of this is learned best by experience, but there are some basic principles that you may want to keep in mind.

+ Always call to confirm an appointment 24 - 48 hours in advance. At that time, if you have another appointment after the one you are calling to confirm, reiterate the fact that you have another appointment at such-and-such a time and will need to leave no later than _____ (time).
+ Check your map before accepting back-to-back appointments and remember to take into consideration things such as rush hour, weather, and the need to stop for gas and meals.

These are but a few ideas. We encourage you to talk with other interpreters in your area to gain additional insights.

Business Policies

You will want to develop a series of business policies in order to protect yourself and the interests of your clients. We encourage you to interview a number of interpreters in private practice to get ideas, but business policies may include such things as:

+ A call-out fee vs. a 2-hour minimum policy — As described above, some interpreters charge an initial "call-out" fee which is greater than their hourly rate, followed by a per-hour charge for time spent

396

beyond the initial hour of work. Other interpreters charge a two-hour minimum fee.

Establishing this policy helps cover associated businesscosts if the job is less than one-hour in duration.

✦ Port-to-port fees — Some individuals "start the clock" from the time they leave their door to go to the place of business and "stop the clock" when they return home or get to the next job. This may be done instead of a call-out fee or a two-hour minimum, and is especially effective where distant travel is involved.

✦ Cancellation Policy — Appointments do cancel and if you have no cancellation policy, you will have no income for the time you booked the appointment. Cancellation policies vary from area to area and interpreter to interpreter. Many interpreters require 50% of the minimum fee if a cancellation takes place with less than 48-hours notification. Others have a policy stating the call out fee or two-hour minimum will be billed if an appointment is cancelled with less that 36 hours notice.

When negotiating a contract in a post-secondary educational setting, a cancellation fee may need to be based on some percentage of the term of the contract. In other words, if you have a contract for 20 hours per week for 16 weeks (an average semester length), you will turn down other work prior to the beginning of the school term. But if the student drops out after two weeks and you have no cancellation agreement in your contract, you will suddenly be without an income. An appropriate cancellation fee in this case may be two to three weeks pay, thus allowing you to have some kind of income while you find other work.

✦ <u>Sliding fee scale</u> — As professional practitioners working with one community which is based on reciprocity and another community based on a fee-for-service
orientation, a number of interpreters have found it
beneficial to develop different pay rates depending on
who is paying the bill. There will generally be a lower
fee if a Deaf client is personally paying for interpreter
services. There may even be a bartering arrangement.

These are just a few examples of policies you need to consider when going into business as a sign language interpreter.

THREATS TO STAYING IN THE FIELD

There are a few things that could cause you to leave the field
prematurely. It is imperative that you are aware of these factors as you consider entering the field and plan for your ongoing
wellness.

Repetitive Strain Injury (RSI)

There has been a frightening surge in the rate of repetitive motion injuries (also known as over-use syndrome) among sign
language interpreters. RSI tends to result in carpal tunnel syndrome, tendonitis, tennis elbow and brachial neuralgia, all of
which can lead to total disability. The best prevention for RSI
includes:

✦ <u>Proper warm up before working</u> — this includes
warming up the hands and arms prior to work and
during any extended breaks in a job; special care must
be taken by interpreters working in cold climates or
air conditioned buildings.
✦ <u>Regular exercise and good nutrition</u> — interpreting is
a physical activity involving the muscles and tendons
of the arms, face, neck and upper body. Further, interpreters must often stand for long periods of time
requiring back and lower body stamina. Maintaining

overall physical conditioning and nutrition will increase your longevity as an interpreter.

✦ Check your signing habits — some interpreters develop particular signing and fingerspelling habits which stress the muscles and tendons. Others actually try to change hand dominance. Ask a teacher or colleague to look at you while signing to see if there are some of these features you can change.

✦ Insist on appropriate working conditions — an interpreter should take a 10 minute break for every 50 minutes worked. Further, if a job is longer than two hours in length, two interpreters should work the job as a team. You may have to advocate actively to obtain working conditions in accord with these restrictions, but the alternative could be total disability!

Emotional Burnout

Working with people day in and day out is stressful. Interpreting requires working with people, many of whom do not understand the work, languages, or cultures involved. In addition, our work often takes us into situations which involve emotional extremes — the exhilaration of the birth of a baby, the pain at being diagnosed with a fatal disease, or the agony of being fired from a job. We go into settings that are stressful in themselves: prisons, lock-up psychiatric wards and intensive care units for example.

If you want to be an interpreter, it is essential that you have well-developed stress management and support systems in place. The failure to do so may result in emotional burnout and an early departure from the field.

Job Market

There is a critical shortage of sign language interpreters throughout North America in every employment area. The job market for sign language interpreters varies, depending on the geographical location (urban vs. rural), the type of interpreting being performed (educational vs. legal, etc.), and the management structure under which the interpreter is hired (employee, contract worker for an agency, or self-employed practitioner).

Types Of Employment
- ✦ staff interpreter — full-time working for a business, school or agency; likely to receive benefits.
- ✦ contract interpreter — working hourly for a school or an interpreting agency; no benefits as a rule;
- ✦ self-employed practitioners — part-to-full-time work, depending on demand; benefits must be paid by the individual interpreters.

Pay Rates vary from $20.00 to $75.00 per hour depending on a number of factors including certification, experience, setting, level of difficulty involved, etc. Supply and demand will influence the rate that can be charged.

Cost Of Doing Business As A Private Practitioner
When calculating pay rates, one must remember to calculate the cost of: transportation, office expenses, business clothing and purchase of personal health and malpractice insurance. In addition, one must plan for the time when business is slow, resulting in reduced income.

Employment Trends
Most interpreters work in education, employment, medical, legal or social services settings. There are also opportunities for employment with state/provincial and federal governments.

Part-time opportunities for employment may be found in all of the above plus the areas of performing arts, travel documentaries and tours, and for various religious services and programs.

Preparing To Do Business

In addition to skills and knowledge related to interpretation, you need to develop business skills related to the work you will be doing. This will include:

+ Writing resumés
+ Writing business letters
+ Basic bookkeeping and techniques for developing invoices and collecting money owed
+ Schedule maintenance
+ Developing appropriate business policies

Trends In The Field

There are more full-time job openings, especially after the passage of ADA in the U.S. Other trends include new opportunities to specialize (medical, mental health, legal). New entries into the field include more men, more non-white individuals, more people with no Deaf family members.

Interpreting In Private Practice can be quite lucrative but is not the best place for a beginning-level interpreter since s/he needs to develop skills to a higher level, develop clientele, and interact with the Deaf community more to build a trust relationship.

Threats To Staying In The Field

Sign language interpreters must develop strategies to avoid repetitive strain injury (RSI) and emotional burnout in order to sustain a long career in this field. RSI can result in total physical disability, and emotional burnout results in depressed, pessimistic individuals who lose their passion for the work.

THOUGHT QUESTIONS

1. Compare the sign language interpreter job market of today with that of the 1960's. What has contributed to the changes noted?
2. Explain what equal access means in general as applied to the Deaf population. How do interpreters fit into this concept of equal access?
3. Where are entry-level interpreters most likely to be hired? Why?

CD STUDY GUIDE

The various activities in the guided Chapter 14 Study Guide on CD will allow you to understand the concepts in this chapter more completely and to apply them to your life experience. Work through the Chapter 14 Study Guide on CD, completing all activities, then submit to your instructor or share with your learning partner.

SUGGESTED ACTIVITIES

+ Design a name, logo, and business card for your private interpreting business.
+ Describe the area in which you hope to work as an interpreter. Study the factors outlined in the chapter and determine the wage you would charge per hour as an interpreter. Give your rationale.
+ Invite to the classroom a panel of interpreters who work in a variety of settings and in various geographical areas. Let them describe their view of the points made in this chapter and answer student questions.
+ Arrange for students to "shadow" a working interpreter for a day. Share these experiences with the class.

Endnotes

1. RID Views (1983)
2. NTID (1989)
3. Palmer (1995, 2001)

APPENDIX A

THE CLAGGETT STATEMENT

The following document was developed by a group of deaf and hearing individuals in 1984 to openly recognize the historic oppressed experience of deaf individuals in relation to churches throughout North America.

I.   WE BELIEVE:

God created the world and saw that it was good. God created women and men to live with dignity and self-respect as children of God. God wants people to live together with justice, equality, freedom and mutual love.

Instead of trusting God's plan, people made themselves into false gods, oppressing each other and creating injustice, wars, suffering and death. But God did not give up on them (us). God sent Jesus as a visible sign of God's liberating love.

Jesus grew up poor. He loved and intimately associated with poor and oppressed people. He knew their suffering and their needs. In relation with these poor and oppressed ones, Jesus showed us God's compassionate love and God's desire for us all to live with justice and freedom.

Instead of accepting Jesus' way, people rejected the Truth. And Jesus suffered the depths of human pain, degradation, and death. But praise be to God who enabled Jesus to break through the shackles of deceit and death, and raised Jesus to new life. The Holy Spirit too can break through the shackles of arrogance and oppression.

II.   WE RECOGNIZE:

A variety of experiences of hearing loss. Some people are deafened as adults; some as children; and some are deaf from birth. All have suffered.

Many deaf people share a common culture, a common language (American Sign Language or "ASL" in the United State and many parts of Canada) and a common heritage of oppression. These deaf people, collectively, are often called the "Deaf community".

Deaf people have long been shackled, often by the "good" intentions of hearing people who haven't understood them. Deaf people lack meaningful representation and leadership in the major educational, professional, and political institutions that affect their lives. This lack grows out of both the intentions and ignorance of the hearing people in power and the "successfully oppressed" condition of deaf people who experience themselves as powerless and incompetent.

Beginning at a young age and continuing into adulthood, deaf people characteristically view themselves as intellectually, emotionally and spiritually inferior to hearing people. This low sense of self-worth is widely known in the psychological studies in deafness.

The majority of deaf children have hearing parents who did not want to have a deaf child and who grieve over their child's deafness. Large numbers of these parents do not accept their child's deafness for a long time. Some never accept it. Many, perhaps most, of the medical, social service and educational institutions which "serve" deaf children and adults encourage the parents to resist acceptance of the child's deafness. They are encouraged to try in every new way possible to make the child look an act like a hearing person.

This regularly takes one of two general forms: The first is the extreme oralist position of the Alexander Graham Bell Society which insists deaf children can and should learn to hear and speak. The second is the so-called "total communication" position of the majority of educators in the United States and Canada. This second approach tolerates the use of signs because they are considered necessary for the acquisition of "language". "Language" in this context always means "English". The type of signing usually prescribed in this context is some form of signed English.

Deaf children attend school in a variety of educational settings. In residential schools for the deaf, the teachers typically are hearing persons who do not understand the children's peer language, do not know American Sign Language, and believe the children to be intellectually and psychologically inferior to hearing children. The primary focus of their educational program is the acquisition of spoken, written and/or signed English. Often the children do not understand the teachers. Most 'communication' is one way, teacher to student.

Most deaf children mainstreamed into public schools are partially or completely isolated from groups of other deaf children like them. Thus, they do not experience the comforting reassurance of sameness and peer group identity. Most schools do not provide interpreters for these children and they miss much or most of what is being taught and said in their classes. Many try to catch up by frantic reading outside the classroom.

Some deaf children do have access to "interpreters". However, most interpreters are not even minimally conversant in American Sign Language. The majority simply try to code the spoken English into a signed form of English (which many argue does not make meaningful sense). Most deaf children have very limited skills in English, and have a hard time understanding a (presumably) signed form of English. However, even those who have good reading and writing skills often say they have a hard time with English-based forms of signing.

Most deaf adults do not understand most "interpreters". But deaf people have become accustomed to not understanding. They tolerate it, usually because they blame themselves – blame their own presumed ignorance. With so few interpreters fluent in ASL, the majority of deaf people have never seen spoken English properly interpreted into a form of communication they readily understand. Also, because most interpreters are unable to accurately convey the meaning of an ASL message into spoken English, most deaf people have never had the opportunity to express themselves as freely in a hearing context, and often have been misinterpreted in important settings. These instances of misinterpretation have furthered the myths that deaf people are inferior, inarticulate, immature, etc.

Most (signing) deaf people marry people who are also deaf, and socialize primarily with other deaf people. The language they use for such social interaction is usually American Sign Language. However, most of them do not believe that their indigenous language is really a "language", but rather that it is an inferior, make-do form of communication. This is what they have been taught by their hearing teachers, counselors, speech therapists, audiologists, and other professionals. ASL is rarely, if ever, taught to any deaf children in school. Instead, they learn it from deaf children of deaf parents, older students, and deaf adults, generally, deaf people do not realize that their community has a "culture" and a "language" which is central to that culture.

III.   MANY DEAF PEOPLE:

Reject the Church because its representatives have been as oppressive as their teachers and therapists. "Religion" has become one more place where deaf people feel they are told to stop being "deaf" and try to be "hearing". They must try to fit into hearing forms of worship with its heavy emphasis on music, its wordy English liturgies and its love for ancient phrases – all through an interpreter they frequently can't understand.

Unfortunately, even the separate deaf churches and/or programs, there has been little development of indigenous worship forms that reflect the experience of deaf people. All of this has led to alienation and/or superficial involvement in the Church. Clearly the situation has not encouraged any real understanding of God and the message of Jesus. Exceptions exist, of course, but unfortunately the exceptions are all-too-few.

The Church generally has not looked upon deaf people as a potential gift or resource to the broader Christian community. The Church has considered deaf people to be "handicapped" and, relatedly, has thought deaf people to be intellectually and morally inferior, unable to learn properly and/or spiritually inhibited by a lack of adequate language. Burdened with such stereotypes, deaf people have not been accepted as equal members of the Body of Christ. The Church has not recognized deaf people as persons equipped with theological and cultural gifts with which to enrich the life of the whole Church.

IV. WE BELIEVE:

That the message of Jesus is a message of liberation – not liberation from deafness, per se, but liberation from all forms of oppression, which include the denial of basic human needs for things like unencumbered communication, healthy human interaction, self-esteem, positive recognition of one's culture and language, and meaningful education.

We do not view deafness as a sickness or handicap. We view it as a gift from God, which has led to the creation of a unique language and culture, worthy of respect and affirmation.

We believe that it is necessary to stop trying to communicate the Gospel through hearing people's eyes, through their interpretation and understanding of the Bible, and through their methods. Deaf people have a right to know the Gospel in their own language and relevant to their own context.

We believe that American Sign Language is indeed a language – and worthy and powerful vehicle for expressing the Gospel.

We believe the Holy Spirit is leading all of us to work for a new day of justice for all deaf people. We believe the Holy Spirit is leading deaf people to develop indigenous forms of worship that can adequately convey the praise and prayers of the deaf Christian community.

We stand in solidarity with the oppressed people of the world. We believe that God empowers the oppressed to become free. By the act of attaining their own freedom, the oppressed can also help liberate those who have oppressed them.

We believe that God is calling the Church to a new vision of liberation of both deaf and hearing people. This vision is deeply rooted in the Gospel of Jesus Christ, and in an understanding of the spiritual, socio-economic, political, and educational struggles of the deaf community.

We believe God has given deaf people a unique perspective and unique gifts. The Body of Christ remains broken and fragmented while deaf people are separate and their gifts unknown and strange to most Christians. We believe God is calling us to wholeness.

We commit ourselves to this vision, and trust God's Spirit to lead, to strengthen, and to empower us in this task. And we call upon deaf and hearing Christians alike to join together in this struggle toward freedom.

Participants/Co-authors

Dr. Mary Weir, Theologian, Teacher
Shelia Stopher Yoder, Social Worker in Christian Ministry
Mary Anne Royster, Interpreter, Teacher
Bill Millar, Pastor
Susan R. Masters, Interpreter, Social Worker
Ella Mae Lentz, ASL Teacher, Translator, Poet
Dr. Jan Kanda (Humphrey), Interpreter, Teacher, Author
Patrick Graybill, Teacher, Actor, ASL Translator,
Deacon in Roman Catholic Church
Pam Dintaman, Christian Ministries
Dr. Charlotte Baker-Shenk, ASL Linguist, Teacher, Author

APPENDIX B

NAD–RID CODE OF PROFESSIONAL CONDUCT
(Adopted July 2005)

Scope
The National Association of the Deaf (NAD) and the Registry of Interpreters for the Deaf, Inc. (RID) uphold high standards of professionalism and ethical conduct for interpreters. Embodied in this Code of Professional Conduct (formerly known as the Code of Ethics) are seven tenets setting forth guiding principles, followed by illustrative behaviors.

The tenets of this Code of Professional Conduct are to be viewed holistically and as a guide to professional behavior. This document provides assistance in complying with the code. The guiding principles offer the basis upon which the tenets are articulated. The illustrative behaviors are not exhaustive, but are indicative of the conduct that may either conform to or violate a specific tenet or the code as a whole.

When in doubt, the reader should refer to the explicit language of the tenet. If further clarification is needed, questions may be directed to the national office of the Registry of Interpreters for the Deaf, Inc.

This Code of Professional Conduct is sufficient to encompass interpreter roles and responsibilities in every type of situation (e.g., educational, legal, medical). A separate code for each area of interpreting is neither necessary nor advisable.

Philosophy
The American Deaf community represents a cultural and linguistic group having the inalienable right to full and equal communication and to participation in all aspects of society. Members of the American Deaf community have the right to informed choice and the highest quality interpreting services.

Recognition of the communication rights of America's women, men, and children who are deaf is the foundation of the tenets, principles, and behaviors set forth in this Code of Professional Conduct.

Voting Protocol
This Code of Professional Conduct was presented through mail referendum to certified interpreters who are members in good standing with the Registry of Interpreters for the Deaf, Inc. and theNational Association of the Deaf. The vote was to adopt or to reject.

Adoption of this Code of Professional Conduct
Interpreters who are members in good standing with the Registry of Interpreters for the Deaf, Inc.and the National Association of the Deaf voted to adopt this Code of Professional Conduct, effective July 1, 2005. This Code of Professional Conduct is a working document that is expected to change over time. The aforementioned members may be called upon to vote, as may be needed from time to time, on the tenets of the code.

The guiding principles and the illustrative behaviors may change periodically to meet the needs and requirements of the RID Ethical Practices System. These sections of the Code of Professional Conduct will not require a vote of the members. However, members are encouraged to recommend changes for future updates.

Function of the Guiding Principles
It is the obligation of every interpreter to exercise judgment, employ critical thinking, apply the benefits of practical experience, and reflect on past actions in the practice of their profession. The guiding principles in this document represent the concepts of confidentiality, linguistic and professional competence, impartiality, professional growth and development, ethical business practices, and the rights of participants in interpreted situations to informed choice. The driving force behind the guiding principles is the notion that the interpreter will do no harm.

When applying these principles to their conduct, interpreters remember that their choices are governed by a "reasonable interpreter" standard. This standard represents the hypothetical interpreter who is appropriately educated, informed, capable, aware of professional standards, and fair-minded.

CODE OF PROFESSIONAL CONDUCT

Tenets

1. Interpreters adhere to standards of confidential communication.

2. Interpreters possess the professional skills and knowledge required for the specific interpreting situation.

3. Interpreters conduct themselves in a manner appropriate to the specific interpreting situation.

4. Interpreters demonstrate respect for consumers.

5. Interpreters demonstrate respect for colleagues, interns, and students of the profession.

6. Interpreters maintain ethical business practices.

7. Interpreters engage in professional development.

Applicability

a) This Code of Professional Conduct applies to certified and associate members of the Registry of Interpreters for the Deaf, Inc., Certified members of the National Association of the Deaf, interns, and students of the profession.

b) Federal, state or other statutes or regulations may supersede this Code of Professional Conduct. When there is a conflict between this code and local, state, or federal laws and regulations, the interpreter obeys the rule of law.

c) This Code of Professional Conduct applies to interpreted situations that are performed either face-to-face or remotely.

Definitions

For the purpose of this document, the following terms are used:

Colleagues: Other interpreters.

Conflict of Interest: A conflict between the private interests (personal, financial, or professional) and the official or professional responsibilities of an interpreter in a position of trust, whether actual or perceived, deriving from a specific interpreting situation.

Consumers: Individuals and entities who are part of the interpreted situation. This includes individuals who are deaf, deaf-blind, hard of hearing, and hearing.

1.0 CONFIDENTIALITY

Tenet: Interpreters adhere to standards of confidential communication.

Guiding Principle: Interpreters hold a position of trust in their role as linguistic and cultural facilitators of communication. Confidentiality is highly valued by consumers and is essential to protecting all involved.

Each interpreting situation (e.g., elementary, secondary, and post-secondary education, legal, medical, mental health) has a standard of confidentiality. Under the reasonable interpreter standard, professional interpreters are expected to know the general requirements and applicability of various levels of confidentiality. Exceptions to confidentiality include, for example, federal and state laws requiring mandatory reporting of abuse or threats of suicide, or responding to subpoenas.

Illustrative Behavior – Interpreters:

1.1 Share assignment-related information only on a confidential and "as-needed" basis (e.g., supervisors, interpreter team members, members of the educational team, hiring entities).

1.2 Manage data, invoices, records, or other situational or consumer-specific information in a manner consistent with maintaining consumer confidentiality (e.g., shredding, locked files).

1.3 Inform consumers when federal or state mandates require disclosure of confidential information.

2.0 PROFESSIONALISM

Tenet: Interpreters possess the professional skills and knowledge required for the specific interpreting situation.

Guiding Principle: Interpreters are expected to stay abreast of evolving language use and trends in the profession of interpreting as well as in the American Deaf community.

Interpreters accept assignments using discretion with regard to skill, communication mode, setting, and consumer needs. Interpreters possess knowledge of American Deaf culture and deafness-related resources.

Illustrative Behavior – Interpreters:

2.1 Provide service delivery regardless of race, color, national origin, gender, religion, age, disability, sexual orientation, or any other factor.

2.2 Assess consumer needs and the interpreting situation before and during the assignment and make adjustments as needed.

2.3 Render the message faithfully by conveying the content and spirit of what is being communicated, using language most readily understood by consumers, and correcting errors discreetly and expeditiously.

2.4 Request support (e.g., certified deaf interpreters, team members, language facilitators) when needed to fully convey the message or to address exceptional communication challenges (e.g. cognitive disabilities, foreign sign

language, emerging language ability, or lack of formal instruction or language).

2.5 Refrain from providing counsel, advice, or personal
opinions.

2.6 Judiciously provide information or referral regarding
available interpreting or community resources without in-
fringing upon consumers' rights.

3.0 CONDUCT

Tenet: Interpreters conduct themselves in a manner appropriate to
the specific interpreting situation.

Guiding Principle: Interpreters are expected to present themselves
appropriately in demeanor and appearance. They avoid situations that
result in conflicting roles or perceived or actual conflicts of interest.

Illustrative Behavior – Interpreters:

3.1 Consult with appropriate persons regarding the interpreting situation to determine issues such as placement
and adaptations necessary to interpret effectively.

3.2 Decline assignments or withdraw from the interpreting profession when not competent due to physical, mental, or emotional factors.

3.3 Avoid performing dual or conflicting roles in inter-
disciplinary (e.g. educational or mental health teams) or
other settings.

3.4 Comply with established workplace codes of conduct,
notify appropriate personnel if there is a conflict with this
Code of Professional Conduct, and actively seek resolution where warranted.

3.5 Conduct and present themselves in an unobtrusive
manner and exercise care in choice of attire.

3.6 Refrain from the use of mind-altering substances before or during the performance of duties.

3.7 Disclose to parties involved any actual or perceived conflicts of interest.

3.8 Avoid actual or perceived conflicts of interest that might cause harm or interfere with the effectiveness of interpreting services.

3.9 Refrain from using confidential interpreted information for personal, monetary, or professional gain.

3.10 Refrain from using confidential interpreted information for the benefit of personal or professional affiliations or entities.

4.0 RESPECT FOR CONSUMERS

Tenet: Interpreters demonstrate respect for consumers.

Guiding Principle: Interpreters are expected to honor consumer preferences in selection of interpreters and interpreting dynamics, while recognizing the realities of qualifications, availability, and situation.

Illustrative Behavior – Interpreters:

4.1 Consider consumer requests or needs regarding language preferences, and render the message accordingly (interpreted or transliterated).

4.2 Approach consumers with a professional demeanor at all times.

4.3 Obtain the consent of consumers before bringing an intern to an assignment.

4.4 Facilitate communication access and equality, and support the full interaction and independence of consumers.

5.0 RESPECT FOR COLLEAGUES

Tenet: Interpreters demonstrate respect for colleagues, interns and students of the profession.

Guiding Principle: Interpreters are expected to collaborate with colleagues to foster the delivery of effective interpreting services. They also understand that the manner in which they relate to colleagues reflects upon the profession in general.

Illustrative Behavior – Interpreters:

5.1 Maintain civility toward colleagues, interns, and students.

5.2 Work cooperatively with team members through consultation before assignments regarding logistics, providing professional and courteous assistance when asked and monitoring the accuracy of the message while functioning in the role of the support interpreter.

5.3 Approach colleagues privately to discuss and resolve breaches of ethical or professional conduct through standard conflict resolution methods; file a formal grievance only after such attempts have been unsuccessful or the breaches are harmful or habitual.

5.4 Assist and encourage colleagues by sharing information and serving as mentors when appropriate.

5.5 Obtain the consent of colleagues before bringing an intern to an assignment.

6.0 BUSINESS PRACTICES

Tenet: Interpreters maintain ethical business practices.

Guiding Principle: Interpreters are expected to conduct their business in a professional manner whether in private practice or in the employ of an agency or other entity. Professional interpreters are entitled to a living wage based on their qualifications and expertise.

Interpreters are also entitled to working conditions conducive to effective service delivery.

Illustrative Behavior – Interpreters:

6.1 Accurately represent qualifications, such as certification, educational background, and experience, and provide documentation when requested.

6.2 Honor professional commitments and terminate assignments only when fair and justifiable grounds exist.

6.3 Promote conditions that are conducive to effective communication, inform the parties involved if such conditions do not exist, and seek appropriate remedies.

6.4 Inform appropriate parties in a timely manner when delayed or unable to fulfill assignments.

6.5 Reserve the option to decline or discontinue assignments if working conditions are not safe, healthy, or conducive to interpreting.

6.6 Refrain from harassment or coercion before, during, or after the provision of interpreting services.

6.7 Render pro bono services in a fair and reasonable manner.

6.8 Charge fair and reasonable fees for the performance of interpreting services and arrange for payment in a professional and judicious manner.

7.0 PROFESSIONAL DEVELOPMENT

Tenet: Interpreters engage in professional development.

Guiding Principle: Interpreters are expected to foster and maintain interpreting competence and the stature of the profession through ongoing development of knowledge and skills.

Illustrative Behavior – Interpreters:

7.1 Increase knowledge and strengthen skills through activities such as:

> ➤ pursuing higher education;
> ➤ attending workshops and conferences;
> ➤ seeking mentoring and supervision opportunities;
> ➤ participating in community events; and
> ➤ engaging in independent studies.

7.2 Keep abreast of laws, policies, rules, and regulations that affect the profession.

APPENDIX C

AVLIC Code of Ethics
RATIFIED: JULY 2000 AVLIC AGM

The purpose of the Code of Ethics is to provide guidance for inter-preters, and in so doing, to ensure quality of service for all persons involved. Adherence to the following tenets are essential for maintaining national standards; professional discretion must be exercised at all times.

The Association of Visual Language Interpreters of Canada (AVLIC) expects its members to maintain high standards of professional conduct in their capacity and identity as an interpreter. Members are required to abide by the Code of Ethics and follow the Guidelines for Professional Conduct as a condition of membership in the organization.

This document articulates ethical principals, values, and standards of conduct to guide all members of AVLIC in their pursuit of professional practice. It is intended to provide direction to interpreters for ethical and professional decision making in their day-to-day work. The Code of Ethics and Guidelines for Professional Conduct is the mechanism by which the public is protected in the delivery of service.

VALUES UNDERLYING THE CODE OF ETHICS & GUIDELINES FOR PROFESSIONAL CONDUCT

AVLIC values:

1. *Professional accountability:*
   Accepting responsibility for professional decisions and actions.
2. *Professional competence:*
   Committing to provide quality professional service throughout one's practice.
3. *Non-discrimination:*
   Approaching professional service with respect and cultural sensitivity.

4. Integrity in professional relationships:
Dealing honestly and fairly with consumers and colleagues.
5. Integrity in business practices:
Dealing honestly and ethically in all business practices.

Members are to understand that each of these core values and accompanying sections are to be considered when making ethical and professional decisions in their capacity and identity as an interpreter. These values are of equal weight and importance.

Code of Ethics and Guidelines
for Professional Conduct

1.0 PROFESSIONAL ACCOUNTABILITY:
Interpreters accept responsibility for all professional decisions made and actions taken.

1.1 Confidentiality

1.1.1 Members will respect the privacy of consumers and hold in confidence all information obtained in the course of professional service. Members may be released from this obligation only with their consumers' authorization or when ordered by law.

1.1.2 Where necessary, a member may exchange pertinent information with a colleague in order to provide consistent quality of service. This will be done in a manner that protects the information and the consumers.

1.1.3 Members need to be aware that other professional codes of conduct may impact upon their work. In such circumstances, members will make appropriate professional decisions and conduct themselves in a manner benefiting the setting and the profession.

1.2 Professional Conduct

1.2.1 Members will hold the needs of consumers primary when making professional decisions.

1.2.2 Members shall recognize that all work undertaken by them on an individual basis, whether pro bono or paid, will ultimately reflect the integrity of themselves and of the profession.

1.2.3 Members shall conduct themselves in a professional manner at all times. They shall not badger or coerce individuals or agencies to use their professional services.

1.2.4 Members shall take into account the limitations of their abilities, knowledge and the resources available to them prior to accepting work. They will remove themselves from a given setting when they realize an inability to provide professional service.

1.2.5 Members must be aware of personal circumstances or conflict of interested that might interfere with their effectiveness. They will refrain from conduct that can lead to substandard performance and/or harm to anyone including themselves and consumers.

1.2.6 Members are accountable to AVLIC and to their local chapter affiliate for their professional and ethical conduct. Further, members are responsible to discuss and resolve, in a professional manner, issues arising from breaches of ethical or professional conduct on the part of individual colleagues after they are observed. In the case where these breaches are potentially harmful to others or chronic, and attempts to resolve the issue have not been successful, such conduct should be reported to AVLIC and/or their local chapter affiliate in a manner directed by the appropriate grievance procedure.

1.3 Scope of Practice

1.3.1 Members will refrain from using their professional role to perform other functions that lie beyond the scope of an interpreting assignment and the parameters of their professional duties. They will not counsel, advise, or interject personal opinions.

1.3.2 When functioning as part of a professional team (e.g. education, legal, medical and mental health settings) it is understood that members will limit their expertise to interpreting. In such settings, it may be appropriate for members to comment on the overall effectiveness of communication, the interpreting process and to suggest appropriate resources and referrals. This should be done only within the context of the professional team.

1.3.3 Members will refrain from manipulating work situations for personal benefit or gain. When working as independent contractors, member may promote their professional services within the scope of their practice. When working under the auspices of an agency or other employer, it is not ethical for the members to promote their professional services independent of the agency or employer.

1.4 Integrity of Service

Members will demonstrate sound professional judgment and accept responsibility for their decisions. Members will make every attempt to avoid situations that constitute a real or perceived conflict of interest. Members will ensure there is full disclosure to all parties should their ancillary interest be seen as a real or perceived conflict of interest.

2.0 PROFESSIONAL COMPETENCE:

Interpreters provide the highest possible quality service through all aspects of their professional practice.

2.1 Qualifications to Practice

Members shall understand the difference between professional and social interactions. They will establish and maintain appropriate boundaries between themselves and consumers. Members will assume responsibility to ensure relationships with all parties involved are reasonable, fair, and professional.

2.2 Faithfulness of Interprettion

Every interpretation shall be faithful to and render exactly the message of the source text. A faithful interpretation. The fidelity of an interpretation includes an adaptation to make the form, the tone, and the deeper meaning of the source text felt in the target language and culture.

2.3 Accountability for Professional Competence

2.3.1 Members will accept full responsibility for the quality of their own work and will refrain from making inaccurate statements regarding their competence, education, experience or certification.

2.3.2 Members are responsible for properly preparing themselves for the work contrcted.

2.3.3 Members will accept contracts for work only after determining they have the appropriate qualifications and can remain neutral throughout the assignment.

2.4 Ongoing Professional Development

2.4.1 Members will incorporate current theoretical and applied knowledge, enhance that knowledge through continuing education throughout their professional careers and will strive for AVLIC certification.

2.4.2 Members will aim to be self-dircted learners, pursuing educational opportunties which are relevant to their professional practice. This could include but is not limited to peer review, collegial consultation, mentoring and regular feedback regarding specific areas of skill development.

3.0 NON-DISCRMINATION:

Interpreters approach professional sevices with respect and cultural sensitivity towards all participants.

3.1 Non-discrimination

Members will respect the individuality, the right to self-determination, and the autonomy of the people with whom they work. They will not discriminate based on ethnicity, gender, age, disability, sexual orientation, religion, personal beliefs and practices, social status or any other factor.

3.2 Communication Preferences

Members will respect and use the form of communication preferred by those deaf and hard of hearing consumers for whom they provide service.

3.3 Deaf Interpreters

The services of a Deaf interpreter may be required when working with individuals who use regional sign dialects, non-standard signs, foreign sign languages, and those with emerging language use. They may also be used with individuals who have disabling conditions that impact on communication. Members will recognize the need for a Deaf interpreter and will ensure their inclusion as a part of the professional interpreting team.

4.0 INTEGRITY IN PROFESSIONAL RELATIONSHIPS:

Interpreters deal honestly and fairly with consumers and colleagues while establishing and maintaining professional boundaries.

4.1 Professional Relationships

Members shall undestand the difference between professional and social interactions. They will establish and maintain appropriate boundaries between themselves and consumers. Members will assume responsibility to ensure relationships with all parties are reasonable , fair, and professional.

4.2 Impartiality

4.2.1 Members shall remain neutral, impartial, and objective. They will refrain from altering a message for political, religious, moral, or philosophical reasons, or any other biased or subjective consideration.

4.2.2 Should a member not be able to put aside personal biases or reactions which threaten impartiality, the member will examine options available to them. This may include not accepting the work or withdrawing their services from the assignment or contract.

4.3 Respect for Colleagues

4.3.1 Members will act toward colleagues in a spirit of mutual cooperation, treating and portraying them to others with respect, courtesy, fairness and good faith. Members are encouraged to share their knowledge with their colleagues in a spirit of mutual assistance.

4.3.2 Members have a professional obligation to assist and encourage new interpreting practitioners in the profession.

4.3.3 Members shall not abuse the good faith of other members or be guilty of a breach of trust or the use of unfair tactics.

ization.

4.4 Support for Professional Associations

Members shall support AVLIC, its affiliates, and other organizations representing the profession and the Deaf community.

5.0 INTEGRITY IN BUSINESS RELATIONSHIPS:

Interpreters establish and maintain professional boundaries with consumers and colleagues in a manner that is honest and fair.

5.1 Business Practices

5.1.1 Members will refrain from any unfair competition with their colleagues, including but not limited to: (a) engaging in comparative advertising (b) willfully under-cutting; or (c) artificially inflating fees during times when market demand exceeds supply.

5.1.2 Members will conduct themselves in all phases of the interpreting situation in a manner benefitting the profession, including negotiating work and contracts, obtaining suitable preparation material, and choice of attire and professional demeanor.

5.1.3 Members will honour professional commitments made when accepting work, and will follow through on their obligations. Members may not unilaterally terminate work or a contract unless they have fair and reasonable grounds to do so.

5.1.4 Members shall take reasonable care of material and/or property given to them by a consumer and may not lend such or use it for purposes other than those for which it was entrusted to them.

5.1 Accurate Representation of Credentials

5.2.1 Members shall not by any means engage in, nor allow the use of, statements that are false, misleading, incomplete, or likely to mislead consumers or members of the public.

5.2.2 Members will refrain from making inaccurate statements regarding their competence, education, experience or certification. Only members certified by AVLIC (COI) or RID (CI/CT or CSC) may use the term "certified" in printed, electronic, signed, or oral transmission. This may include, but is not limited to, interpreter directories, business cards and forms, promotional materials, resume's, or publications they have authored.

5.3 Reimbursement for Services

5.3.1 Members will bill only for services provided. Members will negotiate fees, including cancellation policies, preferably in writing or contract form before service is provided. Members will be sensitive to professional and community norms when establishing fees for service.

5.3.2 Members may also provide bartered or pro bono service in situations where the profession of interpreting and the livelihood of other practitioners will not be threatened.

APPENDIX D

Kohlberg's Stages of Moral Development

THE PRE CONVENTIONAL LEVEL

An individual at this level of development is responsive to cultural definitions of good and bad, right or wrong. These labels are interpreted in terms of either the physical consequences of action (punishment, reward, exchange of favors) or in terms of the physical power of those who make the rules..

STAGE ONE: PUNISHMENT AND OBEDIENCE ORIENTATION

Choices are made to avoid punishment; there is unquestioning deference to those in power.

STAGE TWO: INSTRUMENTAL RELATIVIST ORIENTATION

Choices are made which reap a desired reward; there is some sense of "fairness" based on a "you do for me, I'll do for you" basis,

CONVENTIONAL LEVEL

At this level, living up to the expectations of one's family, group of affiliation, or nation is seen as valuable in its own right, regardless of immediate and obvious consequences. The attitude includes (a) conformity to group expectations and social order, (b) loyalty, (c) actively maintaining, supporting, and justifying the "rules", and (d) identifying with the persons or group making the rules.

STAGE THREE: "GOOD BOY-NICE GIRL" ORIENTATION

Choices are made based on what is approved of by others; there is a great deal of conformity to what the majority does

STAGE FOUR: "LAW AND ORDER" ORIENTATION

Choices are made based on authority, fixed rules, and the maintenance of social order; there is a sense that one must "do his/her duty"

POST-CONVENTIONAL, AUTONOMOUS, OR PRINCIPLED, LEVEL

At this level there is a clear effort to define moral values and principles that have validity and meaning apart from authority figures holding these principles and apart from the individual's own identification with any groups.

STAGE FIVE: SOCIAL CONTRACT LEGALISTIC ORIENTATION

Right and wrong tends to be defined in terms of general individual rights and in terms of standards that have been critically examined and agreed upon by the whole society

STAGE SIX: UNIVERSAL ETHICAL-PRINCIPLE ORIENTATION

Right and wrong is defined by a decision of conscience in accord with self-chosen ethical principles appealing to logic, universality, and consistency. Based on a belief in universal principles of justice, reciprocity, equality of human rights, and respect for the dignity of human beings as individual persons.

While we typically think of each stage as being appropriate for a particular age range, it is possible for someone to become "locked" into a particular stage of development. Research suggests that only 5 percent of the population reaches stage 6 and most individuals are about 30-years of age when they reach that level of thinking. Research also indicates that 20% of our decisions are consciously made. Further, our decisions and behaviors are motivated by unconscious factors from deep within us.

Thus the experiences we have gone through on our way to adulthood determine our self-concept. Our self-concept dictates how far we are able to progress through the stages of moral development and defines our values. Our definition of morality and what is ethical is based on our self-concept.

GLOSSARY

ABSTRACT CLASSIFIERS: classifiers that are smaller than life-size, the shape and movement of which does not necessarily have iconic features.

ABSTRACT LANGUAGE: generic and lacking in specificity.

ACCESSIBILITY: modification to building design, program delivery, or forms of communication which will allow Deaf and disabled individuals to gain access to services provided by an institution or agency; e.g. sign language interpreters make the information accessible to a person who cannot hear what is being said.

ADVENTITIOUS DEAFNESS: to become deaf at some point after birth.

AFFECT: refers to emotions or feelings.

A-LANGUAGE or L1: one's first language, usually the language your parents speak although this is not always the case, also known as mother tongue or native language.

AMBIVALENCE: having both negative and positive feelings about something; common reaction of members of the oppressed group who have both positive and negative feelings about themselves and the minority group they are affiliated with.

AMERICAN SIGN LANGUAGE (ASL): a visual-gestural language incorporating facial grammatical markers, physical affect markers, spatial linguistic information and fingerspelling, as well as signs made with the hands. ASL is a distinct language with its own grammar and syntax, it is not based on, nor derived from, a spoken language; the natural language of the Deaf community, ASL is an integral part of Deaf culture. Varieties include old, traditional and modern.

ANGLICIZED ASL: a form of signing which blends ASL with English-based signs; a contact variety more closely affiliated with ASL than English.

ANGLOPHONE: a person who uses English-based communication, as compared to French-based communication (common term in Canada for English-speaking people).

ASSOCIATION OF VISUAL LANGUAGE INTERPRETERS OF CANADA (AVLIC): the national professional association and certifying body of sign language interpreters in Canada; has provincial chapters and a central office in Edmonton, Alberta.

AUDISM: an attitude based on pathological thinking that results in a negative stigma toward anyone who does not hear; like racism or sexism, audism judges, labels, and limits individuals on the basis of whether a person hears and speaks (coined by Tom Humphries).

AUDITORY FEEDBACK LOOP: the channel through which hearing people hear (and monitor) their own voice as they speak (alternate term: back-channel feedback).

AURAL-ORAL LANGUAGES: languages based on a structured set of linguistic rules in which the communication is based on sound; spoken languages throughout the world fall into this category.

BENEFACTORS ARE PERFECT: an idea frequently held by members of marginalized groups that members of the oppressor group are somehow super-beings; also refered to as "magical thinking."

BICULTURAL: refers to an individual (1) who has knowledge about two cultures, and (2) who has developed socially appropriate behaviors necessary to fit in each of the two cultures. Further, it implies that the individual has the ability to shift from culture to culture, displaying socially appropriate behaviors at the right time with the appropriate group.

BILINGUAL-BICULTURAL (BI-BI) PHILOSOPHY OF INTERPRETATION: a philosophy of interpreting based on the belief that effective interpretation requires cultural and linguistic mediation in order to accomplish speaker goals and maintain dynamic equivalence; based on the recognition of Deaf people as members of an oppressed minority; accepts ASL as a language and Deaf culture as that which encompasses the norms, values, and traditions of this community of people.

BILINGUAL-BICULTURAL EDUCATION (bi-bi): an approach which stresses ASL as the instructional language for all subjects except English, with an ultimate goal of developing competency in both English and American Sign Language; based on the recognition of Deaf people as members of an oppressed minority; accepts ASL as a language and Deaf culture as that which encompasses the norms, values, and traditions of this community of people; students in a bi-bi program study ASL (public signing, grammar, etc.), Deaf culture, Deaf heritage/history, and Deaf studies. This approach to deaf education is becoming more and more popular as its successes are being experienced.

B-LANGUAGE or L2: refers to one's second language, one acquired by living in a country where that language is spoken, by interacting frequently with people using that language or by studying the language formally.

CERTIFICATE OF INTERPRETATION (COI): the professional
certificate awarded by the Association of Visual Language Interpreters of
Canada (AVLIC) to individuals who successfully complete both a knowledge
and skills assessment in effect so long as the member adheres to the AVLIC
Code of Ethics and maintains annual active membership with fees paid in
fulll

CERTIFIED DEAF INTERPRETER (CDI): a deaf interpreter who has taken
and passed the RID certification for Deaf Interpreters.

C-LANGUAGE: a language one can "manage" to comprehend what is
spoken/signed, however the individual speaks/ signs with a heavy accent,
improper grammatical structure and frequent semantic errors.

CLASSIFIERS: a specific set of signs that serve several functions in ASL;
some are iconic (look somewhat like the object they represent), others are
arbitrary (there is no obvious reason for that sign or hand shape to be used
as a classifier for the noun it represents); a classifier generally cannot be used
until the noun it is representing has been signed. Classifiers can convey: (a)
the relationship of a noun to a noun; (b) the way a noun moves; and
(c) describe a variety of nouns.

CLIENTS: a term used to refer to those for whom sign language interpreters
work; includes both Deaf and hearing consumers or clients; sign language
interpreters provide spoken English interpretation/transliteration for hearing clients or ASL/Signed English interpretation/ transliteration for Deaf
consumers (alternate term: consumer).

CLOZE SKILLS: the ability to mentally fill-in-the-blanks when part of an
utterance is obscured or when the receiver does not understand a term or
phrase (also termed "closure".)

CODE OF ETHICS: a set of guidelines that require an individual to develop
effective decision making skills, a clear sense of her/his own beliefs and
values, understand how society defines right/wrong, good/bad, and have the
ability to apply all of this to spur of the moment, professional interactions;
most professions have a code to guide practitioners and consumers in their
fields.

CODE SWITCHING: the conscious or unconscious movement from ASL
into English-like signing or from English-like signing to ASL; this often occurs due to the experience of oppression common to Deaf people in Canada
and the U.S.

COMMUNICATION DYNAMICS: the way people in a communication interaction react to or engage with one another and to the overall interaction.

COMMUNICATION FACILITATION PHILOSOPHY: a set of beliefs regarding Deaf individuals, ASL, and communication dynamics that influences the way a person views her/his role and work as an interpreter; includes a belief of Deaf people as handicapped, ASL as a means of communicating only with less educated individuals, sensitivity to environmental factors that influence communication.

COMMUNICATION: a continuous, transactional process involving two or more people who occupy different but overlapping environments; as they seek to share information or ideas, they create a relationship by simultaneously sending and receiving messages, some of which are clearly and overtly delivered, other that carry implied and unstated information; messages are often distorted by physical and psychological noise.

CONCEPTUALLY ACCURATE SIGNED ENGLISH (CASE) or SIGNED ENGLISH (SE): a manual code for English which combines English grammatical order with ASL signs and some invented initialized signs; choices of signs based on the intended concept or idea of the speaker.

CONDUIT or MACHINE PHILOSOPHY: a set of beliefs regarding Deaf individuals, ASL, and communication dynamics that influences the way a person views her/his role and work as an interpreter; includes a belief of Deaf people as handicapped and needing to learn to take care of themselves; word-for-sign equivalents between signs and spoken English; and the interpreter as having no responsibility for the interaction or communication dynamics taking place.

CONFERENCE OF INTERPRETER TRAINERS (CIT): an American organization of educators who teach interpretation; membership is international.

CONFIDENTIALITY: the agreement that information that takes place in a professional relationship is not to be shared with others outside of the specific setting and relationship; based on a trust relationship between the professional and her/his clients.

CONGENITAL DEAFNESS: to be born deaf or hard-of-hearing.

CONSECUTIVE INTERPRETATION: the process of interpreting into the target language after the speaker completes one or more ideas in the source language and pauses while the interpreter transmits that information; more accurate than simultaneous interpretation.

CONSULTATIVE: when consultative register is used, one of the individuals involved in the interchange has "expert" status or an enhanced command of the topic at hand.

CONSUMER: a term used to refer to those for whom sign language interpreters work; includes both Deaf and hearing consumers or clients; sign language interpreters provide spoken English interpretation/transliteration for hearing clients or ASL/Signed English interpretation/ transliteration for Deaf consumers (alternate term: client).

CONTACT VARIETIES: a mixture of two languages resulting from prolonged language contact between members of different linguistic communities — includes code-switching, code-mixing, and lexical borrowing; sometimes referred to as Pidgin Signed English (PSE) although it does not satisfy the linguistic requirements of a true pidgin.

CRITICAL THINKING SKILLS: the ability to break the whole into its parts, to examine in detail, to look more deeply into a text and determine its nature by engaging in disciplined reasoning, inferring and deducing in order to extract the message carried "below the words/signs" or "between the lines" as well as the information explicitly stated.

CULTURAL AND LINGUISTIC MEDIATION: interpreting in such a way that information has equivalent meaning and impact for individuals with different languages and cultural schema; requires an interpreter to make cultural and linguistic expansions and reductions.

CULTURAL EXPANSION: providing the contextual information required to make sense out of something that is signed or said to someone without the requisite schema or experiential frame; done within the form of the interpretation.

CULTURAL REDUCTION: reducing the volume and sometimes the detail of information within an interpretation without affecting the meaning intended; done to meet communication and cultural norms of the target language.

CULTURAL VIEW OF DEAF PEOPLE: accepts Deaf people as normal, capable human beings rather than as disabled, abnormal, etc.; interprets differences as cultural and experiential.

CULTURE: that complex whole which includes knowledge, beliefs, art, morals, laws, customs and any other capabilities and habits acquired as a member of society (Tyler); set of learned behaviors of a group of people who have their own language, values, rules of behavior, and traditions (Padden); consists of 3 subsets: (a) materialistic — including material things such as food, clothing, other tangible items, (b) behavioral — rules for behavior which can be observed, taught and learned, and (c) cognitive — that "appropriate" behavior learned and developed as a child, which has a deeper meaning and which is not easily observed or understood (Philip).

DEAF (capital "D"): used to denote individuals who, in addition to having a significant hearing loss, function by choice as members of the Deaf community, subscribing to the unique cultural norms, values, and traditions of that group.

DEAF (Deaf view): a label of pride and solidarity for those who have similar experiences, use a shared form of communication and who subscribe to Deaf cultural values, norms, and traditions.

DEAF (hearing view): refers to the inability to hear as compared to "normal" hearing, generally seen as a deficit or an impairment; measured by decibels (alternative terms: hearing impaired or mild, moderate, severe, profound hearing loss).

DEAF INTERPRETER (DI): A Deaf person, trained in the art of interpretation, who facilitates communication between a deaf individual who is using non-standard ASL, a regional dialect or some other form of visual communication and a hearing interpreter. The hearing interpreter interprets information the DI interprets from the deaf consumer to the hearing consumer and signs what the hearing consumer is saying to the DI for transmittal to the deaf consumer.

DECIBELS (db): a unit for expressing the relative intensity of sounds on a scale from zero for the average least perceptible sound to about 130 for the average level where sound induces pain.

DEPENDENCE ON THE "BENEFACTOR": the phenomena of minority group members being dependent upon members of the power group for certain things they perceive they are unable to do for themselves.

DISCOURSE STYLE: the way a language requires that information be presented in a monologue or dialogue.

DYNAMIC EQUIVALENCE: in an interpreted event, maintaining the "chemistry" between a speaker and her/his audience that allows a connection to be made and the speaker's goals to be accomplished.

EMPOWERMENT OF THE CLIENT: behaving in a way that supports another's right to make decisions within an interpersonal interaction by vesting control in the hands of consumers rather than solely in the hands of the interpreter; avoiding the imposition of one's own opinions, advice, sense of values, or preferred form of communication on others.

EMPOWERMENT: a process of reclaiming one's own power in order to take charge of one's own life.

ENGLISH-BASED SIGNS: a generic term used to refer to a variety of signing systems based on English structure, rather than the structure of American Sign Language (ASL); includes the Rochester Method, SEE1, SEE2, and Conceptually Accurate Signed English (CASE).

ENVIRONMENTAL FACTORS: phenomena in the area surrounding communication that can affect the interaction, including lights, extraneous auditory or visual noise, distance from the interpreter to the speaker, distance from the interpreter to the audience, etc.

EQUIVOCAL LANGUAGE: words, signs or phrases that can be interpreted in more than one way; often misleading or confusing to the listener.

ETHICAL BEHAVIOR: making choices and acting in a way that respects others; grows out of a strong moral sense; requires the ability to think critically and the courage to choose to do the right thing.

ETHICS: behavioral standards — a set of principles that defines what is judged appropriate or inappropriate, right or wrong

ETHNOCENTRIC: an attitude that one's own race or culture is superior to all others.

EUPHEMISTIC LANGUAGE: is the use of socially acceptable terms and phrases in place of blunt, descriptive words/phrases (e.g. the "powder room").

EXTERNAL NOISE: actual, physical factors that interfere with communication; includes things like the flickering of an overhead florescent light, the squeal of a poorly connected microphone, or the incessant coughing of someone in the room.

FATALISM OR PASSIVITY: the tendency of members of an oppressed group to feel powerless to change or strike back at "the system"; a "go with the flow" and "don't rock the boat" attitude.

FEAR OF FREEDOM: a lack of determined action that might lead to true equality and empowerment based on fear and sense of inferiority that "paralyzes" oppressed individuals; this response is common among members of an oppressed group, in spite of their anger about the injustice, discrimination and marginalization they experience.

FRANCOPHONE: a term used in Canada to refer to people who use French-based communication, as compared to English-based communication.

Glossary

FROZEN FORM: information or texts that are "fixed" — written, videotaped or audio taped.

FROZEN LINGUISTIC REGISTER: "fixed" texts that are repeated verbatim every time used (e.g. The Lord's Prayer, the national anthem); meaning is found more in the actions accompanying the text than in the words themselves.

GROUP OPPRESSION: a situation in which the dominant group denigrates members of a minority, including their self-worth, abilities, intelligence, and right to be different and affirmed in that difference; includes a denial of the minority group's language and opportunities to use it and a denigration of their culture.

HEARING IMPAIRED: a term used by some hearing people in an attempt to politely refer to Deaf and hard-of-hearing individuals; viewed by Deaf and hard of hearing people as negative and stigmatizing. Preferred term: Deaf and hard-of-hearing.

HELPER PHILOSOPHICAL FRAME: views Deaf people as handicapped, limited, unable to fully manage their personal and business affairs; believes that Deaf people are mentally, emotionally, or experientially incapable of fully understanding the world around them; views the interpreter as a caretaker whose purpose is to help.

HIGH VISUAL ORIENTATION (HVO): a term used to refer to individuals who have no language skills in ASL, LSQ, English, French, or any other language resulting from a developmental disability or because of educational or social deprivation; alternate terms: minimal language skills or minimal language competency.

HORIZONTAL HOSTILITY: the tendency of members of a minority group to turn its anger on other members of its own group; results range from barbed comments and putdowns to verbal or physical attacks and physical violence.

INSTITUTIONALIZED OPPRESSION: attitudes taught overtly or covertly in schools, through the media, and in homes and churches that result in the denigration of a minority group's language, culture, and personhood; a result of individual and group oppression; members of the minority group have no power in the institutions that impact their lives or opportunities for self-determination.

INTERPRETATION: the process of changing a message from one language to another, conveying all essential elements of meaning and maintaining dynamic equivalence; a highly sophisticated and demanding mental task involving complex thinking and analytical strategies.

437

INTERPRETER: one who takes a source language message and, after working through a complex mental process, expresses that same message into the target language, maintaining essential elements of meaning and dynamic equivalence.

LA LANGUE DES SIGNES QUEBECOISE (LSQ): the rule-governed language used by most Deaf people in Francophone areas of Canada; a complete and complex language, accepted as the natural language of the Deaf community. LSQ is an integral part of French Canadian Deaf culture.

LAG TIME: the time used by the interpreter to analyze a source language utterance and to make cultural and linguistic adjustments before producing an equivalent message in the target language (alternate term: processing time).

LINEAGE OF DEAF CHILDREN: ninety percent (90%) of all Deaf children are born to hearing families who have no deafness in their immediate or extended families; this rate is higher among African Americans where the rate of hereditary deafness is lower.

LINEAR GRAMMAR: grammatical structure of a language wherein lexical items and parts of speech are produced singularly, one at a time, in a string of single lexical units.

LINGUISTIC AND CULTURAL EXPANSIONS/REDUCTIONS: manipulating target language output so it contains all of the essential elements of meaning expressed in the source language in such a way as to fit the target language communication norms; decisions regarding expansions and reductions are based on one of three reasons: (a) linguistic need; (b) cultural need; or (c) difference in experiential frame.

LINGUISTIC EXPANSION: stating implied or "understood" information or ideas present in the source language message overtly in the interpretation when this information is required by the cultural and communication norms of the target language.

LINGUISTIC FLUENCY: being able to manipulate a language with the finesse of a native or near-native user of the language; this includes being able to properly shift registers, to discuss a variety of technical and non-technical topics, and to "play" with the language (play on words or play on signs); one cannot be linguistically fluent without knowing the intricate cultural meanings and interpretations of certain utterances, therefore bicultural skills are intrinsically linked to linguistic fluency.

LINGUISTIC REDUCTION: reducing the volume and sometimes the detail of information present in the source language without affecting the meaning intended; done due to the linguistic norms and expectations in the target language.

LINGUISTICS: the study of languages and the structures of which they are composed.

MACHINE PHILOSOPHY: a set of beliefs regarding Deaf individuals, ASL, and communication dynamics which influences the way a person views her/his role and work as an interpreter; includes a belief of Deaf people as handicapped and needing to learn to how to take care of themselves; word-for-sign equivalence between signs and spoken English; and the interpreter as having no responsibility for the interaction or communication dynamics taking place (alternate term: conduit philosophy).

MANUALLY CODED ENGLISH (MCE): a variety of English based signing systems used to represent the aural/oral language of English. Includes the Rochester method, Seeing Essential English (SEE1), Signing Exact English (SEE2), and Conceptually Accurate Signed English (CASE).

MENTORING or TWINNING: an arrangement in which a more experienced interpreter "adopts" a less experienced interpreter, showing her the ropes, introducing her to the Deaf and interpreting communities, and serving as a sounding board to review and evaluate the less-experienced interpreter's professional behavior, decision-making, and quality of interpretation or transliteration.

MINIMAL LANGUAGE COMPETENCY (MLC): term used to refer to individuals who have no language skills in ASL, LSQ, English, French, or any other language due to brain damage or educational or social deprivation; alternate terms: minimal language skills (MLS) or high visual orientation (HVO).

MODALITY: the channel through which a message is expressed, specifically spoken (aural/oral) or signed (visual/ gestural).

MULTI-LEVELED GRAMMAR: the ability of a language to produce more than one lexical item or more than one part of speech simultaneously.

MYTH OF THE MISGUIDED CHILD: a belief by members of a majority group that individuals in a particular minority group don't know what is best for them and thus require "guidance" by the majority group.

MYTHS: traditional stories that ostensibly explain the world view of a particular group of people or that explains a practice or belief.

NEED FOR APPROVAL FROM MARGINALIZED GROUP MEMBERS: the expectation and need for some expression of appreciation and gratitude to the majority group from the minority group; failure to receive approval often results in a sense of victimization.

NEGATIVE VIEW OF THE OPPRESSED GROUP: stigmatization of members of the minority group because they do not measure up to standards established by the majority; the stigmatized group is marginalized — systematically shut out of opportunities that lead to inclusion and equality.

NON-MANUAL SIGNALS (NMS): a set of facial/physical markers (behaviors) that accompany signs in ASL; conveys linguistic, grammatical and affective information; signs absent the non-manual signals result in non-linguistic and nonsensical utterances.

OPPRESSION: unjust or excessive exercise of power or position; results in the disenfranchisement of others.

ORAL DEAF PEOPLE: deaf individuals who do not use sign language, preferring to use speech and speech-reading as their primary form of communication.

ORAL TRANSLITERATION: making spoken English visible for an oral Deaf individual; includes repeating what is being said without speech, selecting words that are most easily speech-readable and sometimes using a gesture for clarification.

ORAL TRANSLITERATOR: one who listens to a spoken English message, then rephrases that message into clearly speech-readable forms for a Deaf consumer who uses speech and speech reading as primary forms of communication.

PARALINGUISTIC ELEMENTS: elements that accompany and add meaning to the expression of language; includes such things as gestures, tone of voice/size of signs, visual/vocal affect, etc.

PASSIVE VOICE: a type of sentence construction in which the actor performing the action indicated by the verb is not overtly identified.

PATERNALISM AND POSSESSIVE CONSCIOUSNESS: a caretaker attitude by members of the dominant group toward minority group members based on the assumption that they are unable to make appropriate decisions and need to be taken care of.

pathological view of Deaf people: a view of Deaf individuals as disabled, imperfect human beings. This view is reflected in the stereotypical labels historically assigned to Deaf people in professional literature.

PHYSIOLOGICAL NOISE biological factors that interfere with communication; includes such things as illness, exhaustion, or hunger;

Glossary

PIDGIN SIGN ENGLISH (PSE): an older (an incorrect) term used to refer to contact varieties or blended forms of English and ASL often used when Deaf and hearing people attempt to communicate.

PRAGMATIC USE OF LANGUAGE: the way a language is actually used rather than language function; helps us make sense of the language we encounter in our interactions with others and determine the meaning of the utterance within the given context.

PROCESS MODELS OF INTERPRETATION: attempts to graphically demonstrate the complex mental activities, decisions made and the factors influencing an interpretation; some models are based on formal research and others have been developed by long-time practitioners based on reflection and introspection of the pro.

PROCESSING TIME: the time used by the interpreter to analyze the source language utterance and to make cultural and linguistic adjustments before producing an equivalent message in the target language (alternate term: lag time).

PROFESSIONAL COMPETENCE: having the knowledge and skills base, as well as ethical judgment, to perform the task of a professional in a given field.

PROFESSIONAL DISTANCE: a social, psychological and physical boundary established to insure individuals function within appropriate professional roles; protects both the professional and the client.

PROFESSIONALS: practitioners working in a field in which they are expected to hold the interests of their clients paramount in all decisions made; have special knowledge, licensure or certification, adhere to a clearly articulated set of values or code of ethics; expected to be trustworthy, come to the task prepared, able to deal with sensitive information in a discrete manner and avoid inappropriate emotional involvement with clients.

PROSODY: the rhythm of a language including stress, inflection, intonation, pausing and phrasing that help listeners determine meaning and predict what the speaker will say next.

PSYCHOLOGICAL NOISE: realities that exist in the heads of all participants in the communication environment and distract from or interferes with the communication; includes things like internal stress, personal judgments about the other participants, and random thoughts that pop into one's mind.

REAL WORLD CLASSIFIERS: classifiers that take on life-size proportions and sometimes look a bit like a reduced form of mime when being produced.

RECIPROCAL SIGNALS: certain eye behaviors, head nods, verbal utterances (e.g., right, uh-huh) to indicate that one is attending and comprehending (or not comprehending) the messages being received.

RECIPROCITY OF PERSPECIVES: an assumption that the experiences and values of another group are identical to your own. Thus, if you traded places, members of the second group would come to view the world like yourself and develop concomitant values.

REGISTER: identifiable variations within all languages which mark the formality or informality of an interaction; Joos identifies five registers, including frozen, formal, consultative, informal and intimate; each register has specific characteristics and unwritten rules determining: (a) turn-taking and interaction between the speaker and listener; (b) complexity/completeness of sentence structure; and (c) choice of vocabulary.

REGISTRY OF INTERPRETERS FOR THE DEAF (RID): the national professional interpreter association and interpreter certifying body of the United States.

REPETITIVE STRAIN INJURY (RSI): a condition resulting from frequently using particular sets of muscles and tendons in the performance of one's work; RSI tends to result in carpal tunnel syndrome, tendonitis, tennis elbow, and brachial neuralgia (also known as overuse syndrome).

RESIDUAL HEARING: the ability to hear to some degree or at some frequencies in spite of a partial hearing loss.

RESISTANCE TO ATTEMPTS FOR LIBERATION: a fear on the part of members in the power group toward any attempts on the part of the oppressed group toward liberation or equality.

ROCHESTER METHOD: a manual code for English wherein each letter of the English alphabet is assigned a hand shape and all words communicated, with the exception of AND, are fingerspelled.

SCHEMA: an organizational or conceptual pattern in the mind; the contextual frame or "script" that helps us interpret what is happening; learned informally from our social and cultural interactions.

SEEING ESSNTIAL ENGLISH (SEE1): a manual code for English wherein each syllable is given a separate manual movement.

SEMANTICS: the way meaning is created by the use and interrelationship of words, phrases and sentences; precise shades of meaning applied to words/ signs in context.

SIGHT TRANSLATION: changing a message from the frozen form of one language (written or taped) into another signed or spoken language done on first sight, without the time normally required to prepare a formal translation; Deaf individuals hold a fairly common expectation that interpreters will be able to provide this service to them.

SIGN SUPPORTED SPEECH (SSS): a broad term used to refer to a variety of English-based signing systems; composed of invented hand movements that attempt to represent English in a manual/visual form, relying entirely upon the lexicon and syntax of English, and usually accompanied with speech or lip movements (formerly referred to as Manually Coded English).

SIGNED ENGLISH (SE): combines English grammatical order with ASL signs as well as some invented initialized signs.

SIGNING EXACT ENGLISH (SEE2): a manual code for English which is a combination of SEE1, invented initialized signs, and some ASL signs; the "proper" sign for various words is determined by the "two-out-of-three rule."

SIGN-TO-VOICE: the part of the interpretation process in which the source language message is signed (ASL, LSQ or a manual form of English) and the output is spoken in English, French or another auditory language.

SIMULTANEOUS COMMUNICATION: speaking and signing at the same time (sometimes referred to as sim-com); research has demonstrated a variety of problems that result from the simultaneous communication of hearing people including the omission of signs, semantic errors, unclear production of signs, and confused mouth markers (alternate term: sign supported speech).

SIMULTANEOUS INTERPRETATION or SIMULTANEOUS TRANS-LITERATION: the process of interpreting/ transliterating into the target language/code at the same time that the source language message is being delivered.

SIZE AND SHAPE SPECIFIERS (SASSes): a specific subset of classifiers that function to describe various nouns; functions like English adjectives.

SOURCE LANGUAGE (SL): the language in which an original message is conveyed and upon which interpretation is based.

SPEAKER GOAL: the motivating purpose behind communication; includes a variety of things such as teaching, inspiring, counseling or guiding, teasing, scolding, threatening, clarifying, explaining, requesting, selling, and convincing.

SPEAKER GOAL: the outcome anticipated or desired effect of saying or signing something to another, includes such things as persuading, teaching, and reprimanding.

SPEECH-READING: a skill employed by some deaf and hard-of-hearing individuals to comprehend spoken communication; involves a combination of deciphering lip, cheek, and throat movements, clarifying gestures and use of closure skills to determine meaning.

STEREOTYPE: a standardized mental picture that is held in common by members of a group and that represents an oversimplified opinion, affective attitude, or uncritical judgment (Webster, 1976).

SUPPORT GROUP: a small group of professional peers committed to confidentiality, growth, honesty and integrity.

TARGET LANGUAGE (TL): the language into which a message is interpreted with equivalent meaning.

TEST OF INTERPRETATION (TOI): the test of interpreting skill required for certification in Canada, administered by the Association of Visual Language Interpreters of Canada (AVLIC); requires first passing the Written Test of Knowledge (WTK).

TOTAL COMMUNICATION: in its original conception (coined by Roy Holcomb), defined as using any means necessary to successfully communicate with a Deaf child; adopted and redefined by the education system to mean speaking and signing at the same time (see simultaneous communication above).

TRANSLATION: changing a message from the frozen form of one language into the frozen form of another language; this is an emerging field for Deaf individuals (e.g. videotaped translations of textbooks, plays and poems).

TRANSLATORS: individuals who perform the work of translation.

TRANSLITERATION: as used in the field of sign language interpretation, is the result of taking a source language message, refers to conveying information between a spoken and signed form of English.

VISUAL-GESTURAL LANGUAGES: based on a structured set of linguistic rules in which the communication base is the movement of the face and body rather than sound; sign languages throughout the world fall into this category.

VOICE-TO-SIGN: the part of the interpretation process in which the source language message is spoken and the output is signed ASL, LSQ or a manual form of English)

WORK SETTINGS: location where interpretation takes place and the number of clients being served; includes one-on-one, small groups, and large groups in such places as education, legal, medical, mental health, and social service settings; the number of clients present and the type of interaction taking place are significant because the use of language, the purpose of speakers, the types of appropriate turn-taking, appropriate volume, etc., change depending on the setting in which interpreters work.

WRITTEN TEST OF KNOWLEDGE (WTK): the test of knowledge required as the first step toward certification in Canada, administered by the Association of Visual Language Interpreters of Canada (AVLIC); does not constitute "partial certification" — in the AVLIC system, an individual is only able to claim certification status after taking and passing the Test Of Interpretation (TOI).

References and Resources

Abudabbeh, N. "Arab families," p 333-46 in M. McGoldrick, J. Giordano, and JK Pearce (Eds.). *Ethnicity and family therapy,* 2nd ed. New York: Guilford Press, 1996.

Adler, R. and N. Towne. 1998. Looking out/looking in: Interpersonal communication (2nd edition). New York: Holt, Rinehart, and Winston.

Adler, R., L. Rosenfeld, & N. Town. 1992. Interplay: the process of interper sonal communication (5th edition). Fort Worth: Harcourt, Brace, & Jovanovich College Publishers.

Akamatsu, C.T. 1992. Teaching deaf Asian and Pacific Island American children. In K.M. Christensen & G.L. Delgado (Eds.), *Multicultural issues in deafness,* pp 127-142. White Plains, NY: Longman Publishing Group.

Alba, A. 1990. *Ethnic identity: the transformation of White America.* New Haven: Yale University Press.

Alberta Ministry of Education. 1988. The use of an interpreter in an educational setting: Guidelines and standards. Edmonton, AB: Alberta Education Response Centre.

Alcorn, B. Reflections, TBC News, Vol. 18, Oct. 1989. Translation by J. Kanda.

Alcorn, B. 1990. Unpublished workshop handouts.

Alcorn, B. and J. H. Kanda. 1989a. (video) Growing up deaf. Austin, Texas: ISSLI.

Alcorn, B. and J. Humphrey. 1988. Unpublished workshop handouts.

Alcorn, B. and J. Humphrey. 1989. Unpublished workshop handouts.

Alcorn, B. and J. Kanda. 1989b. (video) Issues in deafness. Austin, Texas: International School of Sign Language and Interpretation.

Altman, S. 1997. *The encyclopedia of African-American heritage.* New York: Facts of File.

Anderson, G. B. 1994. Tools for a healthier wiser black deaf community. In M.D. Garretson (Ed.) *Deafness: Life and Culture*. A Deaf American Monograph Series, Vol. 44, 1-4. Silver Spring, MD: National Association of the Deaf.

Anderson, G. B. and C. Grace. Black deaf adolescents: A diverse and under served population. IN *The Volta Review*, 93 (5), pp. 73-86.

Anderson, G. and F. Bowe. "Racism within the Deaf community" in *Bragg, L. (ed Deaf world: A historical reader and primary sourcebook.*. New York: New York University Press, pp. 305-308.

Anderson, G. and Watson, D. (Eds.) 1993. *The black Deaf experience: Excellence and equity*. Little Rock, AR: University of Arkansas Rehabilitation Research and Training Center for Persons who are Deaf or Hard of Hearing.

Anderson, G., J. Nishimura, J. Hopkins, F. Martinez and M. Mooney. 1996. "Enhancing racial and ethnic diversity in the interpreting profession. Telecourse. Sugar Grove, Ill: Waubonsee Community College

Anderson, M. and P. Hill Collins. 1992. Race, class and gender: An anthology. Belmont, Ca: Wadsworth Publishing Co.

Anderson. G. 1993. A new agenda for deafness rehabilitation: Embracing multicultural diversity. *Journal of the American Deafness and Rehabilitation Association*, 27 (3), 27-32.

Anthony, D 1971. Seeing essential English, Vol. 1 & 2. Anaheim, CA: Anaheim Union high School District.

Anthony, D. 1966. Seeing essential English. Unpublished Master's Thesis. University of Michigan, Ann Arbor.

Aramburo, A.J. 1989. Sociolinguistic aspects of the black deaf community. In C. Lucas (Ed.), *The sociolinguistics of the Deaf community*, pp 103-119. San Diego, CA: Academic Press.

Arjona, E. 1978. Intercultural communication and the training of interpreters at the Monterey institute of foreign studies. In (Gerver and Sinaiko, Eds.) Language interpretation and communication. New York, NY: Plenum Press. NATO Conference Series, Series III: Human Factors.

Arjona, E. 1984-1985. Unpublished documents and personal correspondence.

Arjona, E. 1984a. Education of translators and interpreters. In (McIntire, Ed.), New dialogues in interpreter education (Proceedings of the fourth national conference of interpreter trainers convention). Silver Spring, Md.: RID Publications.

Arjona, E. 1984b. Testing and evaluation. In (McIntire, Ed.), New dialogues in interpreter education (Proceedings of the fourth national conference of interpreter trainers convention). Silver Spring, Md.: RID Publications.

Association of Visual Language Interpreters of Canada. 1991. AVLIC News. (Fall, 1991). Ottawa: Association of Visual Language Interpreters of Canada.

Association of Visual Language Interpreters of Canada. 1992. Injured interpreters study. Ottawa: Association of Visual Language Interpreters of Canada.

Association of Visual Language Interpreters of Canada. 1992. Interpreters in the educational setting. (A Resource Document) Ottawa, Ontario Canada: Association of Visual Language Interpreters of Canada.

Association of Visual Language Interpreters of Canada. 1992. Repetitive strain injury. Ottawa, Ontario Canada: Association of Visual Language Interpreters of Canada.

Association of Visual Language Interpreters of Canada. 1993. AVLIC's position on the prevention of repetitive strain injuries. Ottawa: Association of Visual Language Interpreters of Canada.

Association of Visual Language Interpreters of Canada. 1993. Interpreter safety and health issues committee: Repetitive strain injuries. AVLIC News, Winter.

Atwood, A. 1988. (Patri, Ed.) Anthology of interpreting papers. Washington, D.C.: Gallaudet University.

Ayvazian, A.1995. "Interrupting the cycle of oppression: The role of allies as agents of change." Fellowship (January/February 1995:7-10.

Babcock, L. 1992. Personal communication.

Baker, C 1978. How does "sim-com" fit into a bilingual approach to education? In (Caccamise and Hicks, Eds.), American sign language in a bilingual, bicultural context (Proceedings of the second national symposium on sign language research and teaching). Silver Spring, MD: National Association of the Deaf.

Baker, C 1983. Implications of linguistic research. In (McIntire, Ed.) New dialogues in interpreter education (Proceedings of the fourth national conference of interpreter trainers convention). Silver Spring, Md.: RID Publications.

Baker, C and Battison, R. (Eds.) 1980. Sign language and the deaf community: Essays in honor of William C. Stokoe. Silver Spring, Md.: National Association of the Deaf.

Baker, C and Cokely, D. 1980. American sign language: A teacher's resource text on grammar and culture. Silver Spring, Md.: TJ. Publishers.

Baker, C and Padden, C. 1978. Focusing on the nonmanual components of American Sign Language. In (Siple, Ed.), Understanding language through sign language research. New York: Academic Press.

Baker, C. 1977. Regulators and turn-taking in American Sign Language discourse. In (Friedman, Ed.) On Hand: New Perspectives on American Sign Language. New York: Academic Press.

Baker-Shenk, C 1986. Characteristics of oppressed and oppressor peoples: their effect on the interpreting context. In (McIntire, Ed.) Interpreting: The art of cross cultural mediation (Proceedings of the 1985 RID Convention). Silver Springs, Md.: RID Publications.

Baker-Shenk, C 1992. The interpreter: Machine, advocate, or ally? In (Plant-Moeller, Ed) Expanding horizons. (Proceedings of the 12th national convention of the Registry of Interpreters for the Deaf). Silver Spring, Md.: RID Publications.

Baker-Shenk, C and Cokely, D. 1980. American sign language: A teacher's resource on grammar and culture. Silver Spring, Md.: TJ Publishers.

Baker-Shenk, C. 1995. Personal communication.

Barnartt, S. and J. Christiansen. 2001. Into their own hands: The president now protest and its consequences" in Bragg, L. (Ed.) *Deaf world: A historical reader and primary sourcebook.*. New York: New York University Press, p. 333-347.

Barth, Gunther. 1964. Bitter Strength: A History of the Chinese in the United States, 1850-1870. Cambridge, MA:

Barth, Gunther. Chinese Sojourners in the West: The Coming, in Southern California Quarterly, 46 (1964), 55-67;

Barth, Gunther. Perrin, Coming to America, 21ff.

Battison, R. 1974. Phonological delation in American Sign Language. Sign Language Studies, 5:1-19.

Beard, L. 1976. Personal communications in preparation for Miss Lillian by Ricks and Seale.

Beattie, M. 1987. Codependent no more. Deerfield Beach, Fla.: Health Com munications.

Bellugi, U. and S. Fischer. 1972. A comparison of sign language and spoken language: Rate and grammatical mechanisms. Cognition 1:173-200.

Berger, Kathleen Stassen. 1998. New York, NY: Worth Publishers. The Developing Person Through the Life Span (4th Edition).

Berne, E. 1974. Games people play. New York: Grover Press.

Bernstein, M., M. Maxwell & K. Matthews. 1985. Bimodal & bilingual communication in schools for the deaf. Sign Language Studies, 47: 127-140.

Berrigan, D. 1983. ASL and me. The Reflector, 5:7-9.

Bienvenu, MJ. 1984. A Road Being Built ... The Reflector (Spring).

Bienvenu, MJ. 1987. Third culture: Working together. In (McIntire, Ed.) Journal of interpretation. (translated by Marina McIntire). Silver Spring, Md.: Registry of Interpreters for the Deaf. Vol. IV, 1987.

Bienvenu, MJ. 1991. Can deaf people survive 'deafness'? Perspectives in deafness: A deaf American monograph. Vol. 41, Nos. 1-2, pp. 21-25.

Bienvenu, MJ. 1992. Blueprints for the Future; Two Programs. In (Walworth, Moores and O'Rourke, Eds.) A free hand: Enfranchising the education of deaf children, (pp. 3-19). Silver Spring, Md.: TJ Publishers

Bienvenu, MJ. and B. Colonomos. 1985-1988. An introduction to American deaf culture series (video series). Burtonsville, Md.: Sign Media, Inc..

Bienvenu, MJ. and B. Colonomos. 1989. Incorporating systems, cardinal and ordinal systems, unique systems. (3-part video series of ASL numbering systems). Burtonsville, Md.: Sign Media, Inc.

Bienvenu, MJ. and B. Colonomos. 1992. Relay interpreting in the '90's. In (Swabey, Ed.) The challenge of the 90's: New standards in interpreter education. (Proceedings of the CIT Eighth National Convention) Conference of Interpreter Trainers.

Bienvenu, MJ. TBC News #9, #18 and #21. Riverdale, Md.: The Bicultural Center.

Billingsley, A. 1990. Understanding African-American family diversity. In J Dewart(Ed.) *the state of black America 1990*. New York, NY: National Urban League, 85-108.

Bishop, A. 1994. Becoming an ally: Breaking the cycle of oppression. Fernwood Publishing.

Bornstein, H 1990. Signed English. In (Bornstein, Ed.) Manual communication: Implications for education, pp. 128-138. Washington, D.C.: Gallaudet University Press.

Bornstein, H and K. Saulnier. 1981. Signed English: A brief follow-up to the first evaluation. American annals of the deaf, 127:69-72.

Bornstein, H L. Hamilton, and K. Saulnier. 1983. The comprehensive signed English dictionary. Washington, DC: Gallaudet University Press.

Bornstein, H, L Hamilton, and K. Saulnier. 1980. Signed English: A first evaluation. American annals of the deaf, 125:467-481.

Bornstein, H. (Ed.). 1990. Manual communication: Implications for education. Washington, D.C.: Gallaudet University Press.

Boso, E and M. Kuntze. 1991. Blazing trails for bilingual-bicultural education in the west. In (Garretson, Ed.) Perspectives on deafness: A deaf American monograph. Vol. 41, Nos. 1-2, pp. 29-32. Silver Spring, Md.: National Association of the Deaf.

Bradshaw, J. 1990. Home coming: Reclaiming and championing your inner child. New York: Bantam Books.

Bragg, B. 1973. Ameslish: Our national heritage. American annals of the deaf, 118:672-674.

Bragg, B. 1989. A wake-up call for hearing signers. A Deaf American Monograph.

Bragg, L. (Ed.) 2001. *Deaf world: A historical reader and primary source book.*. New York: New York University Press.

Brislin, R, K. Cushner, C. Cherri and M. Young. 1986. Intercultural interactions: A practical guide. Beverly Hills: Sage Productions.

Brislin, R. 1981. Cross-cultural encounters. New York: Pergamon Press.

Brislin, R. 1991. Canadian evaluation system. Ottawa: Association of Visual Language Interpreters of Canada.

Caccamise, F, J. Stangarone, M. Mitchell-Caccamise (Eds.) A century of deaf awareness (Proceedings of the 1980 RID convention). Silver Spring, Md.: RID, Inc.

Caccamise, F. & D. Hicks (Eds.). 1978. American sign language in a bilingual, bicultural context (Proceedings of the Second National Symposium on Sign Language Research and Reaching). Silver Spring, Md.: National Association of the Deaf.

Carter, R.1997. "Is White a race? Expressions of White racial identity." Pp. 198-209 in M. Fine, L Weis, LC Powell and LM Wong (Eds.) *Off White: readings on race, power and society.* New York: Routledge.

Carver, R 1989. Deaf illiteracy: A genuine educational puzzle or an instrument of oppression? A critical review. Edmonton: Canadian Association of the Deaf.

Carver, R and M. Rodda. 1987. Parental stress and the deaf child. The ACEHI Journal/La Revue ACEDA, 13:79-89.

Carver, R. 1995. Personal communication.

Carver, S. and K. Malcolm, 1993. AVLIC certification/RID certification: A comparison. AVLIC News. Fall. Ottawa: Association of Visual Language Interpreters of Canada.

Cayton, M. 1991. Writers as outsiders: academic discourse and marginalized faculty. College English, Vol. 53, #6, October 1991, 647-660.

Cetron, Marvin. American Renaissance: Our life at the turn of the twenty-first century

Cheng, L.L. 1993. Deafness: An Asian/Pacific island perspective. In K.M. Christensen & G.L. Delgado (Eds.), *Multicultural issues in deafness*, pp 113-126. White Plains, NY: Longman Publishing Group.

Chong, J. et al. 1987 Occupational health problems of musicians. Canadian family physician, Vol. 35, November.

CLDC. 1984. The claggett statement. Elkhorn, Ind.: Mennonite Board of Missions.

Cohen, O.P, Fischgrund, J.E. and Redding, R. 1990. Deaf children from ethnic, linguistic and racial minority backgrounds: An overview. *American Annals of the Deaf.* Reference Issue, 135 (2) 67-73.

Cohen, O.P. 1993. Multicultural education and the deaf community: A conversation about survival. In M.D. Garretson (Ed.), *Deafness 1993-2013.* A Deaf American Monograph Series, Vol. 43, 23-27 Silver Spring, MD: National Association of the Deaf.

Cokely, D 1978. Comparative varieties of manual communication.

Cokely, D 1981a. Sign language interpreters: a demographic survey. Sign Language Studies. 32:261-186.

Cokely, D 1981b. Demographic characteristics of interpreters. The Reflector, 1:21-28.

Cokely, D 1982. The interpreted medical interview: it loses something in the translation. The Reflector, 3:5-10.

Cokely, D 1983a. When is pidgin not a pidgin? An alternate analysis on the ASL-English contact situation. Sign Language Studies, Spring 1983.

Cokely, D 1983b. Metanotative qualities: How accurately are they conveyed by interpreters? The Reflector, 5:16-22.

Cokely, D 1984a. Editor's comments. The Reflector. 8:3-4.

Cokely, D 1984b. Editor's comments. The Reflector. 9:3-4.

Cokely, D 1985. Towards a sociolinguistic model of the interpretation pro cess: Focus on ASL and English, Ph.D. dissertation Geogetown University, Washington, D.C.--

Cokely, D 1986. The effects of lag time on interpreter errors. Sign Language Studies, 53:341-376.

Cokely, D. (1992). Interpretation: A Sociolinguistic Model. Burtonsville, MD: Linstok Press.

Cokely, D. 1992. Interpretation: A sociolinguistic model. Burtonsville, MD: Linstok Press (Dissertation Series).

Colonomos, B 1982. Reflections of an interpreter trainer in Cokely (Ed.) The Reflector, 2:5-14.

Colonomos, B 1983. Personal notes taken on workshop presentation at Johnson County Community College.

Colonomos, B 1984. A semantic look at sign glosses. The Reflector, 9:5-11.

Colonomos, B. (1980, 1983, 1984, 1987, 1988). Interpreting process: a working model. Unpublished papers.

Colonomos, B. (1983). Interpretation: A Working Model. Riverdale, MD. The Bicultural Centre. Unpublished workshop materials.

Conwell , Russell H. Why and How. 1971. Boston, MA: Lee & Shepard Co.

Crandall, K. 1978. Inflectional morphemes in the manual English of young hearing-impaired children & their mothers. Journal of speech & hearing research, 21: 372-386.

Cross, W.E. Jr. 1991. *Shades of Black: Diversity in African-American identity.* Philadelphia: Temple University Press.
cross-cultural perspective on the education of deaf children"

Cummins, J. 1980. The construct of language proficiency in bilingual education. In Alaitis (Ed.) Current issues in bilingual education. Washington, DC: Georgetown University Press.

Cundy, L. 1993. The professional interpreter - A deaf consumer's perspective. AVLIC News. Fall. Ottawa: Association of Visual Language Interpreters of Canada.

Danks, J. et al. (Eds.) 1997. Cognitive processes in translation and interpreting. Thousand Oaks, CA: Sage Publications.

Davila, R. 1991. Guest presentation made at the 1992 RID Convention. In (Plant-Moeller, Ed.) Expanding horizons. (Proceedings of the 12th national convention of the Registry of Interpreters for the Deaf). Silver Spring, Md.: RID Publications.

Davis, J. 1986. Reanalyzing the sign language continuum: Implications for practitioners, trainers, and students of interpretation. In (McIntire, Ed.) The art of cross-cultural mediation (Proceedings from the RID 1987 National Convention Interpreting). Rockville, Md.: Registry of Interpreters for the Deaf Press.

Davis, J. 1989. Distinguishing language contact phenomena in ASL interpretation. In (Lucas, Ed.) The sociolinguistics of the deaf community, San Diego: Academic Press.

Delgado, G.L. 1984. *The Hispanic deaf.* Washington, DC: Gallaudet University Press.

Delgado-Gaitan, C. 1990. *Literacy for empowerment: The role of parents in children's education.* New York: Falmer Press.

Di Pietro, L. (Ed.) 1978. Guidelines on interpreting for deaf-blind persons. Washington, DC: Public Service Programs, Gallaudet College

Di Pietro, R. 1978. Code-switching as a verbal strategy among bilinguals. In (M. Paradis, Ed.), Aspects of bilingualism, pp. 275-282. Columbia, SC: Hornbeam Press.

Di Pietro, R. 1991. Why do the tulips taste so nice? or the evolution of a hard of hearing person. Perspectives on deafness: A deaf American monograph. Vol. 41, Nos. 1-2, pp. 49-53.

Dolnick, E. 1993. Deafness as culture. The Atlantic, September, 272 (3), 38.

Domingue, R. and B. Ingram. 1977. Sign language interpretation: the state of the art. In Gerver and Sinaiko (Eds.), 81-86.

Douglas College Program of Sign Language Interpretation. (1996). Preceptor's Guide and Student Guide. Vancouver, BC: Douglas College.

Dowling, C. 1981. The Cinderella complex: Women's hidden fear of independence. New York: Pocket Books).

Duffey, T. 1987. The sharing of power. Unpublished paper.

Duncan, E., Prickett, H., Finkelstein, D., Vernon, M., & Hollingsworth, T. 988. Usher's syndrome: What it is, how to cope, and how to help. Springfield, IL: Charles C. Thomas.

Eldridge, N. 1993. Culturally affirmative counseling with American Indians who are deaf. *Journal of the American Deafness and Rehabilitation Association*, 26 (4), 1-14.

Erting. C. 1985. Cultural conflict in a school for deaf children. Anthropology and Education Quarterly, 16:225-243.

Erting. C. 1985. Sociocultural dimensions of deaf education: Belief systems and communicative interaction. Sign Language Studies 17:11-126.

Evans, G. 1993. Letter to the editors and Name change committee report. AVLIC News (Winter). Ottawa: Association of Visual Language Interpreters of Canada.

Ewing, B. 1990. Ethics in public education -- All we didn't learn in kindergarten and now need to know. In (Goldsmith & Ciuccio, Eds.) Reflections on ethics: A compilation of articles inspired by the May 1990 ASHA ethics colloquium. Rockville, Md.: American Speech-Language-Hearing Association.

Fant., L. 1972. Ameslan. Silver Spring, Md.: National Association of the Deaf.

Fant., L. 1990. Silver threads. Silver Spring, Md.: RID Publications.

Fischer, S. 1975. Influences on word-order change in American sign language. In (C. Li, Ed.) Word Order And Word Order Change. Austin: University of Texas Press.

Fischer, S. 1982. Sign language and manual communication. In (Sims, Walter, and Whitehead, Eds.) Deafness and communication, assessment and training. Baltimore, Md.: Williams and Wilkins.

Fischer, S. and B. Gough. 1978. Verbs in American Sign Language. Sign Language Studies. 18:17-48.

Fitzhugh, K. 1983. Free lance interpreting: A professional method for billing. The Reflector, 7:19-23.

Forestal, E. 1994. "Understanding the dynamics of Deaf consumer-Interpreter Relations." Telecourse. Westminster, CO: Front Range Community College.

Freire, P. 1970. Pedagogy of the Oppressed. New York: Continuum.

Freire, P. 1973. Education for critical consciousness. New York: Seabury.

Freire, P. 1989. Paulo Freire & John Vasconcillos: a dialogue. (CSUN, May 15, 1989.)

Friedman, L. (Ed.) 1977. On the other hand: New perspectives on American sign language. New York: Academic Press.

Friedman, L. 1975. Space, time and person reference in American Sign Language. Language 51:696-719.

Friedman, L. 1976. The manifestation of subject, object, and topic in American Sign Language. In (Charles, Ed.) Subject and topic. New York: Academic Press.

Frishberg, N. 1986. Interpreting: An introduction. Silver Spring, Md.: RID Publications. (Revised and reprinted, 1990).

Fritsch-Rudser, S. 1980. The revised code of ethics: Some issues and implications. In (Caccamise, et. al., Eds.) A century of deaf awareness (Proceedings of the 1980 RID convention). Silver Spring, Md.: RID, Inc.

Fritsch-Rudser, S. and M. Strong. An examination of some personal characteristics & abilities of sign language interpreters. Sign Language Studies, 53:315-331.

Garretson, M. (Ed.) 1991. Perspectives on deafness: A deaf American monograph. Vol. 41, Nos. 1-2. Silver Spring, Md.: National Association of the Deaf.

Garretson, M. 1990. Communication issues among deaf people. Eyes, hands, voices, 40 (1,2,3,4)

Gee, J. & W. Goodhard. 1985. Nativization, linguistic theory & deaf language acquisition. Sign Language Studies, 49:291-342.

Gerner de Garcia, B. 1993. Addressing the needs of Hispanic deaf children. In K.M. Christensen & G.L. Delgado (Eds.), *Multicultural issues in deafness*, pp69-90. White Plains, NY: Longman Publishing Group.

Gerver, D. & Sinaiko, H. W. (Eds.) 1978. Language interpretation and communication. New York, NY: Plenum Press. NATO Conference Series, Series III: Human Factors.

Goffman, E. 1963. Stigma: Notes on the management of spoiled identity. Englewood Cliffs, NJ: Prentice Hall.

Granfield, K. 1993. Exercise: What do I do? AVLIC News. Fall. Ottawa: Association of Visual Language Interpreters of Canada.

Granfield, K. and G. McKnight. 1991. Repetitive motion injuries. AVLIC News. Fall. Ottawa: Association of Visual Language Interpreters of Canada.

Gregory, M. & S. Carroll. 1978.Language and Situation: Language Varieties and their social contexts. London: Routledge.

Griffith, M.. 1989. A Church for the Twenty-First Century: A Planning Resource for the Future. Dayton, Ohio: Office of Research, General Council on Ministries, p. 3.

Groce, N.E. 1985. Everyone here spoke sign language. Cambridge, Mass: Harvard University Press.

Grosjean, F 1977. The perception of rate in spoken language and sign languages. Journal of psycholinguistic research. 22:408-13.

Grosjean, F. 1982. Life with two languages: An introduction to bilingualism. Cambridge, MA: Harvard University Press.

Gumperz, J and E. Hernandez-Chavez. 1971. Bilingualism, bidialectalism and classroom interaction. In (Anwar, Ed.) Language in social groups: Essays by John J; Gumperz, pp. 311-339. Stanford, CA: Stanford University Press.

Gumperz, J. 1976. The sociolinguistic significance of conversational code switching. Papers on Language and Context (Working papers of the Language Behavior Research Laboratory, No. 46). Berkeley: University of California.

Gustason, G., 1990. In a presentation made on the subject at CSUN.

Gustason, G., 1990. Signing exact English. In (Bornstein, Ed.) Manual communication: Implications for education, pp. 108-109. Washington, D.C.: Gallaudet University Press.

Gustason, G., 1992. Wall, after wall, after wall. The Deaf American Monograph. Silver Spring, Md.: National Association of the Deaf. Vol. 42, 1992.

Gustason, G., D. Pfetzing, and E. Zawolkow. 1980. Signing exact English. Los Alamitos, CA: Modern signs Press. (Earlier editions printed in 1975, 1973, and 1972).

Hahn, R. 1993. The professional interpreter - An employer's perspective. AVLIC News. Fall. Ottawa: Association of Visual Language Interpreters of Canada.

Hairston, E. & Smith, L. 1983. *Black and deaf in America: are we that different?* Silver Spring, MD: TJ Publishers, Inc.

Hall, E.T. and M. Hall. 1989. Understanding cultural differences: Germans, French and Americans. Yarmouth, ME: Intercultural Press.

Hamlet, J. D. 1998. *Afrocentric visions: Studies in culture and communica tion.* Thousand Oaks, CA: SAGE Publications

Hammond, S.A. & Meiners, L.H. 1993. American Indian deaf children and youth. In K.M. Christensen & G.L. Delgado (Eds.), *Multicultural issues in deafness*, pp. 143-166. White Plains, NY: Longman Publishing Group.

Hayward, D. 1994, 1995 Personal communication.

Heath, K. & D. Lee. 1982. Interpreters as boring monotones: A solution. The Reflector, 4:27-30.

Heller, B, M Stansfield, G. Stark and D. Langholtz. 1985. Sign language interpreter stress: An exploratory study. In Proceedings of the 1985 convention of the American deafness and rehabilitation association. Baltimore, Md.

Herrmann, N 1984. Male/female brain dominance characteristics. Unpublished paper. Lake Lure, North Carolina: The Whole Brain Corporation.

Herrmann, N 1986b. The application of brain dominance technology to the training profession. Lake Lure, North Carolina: The Whole Brain Corporation.

Herrmann, N 1982. Excerpt from the question and answer period following Ned Herrmann's presentation. DACIE conference, August, 1982.

Herrmann, N 1983. Whole brain teaching and learning. College Industry Education Conference Proceedings.

Herrmann, N. l986a. Design and delivery approaches for the specialized modes of the four quadrants. Lake Lure, North Carolina: The Whole Brain Corporation.

Higgins, P. 1980. Outsiders in a hearing world. Beverly Hills: Sage Publications.

Hill, D. 1990. Leadership and professional ethics. In Reflections on ethics: A compilation of articles inspired by the May 1990 ASHA ethics colloquium. Silver Spring, Md.: American Speech and Hearing Association.

Holcomb, Roy. 1968. Total communication.

Holcomb, T. K. 1997."Development of Deaf bicultural identity." American Annals of the Deaf 142, No. 2.

Hoza, J. Doing the right thing: Interpreter role and ethics within a bilingual-bicultural model. In (Swabey, Ed.) The challenge of the 90's: New standards in interpreter education. (Proceedings of the CIT Eighth National Convention) Conference of Interpreter Trainers.

Humphrey, J. and Alcorn, B. (1995). So You Want To Be An Interpreter: An Introduction To Sign Language Interpreting. Amarillo, TX: H & H Publishers.

Humphrey, J. and Alcorn, B. 1988. Unpublished workshop and classroom handouts on comparative cultures.

Humphrey, J. and B. Alcorn. 1994. So you want to be an interpreter?: An introduction to sign language interpreting (1st edition). Amarillo, TX: H&H Publishers.

Humphrey, J., S. Washington, A. Kashar, and B. Alcorn. 1993. Interpreting in the American judicial system: English/ASL. Northridge, Ca.: CSUN.

Humphries, T. 1977. Communicating across cultures (Deaf/hearing) and language learning. (dissertation). Union Graduate School: Cincinnati, Ohio.

Humphries, T. 2001. "Of Deaf-mutes, the strange, and the modern Deaf self" in Bragg, L. (Ed.) Deaf world: A historical reader and primary sourcebook.. New York: New York University Press, pp. 348-364. in Christensen and Delgado (Eds.,) Multicultural issues in deafness,

Ingram, R 1978. Sign language interpretation and general theories of language, interpretation and communication. In (Gerver and Sinaiko, Eds.) Language Interpretation and Communication, p. 109-118. New York, NY: Plenum Press. NATO Conference Series, Series III: Human Factors.

Ingram, R 1984. Teaching decalage skills. In McIntire (Ed.), New dialogues in interpreter education: Proceedings of the Fourth National Con ference of Interpreter Trainers Convention (pp. 291-308). Silver Spring, MD: RID Publications.

Ingram, R 1985. Simultaneous interpretation of sign languages: Semiotic and psycholinguistic perspectives. Multilingual, 4:2, 91-102.

Ingram, R and B. Ingram (Eds.). 1975. Hands across the sea: (Proceedings of the first international conference on interpreting). Silver Spring, Md.: RID, Inc.

Ingram, R. 1988. Interpreter's recognition of structure and meaning. Sign Language Studies, 58:21-36.

Isenhath, J. 1990. The linguistics of American sign language. Jefferson, N.C.: McFarland & Company, Inc.

Isham, W. 1983. Beyond the classroom: Self-directed growth for interpreters. The Reflector, 6:15-17.

Isham, W. 1986. Message analysis. In (McIntire, Ed.) Interpreting: The art of cross cultural mediation (Proceedings of the 1985 RID Conven tion). Silver Springs, Md.: RID Publications.

Johnson R., and C. Erting. 1984. Linguistic socialization in the context of emergent deaf ethnicity. In (Brukman, Ed.) Working paper series, Wenner-Gren Foundation.

Johnson R., and C. Erting. 1989. Ethnicity and socialization in a classroom for deaf children. In (Lucas, Ed.), The sociolinguistics of the Deaf Community, 41-83. San Diego: San Diego Press.

Johnson R., S. Liddell, and C. Erting. 1989. Unlocking the curriculum: Principles for achieving access in deaf education. Washington, D.C.: Gallaudet University.

Johnson, K. Miscommunication in interpreted classroom communication. Sign Language Studies, 70:1-34.

Joos, 1967. The five clocks. New York, NY: Harbinger Books.

Joos, Martin. 1961. The Five Clocks. NY: Harcourt.

Kanda, J 1984. Response to Sylvie Lambert on consecutive interpretation. In (McIntire, Ed.), New dialogues in interpreter education (Proceedings of the Fourth National Conference of Interpreter Trainers Convention). Silver Spring, Md.: RID Publications.

Kanda, J 1987. Interpreter Training. In Van Cleve (Ed.) Gallaudet Encyclopedia of Deaf People and Deafness, p. 96-98.

Kanda, J 1988b. (dissert) A comprehensive description of certified sign language interpreters including brain dominance. Provo, UT: Brigham Young University.

Kanda, J and Alcorn, B. 1982. Legal interpreting (English). Overland Park, Ks.: Johnson County Community College.

Kanda, J and Alcorn, B. 1984 Team interpreting. In Proceedings of the 1983 RID Convention. Silver Spring, Md.: RID Publications.

Kanda, J and B. Alcorn. 1984. Explanation of the Colonomos model. Unpublished paper.

Kanda, J and B. Alcorn. 1984. New Directions in interpreter training. The Reflector, 8:18-22.

Kanda, J and B. Alcorn. 1988. We can communicate (video). Council Bluffs, IA.: Deaf Missions of Iowa.

Kanda, J and B. Alcorn. 1989. Seven, eight, sign it straight: Interpreting embedded numbers (video). Austin, Texas: ISSLI.

Kanda, J. 1988a. Introduction to consecutive interpretation. In University of New Brunswick Sign Language Interpreter Training Curriculum, pp. 135-141.

Kannapell, B. 1978. Linguistic and sociolinguistic perspectives on sign systems for educating deaf children: Toward a true bilingual approach. In (Caccamise & Hicks, Eds.) American sign language in a bilingual, bicultural context (The proceedings of the second national symposium on sign language research and teaching). Silver Spring, Md.: National Association of the Deaf.

Kannapell, B. 1980. Personal awareness and advocacy in the deaf community. In (Baker and Battison, Eds.) Sign language and the deaf com munity: Essays in honor of William C.. Stokoe. Silver Spring, Md.: National Association of the Deaf.

Karpman, S. 1968. Script drama analysis. Transactional analysis bulletin 7:26, April 1968.

Keenan, D., & Smith, M. l983. Sex discrimination and cerebral bias: Implications for the reading curriculum. Reading Improvement 20:50-53.

Kelly, L.1979. The true interpreter: A history of translation theory and practice in the west. New York: St. Martin's Press.

Kemp, M. 1992. The invisible line in the deaf community. A deaf American monograph. Silver Spring, Md.: National Association of the Deaf. Vol. 42, 1992.

Kimura, D. l985. Male brain, female brain: The hidden difference. Psychology Today, 19, (11), 50-58.

Klima, E. and U. Bellugi. 1979. The signs of language. Cambridge, MA: Harvard University Press.

Kluwin, T. 1981. A rationale for modifying classroom signing systems. Sign Language Studies, 31:1790188.

Knoll, Tricia. 1982. Becoming Americans. Portland, OR: Coast to Coast Books.

Kohlberg, L. Collected papers on moral development and moral education. Cambridge, MA: Harvard Graduate School of Education, Spring 1973.

Kristberg, W. 1985. The adult children syndrome. Pompano Beach, Fla.: Health Communications, Inc.

Kyle, J.G. and G. Pullen. 1988. "Cultures in contact: deaf and hearing people" in *Disability, handicap and Society,* Vol. 3, No. 1, 1988, pp. 49-61.

LaBarbera, P. & S. Feyne. 1987. Professional standards for the use of sign language interpreters. In (McIntire, Ed.) Journal of interpretation. Silver Spring, Md.: Registry of Interpreters for the Deaf. Vol. IV, 1987.

Ladashevska, B. 1993. Professionalism = respect/integrity -- An interpreter's perspective. AVLIC News. Fall. Ottawa: Association of Visual Language Interpreters of Canada.

Lambert, S 1988. Personal interview at the Conference of Interpreter Trainers, Traverse City, Michigan.

Lambert, S. 1984. An introduction to consecutive interpretation. In (McIntire , Ed.) New dialogues in interpreter education (Proceedings of the Fourth National Conference of Interpreter Trainers Convention). Silver Spring, Md.: RID Publications.

Lane, H & F. Grosjean (Eds.). Recent perspectives on American Sign Language. Hillsdale, NJ: Lawrence Erlbaum Associates, Publishers.

Lane, H 1980. Some thoughts on language bigotry. (An address at Northeastern University on Professional Day, Spring, 1980).

Lane, H 1984. When the mind hears: A history of the deaf. New York: Random House.

Lane, H 1987. Language research: New views of how the brain works. San Diego: Salk Institute for Biological Studies. Summer 1987.

Lane, H and F. Grosjean. Perception of reading rate by speakers and listeners. Journal of Experimental Psychology, 2:141-147.

Lane, H. 1992. The mask of benevolence. New York: Alfred A. Knoff.

Lane, H., R. Hoffmeister, and B. Bahan. 1996. *A journey into the deaf-world.* San Diego, CA: DawnSignPress.

Larson, M. 1984. Meaning-based translation: A guide to cross-language equivalence. Lanham, Md.: University Press of America.

Lawrence, S. 1994. Presentation made at the 1994 Conference of Interpreter Trainers, Charlotte, NC.

Lee, D. 1983. Sources and aspects of code-switching in the signing of a deaf adult and her interlocutors. Unpublished doctoral dissertation, University of Texas at Austin.

Lee, Jung Young. 1995. Marginality: The Key to Multicultural Theology. MN: Fortress Press.

Letourneau, W. 1987. Study guide for AVLIC written test of knowledge. Ottawa: Association of Visual Language Interpreters of Canada.

Letourneau, W. 1993. Interpreter for the deaf versus visual language interpreter and Memorable events while I was president. AVLIC News. Winter. Ottawa: Association of Visual Language Interpreters of Canada.

Liddell, S. 1980. American sign language syntax. New York: Mouton.

Livingston, S B. Singer and T. Abrahamson. 1994. Effectiveness compared: ASL interpretation vs. transliteration. Sign Language Studies, Spring 1994.

Livingston, S. 1983. Levels of development in the language of deaf children. Sign Language Studies 40:193-286.

Livingston, S., Singer, B. & Abramson, T. (1994). "Effectiveness Compared: ASL interpretation vs. transliteration." Sign Language Studies, 82 Spring.

Lucas, C and C. Valli. 1989. Language contact in the American deaf community. In (Lucas, Ed.) The sociolinguistics of the deaf community, pp. 11-40. New York: Academic Press.

Lucas, C. (Ed.) 1989. The sociolinguistics of the deaf community, New York: Academic Press.

Lyman, Stanford 1974. Chinese Americans. NY: Random House.

Lyman, Stanford. 1977. The Asian in north America. Santa Barbara, CA: ABC-Clio, Inc.

Marmor, G & L. Petitto. 1979. Simultaneous communication in the class room: How well is English grammar represented? Sign Language Studies, 23:99-136.

Mathers, C. & White, F. 1986. Cross-cultural, cross-racial mediation. In M.L. McIntire (Ed.), *Proceedings of the Ninth National Convention of the Registry of Interpreters for the Deaf.* Silver Spring, MD: RID Publications, 97-106.

Maxwell, M. 1990. Simultaneous communication: The state of the art & proposals for change. Sign Language Studies, Vol. 69 (Fall 1990).

Maxwell, M. and M. Bernstein. 1985. The synergy of sign & speech in simultaneous communication. Applied Psycholinguistics, 6:63-81.

McCay, V. and J. Wallrabenstein. 1994. Historical, cultural, psychological and educational aspect of American sign language. The Deaf American, 41:1-2.

McDermott, R. 1974. Achieving school failure: An anthropological approach to illiteracy and social stratification. In (Spindler, Ed.) Education and Cultural Process. New York: Holt, Rinehart & Winston.

McEdwards, M. 1968. Introduction to Style. Dickenson Publishing Co.

McIntire, M (Ed.) 1984. New dialogues in interpreter education (Proceedings of the Fourth National Conference of Interpreter Trainers Convention). Silver Spring, Md.: RID Publications.

McIntire, M (Ed.). 1985. New dimensions in interpreter education: task analysis--theory and application. (Proceedings from the Fifth National Conference of Interpreter Trainers Convention). Silver Spring, Md.: RID Publications.

McIntire, M (Ed.). 1986. New dimensions in interpreter education: curriculum and instruction. (Proceedings from the Sixth National Conference of Interpreter Trainers Convention). Silver Spring, Md.: RID Publications.

McLaughlin, B. 1984. The effects of early bilingualism. In (McLaughlin, Ed.) Second language acquisition in childhood, Vol. I (2nd Ed). Hillsdale, NJ: Erlbaum Associates.

Mellody, P. 1990. Facing codependence. Deerfield Beach, Fla.: Health Communications.

Miles, J, J. Davis, S. Ferguson=Roberts, R. Giles. (Eds.) *Almanac of African American heritage*. 2001. New York: Prentice Hall

Miller, J. 1976. Humanizing the classroom. New York, NY: Praeger Publishers.

Miller, K. 1991. A hunger for healing. New York: Harper Collins Publishers.

Miller, M. and D. Mathews. 1986. Warning! Crossing cultures can be hazardous to your health: A look at communication between deaf and hearing cultures. In Interpreting: The art of cross-cultural mediation. Silver Spring, Md.: Registry of Interpreters for the Deaf Publications.

Mindess, A. 1999. Reading between the signs: Intercultural communication for sign language interpreters. Yarmouth, ME: Intercultural Press.

Minirth, F., P. Meier, R. Hemfelt, S. Sneed, and D. Hawkins. 1990. Love hunger. Nashville, TN: Thomas Nelson Publishers.

Moore, N. (Ed.) 1991. Deaf minority groups: Looking back, looking forward. *Gallaudet Today*, 21 (2).

Moores, D 1977. Issues in the utilization of manual communication. In Proceedings of national symposium on sign language research and teaching. Silver Spring, Md.: National Association of the Deaf.

Moores, D. 1992. What do we know and when did we know it? In (Walworth, Mores and O'Rourke, Eds.) A free hand: Enfranchising the education of deaf children. Silver Spring, Md.: TJ Publishers, pp. 67-88.

Moser, B. 1997. Beyond curiosity: Can interpreting research meet the challenge? In J. Danks, et al. (Eds.). Cognitive processes in transla tion and interpreting (pp. 17-195). Thousand Oaks, CA: Sage Publications.

Nash, J and A. Nash. 1981. Deafness in society. Lexington, MA: Lexington Books.

Nash, K., 1992. The changing population: A challenge for postsecondary education. In S. Foster & G. Walter (Eds.), *Deaf students in postsec ondary education* (pp. 3-23). New York, NY: Routledge Publishing.

Neuman Solow, S 1980. Sign language interpreting: A basic resource book. Silver Spring, Md.: National Association of the Deaf.

Neuman Solow, S. 1991. In (Witter-Merithew) Interpreting in the American Judicial System: ASL/English. Northridge, CA: CSUN (unpub lished).

Newell, W, M. Stinson, D. Castle, D. Mallery-Ruganis, and B. Holcomb. 1990. Simultaneous communication: A description by deaf professionals working in an educational setting. Sign Language Studies, 69:391-414.

Northcott, W. 1984. Oral interpreting: Principles and practices (Perspectives in Audiology series). Baltimore: University Park Press.

NTID, 1989. Documents regarding overuse syndrome received via personal correspondence.

NTID. 1989. Repetitive motion injury (personal communication and retreat notes).

Nygren, P. 1987. The real cost of freelance interpreting in the state of Minne sota. In (McIntire, Ed.) Journal of Interpretation. Silver Spring, Md.: Registry of Interpreters for the Deaf. Vol. IV, 1987.

O'Dea, B. 1995. Personal communication.

Ontario Ministry of Education. 1990. The role and responsibilities of interpreters in the educational setting. Ontario: Ministry of Education.

Padden, C. 1980. The deaf community and the culture of deaf people. In (Baker & Battison, Eds.) Sign Language and the Deaf Com munity: Essays in Honor of William C. Stokoe. Washington, DC: National Association of the Deaf.

Padden, C. and T. Humphries. 1988. Deaf in America: Voices from a culture. Cambridge, MA: Harvard University Press.

Palmer, C. 1995. Working for fun AND profit. The Ripple 7:1, February 1995.

Patri, C. 2000. Cognitive Processing Skills in English. San Diego, CA: DawnSignPress

Patri, C. Ed.) 1988. (Atwood, A., author) Anthology of interpreting papers. Washington, D.C.: Gallaudet University.

Perrin, Linda. 1980. Coming to America: Immigrants from the Far East. New York: Delacort Press.

Philip, M. 1986a. Presentation at CIT, Oct. 1987. (unpublished personal notes)

Philip, M. 1986b. Keynote address made at the Northern California Registry of Interpreters for the Deaf meeting, Nov. 1986. (unpublished personal notes)

Philip, M. 1993."Cross Cultural Comparisons: American Deaf Culture and American majority culture." Telecourse. Westminster, CO: Front Range Community College.

Philip, M. and A. Small. 1991. The path to bilingualism and biculturalism at the learning center for deaf children. Perspectives on deafness: A deaf American monograph. Vol. 41, Nos. 1-2, pp. 121-124.

Plant-Moeller, J. (Ed.) 1992. Expanding horizons. (Proceedings of the 12th national convention of the Registry of Interpreters for the Deaf). Silver Spring, Md.: RID Publications.

Poplack, S. 1980. Sometimes I'll start a sentence in Spanish y termino en enpañol: Toward a typology of code-switching. Linguistics 18, pp. 581-618.

Pousada, A. 1979. Interpreting for language minorities in the courts. In (Alatis and Tucker, Eds.) Georgetown university round table on language and linguistics 1979: Language in public life. Washington, DC: Georgetown University Press.

Pudlas, K. 1987. Sentence reception abilities of hearing impaired students across five communication modes. American Annals of the Deaf, 123, 5: 558-562.

Raffin, M., J. Davis & L. Gilman. 1978. Comprehension of inflectional morphemes by deaf children exposed to a visual English sign system. Journal of Speech & Hearing Research, 21: 387-400.

Registry of Interpreters for the Deaf. 1983. RID Views. Vol. 3, No. 3, pp. 2-3

Registry of Interpreters for the Deaf. 1992. Introduction to the national testing system. Silver Spring, Md.: RID Publications.

Registry of Interpreters for the Deaf. Position papers: standards of practice articulated in a series of documents available from RID. Include such topics as: Business Practices; Billing Considerations; Men toring:" Multiple Roles; Team Interpreting: Coordinating Inter preters for Conferences; Cumulative Motion Injury; Interpreting in Medical Settings; Professional Sign Language Interpreting; Use of a Certified Deaf Interpreter; Interpreting in Mental Health Settings; Sign Language Interpreters and the Medical/Mental Health Communities: Working Together;

Reid, M. l980. Cerebral lateralization in children: An ontogenetic and organ ismic analysis. Unpublished doctoral dissertation, University of Colorado, Boulder.

Report of the national advisory commission on civil disorder (New York: Bantam Books, 1968. 1

Roach, P. 1983. English phonetics and phonology: a practical course. Cambridge: Cambridge University Press.

Roy, C. 2000. new book here

Russell, D 1991a. Update from the President. AVLIC News. Fall, 1991.

Russell, D 1991b. Presentation made in Saskatchewan , August 21, 1991.

Russell, D 1993. Debra Russell, AVLIC president 1988-1992. AVLIC News. Winter. Ottawa: Association of Visual Language Interpreters of Canada.

Russell, D and K. Malcolm. 1991. Interpreting in Canada. In (Plant-Moeller, Ed.) Expanding Horizons: Proceedings of the 12th national convention of the registry of interpreters for the deaf. Silver Spring, MD: RID Publications.

Russell, D. 2000. Interpreting in legal contexts: Consecutive and simultane ous interpretation (unpublished dissertation). University of Calgary: Dept. of Educational Psychology.

Sacks, O. 1988. The revolution of the deaf. New York review of books 35(9), 23-28.

San Francisco Public Library. American culture: The deaf perspective (a video series based in part on the research of Susan Rutherford.) San Francisco Public Library.

Sanderson, G. 1987. Overuse syndrome among sign language interpreters. In (McIntire, Ed.) Journal of interpretation. Silver Spring, Md.: Registry of Interpreters for the Deaf. Vol. IV, 1987.

Sanderson, G. Various unpublished documents used in workshops regarding overuse syndrome.

Sauerburger, D. 1993 Independence without sight or sound. New York: American Foundation for the Blind; Community-based living options for young adults with deaf-blindness. 1987. Sands Point, NY: TAC-Helen Keller National Center

Savage, E. 1992. Unpublished handouts used at the CSUN course Interpreting in the American Judicial System: English/ASL.

Schein, J, B. Mallory and S. Greaves. 1991. Communication for deaf students in mainstream classrooms. (Research and Development Series No. 2). Alberta, Canada: Western Canadian Centre For Studies In Deafness.

Schein, J. 1989. At home among strangers. Washington, D.C.: Gallaudet University Press.

Schildroth, A. & Hotto, W. 1991. Annual survey of hearing impaired children and youth: 1989-90 school your. *American Annals of the Deaf,* reference Issue, 136 (2) 155-164.

Schlesinger, H. & K. Meadow. 1972. Sound and sign. Berkeley: University of California Press.

Schlesinger, H. 1987. Effects of powerlessness on dialogue and development: Disability, poverty and the human condition. In (Heller, Ed.), Psychosocial interventions with sensorially disabled persons. New York: Grune & Statton.

Seleskovitch, D 1978. Interpreting for international conferences: Problems of language and communication. Washington, DC: Pen and Booth.

Seleskovitch, D, 1992. Interpreting Sense. Telecourse. Westminster, CO: Front Range Community College.

Seleskovitch, D. 1992. Fundamentals of the interpretive theory of translation. In (Plant-Moeller, Ed.) Expanding horizons. (Proceedings of the 12th national convention of the Registry of Interpreters for the Deaf). Silver Spring, Md.: RID Publications.

Seymour, C. 1990. The hunt for absolute goodness. In Reflections on ethics: A compilation of articles inspired by the May 1990 ASHA ethics colloquium.

Shaboltz, Carol J. & Dorothy UL Seyler (ed). 1982. New York: Random House, Inc.

Shaw, R. 1987. "Determining Register in Sign-to-English Interpreting" in Sign Language Studies 57, Winter.

Shuy, R. 1987. A sociolinguistic view of interpreter education. In (McIntire, Ed.) Silver Spring, Md.: RID Publications.

Singer, B. 1994. Presentation made at the Conference of Interpreter Trainers in Charlotte, N.C.

Skutnabb-Kangas, T. 1983. Bilingualism or not: The education of minorities. Boston, MA: Little, Brown.

Smith, J.M. (Ed.), Workshop on Interpreting for the deaf. Ball State Teachers College, 1964.

Smith, T. 1983. What goes around, comes around: Reciprocity and interpreters. The Reflector, 5:5-6.

Smith, T. 1991. In (Witter-Merithew) Interpreting in the American Judicial System: ASL/English. Northridge, CA: CSUN (unpublished).

Smith, Theresa B. 1996. Deaf People in Context. Ph.D. dissertation, University of Washington.

Sowell, Thomas. 1981. Ethnic America: a history. NY: Basic Books, Inc.

Stedt, J and D. Moores. 1990. Manual codes on English and American Sign Language: An historical perspective and current realities. In (Bornstein, Ed.) Manual communication: Implications for education, pp. 1-20. Washington, D.C.: Gallaudet University Press.

Steiner, C 1971. Games alcoholics play. New York: Grover Press, Inc.

Steiner, C. 1981. The other side of power. New York: Grover Press, Inc.

Stokoe, W. 1960. Sign language structure: An outline of the visual communication systems of the American deaf. Studies in Linguistics: Occasional Papers. Buffalo, NY: University of Buffalo. (Revised edition in 1978 from Linstok Press, Silver Spring, Md.)

Stokoe, W. 1969. Sign language diglossia. Studies in Linguistics, 21:27-41.

Stokoe, W. 1978. Sign language structure (rev. ed.). Silver Spring, Md.: Linstok Press.

Stokoe, W. 1980. Sign and culture: A reader for students of American sign language. Silver Spring, Md.: Linstok Press.

Stokoe, W. D. Casterline, & C. Croneberg (Eds.) 1965. A dictionary of American sign language on linguistic principles. Washington, D.C.: Gallaudet College Press. (Reprinted in 1976 by Linstok Press, Silver Spring, Md.).

Stone, W. E. 1984. Occupational repetitive strain injuries. Australian Family Physician. 13:9, September.

Stone, W. E. Grading pain associated with overuse. An excerpt used by G. Sanderson in various workshops and presentations on overuse syndrome.

Stromberg, D. 1990. Key Legal Issues in Professional Ethics. In Reflections on ethics: A compilation of articles inspired by the May 1990 ASHA ethics colloquium.

Strong, M. 1988. A bilingual approach to educating deaf children. In (Strong, Ed.), Language Learning and Deafness. Cambridge, UK: Cam bridge University Press.

Strong, M. and E. Charlson. 1989. Simultaneous communication: How teachers approach an impossible task. American Annals of the Deaf, 134.

Stuart, P. & Gilchrist, A. 1991. A sense of identity: Deaf minorities still struggle for acceptance of their heritage. In N. Moore (Ed.) *Gal laudet Today*, 21 (2), 13.

Stuckless, R., J. Avery, & A. Hurwitz (Eds.). 1989. Educational interpreting for deaf students: Report of the national task force on educational interpreting. Rochester, NY: Rochester Institute of Technology.

Supalla, S. 1986. Manually coded English: The modality question in signed language development. Unpublished mater's thesis, University of Illinois, Champaign-Urbana.

Swabey, L. (Ed.) 1992. The challenge of the 90's: New standards in interpreter education. (Proceedings of the CIT Eighth National Convention) Conference of Interpreter Trainers.

Swabey, L. 1992. Interpreting in community settings: A comparison of sign language and spoken language interpreters. In (Plant-Moeller, Ed.) Expanding horizons. (Proceedings of the 12th national convention of the Registry of Interpreters for the Deaf). Silver Spring, Md.: RID Publications.

Swisher, M. & M. Thompson. 1985. Mothers learning simultaneous communication: The dimensions of the task. American Annals f the Deaf, 130: 212-217

Tatum, B. 1997. *Why are all the black kids sitting together in the cafeteria? And other conversations about race.* New York: Perseus Books Group

Taylor, K. 1994. Deafness and learning. University of Victoria: Distance Education Services.

Texas SHHH. The Ears of Texas, the newsletter of the Texas Chapter of SHHH.

Triandis, H. 1995. *Individualism and collectivism.* Boulder CO: Westview Press.

Valli, C. And C. Lucas. 1992. Linguistics of American Sign Language. Washington, D.C.: Gallaudet University Press.

Van Cleve, J. V. (Ed). 1988. Gallaudet Encyclopedia of Deaf People and Deafness. McGraw Hill Co: New York, NY.

Van Scott, D. 1990. Musings of an interpreting student. Unpublished paper.

Waggoner, K. 1990. Professional ethics, a methodology for decision making: Expert systems in the classroom. In Reflections on ethics: A compilation of articles inspired by the May 1990 ASHA ethics colloquium.

Walls, L. 1993. Welcome to the profession! AVLIC news. Winter. Ottawa: Association of Visual Language Interpreters of Canada.

Walworth, M, D. Moores and T. O'Rourke, Ed. 1992. A free hand: Enfranchising the education of deaf children. Silver Spring, Md.: TJ Publishers.

Wampler, D. 1971. Linguistics of visual English. Santa Rosa, CA: Santa Rosa City Schools.

Wasserman, S. 1987. Teaching for thinking: Louis E. Raths revisited. Phi Delta Kappan, 68:460-466.

Watson, J. 1987. Interpreter burnout. In (McIntire, Ed.) Journal of interpretation. Silver Spring, Md.: Registry of Interpreters for the Deaf. Vol. IV, 1987.

Weber, W. K. 1984. Training translators and conference interpreters. New York: Harcourt Brace Jovanovich, Inc.

Wells, R. 1991. Repetitive strain injuries: An old refrain. In Accident prevention. September.

Werlich, E. 1976. A text grammar of English. Heidelberg: Quelle & Meyer.

Wilcox, P., F. Schroeder, and T. Martinez. 1990. A commitment to profes sionalism: Educational interpreting standards within a large public school system. Sign Language Studies, 68:277-286. Silver Spring, Md.: Linstok Press.

Wilcox, S. 1981 The Myers Briggs type indicator: Personality types of sign language students. RID Interpreting Journal. 1:39-50.

Wilcox, S. 1984. "Stuck" in school: A study of semantics and culture in a deaf education class. Sign Language Studies, 43:141-164.

Wilcox, S. and P. Wilcox. 1985. Schema theory and language interpretation: a study of sign language interpreters. In (McIntire, Ed.), Journal of Interpretation. Silver Spring, Md.: RID Publications.

Wilentz, Joan S. The senses of man. New York: Thomas Y. Crowell, 1968.

Williamson, L. 1985. The question of cultural interpreting. University of Washington, Fall Quarter, unpublished paper.

Winston, E. 1988. Mainstream interpreting: An analysis of the task. Washington, D.C.: Gallaudet University.

Witter Merithew, A. Claiming out destiny, Part I and Part II. RID Views, Winter, 1987 and Spring, 1988. Silver Spring, Md.: RID Publica tions.

Wixtrom, C. (1988) Two views of deafness. The Deaf American (Winter), p. 45.

Woititz, J. 1983. Adult child of alcoholics. Pompano Beach, Fla.: Health Communications, Inc.

Woititz, J. 1985. Struggle for intimacy. Pompano Beach, Fla.: Health Communications, Inc.

Woodward, J. 1972. Implications for sociolinguistic research among the deaf. Sign Language Studies. 1:1-7.

Woodward, J. 1973b. Some characteristics of pidgin sign English. Sign Language Studies, 3:39-46.

Woodward, J. 1974. Implications for sociolinguistic research among the deaf. Sign Language Studies, 1:1-7.

Woodward, J. 1978. Some sociolinguistic problems in the implementation of bilingual education for deaf students. In (Caccamise & Hicks, Eds.) American sign language in a bilingual, bicultural context. (The proceedings of the second national symposium on sign language research and teaching). Silver Spring, Md.: National Association of the Deaf.

Woodward, J. 1982. How you gonna get to heaven if you can't talk with Jesus: On depathologizing deafness. Silver Spring, Md.: TJ Publishers.

Woodward, J. and H. Markowitz. 1975 (1980). Some handy new ideas on pidgins and Creoles: Pidgin sign languages. A paper presented at the 1975 International Conference on Pidgin and Creole Languages, Honolulu, January 1975. Published in (Stokoe, Ed.)., Sign and Culture. Silver Spring, Md.: Linstok Press.

Woodward, J. and T. Allen. 1987. Classroom use of ASL by teachers. Sign Language Studies , 54:1-10.

Woodward, J. Working toward change: A program and a study. In (Walworth, Moores and O'Rourke, Eds.) A free hand: Enfranchising the education of deaf children. Silver Spring, Md.: TJ Publishers (pp. 20-36).

Yapp, V. 1984. Signer-cises. Unpublished document developed by California State University-Northridge student health center.

Yuen, C. 1987. Carpal tunnel syndrome: What is it? In (McIntire, Ed.) Journal of interpretation. Silver Spring, Md.: Registry of Interpreters for the Deaf. Vol. IV.

INDEX

A

Adjectives
  Description of A Person/Place/Thing 216
Adverbs
  Describing Action 217
Advocate 139
Affect Markers 218, 219
African American Culture
  Family/Community 63
  Language 65
  Spirituality and Religion 65
  Time/Status 65
Ally 139
Ambivalence 117
American Sign Language 87, 187
  Conveying Meaning 192
  Visual Conveyance Of Information 195
Americans With Disabilities Act (ADA) 286
Asking for Clarification 248
ASL Vaarieties 87
Association of Visual Language Interpreters Of Canada (AVLIC) 264
  establishment of 265
  membership categories 265
  purposes 266
Audism 107, 112, 123, 124
  affects on Deaf people 123, 129, 130
AVLIC Certification 277
  Test of Interpretation 280
  Written Test of Knowledge (WTK) 278
AVLIC Code of Ethics 302
  values underlying 302

B

BENEFACTORS
  Characteristics of 112
Beneficence 107
bilingual-bicultural 116, 151, 167, 176, 177, 178, 179, 180, 182, 236, 261
Business Communication and Interactions 47

Business Policies
  2-hr minimum 394
  Call-out fee 394
  Cancellation Policy 395
  Port-to-port fees 395
  Sliding fee scale 396
Business Skills
  Basic Bookkeeping 393
  Business Policies 394
  Resumé Writing 392
  Schedule Maintenance 394
  Writing Business Letters 393

C

Certification of Sign Language Interpreters 268
  AVLIC Certification 277
  RID Certification 268
Claggett Statement 129, 403
Classifiers
  Describing Action 217
  Description of A Person/Place/Thing 216
  Relationship Of A Person/Place/Thing To Another Person/Place/
    Thing 214
Communication 1, 3, 9, 27, 29, 33, 43, 45, 47, 50, 51, 58, 61, 71, 81,
    97, 184, 246, 276, 311, 358, 359
  communication competence 4
  contextual environment 2
  external noise 3
  influence of culture on communication 33
  nonverbal aspects 2
  physiological noise 3
  psychological noise 3
  the Communication Process 1
  the importance of 1
Communication competence 4
Conceptually Accurate Signed English 89, 93, 102, 103, 156
Contact Varieties 89, 93, 102, 103, 156
Contrasting 196
Conveying Meaning 192
Cost of Doing Business 391
Couching/Nesting 200
Cultural and linguistic mediation 176, 431
Cultural identity 42, 49, 51, 53, 70, 81, 83

Cultural Sense Of Time 41
Culture
  Business Communication and Interactions 47
  collectivist 37, 38, 59, 60, 64, 66, 69, 70, 72, 73, 75
  culture determines 35
  Definition of Status 41
  Definitions 33
    Padden & Humphries 33
    Tyler 33
    UNESCO 33
  individualist 37, 38, 59, 60, 64, 66, 69, 70, 72, 73, 75
  sense of time 41
  the influence on communication 33
  the role of 35

D

Deaf-Blind 78, 98, 99, 100, 104, 106, 249, 266, 272, 351, 362, 375
Deaf Community
  Audism 109, 130, 134
  Multilingual Nature of 86
  Oppression 109, 130, 134
Deaf Culture
  A Culture Based on Sight 59
  Attention-getting and Signaling Devices 61
  Communication Norms 61
  Emotional Display 63
  Eye Contact and Physical Presence 61
  Introductions, Greetings and Leave-taking 59
  Language of Interaction 59
  Reciprocal Signals 63
Deaf President Now 122, 129
Degree of directness
  Equivocal language 10
  Euphemistic language 11
  Passive voice 12, 212, 224
Dependence 119
Describe Then Do 200
Disclaimers 13, 30
Dynamic equivalence 162, 177

E

Educational Interpreter Performance Assessment (EIPA) 281
Effective communicators 4

Emotional Burnout 397
Ethical Conduct
  Accurate Conveyance Of Information 304
  Confidentiality 304
  Empowerment Of The Client 303
  Philisophical Frame: Influence on Ethical Decision-Making 179
  Professional Competence 306
  Professional Distance 305
  Promote The Profession 307
  Purchase Of Services 305
Ethics
  definition 299
ethics-foundation of
  Knowing Yourself 316

F

Faceting 196
Fear Of Freedom 120
Foreign Sign Languages 95, 103

G

Grammar
  not needed to retain the information 6
Guidelines for Professional Conduct
  reasons for 300

H

Hearing Impaired 85
Hedges 13, 30
Hesitations 13, 17, 30
Hispanic Culture
  Family 67
  Language 67
  Learning Style 67
  Physical Boundaries 67
  Spirituality and Religion 67
  Time 67
History and Professionalization Of Interpreting 259
Home Signs and Gestures 96
Horizontal Hostility 117
Humor
  Deaf Joke 131

Humor
   as a tool for interpreters 131, 136

I

Incorporation of 3-D Information 198
Intensifiers 13, 30
Interpretation
   definition of 147
interpreter
   defined 151
   work of 151
Interpreter Education 284
Interpreter Education Programs 282
Interpreters in Private Practice 389
Interpreting
   with African American Deaf people 63
   with Deaf Hispanic people 65
   with Native Deaf people 69
   with people who identify primarily with Deaf culture 57
Interpreting for Conferences 359
   Pay for Services 360
   Professional and Ethical Considerations 362
   Special Considerations 361
   Supervision and Evaluation 360
   Working Conditions 360
Interpreting in a Team 374
   Placement 376
   Role Delineation 375
Interpreting in Educational Settings 323
   Deaf Community view 335
   Ethical Considerations 333
   Opportunities For Professional Development 331
   Pay For Services 329
   Role Delineation 326
   standard qualifications 323
   Supervision and Evaluation 331
   Two Models 325
   Working Conditions 327
Interpreting in Employment-Related Settings 335
   Knowledge And Skills 336
   Pay For Services 338
   Standard Qualifications 337
   Supervision And Evaluation 337

Working Conditions 338
Interpreting in Legal Settings 351
  Ethical Considerations 355
  Pay For Services & Working Conditions 354
  Placement and Protocol 352
  Standard Qualifications 353
  Supervision And Professional Development 354
Interpreting in Medical Settings
  Pay For Services 349
  Placement 346
  Protocol 347
  Role Delineation 347
  Special Knowledge And Skills 348
  Standard Qualifications 350
  Supervision and Professional Development 349
Interpreting in Mental Health and Psychiatric Settings 357
  Other Considerations 359
  Protocol 359
  Special Knowledge and Skills 357
  Standard Qualifications 358
Interpreting in Personal
  Pay, Working Conditions, Supervision 372
  Role Delineation and Special Considerations 371
  Skills and Special Considerations 374
Interpreting in Personal Settings 369
  Working Conditions 369
Interpreting in Religious Settings 339
  Ethical Considerations 342
  Pay For Services 342
  Role Delineation 342
  Special Considerations 340
  Standard Qualifications 340
  Supervision And Professional Development 344
Interpreting in Social Service Settings
  Special Considerations 369
  Working Conditions 369
Interpreting in Theatrical or Performing Arts Settings 362
  Ethical Considerations 369
  Musical Concerts 362
  Pay For Services 367
  Special Considerations 367
  Standard Qualifications 366
  Supervision and Evaluation 367

Theatrical Performances 363
Working Conditions 368

J

Jan's Gems 27, 219
Job Market 387
　Areas of Employment 387
　Interpreters in Private Practice 389
　Most Common Types Of Employment 388
　Pay Rates 389
　Urban vs. Rural 387

L

Language 5
　communication tool 5
　intended meaning 5, 18, 94, 244
　Pragmatic rules 5
Language Fluency 145
　A-language 145
　B-language 145
　C-language 145
　L-1 145
　L-2 145
Legislative Initiatives 285
　Americans with Disabilities Act (ADA) 286
　PL 89-333The Vocational Rehabilitation Act of 1965 285
　PL 93-112 Rehab Act of 1973 285
　PL 94-142 .Education for All Handicapped Children Act23 286
　PL 95-539 The Court InterpretersAct of 1978 286
　PL 95-602 Rehabilitation Amendments of 1978 286
Liberation Movement 122, 129
Linguistic And Cultural Adaptations 246
Linguistic Register 16, 31
　Casual 17, 18, 149
　Consultative 17, 18, 149
　determines 16
　Formal 17, 18, 149
　Frozen 17, 18, 149
　Informal 17, 18, 149
　Intimate 17, 18, 149
　turn-taking 16

M

Making Ethical Decisions 308
  critical thinking 308
  Steps to 308
Making Visual Sense
  Affect Markers 218
  Contrasting 196
  Degree of Detail 196
  Degree of First-Person Address 196
  Describe and Do 196
  Faceting 196
  Grammatical Structure 196
  Implicit and Explicit Meaning 196
  Incorporation of 3-D Information 196
  Negation/Affirmation 210
  Nesting/Couching 196
  Noun/Verb Modifiers 214
  Noun Listing 196
  Pronouns 221
  Reiterating 196
  Role Shifting 196
  Sequence of Information 196
  Voice 212
  Word Order 196
Mediating ASL and English 177, 187
  cultural or linguistic reduction 177
  deriving meaning 151
  dropping source language form 190
  Linguistic Considerations for Interpreters 187
  linguistic expansion 177
  modalities 151
  volume of lexical units/speed of production 151
Mediating ASL and Engllish
  cultural expansion 177
Message Construction 6
  context of the interaction 8, 10
  context of the message conveyance 6
  degree of directness 6, 30
  direct or implicit 10
  powerful/powerless speech 6
  speaker's goal 6, 161, 304
Minimal Language Skills 96, 103
multi-cultural communities 55

Multi-tasking and Monitoring 247
Myth of Neutrality 137

N

NAD-RID Code of Professional Conduct 301
  Guiding principles behind 301
Native Culture
  Children 73
  Communication 71
  Family 71
  Language 71
  Status and Work Ethic 69
  Time 73
Noun-Listing 198
Numbering Systems 220, 221

O

Oppression 64, 109, 130, 134
  impact on interpreters 109, 130, 134
Opressors
  Characteristics of 112
Oral Communication Systems 97

P

Passive voice 12, 212, 224
Philosophical Frame 152, 169
  Bilingual-Bicultural (Bi-Bi) 176
  The Communication Facilitator 174
  The Helper 169
  The Machine (Conduit) 171
Physiological noise 3
Polite Forms 13
Power 122, 129
  Implications For Interpreters 138
Power and Oppression 130
Powerful/Powerless Speech 12
  "up talk" 13
  Disclaimers 13, 30
  Hedges 13, 30
  Hesitations 13, 17, 30
  Intensifiers 13, 30
  Polite Forms 13

Tag questions 13, 30
Prepositions
    Relationship Of A Person/Place/Thing To Another Person/Place/
        Thing 214
Principles of Professional Practice 297
Privilege 113
Process of Interpreting 231
    models 231
Profession, distinguished by
    limited scope of practice & related body of knowledge 298
    set of values or code of ethics 298
    special monopoly via licensure or certification 298
Pronouns 221
Psychological noise 3

R

Reciprocity Of Perspectives 114
Registry of Interpreters for the Deaf (RID) 259
    establishment 260
    membership categories 263
    purposes of 262
Reiterating 197
Repetitive Strain Injury (RSI) 396
Responsible Language 15
    "But" statements 15
    "I" statements 15
    "It" statements 15
    "You" statements 15
Resumé Writing 392
RID Certification
    Certified Deaf Interpreter — CDI) 272
    National Interpreter Certification (NIC) 273
    Oral Transliteration (OTC) 275
    Specialist Certificate: Legal (SC:L) 276
Role-Shifting 198

S

Schemas 107
    Interactions 107
    Memberships 107
    Physical 107
    Psychological 107
    Roles 107

Sight translation 149, 163
Signed English 89, 93, 102, 103, 156
Signing Exact English 89, 91, 102
Sign Supported Speech 89, 94, 102, 115
Source language 147, 153, 162, 175, 211, 245, 271, 278, 279, 280, 281, 289, 292, 362
Speaker/Signer Goals 7, 22, 24, 26, 30
Spoken Language Interpretation 281
Stereotyping 109
Support Groups and Mentors 317

T

Tactile signs 99
Tag questions 13, 30
Target language 147, 153, 162, 175, 211, 245, 271, 278, 279, 280, 281, 289, 292, 362
The Process of Interpreting 233
  Analyze Deep Structure Meaning 236
    Cognitive Competence 236
    Linguistic and Cultural Requirements 241
  Apply Contextual/Schema Screen 241
    Cohort Groups 241
  Formulate/Rehearse Equivalent Message 244
  Produce Target Language Interpretation 245
  Take in Source Language 234, 235
    Cognitive Competence 235
    Linguistic and Cultural Requirements 235
    Physical Requirements 235
    Social Competence 235
The Rochester Method 90, 102
Translation 149, 163
  defined 151
Transliteration 162
  definition of 147, 151

U

Use of First Person 248

V

Visual Communication
  American Sign Language (ASL) 99
  Conceptually Accurate Signed English 99

Contact Varieties 99
Fingerspelling 99
Home Signs and Gestures 99
Signed English 99
Signing Exact English 99
Speech-Reading 104
The Rochester Method 99

W

Where Interpreters Work 323
Working with Deaf Interpreters 344
  Ethical Considerations 345
  Pay For Services 345
  Role Delineation 345
  Special Considerations 344
  Standard Qualifications 344
  Supervision and Professional Development 346
Working With Rehearsed and/or Read Texts 250
Work of Interpreters
  Business Practices 387
  Cultural and linguistic mediation 176
  Interpretation or Signed/Oral Transliteration 153
  interpretation or signed/oral transliteration 151
  Maintaining dynamic equivalence 162
  Sign-to-Voice 155
  Simultaneous or Consecutive 153
  Voice-to-Sign 155
  Working with Deaf interpreters 155